Fodor's
NAPA &
SONOMA

WELCOME TO NAPA AND SONOMA

In California's premier wine region, the pleasures of eating and drinking are celebrated daily. It's easy to join in at famous wineries and rising newcomers off country roads, or at trendy in-town tasting rooms. Chefs transform local ingredients into feasts, and gourmet groceries sell perfect picnic fare. Yountville, Healdsburg, and St. Helena have small-town charm as well as luxurious inns, hotels, and spas, yet the natural setting is equally sublime, whether experienced from a canoe on the Russian River or the deck of a winery overlooking endless rows of vines.

TOP REASONS TO GO

★ **Fine Wine:** Rutherford Cabernets, Carneros Chardonnays, Russian River Pinots.

★ **Spectacular Food:** Marquee Napa chefs, farmers' markets, Sonoma cheese shops.

★ **Cool Towns:** From chic Healdsburg to laid-back Calistoga, a place to suit every mood.

★ **Spas:** Mud baths, herbal wraps, couples' massages, and more in soothing settings.

★ **Winery Architecture:** Stone classics like Buena Vista, all-glass dazzlers like Hall.

★ **Outdoor Fun:** Biking past bright-green vineyards, hot-air ballooning over golden hills.

Fodor's NAPA & SONOMA

Publisher: Amanda D'Acierno, *Senior Vice President*

Editorial: Arabella Bowen, *Editor in Chief*; Linda Cabasin, *Editorial Director*

Design: Tina Malaney, *Associate Art Director*; Chie Ushio, *Senior Designer*; Randy Glance, *Production Designer*

Photography: Jennifer Arnow, *Senior Photo Editor*; Mary Robnett, *Photo Researcher*

Production: Linda Schmidt, *Managing Editor*; Evangelos Vasilakis, *Associate Managing Editor*; Angela L. McLean, *Senior Production Manager*

Maps: Rebecca Baer, *Senior Map Editor*; David Lindroth, Mark Stroud (Moon Street Cartography) *Cartographers*

Sales: Jacqueline Lebow, *Sales Director*

Marketing & Publicity: Heather Dalton, *Marketing Director*; Katherine Punia, *Publicity Director*

Business & Operations: Susan Livingston, *Vice President, Strategic Business Planning*; Sue Daulton, *Vice President, Operations*

Fodors.com: Megan Bell, *Executive Director, Revenue & Business Development*; Yasmin Marinaro, *Senior Director, Marketing & Partnerships*

Copyright © 2015 by Fodor's Travel, a division of Random House LLC

Writer: Daniel Mangin

Editors: Linda Cabasin, lead editor; Bethany Beckerlegge

Production Editor: Carrie Parker

1st Edition

ISBN 978-1-101-87820-0

ISSN 2375-9453

SPECIAL SALES

CONTENTS

ABOUT THIS GUIDE

Fodor's Recommendations

Everything in this guide is worth doing—we don't cover what isn't—but exceptional sights, hotels, and restaurants are recognized with additional accolades. **Fodor'sChoice★** indicates our top recommendations; and **Best Bets** call attention to wineries in various categories. Care to nominate a new place? Visit Fodors.com/contact-us.

Trip Costs

We list prices wherever possible to help you budget well. Hotel and restaurant price categories from $ to $$$$ are noted alongside each recommendation. For hotels, we include the lowest cost of a standard double room in high season. For restaurants, we cite the average price of a main course at dinner or, if dinner isn't served, at lunch. For attractions, we always list adult admission fees; discounts are usually available for children, students, and senior citizens.

Hotels

Our local writers vet every hotel to recommend the best overnights in each price category, from budget to expensive. Unless otherwise specified, you can expect private bath, phone, and TV in your room. For expanded hotel reviews, facilities, and deals visit Fodors.com.

Top Picks	Hotels &
★ **Fodor'sChoice**	Restaurants
	⌂ Hotel
Listings	↳ Number of
✉ Address	rooms
✉ Branch address	⫶⊙⫶ Meal plans
☎ Telephone	✕ Restaurant
🖷 Fax	⚓ Reservations
⊕ Website	⌂ Dress code
✍ E-mail	▭ No credit cards
▦ Admission fee	$ Price
⊙ Open/closed	
times	**Other**
M Subway	⇨ See also
⊹ Directions or	☞ Take note
Map coordinates	♟ Golf facilities

Restaurants

Unless we state otherwise, restaurants are open for lunch and dinner daily. We mention dress code only when there's a specific requirement and reservations only when they're essential or not accepted. To make restaurant reservations, visit Fodors.com.

Credit Cards

The hotels and restaurants in this guide typically accept credit cards. If not, we'll say so.

EUGENE FODOR

Hungarian-born Eugene Fodor (1905–91) began his travel career as an interpreter on a French cruise ship. The experience inspired him to write *On the Continent* (1936), the first guidebook to receive annual updates and discuss a country's way of life as well as its sights. Fodor later joined the U.S. Army and worked for the OSS in World War II. After the war, he kept up his intelligence work while expanding his guidebook series. During the Cold War, many guides were written by fellow agents who understood the value of insider information. Today's guides continue Fodor's legacy by providing travelers with timely coverage, insider tips, and cultural context.

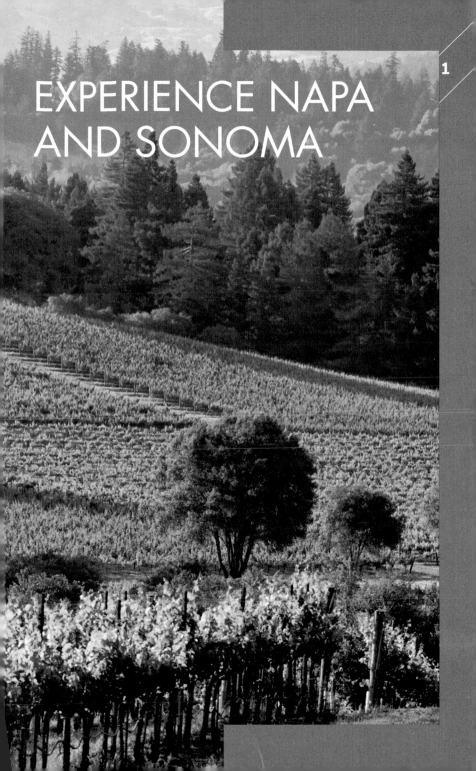

EXPERIENCE NAPA AND SONOMA

1

WHAT'S WHERE

The following numbers refer to chapters.

3 Napa Valley. By far the best known of the California wine regions, Napa is home to some of the biggest names in wine, many producing the Cabernet Sauvignons and Chardonnays that cemented the valley's fame. Densely populated with winery after winery, especially along Highway 29 and the Silverado Trail, it's also home to luxury accommodations and several of the country's best restaurants.

4 Sonoma Valley. Centered on the historic town of Sonoma, the Sonoma Valley goes easy on the glitz, but contains sophisticated wineries and excellent restaurants. Key moments in California and wine-industry history took place here. Part of the Carneros District viticultural area lies within the southern Sonoma Valley. Those who venture into the Carneros will discover wineries specializing in Pinot Noir and Chardonnay. Both grapes thrive in the comparatively cool climate. Farther north Cabernet Sauvignon, Zinfandel, and other warm-weather varietals are grown.

5 Northern Sonoma, Russian River, and West County. Ritzy Healdsburg is a popular base for exploring three important grape-growing areas, the Russian River, Dry Creek, and Alexander valleys. Everything from Chardonnay and Pinot Noir to Cabernet Sauvignon and Petite Sirah grows here. In the county's western parts lie the Sonoma Coast wineries, beloved by connoisseurs for European-style wines from cool-climate grapes.

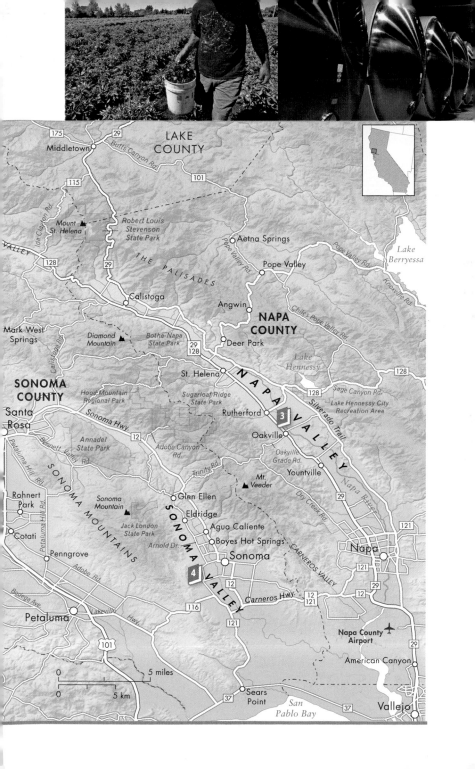

NAPA AND SONOMA PLANNER

About the Restaurants

Farm-to-table Modern American cuisine is the prevalent style in the Napa Valley and Sonoma County, but this encompasses both the delicate preparations of Yountville's Thomas Keller, whose restaurants include The French Laundry, and the upscale comfort food served throughout the Wine Country. The quality (and hype) often means high prices, but you can find appealing, inexpensive eateries, especially in Napa, Calistoga, Sonoma, and Santa Rosa. *For details and price-category information, see the charts in each regional chapter.*

About the Hotels

The fanciest accommodations are concentrated in the Napa Valley towns of Yountville, Rutherford, St. Helena, and Calistoga; Sonoma County's poshest lodgings are in Healdsburg. The spas, amenities, and exclusivity of high-end properties attract travelers with the means and desire for luxury living. The cities of Napa and Santa Rosa are the best bets for budget hotels and inns. *For details and price-category information, see the charts in each regional chapter.*

Getting Here and Around

San Francisco is the main gateway to Napa and Sonoma, which lie due north of the city. Driving is the best way to explore this region. The easiest route to southern Napa and Sonoma counties is to head north across the Golden Gate Bridge on U.S. 101 and east on Highway 37 to Highway 121. Follow signs for the towns of Sonoma (45 miles from San Francisco) and Napa (about 52 miles). Remain on U.S. 101 if your destination is Santa Rosa (55 miles) or Healdsburg (70 miles).

By car. Roads are well maintained here, and distances between towns are fairly short: you can drive from one end to the other of either valley in less than an hour if there's no traffic. The Mayacamas Mountains divide Napa and Sonoma, though, and only a few winding roads traverse the middle sections, so the drive between valleys can be slow. The quicker connector is Highway 121, which runs east–west between southern Napa and Sonoma counties. The far-northern route—from Highway 128 just north of Calistoga, take Petrified Forest Road and Calistoga Road to Highway 12—has a few curves but rewards with great vistas.

By public transportation. Visitors without cars can take van, bus, or limo tours from San Francisco. Taking public transit to Sonoma, Napa, Santa Rosa, and Healdsburg can be time-consuming, but once you arrive at your destination, you can take advantage of taxis and other options. If you're determined not to drive, an enjoyable option from San Francisco is to board the San Francisco Bay Ferry bound for Vallejo. In Vallejo you can transfer to VINE Bus 29, whose stops include the transit hub in downtown Napa. ⇨ *For more information about public transportation, see Getting Here and Around in the Travel Smart chapter. For more information about local bus service, see the Bus Travel sections for the individual towns.*

Planning Your Time

Many first-time visitors to the Wine Country pack as many wineries as possible into a short vacation. Besides being exhausting, this approach goes against the area's laid-back ethos. So you can experience the region without running yourself ragged, we've put together a few strategies for maximizing your wine-tasting fun.

Avoid driving during rush hour. From roughly 4 to 6 pm on weekdays the cars of tourists are joined by those of commuters, resulting in traffic jams. The worst bottlenecks occur on Highway 29 in both directions around St. Helena and southbound between Rutherford and northern Napa.

Get an early start. Tasting rooms are often deserted before 11 am. On the flip side, they're usually the busiest between 3:30 and closing.

Slip off the beaten track. When Napa Valley's tasting rooms along Highway 29 and the Silverado Trail are jammed, those just to the east in Coombsville and Chiles Valley might be nearly deserted. If you're based in Healdsburg, you might find the wineries in the Russian River Valley packed, whereas the ones in the Alexander Valley are comparatively quiet.

Think quality, not quantity. Spend most of your time at a few wineries each day, focusing on your interests. Perhaps you'd like to sample wines from a particular type of grape, or are curious about the different varietals offered by a certain vineyard. Wine-and-food seminars are also a good idea.

Visit on a weekday. From May through October, roads and wineries are less crowded on weekdays. Year-round, tasting rooms are usually the least busy on Tuesday and Wednesday.

Reservations

Book hotels well in advance. Hotel reservations, always advisable, are generally necessary from late spring through October and on many weekends. To be on the safe side, book smaller hotels and inns at least a month ahead. Many of these have two-night minimums on weekends, three nights if Monday is a holiday.

Call restaurants ahead. Reserving a table, or asking your hotel to reserve one for you, can save you time waiting at the door.

Reserve at wineries, too. If you're keen to taste at a specific winery, double-check hours and tour times and, if possible, make a reservation. You can often make reservations for tastings, tours, seminars, and other events. Keep in mind that visits to many wineries are by appointment only, either because their permits require it or because they want to control the flow of visitors to provide a better experience.

NAPA AND SONOMA TOP ATTRACTIONS

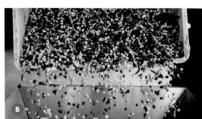

Winery Visits

(A) Tasting wines and touring wineries are favorite Wine Country pastimes. Some places enhance the experience with art galleries, high design, stunning views, or a little razzle-dazzle; others are content to let their wines and gracious hospitality do the talking. Superb wines and amiable guides make Rutherford's Frog's Leap Vineyards an ideal stop.

Luxurious Spa Treatments

Pleasure palaces like the Fairmont's Willow Stream Spa in Sonoma, with its natural thermal pools and luxurious massage and other treatments, deliver the ultimate in self-indulgence. The spa's signature bathing ritual includes exfoliating showers, an herbal steam bath, and a sauna—and that's just the beginning.

Olive Oil Tasting

(B) At classy Round Pond Estate's olive oil tasting in Rutherford, you can dispense with swirling wines and learn to swish the aromatic oils in your mouth like a pro. Tours begin with a walk past olive trees and into the state-of-the-art mill, then proceed to the tasting, which includes red-wine vinegars.

A Meal at The French Laundry

(C) Chef Thomas Keller's Yountville restaurant is considered one of the country's best, and with good reason: the mastery of flavors and attention to detail are subtly remarkable, and the master sommelier's wine pairings elevate Keller's soaring cuisine all the more.

Art Tours at di Rosa

If you've ever wondered what it would be like to purchase every piece of art that tickled your fancy, tour the galleries and grounds of the di Rosa arts center, whose discerning late founder did precisely that. His passion was Northern California art from the 1960s to the present.

Blending Seminars

At Franciscan, Joseph Phelps, Raymond, and elsewhere you can try your hand at fashioning a Bordeaux-style blend from Cabernet Sauvignon and other grapes. In addition to having a fun and educational time, you'll appreciate all the more the skill and knowledge crafting fine wines requires.

Food and Wine Pairings

Paul Hobbs and J Vineyards are among the Sonoma County wineries offering tastings that pair fine wines and small gourmet plates. Tastings over at Jordan are part of an estate tour by Mercedes van with stops at the organic garden that supplies the ingredients and a hilltop vista point with 360-degree views of the 1,200-acre property.

Hot-Air Ballooning

(D) Few experiences in the world are as exhilarating—and yet marvelously serene—as an early-morning balloon ride above the vineyards, a bucket-list staple and deservedly so. Most begin at dawn and end in late morning with brunch and sparkling wine.

Cooking Demos at the CIA

(E) Instructors and guest chefs beguile students and visitors alike during one-hour cooking demonstrations at the Culinary Institute of America's St. Helena campus. Recipes reflect what's in season at the time, and a glass of wine accompanies the dish that's prepared.

Cycling Through the Vineyards

(F) Gentle hills and vineyard-laced farmland make Napa and Sonoma perfect for combining leisurely back-roads cycling with winery stops. Napa Valley Bike Tours and the affiliated Sonoma Valley Bike Tours conduct guided rides that include picnic lunches among the grapevines.

TOP NAPA WINERIES

Far Niente
(A) You can tour the 1885 stone winery and view gleaming classic cars before sitting down to taste Far Niente's famed Cabernet Sauvignon blend and Chardonnay. The small size of the tour groups, the beauty of the grounds, and the quality of the wines make expensive Far Niente worth the splurge.

Artesa Vineyards & Winery
(B) The modern, minimalist layout of Artesa blends harmoniously with the surrounding landscape, yet this Napa winery makes a vivid impression with its outdoor sculptures and fountains. You can savor the wines—and the vineyard views—from tasting bars, indoor seating areas, or outdoor terraces.

Caymus Vineyards
Chuck Wagner started making wine on his Rutherford property in 1972. He's been racking up major awards ever since: Caymus's Special Selection Cabernet Sauvignon is the only two-time *Wine Spectator* Wine of the Year honoree. Wagner's children show promise with wines made for associated labels.

Domaine Carneros
(C) The main building of this Napa winery was modeled after an 18th-century French château owned by the Champagne-making Taittinger family, which co-owns Domaine Carneros. On a sunny day, the experience of sipping a crisp sparkling wine on the outdoor terrace feels noble indeed.

Frog's Leap
A winery that doesn't take itself too seriously, Frog's Leap is known for its entertaining, lighthearted tours. While the guides recount the Rutherford winery's history and offer a glimpse of the organic gardens and deluxe chicken coop, they aren't afraid to crack a few jokes along the way.

Schramsberg

(D) The 19th-century cellars at sparkling-wine producer Schramsberg hold millions of bottles. After you learn how the bubblies at this Calistoga mainstay are made using the *méthode traditionelle* process, and how the bottles are "riddled" (turned every few days) by hand, you can sip generous pours.

Joseph Phelps Vineyards

(E) In good weather, there are few more glorious tasting spots in the Napa Valley than the terrace at this St. Helena winery. Phelps is known for its Cabernet Sauvignons and Insignia, a Bordeaux blend. The wine-related seminars here are smart and entertaining.

The Hess Collection

(F) Before heading to this Napa winery's tasting room to sip excellent Cabernet Sauvignons and Chardonnays, take the time to wander through owner Donald Hess's personal art collection, full of large-scale canvases and other works by important 20th-century artists such as Robert Rauschenberg and Francis Bacon.

Silver Oak Cellars

This winery produces but one wine a year, a Bordeaux-style Cabernet Sauvignon blend, at its Oakville location. It's poured at tastings along with the 100% Cabernet of Silver Oak's other winery, in Sonoma County's Alexander Valley. Tastings also include pours of older Oakville vintages for further comparison.

Tres Sabores

For a pleasing contrast to showplace St. Helena wineries nearby, consider a stop at workaday Tres Sabores, whose organically farmed vineyards lie at the base of the Mayacamas Mountains. Owner-winemaker Julie Johnson is often on hand, but even if she isn't you'll enjoy learning about her and her wines.

TOP SONOMA WINERIES

Benziger Winery

It's best to visit Benziger in fine weather so you can enjoy a tram ride through this Glen Ellen winery's vineyards before tasting wines—most notably the Chardonnays, Cabernet Sauvignons, and Pinot Noirs—made from grapes grown using biodynamic farming methods.

Merry Edwards Winery

(A) Serious Pinot Noir lovers make pilgrimages to this spot in Sebastopol to experience wines that celebrate the singular characteristics of the Russian River Valley appellation. Tastings are offered several times daily—appointments are advised but walk-ins are welcome if there's space.

Iron Horse Vineyards

(B) Proving that tasting sparkling wine doesn't have to be stuffy, this winery on the outskirts of Sebastopol pours its bubblies (and a few still wines) at an outdoor tasting bar, where tremendous views over the vine-covered hills make the top-notch sparklers taste even better.

Copain Wines

(C) The emphasis at this hillside winery outside Healdsburg is on European-style Pinot Noirs whose grapes come from vineyards north of Napa and Sonoma in Mendocino County. Winemaker Wells Guthrie, a master at crafting complex wines from cool-climate grapes, also makes Chardonnays and Syrahs.

MacPhail Family Wines

The word about winemaker James MacPhail is that he's "never met a vineyard he didn't like," but he knows how to pick them. His specialty is Pinot Noir, from grapes grown from Oregon to California's Central Coast. Tastings are at the Barlow, an engaging complex of artisan producers.

Ridge Vineyards
(D) Oenophiles will be familiar with Ridge, which produces some of California's best Cabernet Sauvignon, Chardonnay, and Zinfandel. You can taste wines made from grapes grown here at Ridge's Healdsburg vineyards, and some from its neighbors, along with wines made at its older Santa Cruz Mountains winery.

Ram's Gate Winery
(E) Ultramodern yet rustic Ram's Gate perches grandly on a windswept hill in southern Sonoma, a mere 30 miles northeast of the Golden Gate Bridge. If traffic's light, you can leave San Francisco and be sipping Chardonnays, Pinot Noirs, and other wines in less than an hour.

Matanzas Creek Winery
(F) A sprawling field of lavender makes the grounds of Matanzas Creek especially beautiful in May and June, when the plants are in bloom. But the Santa Rosa winery's Asian-inspired aesthetic makes it delightful year-round, especially if you're a fan of Sauvignon Blanc, Chardonnay, or Merlot.

Patz & Hall
A Napa transplant that relocated to Sonoma in 2014, this respected winery is known for single-vineyard Chardonnays and Pinot Noirs made by James Hall, who consistently surpasses peers who have access to the same high-quality fruit. At Salon Tastings the wines are paired with gourmet bites.

Scribe
Two sons of California walnut growers established this winery on land in Sonoma first planted to grapes in the late 1850s by a German immigrant. Their food-friendly, low-alcohol wines include Riesling, Sylvaner, Chardonnay, Pinot Noir, Syrah, and Cabernet Sauvignon.

IF YOU LIKE

Shopping

Fine wine attracts fine everything else—dining, lodging, and spas—and shopping is no exception. The five towns below stand out for quality, selection, and their walkable downtowns.

Healdsburg. Hands-down the Wine Country's best shopping town, Healdsburg supports stores and galleries selling one-of-a-kind artworks, housewares, and clothing. One not to miss: Gallery Lulo, for its jewelry, small sculptures, and objets d'art.

Napa. A good place to start is the Oxbow Public Market, where stands selling teas, spices, honey, and chef's tools do business alongside upscale eateries. To the west along Main Street the best shopping is between 1st Street and 5th Street, where the chocolate-covered wine bottles at Vintage Sweet Shoppe, in the Napa River Inn, make great gifts.

St. Helena. Galleries, housewares, and clothing and other boutiques are packed into Main Street's 1200 and 1300 blocks. Of note for ladies are Pearl Wonderful Clothing, where celebrities and regular folk pick up the latest fashions, and Footcandy, known for drool-worthy heels.

Sonoma. Shops and galleries ring historic Sonoma Plaza and fill adjacent arcades and side streets. A local trendsetter is Chateau Sonoma, for hip and tasteful French housewares and other imports.

Yountville. The town's one-stop retail spot is V Marketplace. Its many shops include chef Michael Chiarello's NapaStyle, which sells everything you'll need to add Wine Country pizazz to your own home. You'll find additional stylish shopping along Washington Street between Mulberry and Madison.

Spas

Spa choices abound, and with ornate treatments involving brown sugar, Cabernet, and other ingredients, the only real question is how much pampering can your wallet withstand. The four facilities below stand out among other worthy contenders in Napa and Sonoma.

Spa at Bardessono, Yountville. The spa at the Hotel Bardessono brings treatments to guests in their rooms, which are equipped with concealed massage tables, but in the main facility guests and nonguests can enjoy massages, body scrubs, facials, and other relaxing and rejuvenating regimens.

Spa at Kenwood Inn, Kenwood. The experience at the Kenwood Inn's small spa is marvelously ethereal. The signature treatments employ the French line Caudalíe's wine-based Vinothérapie treatments, among them the Honey Wine Wrap and the Crushed Cabernet Scrub.

Spa Dolce, Healdsburg. This popular day spa just off Healdsburg Plaza specializes in skin and body care for men and women and waxing and facials for women. Spa Dolce's signature body-scrub treatment combines brown sugar with scented oil.

Spa Solage, Calistoga. The experts at Solage Calistoga's tranquil spa developed the "Mudslide," a kinder, gentler version of the ooey-gooey traditional Calistoga mud bath. Instead of immersing yourself in volcanic ash you slather on fine mud mixed with French clay in a private heated lounge, then take a power nap in a sound/vibration chair. In addition to enjoying spa treatments, you can take fitness and yoga classes here.

Outdoor Activities

Driving from winery to winery you may find yourself captivated by the incredible landscape. To experience it up close, you can ride in a balloon, hop a bike, paddle a canoe or a kayak, or hike on a trail.

Bicycling. The Wine Country's mostly gentle terrain and pleasant daytime climate make a two-wheeled spin past the vineyards a memorable event. Full packages at outfitters might include bikes, lodging, winery tours, and a guide, or you can just rent a bike and head off on your own with the detailed map provided.

Canoeing and kayaking. The Napa and Russian rivers provide serene settings for canoe and kayaking trips past trees, meadows, vineyards, and small towns. Half- and full-day self-guided trips are the norm. You can float with the current to a pickup spot, from which you'll be whisked by van back to your starting point.

Hiking. Of many worthy hiking spots, two associated with literary lights have unforgettable views, and a third winds through scenic redwoods. A 10-mile hike (a bit steep in spots) in Calistoga's Robert Louis Stevenson State Park leads up Mt. St. Helena, and 20 miles of trails traverse Glen Ellen's Jack London State Historic Park. Over in Guerneville, redwoods tower over trails both easy and strenuous at Armstrong Redwoods State Natural Reserve. In spring and fall you can hike through the grapevines at Healdsburg's Alexander Valley Vineyards.

History

History buffs often head first to Sonoma to view its mission and related sites near Sonoma Plaza. Stops at Buena Vista and Bartholomew Park wineries provide insights into 19th-century California wine making. Over in St. Helena, you can learn the Napa side of the story at Charles Krug and Beringer.

Buena Vista and Bartholomew Park, Sonoma. These two wineries east of Sonoma Plaza occupy land once farmed by Agoston Haraszthy, who ushered in the modern era of California wine making when he planted European grape varietals. Exhibits, photos, and artifacts at each winery illustrate his accomplishments.

Charles Krug and Beringer, St. Helena. The Napa Valley's first winery opened in 1861 after Count Agoston Haraszthy lent Charles Krug a small cider press. Beringer Vineyards, founded in 1876 by brothers Frederick and Jacob Beringer, is the valley's oldest continuously operating property. Tours at both wineries focus on early Napa Valley wine making; for more 19th-century history take the tour at Inglenook in Rutherford.

Sonoma Plaza, Sonoma. The last of 21 California missions established by Franciscan friars sits northeast of Sonoma Plaza. You can tour the mission, its barracks, and a small museum. A tall sculpture in the plaza marks the spot where in 1846 American settlers raised a crudely drawn flag depicting a bear and declared independence from Mexico. The "Bear Republic" lasted only a month, but within five years California had achieved statehood.

WHEN TO GO

Timing Your Trip

High season extends from April through October. Between July and September, expect the days to be hot and dry, the roads filled with cars, and traffic heavy at the tasting rooms. In summer and early fall, it's often necessary to book smaller hotels a month or more in advance, and discounts are rare. November, except for Thanksgiving week, and December before Christmas are less busy, in part because the winter rains will usually have started.

Climate

The weather in Napa and Sonoma is pleasant nearly year-round. Daytime temperatures average from about 55°F during winter to the 80s in summer, when readings in the 90s and higher are common. April, May, and October are milder but still warm. Fall mornings are cool but temperatures can rise quickly.

Festivals and Seasonal Events

Harvesttime sees many festivals and events, but there are high profile events year-round. Below are a few of the most popular ones.

Auction Napa Valley. Dozens of events culminate in the Napa Valley's glitziest night—an opulent dinner and auction of rare wines and other coveted items to benefit local nonprofits. It's held on the first full weekend in June. ⊕ *www.auctionnapavalley.org.*

Flavor! Napa Valley. Several days of dinners, cooking demonstrations, and wine-and-food tastings—many involving top chefs and winemakers—take place the week before Thanksgiving. The event benefits the Culinary Institute of America's scholarship and other programs. ⊕ *www.flavornapavalley.com.*

Kendall-Jackson Heirloom Tomato Festival. Culinary-garden tours, a chefs'-challenge cookoff, and heirloom-tomato-growers' competitions are among the highlights of this late-September outdoor event. ⊕ *www.kj.com/visit-tomato-festival.*

Napa Valley Festival del Sole. This acclaimed mid-July event attracts international opera, theater, dance, and musical performers to Castello di Amorosa and other venues. ⊕ *www.festivaldelsole.org.*

Pinot on the River. Pinot Noir fans flock to the Russian River Valley in late October for a weekend of tastings, seminars, and lively discourse about what makes a great Pinot. ⊕ *www.pinotfestival.com.*

Sonoma County Harvest Fair. This early-October festival in Santa Rosa celebrates agriculture with wine and olive-oil competitions, cooking demos, livestock shows, and the perennially popular Harvest Dog Dash. ⊕ *www.harvestfair.org.*

West of West Wine Festival. Wineries and grape growers along Sonoma County's coastline sponsor this early-August festival to promote their cool-climate Chardonnays, Pinot Noirs, Syrahs, and other wines. ⊕ *www.westsonomacoast.com.*

A Wine & Food Affair. For this event during the first weekend in November, wineries prepare a favorite recipe and serve it with wine. Participants travel from winery to winery to sample the fare. ⊕ *www.wineroad.com.*

Wine Road Barrel Tasting Weekends. In early March, more than 100 wineries open their cellars for tastings of wines right out of the aging barrels. ⊕ *www.wineroad.com.*

Winter Wineland. On the Saturday and Sunday of Martin Luther King Jr. Day weekend (mid-January), nearly all the northern Sonoma County wineries offer tastings, seminars, and entertainment. ⊕ *www.wineroad.com.*

KIDS AND FAMILIES

By its very nature, the Wine Country isn't a particularly child-friendly destination. Don't expect to see many children or to find tons of activities organized with them in mind. That said, you'll find plenty of playgrounds (there's one in Sonoma Plaza, for instance), as well as the occasional family-friendly attraction.

Choosing a Place to Stay

If you're traveling with kids, always mention it when making your reservations. Most of the smaller, more romantic inns and bed-and-breakfasts discourage or prohibit children, and those places that do allow them may prefer to put such families in a particular cottage or room so that any noise is less disruptive to other guests. Larger hotels are a mixed bag. Some actively discourage children, whereas others are more welcoming. Of the large, luxurious hotels, Meadowood tends to be the most child-friendly.

Eating Out

Unless your kid is a budding Thomas Keller, it's best to call ahead to see if a restaurant can accommodate those under 12 with a special menu. You will find inexpensive cafés in almost every town, and places like Gott's Roadside, a retro burger stand in St. Helena, are big hits with kids.

Family-Friendly Attractions

One especially family-friendly attraction is the Charles M. Schulz Museum in Santa Rosa. Its intelligent exhibits generally appeal to adults; younger kids may or may not enjoy the level of detail. The sure bets for kids are the play area outside and the education room, where they can color, draw, and create their own cartoons. Another place for a family outing, also in Santa Rosa, is Safari West, an African wildlife preserve on 400 acres. The highlight is the two-hour tour of the property in open-air vehicles that sometimes come within a few feet of giraffes, zebras, and other animals. You can spend the night in tent-cabins here. At Sonoma Canopy Tours, north of Occidental, families zipline through the redwoods together.

At the Wineries

Children are few and far between at most wineries, but well-behaved children will generally be greeted with a smile. Some wineries offer a small treat—grape juice or another beverage or sometimes coloring books or another distraction.

When booking a tour, ask if kids are allowed (for insurance reasons, wineries sometimes prohibit children under a certain age), how long it lasts, and whether there's another tour option that would be more suitable.

A few particularly kid-friendly wineries include Calistoga's Castello di Amorosa (what's not to like about a 107-room medieval castle, complete with a dungeon?) and Sterling Vineyards, where a short aerial tram ride whisks visitors from the parking lot to the tasting room. In Sonoma County, Benziger conducts vineyard tours in a tractor-pulled tram. The picnic grounds are kid-friendly, as are the ones at Sonoma's Bartholomew Park Winery, which also has hiking trails.

You'll find plenty of kids poolside at the Francis Ford Coppola Winery in Geyserville, and Honig Vineyard & Winery in Rutherford prides itself on making sure kids enjoy a visit as much as their parents do.

THE JOYS OF EATING LOCAL

The concept "eat local, think global" may just be catching on elsewhere in the nation, but it's established doctrine in the Wine Country, home to many artisanal food producers, family farmers, and small ranchers. The catalyst for this culinary and agricultural revolution occurred in nearby Berkeley with the 1971 debut of Chez Panisse, run by food pioneer Alice Waters. Initially called California cuisine, her cooking style showcased local, seasonal ingredients in fresh preparations. It also introduced American chefs to international ingredients and techniques. As the movement spread, it became known as New American cooking and these days often falls under the heading of Modern American.

In the early 1980s, John Ash began focusing on food's relationship to wine. His Santa Rosa restaurant helped set the standard for the variant later dubbed Wine Country cuisine. Ash credits Waters with inspiring him and other chefs to seek out "wholesome and unusual ingredients." Today's appeals to reduce the nation's carbon footprint added another wrinkle to the culinary equation's "think global" component, prompting further emphasis on supporting local agriculture and food production. Much of the back-to-the-earth movement's R&D takes place at Napa and Sonoma's farms and enclaves of artisanal production.

Farms and Gardens

A good way to experience the Wine Country's agricultural bounty and the uses to which chefs put fruits, herbs, vegetables and other ingredients is to visit one of the local farms and gardens that supply produce to top restaurants (some of which have their own gardens as well). In summer and early fall you can visit Jacobsen Orchards as part of a Secret Garden Tour and wine tasting booked through Yountville's Hill Family Estate. The 1.3-acre Jacobsen farm, a five-minute drive from downtown, grows figs, peaches, pears, apricots, heirloom tomatoes, green beans, and culinary flowers—even snails—that appear on plates at chef Thomas Keller's The French Laundry and elsewhere. If you're dining at Keller's restaurant you'll appreciate your meal all the more after tasting, for instance, the difference between fresh basil leaves and flowers and learning that Keller's chefs sometimes use herbs' flowers rather than their leaves to impart more delicate flavors. Over in Santa Rosa, you can tour the 3-acre culinary garden outside the Kendall-Jackson tasting room, which supplies produce for the food and wine pairings there and sends ingredients up the road to Partake by K-J, the winery's restaurant in downtown Healdsburg.

Farmers' Markets

Farmers, of course, sell their goods to local high-end grocers, but a more entertaining way to sample the goodies is to browse the same outdoor farmers' markets that local chefs do. The two biggest ones, both in Sonoma County, are the year-round market in the town of Sonoma and the Healdsburg market, held from May through November. Many a Sonoma chef and even a few from Napa can be spotted at either of these popular markets. Two high-profile Napa Valley markets, one in Crane Park in St. Helena on Friday morning, the other next to Napa's Oxbow Public Market on Tuesday and Saturday morning, operate from May through October. All of these markets are perfect places to assemble items for a picnic, by the way.

Fruit

The Wine Country's diverse climate makes it an ideal place to grow many types of fruit. Healdsburg's Dry Creek Peach & Produce, for instance, grows more than 30 varieties of white and yellow peaches, along with nectarines, plums, figs, persimmons, and other fruit. Rare-fruit varieties grown in Napa and Sonoma include prickly pears, loquats, and pluots, a plum-apricot hybrid. The pluot, a fairly recent creation, involved the reverse engineering of the plumcot, a hybrid developed in Sonoma County by horticulturist Luther Burbank. Another fruit that fares well in these parts is the Meyer lemon.

Vegetables

Some chefs give top billing to their produce purveyors. One recent menu touted a salad containing heirloom tomatoes from Big Ranch Farms of Napa and Solano counties. Over in the Sonoma Valley, another restaurant described the main ingredients in a mushroom salad as all locally grown, in some cases in the wild. There's no equivalent of an appellation for vegetables, but that didn't stop a St. Helena restaurant from informing diners that its Swiss chard came from Mt. Veeder—what's good for Cabernet Sauvignon is apparently also good for leafy greens. Other local vegetables gracing Wine Country menus include artichokes, multihued beets and carrots, and heirloom varieties of butternut squash, beans, and even radishes.

Meat

Family-owned ranches and farms are prominent in the region, with many raising organic or "humane-certified" beef, pork, lamb, and poultry. Upscale restaurants are fervent about recognizing their high-quality protein producers.

A well-known St. Helena restaurant, for example, credits Brandt Farms and Bryan Flannery for various beef cuts on its menu, and you'll see the name Mary's for organic chicken and Liberty for ducks. To delve deeper into what happens to meats between farm and restaurant, you can take a Saturday class at the Fatted Calf Charcuterie in the Oxbow Public Market. Classes that often sell out include Pig + Woman + Knife, a class in hog butchery "taught by women for women."

Seafood

Seafood from local waters abounds, from farm-raised scallops to line-caught California salmon. Around Thanksgiving, California's famous Dungeness crab begins appearing on menus, either steamed whole, in salads, or as a featured ingredient in cioppino, a tomato-based seafood stew that originated in San Francisco. Also look for Hog Island Oysters, whose namesake producer raises more than 3 million oysters a year just south of Sonoma County in Tomales Bay.

Cheese

Restaurant cheese plates, often served before—or in lieu of—dessert, are a great way to acquaint yourself with excellent local cheeses. In Sonoma, Vella Cheese, just north of Sonoma Plaza on 2nd Street East, has been producing Dry Monterey Jack and other cheeses since 1931, the same year that the nearby Sonoma Cheese Factory, on Sonoma Plaza, got its start. At the Epicurean Connection, a few steps from Sonoma Plaza on West Napa Street, try owner Sheana Davis's Delice de la Vallee cheese, a blend of triple-cream cow and goat milk that earned a top prize from the American Cheese Society.

GREAT ITINERARIES

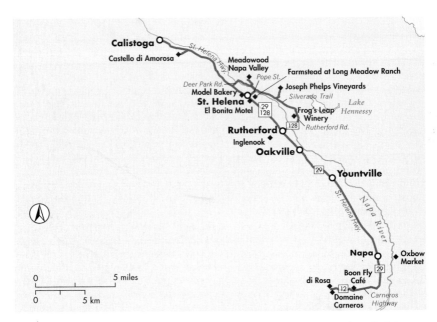

FIRST-TIMER'S NAPA TOUR

On this two-day Napa Valley survey you'll tour key wineries, taste fine wine, learn some history, and shop and dine.

Day 1: History, Tasting, Shopping, Dining

Start your first morning at Napa's **Oxbow Public Market.** Down a brew at Ritual Coffee Roasters, then drive north on Highway 29. At Rutherford stop at film director Francis Ford Coppola's **Inglenook,** whose tour and exhibits provide a fascinating overview of Napa Valley wine making. Continue north on Highway 29 to St. Helena for lunch at **Farmstead at Long Meadow Ranch,** then visit Calistoga's over-the-top **Castello di Amorosa,** off Highway 29, or St. Helena's serene **Joseph Phelps Vineyards,** off the Silverado Trail.

Check into your St. Helena lodgings—luxurious **Meadowood Napa Valley** or pleasantly downscale **El Bonita Motel** are two good options. Poke around St. Helena's shops until dinner, perhaps at Meadowood or **Goose & Gander.**

Day 2: Winery and Art Tours, Lunch, and a Toast

Begin day two over coffee in St. Helena at **Model Bakery,** then drive south on Highway 29 and east on Rutherford Road to **Frog's Leap** (book the winery's entertaining tour in advance). Return to Highway 29 and drive south, then turn west on Highway 121. Stop for lunch at the **Boon Fly Café,** then continue west on Highway 121 to the **di Rosa** arts center and tour its gardens and galleries. Cross Highway 121 to **Domaine Carneros** and toast your trip with some sparkling wine.

SONOMA BACK ROADS TOUR

Stay strictly rural on this easygoing trek through forests, vineyards, and the occasional meadow.

Day 1: From Sebastopol to Forestville

Start day one at the **Barlow** artisan complex in Sebastopol. Have coffee and a pastry at **Taylor Maid Farms** and mosey around, then drive west on Highway 12 to Freestone. Taste cold-climate Chardonnays and Pinot Noirs at **Joseph Phelps Freestone Vineyards.** From Freestone, head north on the Bohemian Highway. Check out the shops in downtown Occidental and have lunch at **Howard Station Cafe.**

After lunch, drive northeast on Graton Road. In Graton, turn northwest on Ross Road and west on Ross Station Road to visit **Iron Horse Vineyards,** known for its sparkling wines. Afterward, backtrack to Highway 116 and turn north. At Martinelli Road, hang a right to reach Forestville's **Hartford Family Winery,** producer of Chardonnays and Pinots. Splurge on a night's rest at the nearby **Farmhouse Inn,** and dine at its stellar restaurant.

Day 2: Healdsburg and Dry Creek

Start day two by taking Wohler Road and then Westside Road north to humble **Porter Creek Vineyards.** After a tasting, continue on Westside to West Dry Creek Road, proceed north, and turn east at Lambert Bridge Road. Assemble a picnic at **Dry Creek General Store,** and continue north on Dry Creek Road to **Truett Hurst Winery.** Taste wines and choose one to have with your picnic here. Backtrack south on Dry Creek Road past the general store, turning east on Lytton Springs Road, which leads to **Ridge Vineyards.** End the day with a Cabernet.

THE ULTIMATE WINE TRIP, 4 DAYS

On this four-day extravaganza, you'll taste well-known and under-the-radar wines, bed down in plush hotels, and dine at restaurants operated by celebrity chefs. Appointments are required for some of the tastings.

Day 1: Sonoma County

Begin your tour in **Geyserville,** about 78 miles north of San Francisco on U.S. 101. Visit **Locals Tasting Room,** which pours the wines of special small wineries. Have lunch at nearby Diavolo or Catelli's, then head south on U.S. 101 and Old Redwood Highway to **Healdsburg's** J Vineyards and Winery, known for sparkling wines, Pinot Grigio, and Pinot Noir. After a tasting, backtrack on Old Redwood to Healdsburg. **Hôtel Les Mars** and **h2hotel** are two well-located spots to spend the night.

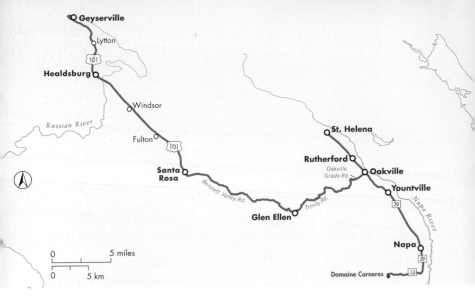

Have dinner at **Chalkboard, Brava de Tapas,** or **Campo Fina,** all close by.

Day 2: Sonoma Wineries

Interesting wineries dot the countryside surrounding Healdsburg, among them **Dry Creek Vineyard, Jordan Vineyard & Winery,** and **Unti Vineyards.** Dry Creek produces Zinfandel, Jordan makes Cabernet Sauvignon and Chardonnay, and Unti specializes in Zinfandel, Sangiovese, and obscure Italian and Rhône varietals. In the afternoon head south on U.S. 101 and east on scenic Highway 12 to **Glen Ellen.** Visit **Jack London State Historic Park,** the memorabilia-filled home of the famous writer. Dine at **Aventine** or **Glen Ellen Star** and stay at the **Olea Hotel.**

Day 3: Napa Valley

On day three, head east from Glen Ellen on Trinity Road, which twists and turns over the Mayacamas Mountains, eventually becoming the Oakville Grade. Unless you're driving, bask in the stupendous **Napa Valley** views. At Highway 29, drive north to **St. Helena.** Focus on history and architecture at **Charles Krug Winery** or let the art and wines at **Hall St. Helena** transport you. Take lunch downtown at **Cindy's Backstreet Kitchen** or **La Condesa.** Check out St. Helena's shopping, then head south on Highway 29 to Yountville for more shopping. Start at celebrity chef Michael Chiarello's **NapaStyle,** inside **V Marketplace.**

Stay overnight at **Bardessono** or the **North Block Hotel,** both within walking distance of Yountville's famous restaurants. A meal at **The French Laundry** is many visitors' holy grail, but dining at **Bouchon, Bistro Jeanty, Redd,** or Chiarello's **Bottega** will also leave you feeling well served.

Day 4: Oakville to Carneros

After breakfast, head north on Highway 29 to **Oakville,** where sipping wine at **Silver Oak Cellars, Nickel & Nickel,** or **B Cellars** will make clear why collectors covet Oakville Cabernet Sauvignons. Nickel & Nickel is on Highway 29; Silver Oak and B Cellars are east of it on Oakville Cross Road. Have a picnic at **Oakville Grocery,** in business on Highway 29 since 1881. Afterward, head south to Highway 121 and turn west to reach the Carneros District. Tour the **di Rosa** arts center (appointment required), then repair across the street to **Domaine Carneros,** which makes French-style sparkling wines. There's hardly a more elegant way to bid a Wine Country adieu than on the Domaine château's vineyard-view terrace.

BEST BOOKS
AND FILMS

BOOKS

Cookbooks

Bottega: Bold Italian Flavors from the Heart of California's Wine Country (2010), by Michael Chiarello. The Food Network star's book takes its name and inspiration from his southern Italian–style Yountville restaurant.

Bouchon Bakery (2012), by Thomas Keller and Sebastien Rouxel. The legendary Keller and his executive pastry chef share recipes that made Yountville's Bouchon Bakery an instant hit.

The Cakebread Cellars American Harvest Cookbook: Celebrating Wine, Food, and Friends in the Napa Valley (2011), by Dolores and Jack Cakebread. This book collects 25 years' worth of recipes from the authors' annual cooking workshops.

The Essential Thomas Keller: The French Laundry Cookbook & Ad Hoc at Home (2010), by Thomas Keller. Recipes inspired by Keller's upscale and down-home Yountville establishments show the chef's great range.

Mustards Grill Napa Valley Cookbook (2001), by Cindy Pawlcyn and Brigid Callinan. Pawlcyn describes her iconic eatery as "a cross between a roadside rib joint and a French country restaurant." She shares recipes and expounds on her culinary philosophy.

Plats du Jour: The Girl & the Fig's Journey Through the Seasons in Wine Country (2011), by Sondra Bernstein. The chef behind Sonoma County's two "fig" restaurants reveals her cooking secrets and adapts some of her signature dishes.

Fiction

Murder Uncorked (2005), *Murder by the Glass: A Wine-Lover's Mystery* (2006), and *Silenced by Syrah* (2007), by Michele Scott. Vineyard manager Nikki Sands is the protagonist of this light and humorous mystery series that unfolds in the Napa Valley.

Nose: A Novel (2013), by James Conaway. A fictitious Northern California wine-making region (couldn't be Napa or Sonoma, could it?) is the setting for a mystery.

Nonfiction

The Emperor of Wine: The Rise of Robert M. Parker, Jr. and the Reign of American Taste (2005), by Elin McCoy. Examination of the American critic's enormous influence considers the sources and worldwide impact of his wine rating system's dominance.

The Far Side of Eden: The Ongoing Saga of Napa Valley (2002), by James Conaway. Conaway's second book on the Wine Country picks up where the first (*Napa, 1992*) left off.

The Finest Wines of California: A Regional Guide to the Best Producers and Their Wines (2011), by Stephen Brook. Part of the World's Finest Wines series, this book profiles 90 top producers.

Harvests of Joy: How the Good Life Became Great Business (1999), by Robert Mondavi and Paul Chutkow. Wine tycoon Robert Mondavi tells his story.

The House of Mondavi: The Rise and Fall of an American Wine Dynasty (2007), by Julia Flynn Siler. The author ruffled many a Napa feather when she published this tell-all book.

Judgment of Paris: California vs. France and the Historic 1976 Paris Tasting That Revolutionized Wine (2005), by George M. Taber. The journalist who originally broke the story of the pivotal event analyzes its history and repercussions.

Matt Kramer's New California Wine: Making Sense of Napa Valley, Sonoma, Central Coast & Beyond (2004), by Matt Kramer. The *Wine Spectator* columnist covers the development of California wine and the wine industry.

Napa Valley: The Land, the Wine, the People (2001), by Charles O'Rear. A former *National Geographic* photographer portrays the valley in this lush book.

The New California Wine: A Guide to the Producers and Wines Behind a Revolution in Taste (2013), by Jon Bonné. The locally influential *San Francisco Chronicle* wine columnist profiles the leaders of the movement to create "wines that show nuance, restraint, and a deep evocation of place."

The New Connoisseurs' Guidebook to California Wine and Wineries (2010), by Charles E. Olken and Joseph Furstenthal. The two authors survey the state's main wine regions.

A New Napa Cuisine (2014), by Christopher Kostow. The much-lauded chef of the Restaurant at Meadowood in St. Helena describes his evolution as a chef and his land-focused approach to cooking.

Postmodern Winemaking: Rethinking the Modern Science of an Ancient Craft (2013), by Clark Smith. A wonky treatise by a longtime winemaker and current Santa Rosa resident, this book ponders the roles of science and art in the creation of great wine.

Sniff, Swirl & Slurp (2002), by Max Allen. This compact handbook provides guidelines on maximizing the wine-drinking experience.

When the Rivers Ran Red: An Amazing Story of Courage and Triumph in America's Wine Country (2009), by Vivienne Sosnowski. The author chronicles the devastating effect of Prohibition on Northern California winemakers.

Zinfandel: A History of a Grape and Its Wine (2003), by Charles Sullivan. The story of America's unique varietal is the story of California wine country.

FILMS AND TV

Bottle Shock (2008). Filmed primarily in the Napa and Sonoma valleys, director Randall Miller's lighthearted, fictionalized feature about the 1976 Paris tasting focuses on Calistoga's Chateau Montelena.

Falcon Crest (1981–1990). This soap opera centered on a winery in the fictional "Tuscany Valley" (aka Napa) may not have aged as well as the best wines made during its era, but it has acquired a nostalgic patina and at its best it's pulpy good fun.

Mondovino (2005). Documentary filmmaker Jonathan Nossiter probes the rocky relationship between the wine industries of California and Europe.

Napa Valley Dreams (2013). Rodney Vance wrote and directed this contemplative love note to the Napa Valley; the 41-minute documentary includes juicy location shots and interviews with major winemakers and other valley residents.

Somm (2012). Some of the scenes in Jason Wise's intense documentary about four sommeliers striving to pass the master sommelier exam were shot in the Napa Valley.

VISITING WINERIES AND TASTING ROOMS

Whether you're a serious wine collector making your annual pilgrimage to Northern California's Wine Country or a newbie who doesn't know the difference between a Merlot and Mourvèdre but is eager to learn, you can have a great time touring Napa and Sonoma wineries. Your gateway to the wine world is the tasting room, where staff members—and occasionally even the actual winemaker—are almost always happy to chat with curious guests.

Tasting rooms range from the grand to the humble, offering everything from a few sips of wine to in-depth tours of the wine-making facilities and vineyards. First-time visitors frequently enjoy the history-oriented tours at Beaulieu, Beringer, Charles Krug, and Inglenook, or the ones at Mondavi, J Vineyards, and Korbel that highlight process as well. The environments at some wineries reflect their founders' other interests: horses at Nickel & Nickel and Tamber Bey, movie making at Francis Ford Coppola and Frank Family, art and architecture at Artesa and Hall St. Helena, and medieval history at the Castello di Amorosa.

These days many wineries describe their tasting room pourers as "wine educators," and indeed some of them have taken online or other classes and have passed an exam to prove basic knowledge of appellations, grape varietals, vineyards, and wine-making techniques. Others are simply well versed in the lore and procedures of their particular wineries. The one constant, however, is a deep, shared pleasure in the experience of wine tasting.

To prepare yourself for your winery visits, we've covered the fundamentals: tasting rooms and what to expect, how to save money on tasting fees, and the types of tours typically offered by wineries. A list of common tasting terms will help you interpret what your mouth is experiencing as you sip. We've also provided a description of the major grape varietals, as well as the specific techniques employed to craft white, red, sparkling, and rosé wines. Because great wines begin in the vineyards, we've included a section on soils, climates, and organic and biodynamic farming methods. A handy Wine-Lover's Glossary of terms, from *acidity* to *zymology*, covers what you may come across in the tasting room or on a tour.

WINE TASTING 101

Don't be intimidated by sommeliers who toss around esoteric adjectives as they swirl their glasses. At its core, wine tasting is simply about determining which wines you like best. However, knowing a few basic tasting steps and a few key quality guidelines can make your winery visit much more enjoyable and help you remember which wines you liked, and why, long after you return home. ■ TIP→ **Above all, follow your instincts at the tasting bar: there is no right or wrong way to describe wine.**

If you watch the pros, you'll probably notice that they take time to inspect, swirl, and sniff the wine before they get around to sipping it. Follow their lead and take your time, going through each of the following steps for each wine. Starting with the pop of the cork and the splashing of wine into a glass, all of your senses play a part in wine tasting.

USE YOUR EYES

Before you taste it, take a good look at the wine in your glass. Holding the glass by the stem, raise it to the light. Whether it's white, rosé, or red, your wine should be clear, without cloudiness or sediments, when you drink it. Some unfiltered wines may seem cloudy at first, but they will clear as the sediments settle.

In the natural light, place the glass in front of a white background such as a blank sheet of paper or a tablecloth. **Check the color.** Is it right for the wine? A California white should be golden: straw, medium, or deep, depending on the type. Rich, sweet, dessert wine will have more intense color, but Chardonnay and Sauvignon Blanc will be paler. A rosé should be a clear pink, from pale to deep, without too much red or any orange. Reds may lean toward ruby or garnet coloring; some have a purple tinge. They shouldn't be pale (the exception is Pinot Noir, which can be quite pale yet still have character). In any color of wine, a brownish tinge is a flaw that indicates the wine is too old, has been incorrectly stored, or has gone bad. If you see brown, try another bottle.

BREATHE DEEP

You might notice that experienced wine tasters spend more time sniffing the wine than drinking it. This is because this step is where the magic happens: aroma plays a huge role in wine's flavor. After you have looked at the wine's color, **sniff the wine once or twice** to see if you can identify any aromas. Then gently move your glass in a circular motion to swirl the wine around. Aerating the wine this way releases more of its aromas. (It's called "volatilizing the esters," if you're trying to impress someone.) Stick your nose into the glass and take another long sniff.

Wine should smell good to you. You might pick up the scent of apricots, peaches, ripe melon, honey, and wildflowers in a white wine; black pepper, cherry, violets, and cedar in a red. Rosés (which are made from red-wine grapes) smell something like red wine, but in a scaled-back way, with hints of raspberry, strawberry, and sometimes a touch of rose petal. You might encounter surprising smells, such as tar—which some people actually appreciate in certain (generally expensive, red) wines.

For the most part, a wine's aroma should be clean and pleasing to you, not "off." If you find a wine's odor odd or unpleasant, there's probably something wrong. Watch out for hints of wet dog or skunk, or for moldy, horsey, mousy, or sweaty smells. Sniff for chemical faults such as sulfur, or excessive vanilla scents (picked up from oak barrels) that overwhelm the other aromas. A vinegar smell indicates that the wine has started to spoil. A rotten wood or soggy cardboard smell usually means that the cork has gone bad, ruining the wine. It's extremely rare to find these faults in wines poured in the tasting rooms, however, because staffers usually taste each bottle before pouring from it.

JUST A SIP

Once you've checked its appearance and aroma, **take a sip**—not a swig or a gulp—of the wine. As you sip a wine, **gently swish it around in your mouth**—this releases more aromas for your nose to explore. Do the aroma and the flavor complement each other, improve each other? While moving the wine around in your mouth, also think about the way it feels: silky or crisp? Does it coat your tongue or is it thinner? Does it seem to fill your mouth with flavor or is it weak? This combination of weight and intensity is referred to as *body*: a good wine may be light-, medium-, or full-bodied.

Do you like it? If not, don't drink it. Even if there is nothing actually wrong with a wine, what's the point of drinking it if you don't like it? A wine can be technically perfect but nevertheless taste strange, unpleasant, or just boring to you. It's possible to learn to appreciate wine that doesn't appeal to your tastes, but unless you like a wine right off the bat, it probably won't become a favorite. In the tasting room, dump what you don't like and move on to the next sample.

The more complex a wine, the more flavors you will detect in the course of tasting. You might experience different things when you first take a sip (*up front*), when you swish (*in the middle* or *at mid-palate*), and just before you swallow (*at the end* or *on the back-palate*). A good table wine should be neither too sweet nor too tart, and never bitter. Fruitiness, a subtle near-sweetness, should be balanced by acidity, but not to the point that the wine tastes sour or makes your mouth pucker. An astringent or drying quality is the mark of tannins, a somewhat mysterious wine element that comes from grape skins and oak barrels. In young reds this can taste almost bitter—but not quite. All these qualities, together with the wine's aroma, blend to evoke the flavors—not only of fruit but also of unlikely things such as leather, tobacco, or almonds.

SPIT OR SWALLOW?

You may choose to spit out the wine (into the dump bucket or a plastic cup) or swallow it. The pros typically spit, because they want to preserve their palates (and sobriety!) for the wines to come, but you'll find that swallowers far outnumber spitters in the winery tasting rooms. Either way, **pay attention to what happens after the wine leaves your mouth**—this is the finish, and it can be spectacular. What sensations stay behind or appear? Does the flavor fade away quickly or linger pleasantly? A long finish is a sign of quality; wine with no perceptible finish is inferior.

TASTING ROOMS AND WINERY TOURS

Some wineries in Napa and Sonoma have opulent faux châteaus with vast gift shops; others welcome guests with rough converted barns where you might have to step over the vintner's dog in the doorway. But it doesn't matter if you're visiting an elaborate tasting room complete with art gallery and upscale restaurant, or you're squeezed into the corner of a cinder-block warehouse amid stacked boxes and idle equipment: either way, tasting rooms are designed to introduce newcomers to the pleasures of wine and to inform visitors about the wines made at that winery. So don't worry if you're new to tasting. Relax, grab a glass, and join in for a good time.

At most wineries, you'll have to pay for the privilege of tasting—from $5 to $25 for a standard tasting of some or all of a winery's current releases and from $15 to $40 (and up at truly high-end wineries) to taste reserve, estate, or library wines. To experience wine making at its highest level, consider splurging for a special tasting at one winery at least.

In general, you'll find the fees slightly higher in Napa than in Sonoma, though there are exceptions to this rule. No matter which region you're in, you'll still find the occasional freebie—though it's likely to be at a spot that's off the major tourist thoroughfares and on some little-traveled back road.

In tasting rooms, tipping is very much the exception rather than the rule. Most frequent visitors to the Wine Country never tip those pouring the wines in the tasting rooms, though if a server has gone out of his or her way to be helpful—by pouring special wines not on the list, for example—leaving $5 or so would be a nice gesture.

Many wineries are open to the public, usually daily from around 10 or 11 am to 5 pm. They may close as early as 4 or 4:30, especially in winter, so it's best to get a reasonably early start if you want to fit in more than a few spots. ■ TIP➔ **Most wineries stop serving new visitors 15 to 30 minutes before the posted closing time, so don't expect to skate in at the last moment.** Some wineries require reservations, and still others are closed to the public entirely. When in doubt, call in advance.

Though you might have the tasting room all to yourself if you visit midweek in winter, in summer, during crush (harvest season), and on weekends it's likely you'll be bumping elbows with other tasters and vying for the attention of the server behind the bar. If you prefer smaller crowds, look for wineries off the main drags of Highway 29 in Napa and Highway 12 in Sonoma. Look for wineries that are open by appointment only; they tend to schedule visitors carefully to avoid big crowds. Keep in mind that many wineries require appointments not to be snooty or exclusive, but because zoning regulations or occupancy restrictions compel them to limit the number of guests they receive. At some wineries, calling from the driveway constitutes sufficient notice, but for others phoning or reserving online a day ahead really is necessary. If the urge suddenly strikes to visit one of the latter, though, it never hurts to call and see if there's an opening that day.

Wineries tend to have fewer tasters early in the morning and get busiest between 3 pm and closing. On weekends, do what the locals do—visit on Sunday rather than Saturday. As many veteran tasting-room pourers will attest, Sunday is generally mellower. Saturday crowds include more people in weekend party mode and on bus and limo tours.

Finally, remember that those little sips add up, so pace yourself. If you plan to visit several wineries, try just a few wines at each so you don't hit sensory overload, when your mouth can no longer distinguish subtleties. (This is called palate fatigue.) ■TIP→ **Choose a designated driver for the day: roads are often narrow and curvy.** You may be sharing your lane with bicyclists and wildlife as well. Although wineries rarely advertise it, many will provide a free nonalcoholic drink for the designated driver; it never hurts to ask.

IN THE TASTING ROOM

In most tasting rooms, a list of the wines available that day will be on the bar or offered by the server. The wines will be listed in a suggested tasting order, starting with the lightest-bodied whites and progressing to the most intense reds. Dessert wines will come at the end.

You'll usually find an assortment of the winery's current releases. There might also be a list of reserve (special in some way) or library (older) wines you can taste for a larger fee. To create a more cohesive experience, tasting rooms sometimes offer "flights" consisting of three or more particular wines selected to complement or contrast with one another. These might be vertical (several vintages of one wine), horizontal (several different varietals from one season), or more intuitively assembled.

Don't feel the need to try all the wines you're offered. In fact, many wineries indicate at the bottom of the list that you're limited to four or five. (In reality, however, servers rarely hold you to this limit if the tasting room isn't too crowded and you're showing a sincere interest in the wines.) If you can't decide which wines to choose, tell the server what types of wines you usually like and ask for a recommendation.

The server will pour you an ounce or so of each wine you select. As you taste it, feel free to take notes or ask questions. ■TIP→ **If you use the list of the wines for your note taking, you'll have a handy record of your impressions at the end of your trip.** There might be a plate of

2

Money-Saving Tips

Those $20 tasting fees can add up awfully quickly if you're not careful, so consider the following tips for whittling down your wine-tasting budget.

■ Many hotels, bed-and-breakfasts, and visitor centers distribute coupons for free or discounted tastings—don't forget to ask. Also check winery websites for similar coupons you can print or send to your smartphone.

■ If you and your travel partner don't mind sharing a glass, servers are happy to let you split a tasting. (This is also a good way to pace yourself to keep from becoming tipsy.)

■ Get off the beaten track. Wineries along heavily traveled routes in Napa and Sonoma typically charge the most. Smaller spots along the back roads often charge less—or sometimes nothing at all.

■ Some wineries refund the tasting fee if you buy a bottle. Usually one fee is waived per bottle, though high-end wineries may require you to buy two or more bottles, or purchase a certain dollar amount. If the tasting list doesn't indicate that the fee is waived with a purchase, it's wise to ask.

crackers on the bar; nibble them when you want to clear your palate before tasting the next selection.

If you don't like a wine, or you've simply tasted enough, feel free to pour the rest into one of the dump buckets on the bar (if you don't see one, just ask).

TAKING A TOUR

Even if you're not a devoted wine drinker, seeing how grapes become wine can be fascinating. Tours tend to be most exciting (and most crowded) in September and October, when the harvest and crushing are under way. In harvest season you'll likely see workers picking in the vineyards and hauling bins and barrels around with forklifts. At other times of the year, the work consists of monitoring wine, "racking" it (eliminating sediment by transferring it from one tank or barrel to another), and bottling the finished wine.

Depending on the size of the winery, tours range from a few people to large groups and typically last 30 minutes to an hour. The guide explains what happens at each stage of the wine-making process, usually emphasizing the winery's particular approach to growing and wine making. Feel free to ask questions at any point in the tour. If it's harvest or bottling time, you might see and hear the facility at work. Otherwise, the scene is likely to be quiet, with just a few workers tending the tanks and barrels.

Some winery tours are free, in which case you usually pay a separate fee to taste the wine. If you've paid for the tour—often from $10 to $30—your wine tasting is usually included in the price. ■**TIP→ Wear comfortable shoes, because you might be walking on wet floors or** stepping over hoses or other equipment. Dress in layers, because many tours take you to facilities where temperatures may be hot or cold.

At large wineries, introductory tours are typically offered several times daily. Less frequent are specialized tours and seminars focusing on such subjects as growing techniques, sensory evaluation, wine blending, and food-and-wine pairing. These events typically cost from $20 to $50, sometimes a bit more if lunch is included. If you're spending a few days in the Wine Country, it's worth making a reservation for at least one of these in-depth experiences.

TOP CALIFORNIA GRAPE VARIETALS

Several dozen grape varietals are grown in the Wine Country, from favorites like Chardonnay and Cabernet Sauvignon to less familiar types like Albariño and Tempranillo. Although you don't need to be on a first-name basis with them all, you'll likely come across many of the following varietals as you visit the wineries.

WHITE

Albariño. One of the most popular wine grapes in Spain (it's also a staple of Portuguese wine making), this cool-climate grape creates light, citrusy wines, often with overtones of mango or kiwi. Some wineries in the Carneros region are experimenting with Albariño.

Chardonnay. California Chardonnays spent many years chasing big, buttery flavor, but the current trend is toward more restrained wines that let the grapes shine through. Because of Napa and Sonoma's warmer, longer growing seasons, Chardonnays from those regions will always be bolder than their counterparts in Burgundy.

Chenin Blanc. This Loire Valley native can produce a smooth, pleasingly acidic California wine. It gets short shrift with a lot of wine reviewers because of its relative simplicity and light body, but many drinkers appreciate the style.

Gewürztraminer. Cooler California climes such as the Russian River Valley are great for growing this German-Alsatian grape, which is turned into a boldly perfumed, fruity wine.

Marsanne. A white-wine grape of France's northern Rhône Valley, Marsanne can produce an overly heavy wine unless handled with care. It's becoming more popular in California in these Rhône-blend-crazy times.

Pinot Gris. Known in Italy as Pinot Grigio, this varietal yields a more deeply colored wine in California. It's not highly acidic and has a medium to full body.

Riesling. Also called White Riesling, this cool-climate German grape has a sweet reputation in America. When made in a dry style, though, it can be crisply refreshing, with lush aromas.

Buying and Shipping Wine

Don't feel obliged to buy a bottle of wine just because the winery has given you a taste, especially if you have paid a tasting fee. Still, many visitors like to buy a bottle or two from small wineries as a courtesy, especially when they have taken more than a few minutes of the staff's time.

If you discover a bottle you particularly like, ask where it's available. Some wines, especially those from bigger operations, are widely distributed, but many are available only at the wineries themselves, and perhaps at a handful of restaurants or shops in the area. You might want to stock up if you won't be able to get a desired wine at home.

If several of a winery's offerings appeal to you and you live in a state that allows you to order wines directly from wineries (most staffers have this information at the ready), consider joining its wine club. You'll receive offers for members-only releases, invitations to winery events, and a discount on all of your purchases.

Ask about the winery's direct-shipment program. Most wineries are happy to ship your wine, as long as you live in a state where it's permitted. Wineries offer the full range of shipping options, and they'll sell you Styrofoam chests or wheeled, padded cases you can use on your flight home. For up-to-date information about whether your state allows shipping, check out the website run by the Wine Institute, ⊕ *www.wineinstitute.org/programs/shipwine.*

Roussanne. This grape from the Rhône Valley makes an especially fragrant wine that can achieve a balance of fruitiness and acidity.

Sauvignon Blanc. Hailing from Bordeaux and France's Loire Valley, this white grape does very well almost anywhere in California. Wines made from this grape display a wide range of personalities, from herbaceous to tropical-fruity.

Viognier. Until the early 1990s, Viognier was rarely planted outside France's Rhône Valley, but today it's one of California's hottest white-wine varietals. Usually made in a dry style, the best Viogniers have an intense fruity or floral bouquet.

RED

Barbera. Prevalent in California thanks to 19th-century Italian immigrants, Barbera yields easy-drinking, low-tannin wines with big fruit and high acid.

Cabernet Franc. Most often used in blends, often to add complexity to Cabernet Sauvignon, this French grape can produce aromatic, soft, and subtle wines. An often earthy, or even stinky, aroma repels some drinkers and makes avid fans of others.

Cabernet Sauvignon. The king of California reds, this Bordeaux grape is at home in well-drained soils. At its best, the California version is dark, bold, and tannic, with black currant notes. On its own it can require a long aging period, so it's often softened with Cabernet Franc, Merlot, and other red varieties for earlier drinking.

Gamay. Also called Gamay Beaujolais, this vigorous French grape variety is widely planted in California. It produces pleasant reds and rosés that should be drunk young.

Grenache. This Spanish grape, which makes some of the southern Rhône Valley's most distinguished wines, ripens best in hot, dry conditions. Done right, Grenache is dark and concentrated and improves with age.

Merlot. This blue-black Bordeaux varietal makes soft, full-bodied wine when grown in California. It's often fruity, and can be complex even when young. Merlot's rep was tarnished by the movie *Sideways* (and by the introduction of cheap, too-sweet versions), but aficionados of the Napa Valley's high-quality representatives have never lost faith.

Mourvèdre. This red-wine grape makes wine that is deeply colored, very dense, high in alcohol, and at first harsh, but it mellows with several years of aging. It's a native of France's Rhône Valley and is increasingly popular in California.

Nebbiolo. The great red-wine grape of Italy's Piedmont region is now widely planted in California. It produces sturdy, full-bodied wines that are fairly high in alcohol and age splendidly.

Petite Sirah. Unrelated to the Rhône grape Syrah, Petite Sirah may be a hybrid created in the mid-19th-century California vineyard—no one is sure. It produces a hearty wine that is often used in blends.

Pinot Noir. The darling of grape growers in cooler parts of Napa and Sonoma, including the Carneros region and the Russian River Valley, Pinot Noir is also called the "heartbreak grape" because it's hard to cultivate. At its best it has a subtle but addictive earthy quality.

Sangiovese. This red grape dominates the Chianti region and much of central Italy. Depending on how it's grown and vinified, it can be made into vibrant, light- to medium-bodied wines, as well as into long-lived, very complex reds.

Syrah. Another big California red, this grape originated in the Rhône Valley. With good tannins it can become a full-bodied, almost smoky beauty (without them it can be flabby and forgettable). California plantings increased rapidly after the mid-1990s, thanks to the soaring reputation of Rhône-style wines and the popularity of Syrah from Australia, where it is called Shiraz.

Tempranillo. The major varietal in Spain's Rioja region, sturdy Tempranillo makes inky purple wines with a beautifully rich texture. Wines made from this grape are great on their own but excel when paired with red-meat and game dishes.

Zinfandel. Celebrated as California's own (though it has distant old-world origins), Zinfandel is rich and spicy. Its tannins can make it complex and well suited for aging, but too often it is made in an overly jammy, almost syrupy, style. Typically grown to extreme ripeness, the grape can produce wines with high alcohol levels.

HOW WINE IS MADE

THE CRUSH

The process of turning grapes into wine generally starts at the **crush pad,** where the grapes are brought in from the vineyards. Good winemakers carefully monitor their grapes throughout the year, but their presence is especially critical at harvest, when ripeness determines the proper day for picking. Once that day arrives, the crush begins.

Wineries pick their grapes by machine or by hand, depending on the terrain and on the type of grape. Some varietals are harvested at night with the help of powerful floodlights. Why at night? In addition to it being easier on the workers (daytime temperatures often reach 90°F [32°C] or more in September), the fruit-acid content in the pulp and juice of the grapes peaks in the cool night air. The acids—an essential component during fermentation and aging, and an important part of wine's flavor—plummet in the heat of the day.

Grapes must be handled with care so that none of the juice is lost. They arrive at the crush pad in large containers called gondolas. Unless the winemaker intends to ferment the entire clusters, which is generally done only for red wines to strengthen the tannins or add flavors or aromas, they are dropped gently onto a conveyor belt that deposits them into a **stemmer-crusher,** which gently separates the grapes from their stems. Then the sorting process begins. At most wineries this is done by hand at sorting tables, where workers remove remaining stems and leaves and reject any obviously damaged berries. Because anything not sorted out will wind up in the fermenting tank, some wineries double or even triple sort to achieve higher quality. Stems, for instance, can add unwanted tannins to a finished wine. On the other hand, winemakers sometimes desire those tannins and allow some stems through. A few high-end wineries use electronic optical grape sorters that scan and assess the fruit. Berries deemed too small or otherwise defective are whisked away, along with any extraneous vegetal matter.

No matter the process used, the sorted grapes are then ready for transfer to a press or vat.

After this step, the production process goes one of four ways, depending on whether a white, red, rosé, or sparkling wine is being made.

WHITE WINES

The juice of white-wine grapes first goes to **settling tanks,** where the skins and solids sink to the bottom, separating from the free-run juice on top. The material in the settling tanks still contains a lot of juice, so after the free-run juice is pumped off, the rest goes into a **press.** A modern press consists of a perforated drum containing a Teflon-coated bag. As this bag is inflated like a balloon, it slowly pushes the grapes against the outside wall and the liquids are gently squeezed from the solids. Like the free-run juice, the press juice is pumped into a stainless-steel **fermenter.**

Press juice and free-run juice are fermented separately, but a little of the press juice may be added to the free-run juice for complexity. Because press juice tends to be strongly flavored and may contain undesirable flavor components, winemakers are careful not to add too much. Most white wines are fermented at 59°F to 68°F (15°C to 20°C). Cooler temperatures, which develop delicacy and fruit aromas, are especially important for Sauvignon Blanc and Riesling.

During fermentation, yeast feeds on the sugar in grape juice and converts it to alcohol and carbon dioxide. Wine yeast dies and fermentation naturally stops in two to four weeks, when the alcohol level reaches 15% (or sometimes more). If there's not enough sugar in the grapes to reach the desired alcohol level, the winemaker can add extra sugar before or during fermentation in a process called **chaptalization.**

To prevent oxidation that damages wine's color and flavor and kills wild yeast and bacteria that produces off flavors, winemakers almost always add sulfur dioxide, in the form of sulfites, before fermenting. A winemaker may also encourage **malolactic fermentation** (or simply *malo*) to soften a wine's acidity or deepen its flavor and complexity. This is done either by inoculating the wine with lactic bacteria soon after fermentation begins or right after it ends, or by transferring the new wine to wooden vats that harbor the bacteria. Malo, which can also happen by accident, is undesirable in lighter-bodied wines because it overpowers the flavor from the grapes.

For richer results, free-run juice from Chardonnay grapes, as well as some from Sauvignon Blanc grapes, might be fermented in oak barrels. **Barrel fermentation** creates more depth and complexity, as the wine picks up vanilla flavors and other harmonious traits from the wood. In many cases the barrels used to make white wines, especially Sauvignon Blanc, are older, "neutral" barrels previously used to make other wines. These neutral barrels can add a fullness to a wine without adding any wood flavors. Sometimes, though, the winemaker uses a percentage of "new oak" (the term for the first time a barrel is used). The barrels used by California winemakers may be made in America or imported from France or Eastern Europe. They are very expensive and can be used for only a few years. In recent years, wineries have begun using "concrete eggs"—egg-shape fermenting tanks made out of concrete—mostly to make white wines. Bigger than a barrel but smaller than most stainless tanks, the eggs, like barrels, are porous enough to "breathe," but unlike wood don't impart flavors or tannins to wines. Some winemakers believe concrete can increase the minerality and the feel in the mouth of wines such as Sauvignon Blanc or Chardonnay. The egg shape is thought to aid in fermentation, because as the wine is fermenting it becomes hotter and starts to bubble like water boiling in a pan. Some winemakers believe that the flavors mix better at this stage than they do in other fermenters. The notion of fermenting wines in concrete receptacles may sound new-fangled, but their use dates back to the 19th century (and some say even farther back).

When the wine has finished fermenting, whether in a tank or a barrel, it is generally **racked**—moved into a clean tank or barrel to separate it

from any remaining grape solids. Sometimes Chardonnay and special batches of Sauvignon Blanc are left "on the lees"—atop the spent yeast, grape solids, and other matter that were in the fermenting tank—for extended periods of time before being racked to pick up extra complexity. Wine may be racked several times as the sediment continues to settle out.

After the first racking, the wine may be **filtered** to take out solid particles that can cloud the wine and any stray yeast or bacteria that can spoil it. This is especially common for whites, which may be filtered several times before bottling. This is a common practice among commercial producers, but many fine-wine makers resist filtering, as they believe it leads to less complex wines that don't age as well.

White wine may also be **fined** by mixing in a fine clay called bentonite or albumen from egg whites. As they settle out, they absorb undesirable substances that can cloud the wine. As with filtering, the process is more common with ordinary table wines than with fine wines.

Winemakers typically blend several batches of wine together to balance flavor. Careful **blending** gives them an extra chance to create a perfect single-varietal wine or to combine several varietals that complement each other in a blend. Premium vintners also make unblended wines that highlight the attributes of grapes from a single vineyard.

New wine is stored in stainless-steel, oak, or concrete containers to rest and develop before bottling. This stage, called **maturation** or **aging,** may last anywhere from a few months to more than a year. Barrel rooms are kept dark to protect the wine from both light and heat, either of which can be damaging. Some wineries keep their wines in air-conditioned rooms or warehouses; others use long, tunnel-like caves bored into hillsides, where the wine remains at a constant temperature.

If wine is aged for any length of time before bottling, it will be racked and perhaps filtered several times. Once it is bottled, the wine is stored for **bottle aging.** This is done in a cool, dark space to prevent the corks from drying out; a shrunken cork allows oxygen to enter the bottle and spoil the wine. In a few months, most white wines will be ready for release.

RED WINES

Red-wine production differs slightly from that of white wine. Red-wine grapes are crushed in the same way, but the juice is not separated from the grape skins and pulp before fermentation. This is what gives red wine its color. After crushing, the red-wine **must**—the thick slurry of juice, pulp, and skins—is fermented in vats. The juice is "left on the skins" for varying amounts of time, from a few days to a few weeks, depending on the type of grape and on how much color and flavor the winemaker wants to extract.

Fermentation also extracts chemical compounds such as **tannins** from the skins and seeds, making red wines more robust than whites. In a red designed for drinking soon after bottling, tannin levels are kept down; they should have a greater presence in wine meant for aging. In a young red not ready for drinking, tannins feel dry or coarse in your mouth, but they soften over time. A wine with well-balanced tannin will maintain its fruitiness and backbone as its flavor develops. Without adequate tannins, a wine will not age well.

Creating the **oak barrels** that age the wine is a craft in its own right. At Demptos Napa Cooperage, a French-owned company that employs French barrel-making techniques, the process involves several elaborate production phases. The staves of oak are formed into the shape of a barrel using metal bands, and then the rough edges of the bound planks are smoothed. Finally, the barrels are literally toasted to give the oak its characteristic flavor, which will in turn be imparted to the wine.

Red-wine fermentation occurs at a higher temperature than that for whites—about 70°F to 90°F (21°C to 32°C). As the grape sugars are converted into alcohol, large amounts of carbon dioxide are generated. Carbon dioxide is lighter than wine but heavier than air, and it forms an **"aerobic cover"** that protects the wine from oxidation. As the wine ferments, grape skins rise to the top and are periodically mixed back in so the wine can extract the maximum amount of color and flavor. This is done either in the traditional fashion by punching them down with a large handheld tool or by pumping the wine from the bottom of the vat and pouring it back in at the top.

At the end of fermentation, the free-run wine is drained off. The grape skins and pulp are sent to a press, where the remaining liquid is extracted. As with white wines, the winemaker may blend a little of the press wine into the free-run wine to add complexity. Otherwise, the press juice goes into bulk wine—the lower-quality, less expensive stuff. The better wine is racked and then perhaps fined; some reds are left unfined for extra depth.

Next up is **oak-barrel aging,** which takes from a half year to a year or longer. Oak, like grapes, contains natural tannins, and the wine extracts these tannins from the barrels. The wood also has countless tiny pores through which water slowly evaporates, making the wine more concentrated. To make sure the aging wine does not oxidize, the barrels have to be regularly **topped off** with wine from the same vintage.

New, or virgin, oak barrels impart the most tannins to a wine. With each successive use the tannins are diminished, until the barrel is said to be "neutral." Depending on the varietal, winemakers might blend juice aged in virgin oak barrels with juice aged in neutral barrels. In the tasting room you may hear, for instance, that a Pinot Noir was aged in 30% new oak and 70% two-year-old oak, meaning that the bulk of the wine was aged in oak used for two previous agings.

The only way even the best winemaker can tell if a wine is finished is by tasting it. A winemaker constantly tastes wines during fermentation, while they are aging in barrels, and, less often, while they age in bottles. The wine is released for sale when the winemaker's palate and nose say it's ready.

A winemaker checks on a vintage being aged in barrels.

SPARKLING WINES

Despite the mystique surrounding them, sparkling wines are nothing more or less than wines in which carbon dioxide is suspended, making them bubbly. Good sparkling wine will always be fairly expensive because a great deal of work goes into making it.

White sparkling wines can be made from either white or black grapes. In France, Champagne is traditionally made from Pinot Noir or Chardonnay grapes, whereas in California sparkling wine might be made with Pinot Blanc, Riesling, or sometimes other white grapes. If black grapes are used, they must be picked very carefully to avoid crushing them. The goal is to minimize contact between the inner fruit (which is usually white) and the skins, where the purplish-red color pigments reside. The grapes are rushed to the winery and crushed very gently, preventing the juice from coming in contact with the pigments and turning red. Even so, some sparklers have more of a pink tinge to them than the winemaker intends.

The freshly pressed juice and pulp, or must, is **fermented with special yeasts** that preserve the characteristic fruit flavor of the grape variety used. Before bottling, this finished "still" wine (wine without bubbles) is mixed with a *liqueur de tirage,* a blend of wine, sugar, and yeast. This mixture causes the wine to ferment again—in the bottle, where it stays for up to 12 weeks. **Carbon dioxide**, a by-product of fermentation, is produced and trapped in the bottle, where it dissolves into the wine (instead of escaping into the air, as happens during fermentation in barrel, vat, or tank). This captive carbon dioxide transforms a still wine into a sparkler.

CLOSE UP

It's All on the Label

If you look beyond the photograph of a weathered château or the quirky drawing of a cartoon creature, a wine's label will tell you a lot about what's inside. If you want to decode the details, look for the following information:

■ **Alcohol content:** In most cases, U.S. law requires bottles to list the alcohol content, which typically hovers around 13% or 14%, but big red wines from California, especially Zinfandel, can soar to 16% or more.

■ **Appellation:** At least 85% of the grapes must have come from the AVA (American Viticultural Area) listed on the bottle. A bottle that says "Mt. Veeder," for example, contains mostly grapes that are grown in the compact Mt. Veeder appellation, but if the label simply says "California," the grapes could have come from anywhere in the state.

■ **Estate or Estate Grown:** Wines with this label must be made entirely of grapes grown on land owned or farmed by the winery.

■ **Reserve:** An inexact term meaning "special" (and therefore usually costing more), *reserve* can refer to how or where the grapes were grown, how the wine was made, or even how long it was aged.

■ **Varietal:** If a type of grape is listed on the label, it means that at least 75% of the grapes in this wine are of that varietal. If there's none listed, it's almost certainly a blend of various types of grapes.

■ **Vineyard name:** If the label lists a vineyard, then at least 95% of the grapes used must have been harvested there. A vineyard name is more commonly, though not exclusively, found on higher-end bottles.

■ **Vintage:** If a year appears on the label, it means that at least 95% of the grapes were harvested in that year (85% if the wine is not designated with an AVA). If no vintage is listed, the grapes may come from more than one year's harvest.

■ **Wine name:** Many wineries will give their wines a catchy name, to help consumers pick it out in a crowd.

New bottles of sparkling wine are stored on their sides in deep cellars. The wine now ages *sur lie,* or "on the lees" (the dead yeast cells and other deposits trapped in the bottle). This aging process enriches the wine's texture and increases the complexity of its bouquet. The amount of time spent *sur lie* has a direct relation to its quality: the longer the aging, the more complex the wine.

The lees must be removed from the bottle before a sparkling wine can be enjoyed. This is achieved in a process whose first step is called **riddling.** In the past, each bottle, head tilted slightly downward, was placed in a riddling rack, an A-frame with many holes of bottleneck size. Riddlers gave each bottle a slight shake and a downward turn—every day, if possible. This continued for six weeks, until each bottle rested upside down in the hole and the sediment had collected in the neck, next to the cork. Simple as it sounds, this process is actually very difficult. Hand-riddling is a fine art perfected after much training. Today most sparkling wines

DID YOU KNOW?

Before tasting a wine, you should always smell it. The odors of fruit, flowers, and spices are not uncommon.

are riddled in ingeniously designed machines called gyro palettes, which can handle 500 or more bottles at a time, though at a few wineries, such as Schramsberg, the work is still done by hand.

After riddling, the bottles are **disgorged.** The upside-down bottles are placed in a very cold solution, which freezes the sediments in a block that attaches itself to the crown cap that seals the bottle. The cap and frozen plug are removed, and the bottle is topped off with a wine-and-sugar mixture called **dosage** and recorked with the traditional Champagne cork. The dosage ultimately determines the sparkler's sweetness.

Sparkling wines with 1.5% sugar or less are labeled **brut,** those with 1.2% to 2% sugar are called **extra dry,** those with 1.7% to 3.5% are called **sec** (French for "dry"), and those with 3.5% to 5% are **demi-sec** (half dry). Sparkling wines labeled **doux** (sweet) have more than 5% sugar. Most sparkling-wine drinkers refuse to admit that they like their bubbly on the sweet side, and this labeling convention allows them to drink sweet while pretending to drink dry. It's a marketing ploy invented in Champagne at least a century ago. A sparkling wine to which no dosage has been added will be bone dry (and taste sour to some) and may be called natural or **extra-brut.**

Most sparkling wines are not vintage dated but are *assembled* (the term sparkling-wine makers use instead of *blended*) to create a **cuvée,** a mix of different wines and sometimes different vintages consistent with the house style. However, sparkling wines may be vintage dated in particularly great years.

Sparkling wine may also be made by time- and cost-saving bulk methods. In the **Charmat process,** invented by Eugene Charmat early in the 20th century, the secondary fermentation takes place in large tanks rather than individual bottles. Basically, each tank is treated as one huge bottle. After the bubbles have developed, the sediments are filtered out and the wine is bottled. This comes at a price: although the sparkling wine may be ready in as little as a month, it has neither the complexity nor the bubble quality of traditional sparklers. In the United States, sparkling wine made in this way must be labeled "Bulk Process" or "Charmat Process." Sparkling wines made in the traditional, time-consuming fashion may be labeled "Méthode Traditionelle" or "Wine Fermented in This Bottle."

ROSÉ WINES

Rosé or blush wines are made from red-wine grapes, but the juicy pulp is left on the skins for a matter of hours—typically from 12 to 36—rather than days. When the winemaker decides that the juice has reached the desired color, it is drained off and filtered. Yeast is added, and the juice is left to ferment. Because the must stays on the skins for a shorter time, fewer tannins are leached from the skins, and the resulting wine is not as full flavored as a red. You might say that rosé is a lighter, fruitier version of red wine, not a pink version of white.

Rosé has gotten a bad rap in recent years, perhaps because it's sometimes confused with inexpensive, sickly sweet white Zinfandels that

The French Connection

Sparkling wines were perfected in Champagne, France's northernmost wine district, where wines tend to be a bit acidic because grapes do not always fully ripen. That's why sparkling wines have traditionally been naturally tart, even austere. Because of their progenitor's birthplace, many sparkling wines are called "Champagne." However, this term designates a specific region, so it shouldn't be used for American wines. That's not to say that Napa and Sonoma County sparkling wines are in any way inferior to French ones. The French Champagne houses are fully aware of the excellence of the California product and have been quick to cash in on the laurels gathered by such pioneers as Hanns Kornell, Schramsberg, and Iron Horse by establishing sparkling-wine cellars in Sonoma and Napa with American partners.

are a similar hue, but the French have been making excellent dry rosés for decades. Many California vintners have jumped on the rosé bandwagon, and it seems like almost every tasting room features at least one of these refreshing wines. The range of tastes and textures is remarkable. Depending on how it's made, Rosé of Cabernet Sauvignon, for instance, can have a velvety and almost savory taste, while Rosé of Pinot Noir or Syrah can might have a crisp and mineral-like taste.

GRAPE GROWING: THE BASICS

Most kinds of wine grapes are touchy. If the weather is too hot, they can produce too much sugar and not enough acid, resulting in overly alcoholic wines. Too cool and they won't ripen properly, and some will develop an unpleasant vegetal taste. And rain at the wrong time of year can wreak havoc on vineyards, causing grapes to rot on the vine. What's more, the wrong type of soil can leave vines with "wet feet," which can seriously hamper their growth. These and many other conditions must be just right to coax the best out of persnickety wine grapes, and Napa and Sonoma have that magical combination of sun, rain, fog, slope, and soil that allows many varieties of wine grape to thrive.

APPELLATIONS: LOCATION, LOCATION, LOCATION

California growers and winemakers generally agree that no matter what high-tech wine-making techniques might be used after the grapes are picked, in fact the wine is really made in the vineyard. This emphasis on *terroir* (a French term that encompasses a region's soil, microclimate, and overall growing conditions) reflects a belief that the quality of a wine is determined by what happens before the grapes are crushed. Even a small winery can produce spectacular wines if it has the right location and grows the grapes best suited to its soil and microclimate.

In the United States, the Alcohol and Tobacco Tax and Trade Bureau (TTB) designates **appellations of origin** based on political boundaries or

Pinot Noir and Chardonnay are widely grown in the Russian River Valley.

unique soil, climate, or other characteristics. California, for instance, is an appellation, as are Napa and Sonoma counties. More significantly to wine lovers, the TTB can designate a unique grape-growing region as an American Viticultural Area (AVA), more commonly called an appellation. Whether the appellation of origin is based on politics or terroir, it refers to the source of a wine's grapes, not to where it was made.

Different appellations—there are more than 100 AVAs in California, with 16 in the county of Napa alone—are renowned for different wines. The Napa Valley is known for Cabernet Sauvignon, for example, the Russian River Valley for Chardonnay and Pinot Noir, and the Dry Creek Valley for Zinfandel. Wineries can indicate the appellation on a bottle's label only if 85% of the grapes were grown in that appellation. Many wineries buy grapes from outside their AVA, so they might label different wines with the names of different regions.

What makes things a little confusing is that appellations often overlap, allowing for increased levels of specificity. The Napa Valley AVA is, of course, part of the California appellation, but the Napa Valley AVA is itself divided into even smaller subappellations, the Oakville and Rutherford AVAs being among the most famous of these. There are even subappellations within subappellations. Over in Sonoma County, the Russian River Valley AVA contains the smaller Green Valley of the Russian River Valley AVA, which earned status as a separate viticultural area by virtue of its soils and a climate cooler and foggier than much of the rest of the Russian River Valley.

When it is to their advantage, winemakers make sure to mention prestigious appellations, and even specific vineyards, on their labels. If the grapes have come from multiple AVAs within a given region—say, the North Coast—the wine can be labeled with the name of the whole region. Wines simply labeled "California" are usually made of grapes from more than one region.

GEOLOGY 101

Wherever grapes are grown, geology matters. Grapevines are among the few plants that give their best fruit when grown in poor, rocky soil. On the other hand, grapes just don't like wet feet. The ideal vineyard soil is easily permeable by water. Until the 1990s, California growers were more interested in climate than geology when deciding where to plant vineyards and how to manage them. As demand for premium wine exploded, though, winemakers began paying much more attention to the soil part of the terroir equation. Geologists now do a brisk business advising growers.

Different grape varieties thrive in different types of soil. For instance, Cabernet Sauvignon does best in well-drained, gravelly soil. If it's too wet or contains too much heavy clay or organic matter, the soil will give the wine an obnoxious vegetative quality that even the best winemaking techniques cannot remove. Merlot, however, can grow in soil with more clay and still be made into a delicious, rich wine. Sauvignon Blanc does quite well in heavy clay soils, but the winegrower has to limit irrigation and use some viticultural muscle to keep the grapes from developing unacceptable flavors. Chardonnay likes well-drained vineyards but will also take heavy soil.

Beltane Ranch is a B&B on a real working ranch near Glen Ellen that grows olives, grapes, and cattle; the ranch was originally a turkey farm.

The soils below Napa Valley's crags and in the valleys of Sonoma County are dizzyingly diverse, which helps account for the unusually wide variety of grapes grown in such a small area. Some of the soils are composed of dense, heavy, sedimentary clays washed from the mountains; others are very rocky clays, loams, or silts of alluvial fans. These fertile, well-drained soils cover much of the valleys' floors. Other areas have soil based on serpentine, a rock that rarely appears aboveground. In all, there are about 60 soil types in the Napa and Sonoma valleys.

In Wine Country you'll hear a lot about limestone, a nutrient-rich rock in which grapevines thrive. Some California winemakers claim to be growing in limestone when in fact they are not. In fact, only small patches of California's Wine Country have significant amounts of limestone. The term is often used to describe the streak of light-color, almost white soil that runs across the Napa Valley from the Palisades to St. Helena and through Sonoma County from the western flanks of the Mayacamas Mountains to Windsor. The band is actually made of volcanic material that has no limestone content.

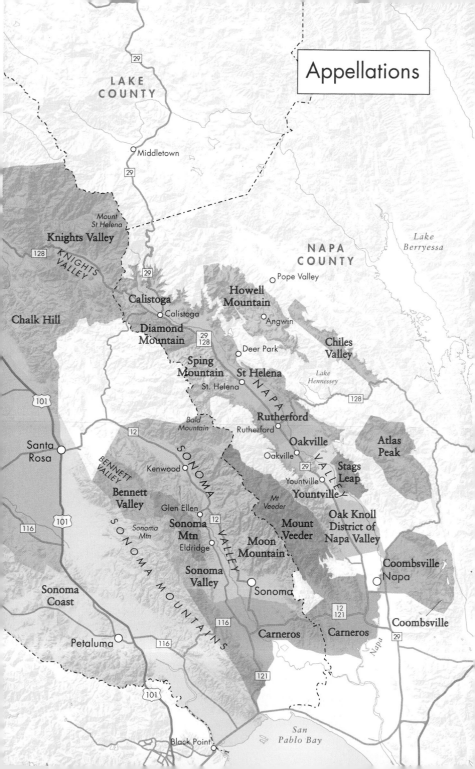

Appellations

LAKE
COUNTY

29

29

Middletown

Mount
St Helena

Knights Valley

KNIGHTS
VALLEY

128

Chalk Hill

NAPA
COUNTY

Lake
Berryessa

Pope Valley

Calistoga

Calistoga

Diamond
Mountain

Howell
Mountain

Angwin

29
128

Deer Park

Chiles
Valley

Spring
Mountain

St Helena

St. Helena

Lake
Hennessey

128

Santa
Rosa

101

12

Bald
Mountain

SONOMA

Rutherford

Rutherford

Oakville

Atlas
Peak

Kenwood

Oakville

VALLEY

29

Stags
Leap

Bennett
Valley

BENNETT
VALLEY

Yountville

Yountville

Glen Ellen

12

Mt
Veeder

Sonoma
Mtn

Sonoma
Mtn

Eldridge

Moon
Mountain

Mount
Veeder

Oak Knoll
District of
Napa Valley

116

101

SONOMA

Sonoma
Valley

Sonoma

Coombsville
Napa

Coombsville

Sonoma
Coast

MOUNTAINS

VALLEY

116

Carneros

Carneros

12
121

Napa

29

Petaluma

116

121

101

San
Pablo Bay

Black Point

DOWN ON THE FARM

Much like a fruit or nut orchard, a vineyard can produce excellent grapes for decades—even a century—if it's given the proper attention. The growing cycle starts in winter, when the vines are bare and dormant. While the plants rest, the grower works to enrich the soil and repair the trellising system (if there is one) that holds up the vines. This is when **pruning** takes place to regulate the vine's growth and the upcoming season's crop size.

In spring, the soil is aerated by plowing, and new vines go in. The grower trains established vines so they grow, with or without trellising, in the shape most beneficial for the grapes. **Bud break** occurs when the first bits of green emerge from the vines, and a pale green veil appears over the winter's gray-black vineyards. A late frost can be devastating at this time of year. Summer brings the flowering of the vines, when clusters of tiny green blossoms appear, and **fruit set,** when the grapes form from the blossoms. As the vineyards turn luxuriant and leafy, more pruning, along with leaf pulling, keeps foliage in check so the vine directs nutrients to the grapes, and so the sun can reach the fruit. As summer advances, the grower will **thin the fruit,** cutting off (or "dropping") some bunches so the remaining grapes intensify in flavor. A look at the vineyards reveals heavy clusters of green or purple grapes, some pea-size, others marble-size, depending on the variety.

Fall is the busiest season in the vineyard. Growers and winemakers carefully monitor the ripeness of the grapes, sometimes with equipment that tests sugar and acid levels and sometimes simply by tasting them. As soon as the grapes are ripe, **harvest** begins amid the lush foliage. In California this generally happens in September and October, but sometimes a bit earlier or later, depending on the type of grape and the climatic conditions. Picking must be done as quickly as possible, within just a day or two, to keep the grapes from passing their peak. Most California grapes are harvested mechanically, but some are picked by hand. After harvest, the vines start to regenerate for the next year.

Sometimes by preference and sometimes by necessity, winemakers don't grow all the grapes they need. Small wineries with only a few acres of grapes are limited in the varietals and quantities they can grow. (The smallest producers don't even have their own wineries, so they pay to use the equipment and storage space at custom crush facilities.) Midsize wineries may aim to get bigger. If it doesn't buy more acreage, a winery that wants to expand production has to buy grapes from independent growers.

Many winemakers purchase at least some of their grapes. Some have negotiated long-term contracts with top growers, buying grapes from the same supplier year after year. This way, the winemaker can control the consistency and quality of the fruit, just as if it came from the winery's own vineyard. Other wineries buy from several growers, and many growers sell to more than one winery.

Winemakers who buy from growers face a paradoxical problem: it's possible to make a wine that's too good and too popular. As the demand for a wine—and its price—rises, so will the price of the grapes used to make it. Other wineries sometimes bid up the price of the grapes, meaning that a winemaker can no longer afford the grapes that made a wine famous. This competitiveness among winemakers for specific batches of grapes underscores the faith put in the importance of growers.

ORGANIC AND BIODYNAMIC

If, as many grape growers insist, a wine is only as good as the vineyard it comes from, those who have adopted organic and biodynamic agricultural methods may be on to something. But when using terms like *organic* and *biodynamic,* what do vintners mean? Although organic viticulture is governmentally recognized and regulated, it is vaguely defined and its value is hotly debated—just like the rest of organic farming. It boils down to a rejection of chemical fertilizers, pesticides, and fungicides. Biodynamic farmers also reject these artificial agents, and their vineyard maintenance involves metaphysical principles as well.

Partly because it's difficult and expensive to qualify for official certification, partly because organic vineyards have smaller yields, and partly because it's hard to grow grapes organically except in warm, dry climates, organic viticulture remains the exception rather than the rule, although more vineyards are being certified organic every year.

Even rarer than wines produced from organically grown grapes are completely organic wines. For a wine to be certified as organic, not only do the grapes have to come from organic vineyards, but the processing must use a minimum of chemical additives. Some winemakers argue that it is impossible to make truly fine wine without using additives like sulfur dioxide, an antioxidant that protects the wine's color, aroma, flavor, and longevity.

Many wineries that might qualify as partially organic resist the label, wary of its effect on their reputation. Still, the movement is gaining momentum. Many major players, even if they are not certified organic, have taken steps to reduce their use of pesticides or implement other eco-friendly policies. Others grow some or all of their grapes organically. Very few producers make completely organic wine.

If demand for organic products continues to grow, supply will no doubt follow suit. In the meantime, if you want organic wine, read the label carefully. To be called organic, a wine must contain certified organic grapes and have no added sulfites. Remember that some wines made from certified organic grapes still contain sulfites.

Their interest in organic farming has led some winery owners and vineyard managers to adopt biodynamic farming methods. The principles of biodynamic agriculture were conceived in the 1920s by the Austrian scholar and mystic Rudolf Steiner and refined in the 1930s by Ehrenfried Pfeiffer, a German scientist and specialist in soil management.

Biodynamic farmers view the land as a living, self-sustaining organism requiring a healthy, unified ecosystem to thrive. To nurture the soil, for instance, vineyard workers spray specially formulated herbal "teas" (the ingredients include yarrow, dandelion, valerian, and stinging nettle flowers) onto compost spread in the fields. Grazing animals such as sheep or goats maintain the ground cover between the vines (the animals' manure provides natural fertilizer), and natural predators, among them insect-eating bats, control pests that might damage the crop. Steiner and his successors believed that the movements of the sun and the moon influence plant development, so astronomical calendars play a role in the timing of many vineyard activities.

At its most elevated level, the biodynamic philosophy recognizes a farm as a metaphysical entity that requires its human inhabitants not merely to tend it but to form a spiritual bond with it, a notion that other organic farmers share in theory even if their methods sometimes diverge. Among wineries whose practices have been certified organic are Hall in the Napa Valley, and Preston of Dry Creek in Northern Sonoma County. The Napa Valley's Robert Sinskey Vineyards is certified both organic and biodynamic, as is the Sonoma Valley's Benziger Family Winery.

WINE-LOVER'S GLOSSARY

Like most activities, wine making and tasting require specialized vocabularies. Some words are merely show-off jargon, but some are specific and helpful.

Acidity. The tartness of a wine, derived from the fruit acids of the grape. Acids stabilize a wine (i.e., preserve its character), balance its sweetness, and bring out its flavors. Too little or too much acid spoils a wine's taste. Tartaric acid is the major acid in wine, but malic, lactic, and citric acids also occur.

Aging. The process by which some wines improve over time, becoming smoother and more complex and developing a pleasing bouquet. Wine is most commonly aged in oak vats or barrels, slowly interacting with the air through the pores in the wood. Sometimes wine is cellared for bottle aging. Today many wines are not made for aging and are drunk relatively young, as soon as a few months after bottling. Age can diminish a wine's fruitiness and also dull its color: whites turn brownish, rosés orange, reds brown.

Alcohol. Ethyl alcohol is a colorless, volatile, pungent spirit that not only gives wine its stimulating effect and some of its flavor but also acts as a preservative, stabilizing the wine and allowing it to age. A wine's alcohol content must be stated on the label, expressed as a percentage of volume, except when a wine is designated table wine.

American Viticultural Area (AVA). More commonly termed an *appellation.* A region with unique soil, climate, and other grape-growing conditions can be designated an AVA by the Alcohol and Tobacco Tax and Trade Bureau. When a label lists an appellation—Napa Valley or Mt. Veeder, for example—at least 85% of the grapes used to make the wine must come from that AVA.

Ampelography. The science of identifying varietals by their leaves, grapevines, and, more recently, DNA.

Appellation. *See American Viticultural Area.*

Aroma. The scent of young wine derived directly from the fresh fruit. It diminishes with fermentation and is replaced by a more complex bouquet as the wine ages. The term may also be used to describe special fruity odors in a wine, such as black cherry, green olive, ripe raspberry, or apple.

Astringency. The puckery sensation produced in the mouth by the tannins in wine.

AVA. *See American Viticultural Area.*

Balance. A quality of wine in which all desirable elements (fruit, acid, tannin) are present in the proper proportion. Well-balanced wine has a pleasing nose, flavor, and mouth feel.

Barrel fermenting. The fermenting of wine in small oak barrels instead of large tanks or vats. This method allows the winemaker to keep grape lots separate before blending the wine. The cost of oak barrels makes this method expensive.

Barrique. An oak barrel used for aging wines.

Biodynamic. An approach to agriculture that focuses on regarding the land as a living thing; it generally incorporates organic farming techniques and the use of the astronomical calendar in hopes of cultivating a healthy balance in the vineyard ecosystem.

Blanc de blancs. Sparkling or still white wine made solely from white grapes.

Blanc de noirs. White wine made with red grapes by removing the skins during crush. Some sparkling whites, for example, are made with red Pinot Noir grapes.

Blending. The mixing of several wines to create one of greater complexity or appeal, as when a heavy wine is blended with a lighter one to make a more approachable medium-bodied wine.

Body. The wine's heft or density as experienced by the palate. A full body makes the mouth literally feel full. It is considered an advantage in the case of some reds, a disadvantage in many lighter whites. *See also Mouth feel.*

Bordeaux blend. A red wine blended from varietals native to France's Bordeaux region—Cabernet Sauvignon, Cabernet Franc, Malbec, Merlot, and Petit Verdot.

Botrytis. *Botrytis cinerea,* a beneficial fungus that can perforate a ripe grape's skin. This dehydrates the grape and concentrates the remaining juice while preserving its acids. Botrytis grapes make a sweet but not cloying wine, often with complex flavors of honey or apricot.

Bouquet. The odors a mature wine gives off when opened. They should be pleasantly complex and should give an indication of the wine's grape variety, origin, age, and quality.

Brix. A method of telling whether grapes are ready for picking by measuring their sugars. Multiplying a grape's Brix number by .55 approximates the potential alcohol content of the wine.

Brut. French term for the driest category of sparkling wine. *See also Demi-sec, Sec.*

Case. A carton of 12 750-ml bottles of wine. A magnum case contains six 1.5-liter magnum bottles. Most wineries will offer a discount if you purchase wine by the case (or sometimes a half case).

Cask. A synonym for *barrel*. More generally, any size or shape wine container made from wood staves.

Cellaring. Storage of wine in bottles for aging. The bottles are laid on their sides to keep the corks moist and prevent air leakage that would spoil the wine.

Champagne. The northernmost wine district of France, where the world's only genuine Champagne is made. The term is often used loosely in America to denote sparkling wines in general.

Cloudiness. The presence of particles that do not settle out of a wine, causing it to look and taste dusty or even muddy. If settling and decanting do not correct cloudiness, the wine has been badly made or is spoiled.

Complexity. The qualities of good wine that provide a multilayered sensory experience to the drinker. Balanced flavors, harmonious aromas or bouquet, and a long finish are components of complexity.

Corked. Describes wine that is flawed by the musty, wet-cardboard flavor imparted by cork mold, technically known as TCA, or 2,4,6-Trichloroanisole.

Crush. American term for the harvest season. Also refers to the year's crop of grapes crushed for wine.

Cuvée. Generally a sparkling wine, but sometimes a still wine, that is a blend of different wines and sometimes different vintages. Most sparkling wines are cuvées.

Decant. To pour a wine from its bottle into another container either to expose it to air or to eliminate sediment. Decanting for sediment pours out the clear wine and leaves the residue behind in the original bottle.

Demi-sec. French term that translates as "half-dry." It is applied to sweet wines that contain 3.5%–5% sugar.

Dessert wines. Sweet wines that are big in flavor and aroma. Some are quite low in alcohol; others, such as port-style wines, are fortified with brandy or another spirit and may be 17%–21% alcohol.

Dry. Having very little sweetness or residual sugar. Most wines are dry, although some whites, such as Rieslings, are made to be "off-dry," meaning on the sweet side.

Estate bottled. A wine entirely made by one winery at a single facility. The grapes must come from the winery's own vineyards or vineyards farmed by the winery within the same appellation (which must be printed on the label).

Fermentation. The biochemical process by which grape juice becomes wine. Enzymes generated by yeast cells convert grape sugars into alcohol and carbon dioxide. Fermentation stops when either the sugar is depleted and the yeast starves or when high alcohol levels kill the yeast.

Fermenter. Any vessel (such as a barrel, tank, or vat) in which wine is fermented.

Filtering, Filtration. A purification process in which wine is pumped through filters to rid it of suspended particles.

Fining. A method of clarifying wine by adding egg whites, bentonite (a type of clay), or other natural substances to a barrel. As these solids settle to the bottom, they take various dissolved compounds with them. Most wine meant for everyday drinking is fined; however, better wines are fined less often.

Finish. Also known as *aftertaste*. The flavors that remain in the mouth after swallowing wine. A good wine has a long finish with complex flavor and aroma.

Flight. A few wines—usually from three to five—specially selected for tasting together.

Fortification. A process by which brandy or another spirit is added to a wine to stop fermentation and to increase its level of alcohol, as in the case of port-style dessert wines.

Fruity. Having aromatic nuances of fresh fruit, such as fig, raspberry, or apple. Fruitiness, a sign of quality in young wines, is replaced by bouquet in aged wines.

Fumé Blanc. A nonspecific term for wine made with Sauvignon Blanc. Robert Mondavi originally coined the term to describe his dry, crisp, oak-aged Sauvignon Blanc.

Green. Said of a wine made from unripe grapes, with a pronounced leafy flavor and a raw edge.

Horizontal tasting. A tasting of several different wines of the same vintage.

Late harvest. Wine made from grapes harvested later in the fall than the main lot, and thus higher in sugar levels. Many dessert wines are late harvest.

Lees. The spent yeast, grape solids, and tartrates that drop to the bottom of the barrel or tank as wine ages. Wine, particularly white wine, gains complexity when it is left on the lees for a time.

Library wine. An older vintage that the winery has put aside to sell at a later date.

Malolactic fermentation. A secondary fermentation in the tank or barrel that changes harsh malic acid into softer lactic acid and carbon dioxide. Wine is sometimes inoculated with lactic bacteria or placed in wood containers that harbor the bacteria to enhance this process. Often referred to as *ML* or *malo*. Too much malo can make a wine too heavy.

Meritage. A trademarked name for American (mostly California) Bordeaux blends that meet certain wine-making and marketing requirements and are made by member wineries of the Meritage Association.

Méthode champenoise. The traditional, time-consuming method of making sparkling wines by fermenting them in individual bottles. By agreement with the European Union, sparkling wines made in California this way are labeled *méthode traditionelle*.

Mouth feel. Literally, the way wine feels in the mouth. Mouth feel, such as smoothness or astringency, is detected by the sense of touch rather than of smell or taste.

Must. The slushy mix of crushed grapes—juice, pulp, skin, seeds, and bits of stem—produced by the stemmer-crusher at the beginning of the wine-making process.

Neutral oak. The wood of older barrels or vats that no longer pass much flavor or tannin to the wine stored within.

New oak. The wood of a fresh barrel or vat that has not previously been used to ferment or age wine. It can impart desirable flavors and enhance a wine's complexity, but if used to excess it can overpower a wine's true character.

Noble rot. *See Botrytis.*

Nonvintage. A blend of wines from different years. Nonvintage wines have no date on their label. Wine may be blended from different vintages to showcase strong points that complement each other, or to make a certain wine taste the same from one year to the next.

Nose. The overall fragrance (aroma or bouquet) given off by a wine; the better part of its flavor.

Oaky. A vanilla-woody flavor that develops when wine is aged in oak barrels. Leave a wine too long in a new oak barrel and that oaky taste overpowers the other flavors.

Organic viticulture. The technique of growing grapes without the use of chemical fertilizers, pesticides, or fungicides.

Oxidation. Undesirable flavor and color changes to juice or wine caused by too much contact with the air, either during processing or because of a leaky barrel or cork. Most often occurs with white wine, especially if it's over the hill.

pH. Technical term for a measure of acidity. It is a reverse measure: the lower the pH level, the higher the acidity. Most wines range in pH from 2.9 to 4.2, with the most desirable level between 3.2 and 3.5. Higher pHs make wine flabby and dull, whereas lower pHs make it tart.

Phylloxera. A disease caused by the root louse *Phylloxera vastatrix*, which attacks and ultimately destroys the roots. The pest is native to the United States; it traveled to France with American grape vines in the 19th century and devastated nonresistant vineyards.

Pomace. Spent grape skins and solids left over after the juice has been pressed, commonly returned to the fields as fertilizer.

Racking. Moving wine from one tank or barrel to another to leave unwanted deposits behind; the wine may or may not be fined or filtered in the process.

Reserve wine. Inexact term applied by vintners to indicate that a wine is better in some way (through aging, source of the grapes, and so on) than others from their winery.

Residual sugar. The natural sugar left in a wine after fermentation, which converts sugar into alcohol. If the fermentation was interrupted or if the must has very high sugar levels, some residual sugar will remain, making a sweeter wine.

Rhône blend. A wine made from grapes hailing from France's Rhône Valley, such as Marsanne, Roussanne, Syrah, Cinsault, Mourvèdre, or Viognier.

Rosé. Pink wine, usually made from red-wine grapes (of any variety). The juice is left on the skins only long enough to give it a tinge of color.

Rounded. Said of a well-balanced wine in which fruity flavor is nicely offset by acidity—a good wine, though not necessarily a distinctive or great one.

Sec. French for "dry." The term is generally applied within the sparkling or sweet categories, indicating the wine has 1.7%–3.5% residual sugar. Sec is drier than demi-sec but not as dry as brut.

Sediment. Dissolved or suspended solids that drop out of most red wines as they age in the bottle, thus clarifying their appearance, flavors, and aromas. Sediment is not a defect in an old wine or in a new wine that has been bottled unfiltered.

Sparkling wines. Wines in which carbon dioxide is dissolved, making them bubbly. Examples are French Champagne, Italian prosecco, and Spanish cava.

Sugar. Source of grapes' natural sweetness. When yeast feeds on sugar, it produces alcohol and carbon dioxide. The higher the sugar content of the grape, the higher the potential alcohol level or sweetness of the wine.

Sulfites. Compounds of sulfur dioxide that are almost always added before fermentation to prevent oxidation and to kill bacteria and wild yeasts that can cause off flavors. Sulfites are sometimes blamed as the culprit in headaches caused by red wine, but the connection has not been proven.

Sustainable viticulture. A viticultural method that aims to bring the vineyard into harmony with the environment. Organic and other techniques are used to minimize agricultural impact and to promote biodiversity.

Table wine. Any wine that has at least 7% but not more than 14% alcohol by volume. The term doesn't necessarily imply anything about the wine's quality or price—both super-premium and jug wines can be labeled as table wine.

Tannins. You can tell when they're there, but their origins are still a mystery. These natural grape compounds produce a sensation of drying or astringency in the mouth and throat. Tannins settle out as wine ages; they're a big player in many red wines.

Tartaric acid, Tartrates. The principal acid of wine. Crystalline tartrates form on the insides of vats or barrels and sometimes in the bottle or on the cork. They look like tiny shards of glass but are not harmful.

Terroir. French for "soil." Typically used to describe the soil and climate conditions that influence the quality and characteristics of grapes and wine.

Varietal. A wine that takes its name from the grape variety from which it is predominantly made. California wines that qualify are almost always labeled with the variety of the source grape. According to U.S. law, at least 75% of a wine must come from a particular grape to be labeled with its variety name.

Vat. A large container of stainless steel, wood, or concrete, often open at the top, in which wine is fermented or blended. Sometimes used interchangeably with *tank*.

Veraison. The time during the ripening process when grapes change their color from green to red or yellow and sugar levels rise.

Vertical tasting. A tasting of several vintages of the same wine.

Vinification. Wine making, the process by which grapes are made into wine.

Vintage. The grape harvest of a given year, and the year in which the grapes are harvested. A vintage date on a bottle indicates the year in which the grapes were harvested rather than the year in which the wine was bottled.

Viticulture. The cultivation of grapes.

Woody. Describes excessively musty wood aromas and flavors picked up by wine stored in a wood barrel or cask for too long. The term *woody* is always a negative.

Yeast. A minute, single-celled fungus that germinates and multiplies rapidly as it feeds on sugar with the help of enzymes, creating alcohol and releasing carbon dioxide in the process of fermentation. Some wine-makers prefer allowing grapes to ferment in natural yeasts acquired in the vineyard, believing that this leads to more complex flavors. Other winemakers rely on commercial yeasts to aid in fermentation because the results are more consistent.

Zymology. The science of fermentation.

NAPA VALLEY

Visit Fodors.com for advice, updates, and bookings

WELCOME TO NAPA VALLEY

TOP REASONS TO GO

★ **Art and architecture:** Several wineries are owned by art collectors whose holdings grace indoor and outdoor spaces, and the valley contains remarkable specimens of winery architecture.

★ **Balloon rides:** By the dawn's early light, hot-air balloons soar over the vineyards, a magical sight from the ground and even more thrilling from above. Afterward, enjoy a champagne brunch.

★ **Fine dining:** It may sound like hype, but a meal at one of the valley's top-tier restaurants can be a revelation—about just how satisfying the act of eating can be and about how well quality wines pair with food.

★ **Spa treatments:** Work-hard, play-hard types and inveterate sybarites flock to spas for pampering.

★ **Wine tasting:** Whether you're on a pilgrimage to famous Cabernet houses or searching for hidden-gem wineries and obscure varietals, the valley supplies plenty of both.

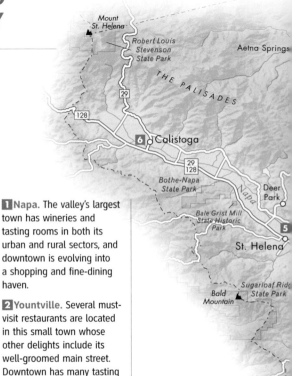

1 Napa. The valley's largest town has wineries and tasting rooms in both its urban and rural sectors, and downtown is evolving into a shopping and fine-dining haven.

2 Yountville. Several must-visit restaurants are located in this small town whose other delights include its well-groomed main street. Downtown has many tasting rooms; most of Yountville's wineries are to the east, with a few to the north and south.

3 Oakville. With a population of less than 100, this town is all about its vineyards, mostly of Cabernet. Fans of this noble grape could get lost for several days here sampling the many fine wines made from it.

4 Rutherford. "It takes Rutherford dust to grow great Cabernet," a renowned winemaker once said, and with several dozen wineries in this appellation, there are plenty of opportunities to ponder what this means.

5 St. Helena. Genteel St. Helena's Main Street evokes images of classic Americana; its wineries range from valley stalwarts Beringer and Charles Krug to boutique wineries tucked away in the hills.

6 Calistoga. The spa town Sam Brannan started in the 19th century still has its Old West–style false fronts, but it's now also home to luxurious lodgings and spas with 21st-century panache.

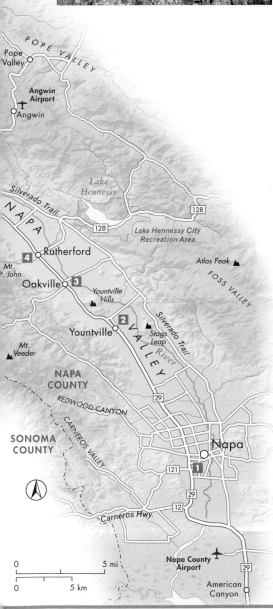

GETTING ORIENTED

3

From the air, the Napa Valley reveals itself as the tiny sliver it is, 5 miles across at the widest point, running for 30 miles from southeast to northwest between the Vaca Range to the east and the Mayacamas Mountains to the west. The main towns—from south to north, Napa, Yountville, Oakville, Rutherford, St. Helena, and Calistoga—straddle Highway 29, known for most of this stretch as the St. Helena Highway.

With more than 500 wineries and many of the biggest brands in the business, the Napa Valley is the Wine Country's star. Napa, the largest town, lures with its cultural attractions and (relatively) reasonably priced accommodations. A few miles farther north, compact Yountville is packed with top-notch restaurants and hotels, and Oakville and Rutherford are renowned for their Cabernet Sauvignon–friendly soils. Beyond them, St. Helena teems with elegant boutiques and restaurants, and casual Calistoga, known for its spas and hot springs, has the feel of an Old West frontier town.

The Napa Valley contains only about an eighth the number of acres planted to grapes of France's Bordeaux region, but past volcanic and other seismic activity have bequeathed the valley diverse soils and microclimates that provide winemakers with the raw materials to craft wines of consistently high quality. More acreage is devoted to Cabernet Sauvignon and Chardonnay than any other varietals, but Cabernet Franc, Merlot, Pinot Noir, Petite Sirah, Sauvignon Blanc, Syrah, Zinfandel, and other wines are also made here. In terms of output, though, the valley's reputation far exceeds the mere 4% of California's wine-grape harvest produced here each year.

So what makes the Napa Valley one of the state's top tourist destinations and a playground for San Francisco Bay Area residents? For one thing, variety. For every blockbuster winery whose name you'll recognize from the shelves of wine stores and the pages of *Wine Spectator*—Robert Mondavi, Beringer, and Caymus, to name a very few—you'll also find low-frills operations that will warmly welcome you into their modest tasting rooms. The local viticulture has inspired a robust passion for food, and several outstanding chefs have solidified the valley's position as one of the country's great restaurant destinations. You will also get a glimpse of California's history, from wine cellars dating back to the late 1800s to the flurry of Steamboat Gothic architecture dressing up Calistoga. Binding all these temptations together is the sheer scenic beauty of the place. Much of Napa Valley's landscape unspools in orderly, densely planted rows of vines. Even the climate cooperates, as the warm summer days and refreshingly cool evenings that are so favorable for grape growing also make perfect weather for traveling.

PLANNER

WHEN TO GO

The Napa Valley is a year-round destination whose charms vary depending on the season. Watching the misty winter fog rising on a rainy day off dark, gnarly grapevines, for example, can be just as captivating a moment as witnessing a summer sunset backlighting flourishing vineyard rows. Because the Napa Valley is the most-visited Wine Country locale, summers draw hordes of tourists, making late spring and early fall, when it's less crowded and temperatures are often cooler, among the best times to come. Harvesttime—from August into November, depending on the grape type and the year's weather—is the best time to visit to see wine making in action. Weekends can be busy year-round. To avoid heavy traffic on summer weekends, it almost always works best to arrive by mid-morning, especially if you need to be back in San Francisco by early evening.

PLANNING YOUR TIME

First things first: even in a month it's impossible to "do" the Napa Valley, whose local vintners' association represents more than 500 wineries. Many visitors find that visiting three or four wineries a day and spending quality time at each of them—with a leisurely lunch to rest the palate—is preferable to cramming in as many visits as possible. You can, of course, add variety with a spa treatment (these can take up to a half day), a balloon ride (expect to rise early and finish in the late morning), shopping, or a bicycle ride.

You can maximize your time touring wineries with a few simple strategies. If you'll be visiting a big operation such as Mondavi, Beringer, or Castello di Amorosa, try to schedule that stop early in the day and then smaller wineries after lunch. You're less likely to be held up by the crowds that way. Even during the week in summertime, the afternoon traffic on Highway 29 can be heavy, so after 3 pm try to avoid wineries along this stretch. Plan your visits to wineries on or just off the Silverado Trail for later in the day.

The town of Napa is the valley's most affordable base, and it's especially convenient if most of your touring will be in the southern half. If you'll be dining a lot in Yountville, staying there is a good idea because you can walk or take the Yountville Trolley back to your lodging. Calistoga is the most affordable base in the northern Napa Valley, though it's not always convenient for touring southern Napa wineries.

GETTING HERE AND AROUND
BUS TRAVEL

VINE Bus 29 Express brings passengers from the BART (Bay Area Rapid Transit) El Cerrito Del Norte station and the Vallejo Ferry Terminal. VINE Bus 25 travels between the towns of Napa and Sonoma. VINE Bus 10 and (weekdays only) Bus 29 run between Napa and Calistoga, with one stop or more in Yountville, Oakville, Rutherford, St. Helena, and Calistoga. Keep in mind that although Bus 10 operates on Sunday many VINE buses do not. ⇨ *For more information about arriving by bus, see Bus Travel in the Travel Smart chapter. For more information about local bus service, see the Bus Travel sections for the individual towns in this chapter.*

Contacts VINE ✉ *Napa* ☎ *707/251–2800, 800/696–6443* ⊕ *www.ridethevine. com.*

CAR TRAVEL

Traveling by car is the most convenient way to tour the Napa Valley. From San Francisco there are two main routes into the valley, both getting you there in about an hour in normal traffic. You can head north across the Golden Gate Bridge and U.S. 101, east on Highway 37 and then Highway 121, and north on Highway 29; or east across the San Francisco–Oakland Bay Bridge and north on Interstate 80, west on Highway 37, and north on Highway 29.

Highway 29, the Napa Valley Highway, heads north from Vallejo first as a busy four-lane highway, then narrows to a two-lane road at Yountville. Beyond Yountville, expect Highway 29 to be congested, especially on summer weekends. Traveling through St. Helena can be particularly slow during morning and afternoon rush hours. You'll probably find slightly less traffic on the Silverado Trail, which roughly parallels Highway 29 all the way from Napa to Calistoga. Cross streets connect the two like rungs on a ladder every few miles, making it easy to cross from one to the other.

■ **TIP➜** The Silverado Trail is your friend: although the Trail can get busy in the late afternoon, too, it's almost always a better option than Highway 29 if you're traveling between, say, St. Helena or Calistoga and the city of Napa.

⇨ *For information about car services and limos, see Getting Here and Around in the Travel Smart chapter.*

RESTAURANTS

Dining out is one of the deep pleasures of a Napa Valley visit. Cuisine here tends to focus on seasonal produce, some of it from gardens the restaurants maintain themselves, and many chefs endeavor to source their proteins locally, too. The French Laundry, the Restaurant at Meadowood, La Toque, Bouchon, Bistro Jeanty, Redd, Solbar, Restaurant at Auberge du Soleil, Press, and Terra often appear at the top of visitors' agendas, and rightfully so: in addition to superb cuisine they all have sommeliers or waiters capable of helping you select wines that will enhance your enjoyment of your meal immeasurably, and the level of service matches the food and surroundings. Another two-dozen restaurants provide experiences nearly on a par with those at the above

DID YOU KNOW?

Sterling Vineyards is perched on a hilltop south of Calistoga. Instead of driving to the winery, you board an aerial tram for the scenic trip up to the tasting room.

establishments, so if your favorite is booked when you visit you'll still have plenty of options.

HOTELS

With the price of accommodations at high-end inns and hotels *starting* at more than $1,000 a night, when it comes to Napa Valley lodging the question at first glance seems to be how much are you willing to pay? If you have the means, you can ensconce yourself between plush linens at exclusive hillside retreats with fancy architecture and even fancier amenities, and you're more or less guaranteed to have a fine time. As with Napa Valley restaurants, though, the decor and amenities the most stylish hotels and inns provide have upped the ante for all hoteliers and innkeepers, so even if you're on a budget you can live swell. Many smaller inns and hotels and even the motels provide pleasant stays for a fairly reasonable price. The main problem with these establishments is that they often book up quickly, so if you're visiting between late May and October, it's wise to reserve your room as far ahead as possible. *Hotel reviews have been shortened. For full information, visit Fodors.com.*

WHAT IT COSTS			
$	**$$**	**$$$**	**$$$$**
Restaurants	under $16	$16–$22	$23–$30	over $30
Hotels	under $201	$201–$300	$301–$400	over $400

Restaurant prices are the average cost of a main course at dinner, or if dinner isn't served, at lunch. Hotel prices are the lowest cost of a standard double room in high season.

APPELLATIONS

Nearly all of Napa County, which stretches from the Mayacamas Mountains in the west to Lake Berryessa in the east, makes up the Napa Valley American Viticultural Area (AVA). This large region is divided into many smaller AVAs, or subappellations, each with its own unique characteristics.

Los Carneros AVA stretches west from the Napa River across the southern Napa Valley into the southern Sonoma Valley. Pinot Noir and Chardonnay are the main grapes grown in this cool, windswept region just north of San Pablo Bay, but Merlot, Syrah, and, in the warmer portions, Cabernet Sauvignon, also do well here. Four of the subappellations north of the Carneros District—Oak Knoll, Oakville, Rutherford, and St. Helena—stretch clear across the valley floor. Chilled by coastal fog, the **Oak Knoll District of Napa Valley AVA** has some of the coolest temperatures. The **Oakville AVA,** just north of Yountville, is studded with both big-name wineries (such as Robert Mondavi and Silver Oak) and awe-inspiring boutique labels (such as the super-exclusive Screaming Eagle). Oakville's gravelly, well-drained soil is especially good for Cabernet Sauvignon.

A sunny climate and well-drained soil make **Rutherford AVA** one of the best locations for Cabernet Sauvignon in California, if not the world.

Best Bets for Napa Valley Wineries

WINE TASTING

Hall St. Helena. A glass-walled tasting area perched over the vineyards supplies a dramatic setting to taste award-winning Cabernets.

Joseph Phelps Vineyards, St. Helena. Tastings at Phelps unfold like everything else here, with class, grace, and precision—an apt description of the wines themselves.

Ma(i)sonry Napa Valley, Yountville. No ordinary tasting facility, this art and design gallery pours vintages from limited-production wineries.

Silver Oak Cellars, Oakville. The sole wine produced here is a respected Cabernet Sauvignon blend available for tasting in a stone struc- ture constructed of materials from a 19th-century flour mill.

WINERY TOURING

Beringer Vineyards, St. Helena. Of three Napa wineries that provide good overviews of California wine making—Beaulieu and Mondavi being the other two—Beringer has perhaps the prettiest site.

Frog's Leap, Rutherford. A light- hearted tone and well-informed tour guides make for entertaining educa- tion at Frog's Leap.

The Hess Collection, Napa. The guided tour of the Hess facilities is enlightening, but the real revelations come on self-guided tours of the owner's modern-art holdings.

Schramsberg, Calistoga. Deep inside 19th-century caves created by Chinese laborers, you'll learn all about crafting *méthode traditionelle* sparkling wines. Back aboveground, you'll taste the fruits of the winemak- er's labors.

SETTING

Artesa Vineyards & Winery, Napa. The tasting room here blends so discreetly into the surrounding landscape that visitors often gasp upon encountering the fountains and artworks near the entrance.

Castello di Amorosa, Calistoga. You have to admire a guy who dreams of building a 107-room replica of a medieval castle—and then makes it happen. Crazy. Eccentric. Worth a peek.

Domaine Carneros, Napa: Sip sparkling wines in style on the outdoor terrace of this Carne- ros District winery part owned by Taittinger, the French champagne producer.

Far Niente, Oakville. Something's always abloom in Far Niente's landscaped gardens. Splurge on the tasting and tour and bask for a moment in the sublime sophistication that is the Napa Valley.

FOOD-WINE PAIRING

B Cellars, Oakville. An open kitchen dominates the B Cellars tasting room, among the clues that this boutique winery, which serves good-size bites at tastings, takes the relationship between food and wine seriously.

Round Pond Estate, Rutherford. Excellent morsels accompany the sips and samples at both the high-tech olive mill and the winery; you can also have lunch or brunch here.

Sequoia Grove, Rutherford. At this winery's enlightening food-pairing seminars you'll learn how sweet- ness, acidity, and other elements of food alter the taste of the wines they accompany.

3

Napa Valley Wine Train passengers get up-close vineyard views from vintage Pullman railroad cars.

North of Rutherford, the **St. Helena AVA** is one of Napa's toastiest, as the slopes surrounding the narrow valley reflect the sun's heat. Bordeaux varietals are the most popular grapes grown here—particularly Cabernet Sauvignon, but also Merlot. Just north, at the foot of Mt. St. Helena is the **Calistoga AVA;** Cabernet Sauvignon does well here, but also Zinfandel, Syrah, and Petite Sirah.

Stags Leap District AVA, a small district on the eastern side of the valley, is marked by dramatic volcanic palisades. As with the neighboring **Yountville AVA,** Cabernet Sauvignon and Merlot are by far the favored grapes. In both subappellations, cool evening breezes encourage a long growing season and intense fruit flavors. Some describe the resulting wines as "rock soft" or an "iron fist in a velvet glove." Also on the valley's eastern edge is the **Coombsville AVA.** Cabernet Sauvignon grows on the western-facing slopes of the Vaca Mountains, with Merlot, Chardonnay, Syrah, and Pinot Noir more prevalent in the cooler lower elevations.

The **Mt. Veeder** and **Spring Mountain AVAs** each encompass parts of the mountains that give them their names. Both demonstrate how stressing out grapevines can yield outstanding results; the big winner is Cabernet Sauvignon. Growing grapes on these slopes takes a certain recklessness—or foolhardiness, depending on your point of view—since many of the vineyards are so steep that they have to be tilled and harvested by hand.

The great variety of the climates and soils of the remaining subappellations—the **Atlas Peak, Chiles Valley, Diamond Mountain District, Howell Mountain,** and **Wild Horse Valley AVAs**—explains why vintners here can make so many different wines, and make them so well, in what in the end is a relatively compact region.

NAPA

46 miles northeast of San Francisco.

Visitors who glimpse Napa's malls and big-box stores from Highway 29 often speed past the town on the way to the more seductive Yountville or St. Helena. But Napa, population 79,000, has changed. After many years as a blue-collar burg detached from the Wine Country scene, Napa has spent the past decade reshaping its image. A walkway that follows the Napa River has made downtown more pedestrian-friendly, and each year more high-profile restaurants and hotels and inns pop up. The nightlife options are arguably the valley's best, shopping has become more chic and varied, and the Oxbow Public Market, a complex of high-end food purveyors, is popular with locals and tourists. If you establish your base in Napa, you'll undoubtedly want to explore the wineries amid the surrounding countryside, but plan on spending at least a half a day strolling the downtown district.

Napa was founded in 1848 in a strategic location on the Napa River, where the Sonoma-Benicia Road (Highways 12 and 29) crossed at a ford. The first wood-frame building was a saloon, and the downtown area still projects an old-river-town vibe. Many Victorian houses have survived, some as beautiful bed-and-breakfast inns, and in the original business district a few older buildings have been preserved. Some of these structures, along with newer ones, were heavily damaged on August 24, 2014, during an early-morning magnitude 6.0 earthquake centered less than 10 miles south of town. The earthquake, the largest in the San Francisco Bay Area in a quarter century, caused an estimated $362 million in damage to private property and public infrastructure, most of it in and around Napa. The wine industry experienced an additional $80 million in losses. Bottles, tanks, and barrels of wine were destroyed, and some historic buildings, including the 1886 Eschol Winery structure at Trefethen Vineyards, suffered damage that will take years to repair. Much of Napa was back to normal within two months, but as you stroll downtown or visit the affected wineries you may detect lingering evidence of the quake's destruction.

GETTING HERE AND AROUND

To get to downtown Napa from Highway 29, take the 1st Street exit and follow the signs for Central Napa. In less than a mile you'll reach the corner of 2nd Street and Main Street. Most of the town's sights and many of its restaurants are clustered in an easily walkable area near this intersection (you'll find street parking and garages nearby). Most of the wineries with city of Napa addresses are on or just off Highway 29 or the parallel Silverado Trail, the exception being the ones in the Carneros District or Mount Veeder AVA. Most of these are on or just off Highway 121. VINE Bus 29 Express serves Napa from BART light rail's El Cerrito Del Norte station and the San Francisco Ferry's Vallejo terminal. Vine Bus 10 passes by some downtown sights.

ESSENTIALS

Contact Do Napa ☎ *707/257–0322* ⊕ *www.donapa.com.*

EXPLORING

TOP ATTRACTIONS

Fodor's Choice ★ **Artesa Vineyards & Winery.** From a distance the modern, minimalist architecture of Artesa blends harmoniously with the surrounding Carneros landscape, but up close its pools, fountains, and the large outdoor sculptures by resident artist Gordon Huether of Napa make a vivid impression. So, too, do the wines crafted by Mark Beringer, who focuses on Chardonnay and Pinot Noir but also produces Cabernet Sauvignon and other limited-release wines such as Albariño and Tempranillo. You can taste wines by themselves or paired with chocolate ($50), cheese ($60), and tapas ($60). ■TIP→ The main tour, conducted daily, explores wine making and the winery. A Friday-only tour covers the art, and from June through October there's a vineyard tour. ⌧ *1345 Henry Rd., off Old Sonoma Rd. and Dealy La.* ☎ *707/224–1668* ⊕ *www.artesawinery. com* ⌧ *Tastings $20–$60, tours $30–$45* ☼ *Daily 10–5, winery tour daily at 11 and 2, art tour Fri. at 10:30; reservations required for some tastings and tours.*

Darioush. Exceptional hospitality and well-balanced wines from southern Napa Valley grapes are the hallmarks of this winery whose flamboyant architecture recalls the ancient Persian capital Persepolis. Several wines, including the signature Napa Valley Cabernet Sauvignon, combine grapes grown high on Mt. Veeder with valley-floor fruit, the former providing tannins and structure, the latter adding mellower, savory notes. Viognier, Chardonnay, Merlot, Pinot Noir, and a distinctive Cab-Shiraz blend are among the other wines made here. ■TIP→ Except on Saturday, walk-in parties can taste at the bar, but an appointment is required at all times for seated tastings that range from a cheese-wine pairing to a sit-down with owner Darioush Khaledi in his private wine cellar. ⌧ *4240 Silverado Trail, near Shady Oaks Dr.* ☎ *707/257–2345* ⊕ *www.darioush.com* ⌧ *Tasting $40–$300* ☼ *Daily 10:30–5, Sat. by appointment only.*

Fodor's Choice ★ **di Rosa.** About 2,000 works from the 1960s to the present by Northern California artists are displayed on this 217-acre art property. They can be found not only in galleries and in the former residence of its late founder, Rene di Rosa, but also on every lawn, in every courtyard, and even on the lake. Some works were commissioned especially for di Rosa, among them Paul Kos's meditative *Chartres Bleu,* a video installation in a chapel-like setting that replicates a stained-glass window from the cathedral in Chartres, France. ■TIP→ You can view the current temporary exhibition and a few permanent works at the Gatehouse Gallery, but to experience the breadth of this incomparable collection you'll need to book a tour. ⌧ *5200 Sonoma Hwy./Hwy. 121* ☎ *707/226–5991* ⊕ *www.dirosaart.org* ⌧ *Gatehouse Gallery $5, tours $12–$15* ☼ *Wed.–Sun. 10–4.*

Fodor's Choice ★ **Domaine Carneros.** A visit to this majestic château is an opulent way to enjoy the Carneros District—especially in fine weather, when the vineyard views are spectacular. The château was modeled after an 18th-century French mansion owned by the Taittinger family. Carved into the hillside beneath the winery, the cellars produce delicate sparkling

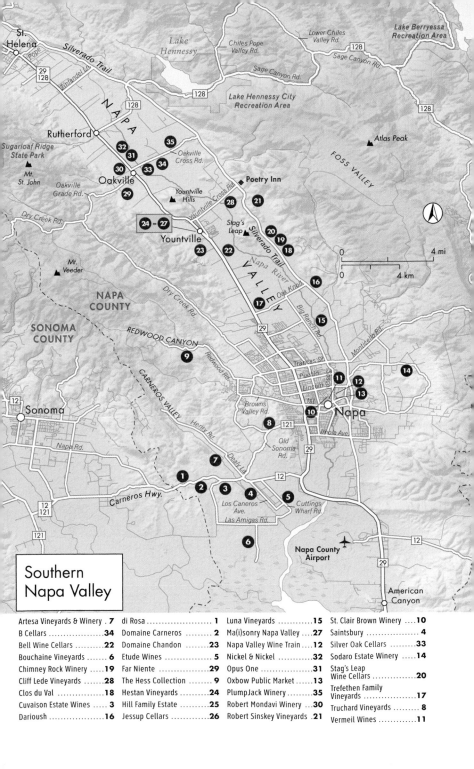

Southern Napa Valley

The main château at Domaine Carneros sits high on a hill.

wines reminiscent of those made by Taittinger, using only Los Carneros AVA grapes. The winery sells full glasses, flights, and bottles of its wines, which also include Chardonnay, Pinot Noir, and other still wines. Enjoy them all with cheese and charcuterie plates, caviar, or smoked salmon. Seating is in the Louis XV–inspired salon or on the terrace overlooking the vines. The tour here covers traditional methods of making sparkling wines. ⊠ *1240 Duhig Rd., at Hwy. 121* ☎ *707/257–0101, 800/716–2788* ⊕ *www.domainecarneros.com* ☜ *Tastings $10–$40, tour $40* ☾ *Daily 10–5:45; tour daily at 11, 1, and 3.*

Etude Wines. You're apt to see or hear hawks, egrets, Canada geese, and other wildlife on the grounds of Etude, known for its sophisticated Pinot Noirs. Though the winery and its light-filled tasting room are in Napa County, the grapes for its flagship Carneros Estate Pinot Noir come from the Sonoma portion of Los Carneros, as do the ones for the rarer Heirloom Carneros Pinot Noir. Chardonnay, Pinot Blanc, Pinot Noir, and other wines made by Jon Priest are poured daily in the tasting room. On Friday and the weekend, Pinot Noirs from California, Oregon, and New Zealand are compared at the Study of Pinot Noir seminars ($45). ■TIP→ Single-vineyard Napa Valley Cabernets are another Etude specialty; the Rutherford and Oakville ones are particularly good. ⊠ *1250 Cuttings Wharf Rd., 1 mile south of Hwy. 121* ☎ *877/586–9361* ⊕ *www.etudewines.com* ☜ *Tastings $15–$45* ☾ *Daily 10–4:30; Study of Pinot Noir tastings Fri.–Sun. at 10, 1, and 3 by appointment.*

Fodor'sChoice
★
The Hess Collection. About 9 miles northwest of Napa, up a winding road ascending Mt. Veeder, this winery is a delightful discovery. The limestone structure, rustic from the outside but modern and airy within,

contains Swiss owner Donald Hess's world-class art collection, including large-scale works by contemporary artists such as Andy Goldsworthy, Anselm Kiefer, and Robert Rauschenberg. Cabernet Sauvignon is a major strength, and the 19 Block Cuvée, Mount Veeder, a Cabernet blend, shows off the Malbec and other estate varietals. ■**TIP→ Food-wine pairings include one with chocolates that go well with the Mount Veeder Cabernet Sauvignon.** ⊠ *4411 Redwood Rd., west off Hwy. 29 at Trancas St./Redwood Rd. exit* ☎ *707/255–1144* ⊕ *www.hesscollection. com* ⌨ *Art gallery free, tastings $20–$85* ⊙ *Daily 10–5:30; guided tours daily 10:30–3:30.*

Fodor's Choice **Oxbow Public Market.** The market's two dozen shops, wine bars, and arti-
★ sanal food producers provide an introduction to Napa Valley's wealth of foods and wines. Swoon over decadent charcuterie at the Fatted Calf, slurp bivalves at Hog Island Oyster Company, or chow down on tacos with homemade tortillas at C Casa. Afterward, sip wine at Ca' Momi Enoteca or sample the barrel-aged cocktails and handcrafted vodka of the Napa Valley Distillery. The owner of C Casa also runs Cate & Co., a bakeshop that makes going gluten-free an absolute delight. ■**TIP→ Locals head to Model Bakery around 3 pm for hot-from-the-oven "late bake" bread.** ⊠ *610 and 644 1st St., at McKinstry St.* ⊕ *www. oxbowpublicmarket.com* ⌨ *Free* ⊙ *Weekdays 9–9, weekends 10–9; merchants hrs vary.*

St. Clair Brown Winery. Tastings at this women-run "urban winery" a few blocks north of downtown take place in an intimate, light-filled greenhouse or the colorful culinary garden outside. Winemaker Elaine St. Clair, well regarded for her stints at Domaine Carneros and Black Stallion, produces elegant wines—crisp yet complex whites and smooth, French-style reds among whose stars are the Cabernet Sauvignon and a Syrah from grapes grown in the Coombsville appellation. The wines are paired with addictive appetizers that include almonds roasted with rosemary, cumin, and Meyer lemon juice. ■**TIP→ You can sip single wines by the glass or half glass, or opt for the four-wine sampler.** ⊠ *816 Vallejo St., off Soscol Ave.* ☎ *707/255–5591* ⊕ *www. stclairbrownwinery.com* ⌨ *Tastings $4–$20* ⊙ *Daily 11–8.*

Saintsbury. This Carneros pioneer helped disprove the conventional wisdom that only the French could produce great Pinot Noir. Back in 1981, when Saintsbury released its first Pinot, the region had yet to earn its current reputation as a setting in which the often finicky varietal could prosper. If you still have doubts, try the earthy, intense Brown Ranch Pinot Noir. As crafted by winemaker Chris Kajani the other Pinot Noirs tend to be lighter in style and more fruit-forward. Named for the English author and critic George Saintsbury (he wrote *Notes on a Cellar-Book*), the winery also makes Chardonnay and a perky Vin Gris. ■**TIP→ When the weather cooperates, the leisurely tastings at this unpretentious operation take place in a rose garden.** ⊠ *1500 Los Carneros Ave., south off Hwy. 121 and east (left) on Withers Rd. for entrance* ☎ *707/252–0592* ⊕ *www.saintsbury.com* ⌨ *Tasting $25* ⊙ *Daily by appointment only.*

3

Fodor's Choice **Trefethen Family Vineyards.** Superior estate Chardonnay, Cabernet Sau-
★   vignon, and Pinot Noir wines are Trefethen's trademark. To find out
how well they age—and what a Napa Valley Pinot Noir from grapes
grown north of the Carneros district tastes like—pay for the reserve
tasting, which includes pours of limited-release wines and one or two
older vintages. The big terra-cotta-colored structure on-site, built in
1886, was designed with a gravity-flow system, with the third story for
crushing, the second for fermenting the resulting juice, and the first for
aging. The wooden building, whose ground floor served for years as
the tasting room, suffered severe damage in the 2014 Napa earthquake.
■TIP➜ Tastings will take place elsewhere until restoration has been
completed (2016 at the earliest), and visits will be by appointment
only. ⊠ *1160 Oak Knoll Ave., off Hwy. 29* ☎ *866/895–7696* ⊕ *www.
trefethen.com* 🗷 *Tasting $25–$35* ⊗ *Daily 10–4:30, by appointment.*

WORTH NOTING

Bouchaine Vineyards. Tranquil Bouchaine lies just north of the tidal
sloughs of San Pablo Bay—to appreciate the setting, walk at least a
portion of the self-guided ¾-mile tour through the vineyards and scan
the skies for hawks and golden eagles soaring above the vineyards.
The alternately breezy and foggy weather in this part of the Carneros
works well for the Burgundian varietals Pinot Noir and Chardonnay.
These account for most of Bouchaine's excellent wines, but also look
for Pinot Blanc, Pinot Gris, Pinot Meunier, Riesling, and Syrah. Tastings
may end with the silky-sweet late-harvest Chardonnay called Bouche
d'Or. ⊠ *1075 Buchli Station Rd., off Duhig Rd., south of Hwy. 121*
☎ *707/252–9065* ⊕ *www.bouchaine.com* 🗷 *Tastings $20–$30* ⊗ *Mid-
Mar.–Oct., daily 10:30–5:30; Nov.–mid-Mar., daily 10:30–4:30.*

Cuvaison Estate Wines. The flagship Carneros Chardonnay is the star at
Cuvaison (pronounced coo-vay-ZON), whose slick, modern tasting
room was constructed from inventively recycled materials. The winery also makes Sauvignon Blanc, Pinot Noir, and Syrah under its own
label, and Brandlin Cabernet Sauvignons and Zinfandel wines from a
historic Mount Veeder estate 1,200 feet above the Napa Valley floor.
Some wines can be purchased only at the winery, or sometimes online.
All tastings are sit-down style, either indoors or, in good weather, on an
outdoor patio whose lounge chairs and vineyard views encourage you
to take the time to savor the wines. ■TIP➜ You must make an appointment to visit, but even on the shortest of notice you can usually get in.
⊠ *1221 Duhig Rd., at Hwy. 121* ☎ *707/942–2455* ⊕ *www.cuvaison.
com* 🗷 *Tasting $20, tour $30* ⊗ *Daily 10–5, by appointment; tour
weekends at 9:30 by appointment.*

Luna Vineyards. Tall oaks shading an ivy-draped roadside wall mark the
entrance to this Tuscan-style winery near the Silverado Trail's southern end. Originally known for Sangiovese and Pinot Grigio, Luna still
makes wines from these grapes—the reserve Pinot Grigio, from estate-
grown fruit, often seduces reds-only partisans—but these days you're
as likely to sip a polished, un-buttery Chardonnay or a Bordeaux-style
Cabernet Sauvignon blend. Winemaker Shawna Miller even puts a winning French spin on the Sangiovese Reserve, using oak the way one
would for a Cab or Merlot and blending in Petite Sirah before bottling.

Both the art and the wine inspire at the Hess Collection.

Most tastings take place under the chocolate-brown coffered ceiling of the indoor salon or on a slate-floored terrace just outside. ⊠ *2921 Silverado Trail, at Hardman Ave.* ☎ *707/255–2474* ⊕ *www.lunavineyards.com* 🖃 *Tasting $25* ⊘ *Daily 10:30–6.*

Napa Valley Wine Train. Several century-old restored Pullman railroad cars and a two-story 1952 Vista Dome car with a curved glass roof travel a leisurely, scenic route between Napa and St. Helena. All trips include a well-made lunch or dinner; for all lunches and Saturday dinner you can combine your trip with a winery tour. Murder-mystery plays and dinners with vintners and winemakers are among the regularly scheduled special events. ■**TIP**➔ **It's best to make this trip during the day, when you can enjoy the vineyard views.** ⊠ *1275 McKinstry St., off 1st St.* ☎ *707/253–2111, 800/427–4124* ⊕ *www.winetrain.com* 🖃 *From $124* ⊘ *Lunch: Jan. and Feb., Fri.–Sun. 11:30; Mar.–Dec., daily 11:30. Dinner: May–Sept., Fri.–Sun. 6:30; Oct., Fri. and Sat. 6:30; Nov.–Mar., Sat. 6:30; Apr., Fri. and Sat. 6:30.*

Sodaro Estate Winery. Upscale-yet-modest Sodaro is a great introduction to the Coombsville AVA. Tours start on a crush pad with a view of rolling vineyards, then head inside the wine cave for a seated tasting of the signature wines: a Cabernet Sauvignon and a Bordeaux-style blend. You might also taste a special limited-release wine. All wines are paired with local cheeses and breadsticks. The tour concludes with a walk through the wine cave itself. It's no surprise that the vibe here is so luxurious: owners Don and Felicity Sodaro also own several area hotels. ⊠ *24 Blue Oak La., east of Silverado Trail (take Hagen Rd. east*

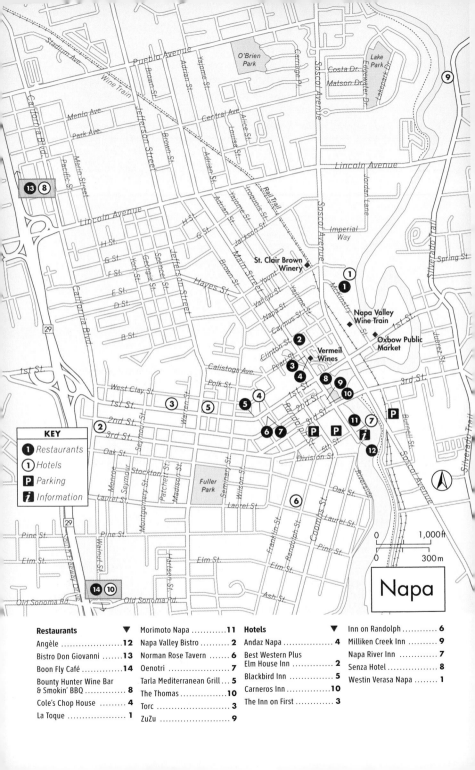

to 3rd Ave. S) ☏ *707/251–8216* ⊕ *www.sodarowines.com* ✉ *Tour and tasting $40* ⊙ *By appointment only.*

Truchard Vineyards. Diversity is the name of the game at this family-owned winery on prime acreage amid the Carneros region's rolling hills. Major Napa Valley vintners purchase most of the grapes grown here, but some of the best are held back for estate-only wines—the Chardonnays and Pinot Noirs the region is known for, along with Roussannes, Zinfandels, Merlots, Syrahs, Cabernet Sauvignons, and a few others. You must call ahead to tour or taste, but if you do, you'll be rewarded with a casual but informative experience tailored to your interests. The tour takes in the vineyards and the wine cave. ■TIP➔ **Climb the small hill near the winery for a photo-op view of the pond and the pen of Angora goats over the ridge.** ✉ *3234 Old Sonoma Rd., off Hwy. 121* ☏ *707/253–7153* ⊕ *www.truchardvineyards.com* ✉ *Tasting $30* ⊙ *Mon.–Sat., by appointment only.*

Vermeil Wines. As a National Football League coach Dick Vermeil, a Napa Valley native, relied on savvy veterans, and he does the same with his eponymous wines, presented in downtown Napa at a casual storefront tasting room. Longtime winemaker Paul Smith crafts restrained, old-style wines that score with critics and connoisseurs. Standouts include the Frediani Vineyard Cabernet Franc and Zinfandel wines and the Jean Louis Vermeil Cabernet Sauvignon. ■TIP➔ **Another Vermeil tasting room is located on Lincoln Avenue in downtown Calistoga.** ✉ *1018 1st St.* ☏ *707/254–9881* ⊕ *www.vermeilwines.com* ✉ *Tastings: $15–$75* ⊙ *Sun.–Wed. 10–10, Thurs.–Sat. 10 am–11 pm.*

WHERE TO EAT

$$$
FRENCH

×**Angèle.** An 1890s boathouse with a vaulted wood-beam ceiling sets the scene for romance at this French bistro. Though the style is casual—tables are close together, and warm, crusty bread is plunked down on paper-top tables—chef Rogelio Garcia's food is always well executed. Look for clever variations on classic French dishes such as roasted quail served with confit of lobster mushrooms. Banana gratin stands out among several homemade desserts. ■TIP➔ **In fine weather, dine under yellow-and-white striped umbrellas at one of the outdoor tables.** ⑤ *Average main: $28* ✉ *540 Main St., at 5th St.* ☏ *707/252–8115* ⊕ *www.angelerestaurant.com.*

$$$
ITALIAN
FAMILY

×**Bistro Don Giovanni.** At this boisterous bistro with a roadhouse feel you can peek past the copper pots hanging in the open kitchen to see the 750°F wood-burning oven. The Cal-Italian food here is simultaneously inventive and comforting: fritto misto usually composed of onions, fennel, calamari, and rock shrimp, lightly battered and deftly deep-fried; pesto ravioli with lemon-cream, tomato, or herb-butter sauce; pepperoni pizza with Jimmy Nardello peppers, tomatoes, and *stracciatella* cheese; and lamb and ricotta meatballs. Depending on your mood (and the weather), you can have your meal in the main dining room, in the bar area, or on the patio or lawn. ⑤ *Average main: $27* ✉ *4110 Howard La., off Hwy. 29* ☏ *707/224–3300* ⊕ *www.bistrodongiovanni.com.*

$$　✕ **The Boon Fly Café.** This small spot melds rural charm with industrial
MODERN　chic. Outside, swings occupy the porch of a modern red barn; inside,
AMERICAN　things get sleek with high ceilings and galvanized-steel tabletops. The
Fodor's Choice　menu of three squares a day updates American classics such as fried
★　chicken (free-range in this case), burgers (but with Kobe beef), and
shrimp and grits. The flatbreads, including a super-creamy smoked
salmon one made with fromage blanc, Parmesan, and lemon crème
fraîche, are worth a try. Chicken and waffles and other daily specials
draw locals, too, and there's a varied selection of wines by the glass.
■ TIP→ Open all day, the Boon Fly makes a convenient mid-morning
or late-afternoon stop. $ *Average main: $22* ⊠ *Carneros Inn, 4048
Sonoma Hwy.* ☎ *707/299–4870* ⊕ *www.boonflycafe.com.*

$$$　✕ **Bounty Hunter Wine Bar & Smokin' BBQ.** A triple threat, Bounty Hunter is
AMERICAN　a wine store, wine bar, and restaurant in one. You can stop by for just a
Fodor's Choice　glass—about 40 choices are available in both 2- and 5-ounce pours—or
★　a bottle, but it's best to come with an appetite. Every dish on the small
menu is a standout, including the pulled-pork and beef brisket sandwiches served with three types of barbecue sauce, the signature beer-can
chicken (only Tecate will do), and meltingly tender St. Louis–style ribs.
The space is whimsically rustic, with stuffed game trophies mounted on
the wall and leather saddles standing in for seats at a couple of tables.
$ *Average main: $26* ⊠ *975 1st St., near Main St.* ☎ *707/226–3976*
⊕ *www.bountyhunterwinebar.com* ⚑ *Reservations not accepted.*

$$$$　✕ **Cole's Chop House.** When only a thick, perfect steak will do, popu-
STEAKHOUSE　lar Cole's is the best choice in town. The prime steaks—New York
Fodor's Choice　and porterhouse—are dry-aged by Allen Brothers of Chicago, purvey-
★　ors to America's top steak houses. New Zealand lamb chops are the
house's nonbeef favorite, and seasonal additions might include veal
chops. Inside an 1886 stone building, Chops hews to tradition with
the starters and sides. Expect oysters Rockefeller, creamed spinach,
grilled asparagus with hollandaise, and other standbys, all prepared
with finesse. The wine list is borderline epic, with the best of the Napa
Valley amply represented. $ *Average main: $38* ⊠ *1122 Main St., at
Pearl St.* ☎ *707/224–6328* ⊕ *www.coleschophouse.com* ⚑ *Reservations
essential* ⊘ *No lunch.*

$$$$　✕ **La Toque.** Chef Ken Frank's La Toque is the complete package: his
MODERN　imaginative Modern American cuisine is served in an elegant dining
AMERICAN　space, complemented by an astutely assembled wine lineup that in 2014
Fodor's Choice　earned a coveted *Wine Spectator* Grand Award, bestowed on only 74
★　establishments worldwide. Built around seasonal local ingredients, the
menu changes frequently, but Rosti potato with Israeli Russian Osetra
caviar routinely appears as a starter, and Moroccan-spiced Liberty Farm
duck breast and Wagyu beef served with Frank's variation on pou-
tine are oft-seen entrées. Four-course ($80) and five-course ($98) tasting menus are offered, but for a memorable occasion consider letting
the chef and sommelier surprise you via the chef's table tasting menu
($195, $95 additional for wine pairings). $ *Average main: $80* ⊠ *Wes-
tin Verasa Napa, 1314 McKinstry St., off Soscol Ave.* ☎ *707/257–5157*
⊕ *www.latoque.com* ⊘ *No lunch.*

$$$$ ✕**Morimoto Napa.** *Iron Chef* star Masuharu Morimoto is the big name
JAPANESE   behind this downtown Napa hot spot. Organic materials such as twisting grapevines above the bar and rough-hewn wooden tables seem
simultaneously earthy and modern, creating a fitting setting for the
gorgeously plated Japanese fare, from sashimi served with grated fresh
wasabi to elaborate concoctions that include sea-urchin carbonara,
made with udon noodles. Everything's delightfully overdone, right
down to the desserts. ■ TIP➡ For the full experience, leave the choice
up to the chef and opt for the omakase menu ($120–$160). ⑤ *Average main: $44* ✉ *610 Main St., at 5th St.* ☎ *707/252–1600* ⊕ *www.
morimotonapa.com.*

$$ ✕**Napa Valley Bistro.** Locals have taken a liking to chef-owner Bernardo
AMERICAN   Ayala's unpretentious bistro, which specializes in perky comfort food—
everything from mac and cheese with bacon and organic fried chicken
to empanadas and vegetarian spring rolls. Other crowd pleasers include
the Niman Ranch St. Louis ribs slathered in molasses barbecue sauce
and the burger made from local lamb and served with feta and a rose-
mary aioli. The restaurant's Sunday brunch is bountiful and popular.
⑤ *Average main: $18* ✉ *975 Clinton St., near Main St.* ☎ *707/666–2383*
⊕ *www.napavalleybistro.net* ☽ *Closed Mon.*

$$ ✕**Norman Rose Tavern.** If downtown Napa had its own version of the bar
AMERICAN   in *Cheers*, it would be the Norman Rose. Casual and family-friendly,
"The Rose" serves such classic American fare as hamburgers, sandwiches, and fish-and-chips. It has a full bar and pours local wines and
regional beers. Happy hour, held on weekdays from 3 to 6 pm, is particularly rollicking, with specials on hot wings (by the pound) and sliders. ■ TIP➡ On warm days, arrive early for a spot on the open-air patio.
⑤ *Average main: $17* ✉ *1401 1st St., at Franklin St.* ☎ *707/258–1516*
⊕ *www.normanrosenapa.com.*

$$$ ✕**Oenotri.** Often spotted at local farmers' markets or in one of two
ITALIAN   gardens he helps tend, Tyler Rodde, Oenotri's ebullient chef-owner
and a Napa native, is ever on the lookout for fresh produce and other
ingredients to incorporate into his rustic southern-Italian cuisine. His
restaurant, a brick-walled contemporary space with tall windows and
wooden tables, is a lively spot to sample house-made salumi and pastas
and Neapolitan-style thin-crust pizzas that always include a simple but
satisfying Margherita pie made with San Marzano tomatoes and buffalo
mozzarella. Entrées might include roasted squab, king salmon, or pork
loin. ⑤ *Average main: $23* ✉ *1425 1st St., at Franklin St.* ☎ *707/252–
1022* ⊕ *www.oenotri.com.*

$$ ✕**Tarla Mediterranean Grill.** The menu at Tarla challenges the Napa Val-
MEDITERRANEAN   ley's notoriously Italo-centric diners to venture deeper into the Medi-
terranean. You can build a meal by combining such traditional mezes
(tapas) as stuffed grape leaves with fresh tzatziki (a thick yogurt sauce
with cucumber, dill, and mint) and spanakopita (phyllo dough stuffed
with spinach and feta) with more contemporary, seasonally offered
creations—perhaps a crab, spinach, and hearts of palm fondue. The
entrées include updates of moussaka and other Mediterranean mainstays, along with fancifully modern items such as beef short ribs
braised with a pomegranate-wine sauce and accompanying them with

a corn-and-white-truffle risotto. $ *Average main: $19* ⊠ *Andaz Napa, 1480 1st St., at School St.* ☏ *707/255–5599* ⊕ *www.tarlagrill.com.*

$$$
MODERN
AMERICAN

✕ **The Thomas.** Brad Farmerie, also the executive chef at New York City's Public restaurant, tickles diners' palates with earthy-yet-lofty preparations, served inside an iconic downtown building that was closed for decades, shrouded in murder and mystery. There's no mystery, though, to the winning approach of Farmerie and chef de cuisine Jonnatan Leiva. Appetizers such as the truffled portobello mushroom mousse with whiskey jelly, perhaps accompanied by a mod cocktail from the first-floor Fagiani's Bar, set the mood for entrées that might include wild king salmon served with shaved fennel and a cucumber emulsion. Even the brussels sprouts, deep-fried and served with a house-made chili-caramel sauce, delight. ■ TIP➔ In good weather head up to the rooftop deck for its river views. $ *Average main: $26* ⊠ *813 Main St., at 3rd St.* ☏ *707/226–7821* ⊕ *www.thethomas-napa.com* ☉ *No lunch weekdays.*

$$$
MODERN
AMERICAN
Fodor's Choice
★

✕ **Torc.** *Torc* means "wild boar" in an early Celtic dialect, and chef Sean O'Toole occasionally incorporates his restaurant's namesake beast into dishes at his eclectic downtown restaurant. Bolognese sauce, for example, might include ground wild boar, tomato, lime, and cocoa. O'Toole has helmed kitchens at top New York City, San Francisco, and Yountville establishments. Torc is the first restaurant he's owned, and he crafts meals with style and precision that are reflected in the gracious service and classy, contemporary decor. ■ TIP➔ The Bengali sweet potato–pakora appetizer, which comes with a dreamy-creamy yogurt-truffle dip, has been a hit since day one. $ *Average main: $25* ⊠ *1140 Main St., at Pearl St.* ☏ *707/252–3292* ⊕ *www.torcnapa.com* ☉ *No lunch weekdays.*

$$$
SPANISH
Fodor's Choice
★

✕ **ZuZu.** The focus at festive ZuZu is on tapas, paella, and other Spanish favorites. Diners down *cava* (Spanish sparkling wine) or sangria with dishes that might include white anchovies with boiled egg and rémoulade on grilled bread. Locals revere the paella, made with Spanish Bomba rice. Latin jazz on the stereo helps make this place a popular spot for get-togethers. In fall 2014, ZuZu's owners opened **La Taberna,** three doors south at 815 Main Street, a bar for *pintxos* (small bites) and cocktails. The signature dish: suckling pig, which goes well with the beers, wines, and other libations. $ *Average main: $29* ⊠ *829 Main St., near 3rd St.* ☏ *707/224–8555* ⊕ *www.zuzunapa.com* ☖ *Reservations not accepted* ☉ *No lunch weekends.*

WHERE TO STAY

$$$
HOTEL
Fodor's Choice
★

▦ **Andaz Napa.** Part of the Hyatt family, this boutique hotel with an urban-hip vibe has luxurious rooms with flat-screen TVs, laptop-size safes, and white-marble bathrooms stocked with high-quality bath products. **Pros:** proximity to downtown restaurants, theaters, and tasting rooms; access to modern fitness center; complimentary beverage upon arrival; complimentary snacks and nonalcoholic beverages in rooms. **Cons:** parking can be a challenge on weekends; unremarkable views from some rooms. $ *Rooms from: $309* ⊠ *1450 1st St.* ☏ *707/687–1234* ⊕ *andaznapa.com* ⇥ *137 rooms, 4 suites* ◖ *No meals.*

At fascinating di Rosa the art treasures can be found indoors and out.

$$
HOTEL
Fodor's Choice
★

⊞ **Best Western Plus Elm House Inn.** In a region known for over-the-top architecture and amenities and prices to match, this inn delivers style and even a touch of grace at affordable prices. **Pros:** polite staff; generous continental breakfasts; complimentary freshly baked cookies in lobby. **Cons:** hot tub but no pool; about a mile from downtown; some road noise in streetside rooms. ⑤ *Rooms from: $244* ⊠ *800 California Blvd.* ☎ *707/255–1831* ⊕ *www.bestwestern.com* ⊃ *22 rooms* ⦿ *Breakfast.*

$
B&B/INN

⊞ **Blackbird Inn.** Arts and Crafts style infuses this home from the turn of the last century, from the lobby's enormous fieldstone fireplace to the lamps that cast a warm glow over the impressive wooden staircase. **Pros:** gorgeous architecture and period furnishings; convenient to downtown Napa; free afternoon wine service. **Cons:** must be booked well in advance; some rooms are on the small side. ⑤ *Rooms from: $185* ⊠ *1755 1st St.* ☎ *707/226–2450, 888/567–9811* ⊕ *www. blackbirdinnnapa.com* ⊃ *8 rooms* ⦿ *Breakfast.*

$$$$
RESORT
Fodor's Choice
★

⊞ **Carneros Inn.** Freestanding board-and-batten cottages with rocking chairs on each porch are simultaneously rustic and chic at this luxurious property. **Pros:** cottages have lots of privacy; beautiful views from hilltop pool and hot tub; heaters on private patios; excellent Boon Fly Café is open all day. **Cons:** a long drive to destinations up-valley; smallish rooms with limited seating options. ⑤ *Rooms from: $600* ⊠ *4048 Sonoma Hwy./Hwy. 121* ☎ *707/299–4900, 888/400–9000* ⊕ *www.the carnerosinn.com* ⊃ *76 cottages, 10 suites* ⦿ *No meals.*

$$
B&B/INN

⊞ **The Inn on First.** Guests gush over this inn whose hosts-with-the-most owners make a stay here one to remember. **Pros:** full gourmet breakfast; varied room choices; garden and patio; away from downtown. **Cons:**

away from downtown; no TVs; children under age 12 not permitted. ⑤ *Rooms from: $300* ✉ *1938 1st St.* ☎ *707/253–1331* ⊕ *www.theinnonfirst.com* ⟿ *10 rooms* ⦿ *Breakfast.*

$$
B&B/INN
⛬ **Inn on Randolph.** A few calm blocks from the downtown action, the restored Inn on Randolph is a sophisticated haven celebrated for its gluten-free breakfasts and snacks. **Pros:** quiet; gourmet breakfasts; sophisticated decor; romantic setting. **Cons:** a bit of a walk from downtown. ⑤ *Rooms from: $285* ✉ *411 Randolph St.* ☎ *707/257–2886* ⊕ *www.innonrandolph.com* ⟿ *5 rooms, 5 cottages* ⦿ *Breakfast.*

$$$
B&B/INN
⛬ **Milliken Creek Inn.** Wine-and-cheese receptions at sunset set a romantic mood in this hotel's intimate lobby, with its terrace overlooking a lush lawn and the Napa River. **Pros:** soft-as-clouds beds; serene spa; breakfast delivered to your room (or elsewhere on the beautiful grounds). **Cons:** expensive; road noise audible in outdoor areas. ⑤ *Rooms from: $379* ✉ *1815 Silverado Trail* ☎ *707/255–1197* ⊕ *www.millikencreekinn.com* ⟿ *12 rooms* ⦿ *Breakfast.*

$$
B&B/INN
⛬ **Napa River Inn.** Part of a complex of restaurants, shops, a nightclub, and a spa, this waterfront inn is within easy walking distance of downtown hot spots. **Pros:** wide range of room sizes and prices; near downtown action; pet friendly. **Cons:** river views could be more scenic; some rooms get noise from nearby restaurants. ⑤ *Rooms from: $249* ✉ *500 Main St.* ☎ *707/251–8500, 877/251–8500* ⊕ *www.napariverinn.com* ⟿ *65 rooms, 1 suite* ⦿ *Breakfast.*

$$$
HOTEL
Fodor'sChoice
★
⛬ **Senza Hotel.** Exterior fountains, gallery-quality outdoor sculptures, and decorative rows of grapevines signal the Wine Country–chic aspirations of this boutique hotel operated by the owners of Hall St. Helena winery. **Pros:** high-style fixtures; fireplaces in all rooms; Wine Country–chic atmosphere. **Cons:** just off highway; little of interest within walking distance; some bathrooms have no tub. ⑤ *Rooms from: $369* ✉ *4066 Howard La.* ☎ *707/253–0337* ⊕ *www.senzahotel.com* ⟿ *41 rooms* ⦿ *Breakfast.*

$$
HOTEL
⛬ **Westin Verasa Napa.** Near the Napa Valley Wine Train depot and the Oxbow market, this spacious resort is sophisticated and soothing. **Pros:** two heated saline pools; most rooms have well-equipped kitchenettes (some have full kitchens); spacious double-headed showers; good value for the price. **Cons:** "amenities fee" added to room rate. ⑤ *Rooms from: $299* ✉ *1314 McKinstry St.* ☎ *707/257–1800, 888/627–7169* ⊕ *www.westinnapa.com* ⟿ *160 suites, 20 rooms* ⦿ *No meals.*

NIGHTLIFE AND PERFORMING ARTS

The bars at popular restaurants and hotels constitute much of the nightlife action in Napa, but because of its size the city attracts big-name performers to a few venues downtown. The wine bars draw a younger and sportier crowd than elsewhere in the Napa Valley.

NIGHTLIFE

Fodor'sChoice
★
1313 Main. Cool, sexy 1313 Main attracts a youngish crowd for top-drawer spirits and sparkling and still wines. The on-site **LuLu's Kitchen** serves bar food—past favorites have included coq au vin wings and corn

Few experiences are as exhilarating yet serene as an early-morning balloon ride above the vineyards.

and shiso fritters—and wild salmon, steak, and other entrées. ✉ *1313 Main St., at Clinton St.* ☎ *707/258–1313* ⊕ *www.1313main.com.*

Cadet Wine + Beer Bar. A snappy 2014 addition to Napa's nightlife scene, Cadet plays things urban-style cool with a long bar, high-top tables, an all-vinyl soundtrack, and a low-lit, generally loungelike feel. The two owners describe their outlook as "unabashedly pro-California," but their lineup of 150-plus wines and beers embraces the globe. The crowd here is youngish, the vibe festive. ✉ *930 Franklin St., at end of pedestrian alley between 1st and 2nd Sts.* ☎ *707/224–4400* ⊕ *www. cadetbeerandwinebar.com.*

City Winery Napa. A makeover transformed the 1879 Napa Valley Opera House into a combination wine bar, restaurant, and live-music venue that features top singer-songwriters and small acts. Many of the three dozen wines on tap are exclusive to the club from prestigious area wineries. ✉ *1030 Main St., near 1st St.* ☎ *707/260–1600* ⊕ *www.city winery.com/napa.*

Silo's. At this club inside the Historic Napa Mill, locals sip wine and listen to excellent live music—mostly jazz, but also rock, blues, and other styles. The cover varies, but it's generally $10 to $25. ✉ *530 Main St., near 5th St.* ☎ *707/251–5833* ⊕ *www.silosnapa.com.*

PERFORMING ARTS

Uptown Theatre. This top-notch live-music venue, a former movie house, attracts Ziggy Marley, Ani DiFranco, Napa Valley resident and winery owner Boz Scaggs, and other performers. ✉ *1350 3rd St., at Franklin St.* ☎ *707/259–0123* ⊕ *www.uptowntheatrenapa.com.*

CLOSE UP

Wine Country Balloon Rides

Thought those vineyards were beautiful from the highway? Try viewing them from an altitude of about a thousand feet, serenely drifting along with the wind, the only sound the occasional roar of the burners overhead.

Many companies organize hot-air-ballooning trips over Napa and Sonoma, offering rides that usually cost between $200 and $250 per person for a one-hour flight, which typically includes brunch or lunch afterward. If you were hoping for the ultimate in romance—a flight with no one else but your sweetie (and an FAA-approved pilot) on board—be prepared to shell out two to four times as much.

Flights typically take off at the crack of dawn, when winds are the lightest, so be prepared to make an early start, and dress in layers. Flights are dependent on weather, and if there's rain or too much fog, expect to be grounded. Hotels can hook you up with nearby companies, some of which will pick you up at your lodgings.

3

SPAS

The Spa at Napa River Inn. All stress will be under arrest after a massage, facial, or other treatment at this spa inside Napa's vaguely late-deco former police station. Among the oft-chosen massages here are the signature Yogi Ohm, which incorporates Asian influences, and Adjust Your Frequency, involving aromatherapy, tuning forks, and other body-aligning procedures. The five-hour Royal Treatment pulls out all the stops with a full-body massage, foot rehab, exfoliation, a body wrap, and a grape-seed facial. ■ TIP→ If you're traveling with a dog in need of TLC, the spa will pamper your pet with a walk, a treat, and a mini massage while you're indulging yourself. ⊠ *500 Main St., at 5th St.* ☎ *707/265–7537* ⊕ *www.napariverinn.com/the-spa* ✉ *Treatments $20–$440* ☉ *Mon.–Sat. 9–9, Sun. 9–7.*

SPORTS AND THE OUTDOORS

BALLOONING

Balloons Above the Valley. This company's personable and professional pilots make its outings a delight. Flights depart from the Napa Valley Marriott, in the city of Napa, and conclude with a champagne brunch there. You can extend the pleasure with packages that include a picnic lunch and winery tours. ☎ *707/253–2222, 800/464–6824* ⊕ *www.balloonrides.com* ✉ *From $179 (for a weekday flight).*

SHOPPING

Napa's most interesting shops and boutiques can be found downtown west of the Napa River, along Pearl and 1st through 5th streets between Main and about Franklin streets. East of the river at the Oxbow Public Market, you'll also find stands worth visiting.

Bounty Hunter Rare Wine & Spirits. The wine shop affiliated with the Bounty Hunter restaurant stocks Napa cult Cabernets and other hard-to-find wines. ⊠ *975 1st St., near Main St.* ☎ *707/255–0622* ⊕ *www.bountyhunterwine.com.*

Lucero Olive Oil. Its well-designed facility and entertaining tastings of olive oils and balsamic vinegars make Lucero worth checking out. You'll learn to recognize the subtle differences between the various extra virgin and infused oils, some of which are so flavor-filled they go well even with ice cream. ⊠ *1012 1st St., at Main St.* ☎ *707/255–4645* ⊕ *www.lucerooliveoil.com/retail-store.*

Napa Premium Outlets. Even travelers zipping through Napa sometimes yield to temptation and detour to this mall where such national chains as Kenneth Cole, J. Crew, Barneys New York, and Coach sell their wares at discounted prices. ⊠ *629 Factory Stores Dr., off Hwy. 29 at 1st St. exit* ☎ *707/226–9876* ⊕ *www.premiumoutlets.com/napa.*

Shackford's Kitchen Store. The gracious Mr. Shackford's shop looks more like a hardware store than the low-key celebration of the art of cooking that it is, but if you need it—kitchenware, accessories, hard-to-find replacement items—he's probably got it. ⊠ *1350 Main St., at Caymus St.* ☎ *707/226–2132.*

YOUNTVILLE

9 miles north of downtown Napa; 9 miles south of St. Helena.

Fodor's Choice ★ These days Yountville is something like Disneyland for food lovers. It all started with Thomas Keller's The French Laundry, one of the best restaurants in the United States. Keller is also behind two more casual restaurants a few blocks from his mother ship, along with a very popular bakery. Perhaps by the time you read this his proposed ice-cream shop will be open, too. And that's only the tip of the iceberg. You could stay here for a week and not exhaust all the options in this tiny town with a big culinary reputation.

Yountville is full of small inns and luxurious hotels catering to those who prefer to be able to walk rather than drive to their lodgings after dinner. But it's also well located for excursions to big-name Napa wineries. Near Yountville, along the Silverado Trail, the Stags Leap District helped put Napa on the wine-making map with its bold Cabernet Sauvignons. Volcanic soil predominates on the eastern slopes of Stags Leap, apparent from the towering volcanic palisades and crags hovering over the vineyards. Though many visitors use Yountville as a home base, touring wineries by day and returning to town for dinner, you could easily while away a few hours in town, wandering through the many shops on or just off Washington Street, or visiting the many downtown tasting rooms.

GETTING HERE AND AROUND

If you're traveling north on Highway 29, take the Yountville exit, stay east of the highway, and take the first left onto Washington Street. Traveling south on Highway 29, turn left onto Madison Street and right onto Washington Street. Nearly all of Yountville's businesses and restaurants

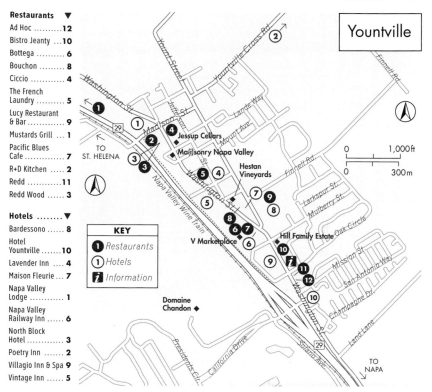

Yountville

KEY

① *Restaurants*
① *Hotels*
🛈 *Information*

are clustered along a half-mile stretch of Washington Street. Yountville Cross Road connects downtown Yountville to the Silverado Trail, where you'll find many of the area's best wineries. VINE Bus 10 and Bus 29 stop in Yountville. The Yountville Trolley circles the downtown area and hits a few spots beyond.

A note about addresses: the city of Napa surrounds Yountville, so many places north of Yountville, and closely associated with the town, are in fact in Napa.

Contact Yountville Trolley ☎ 707/944–1234 10 am–7 pm, 707/312–1509 7 pm–11 pm ⊕ www.ridethevine.com/yountville-trolley.

ESSENTIALS

Contact Yountville Chamber of Commerce ✉ 6484 Washington St., at Oak Circle ☎ 707/944–0904 ⊕ yountville.com.

EXPLORING

TOP ATTRACTIONS

Bell Wine Cellars. With vineyard and winery experience in South Africa, Europe, and California, a hand in the creation of the Los Carneros, Oakville, and Rutherford AVAs, and participation in research that led to the revival of Clone 6, a type of Cabernet Sauvignon, winemaker

Domaine Chandon claims a prime piece of real estate.

Anthony A. Bell had a varied career even before opening his namesake winery in 1991. Bell grows Chardonnay and Merlot on his Yountville property, but he's best known for Cabernet Sauvignons, particular one from Clone 6 fruit grown in Rutherford. His winery, south of town down a long driveway off Washington Street, is a quiet, casual place to sip old world–style wines made from carefully cultivated grapes. ⊠ *6200 Washington St., 1 mile south of town* ☎ *707/944–1673* ⊕ *www.bellwine.com* ⊠ *Tastings $20–$40, tours $40 (includes tasting)* ⊙ *Daily 10–4, by appointment.*

Fodor's Choice **Cliff Lede Vineyards.** Inspired by his passion for classic rock, owner and
★ construction magnate Cliff Lede named his Stag's Leap vineyard blocks after hits by the Grateful Dead and other bands, but the vibe at his efficient, high-tech winery is anything but laid-back. It's worth taking the estate tour to learn about the agricultural science that informs vineyard management here, and to see the production facility in action. Architect Howard Backen designed the winery and its tasting room, where Lede's Sauvignon Blanc, Cabernet Sauvignons, and other wines, along with some from sister winery Fel, which produces much-lauded Anderson Valley Pinot Noirs, are poured. ■TIP➔ **Walk-ins are welcome at the tasting bar, but appointments are required for the veranda outside and a nearby gallery that often displays rock-related art.** ⊠ *1473 Yountville Cross Rd., off Silverado Trail* ☎ *707/944–8642* ⊕ *cliffledevineyards.com* ⊠ *Tastings $25–$45; estate tour and tasting $75* ⊙ *Daily 10–4.*

Domaine Chandon. On a knoll shaded by ancient oak trees, this French-owned maker of sparkling wines claims one of Yountville's prime pieces of real estate. Chandon is best known for bubblies, but the still

A Great Southern Napa Drive

Traffic permitting, you could easily traverse the entire Napa Valley in about 45 minutes, passing scores of wineries along Highway 29. Many visitors do this, but a better strategy would be to tour just the southern Napa Valley at a more leisurely pace.

Have coffee at the Model Bakery in Napa's **Oxbow Public Market,** then drive north on Highway 29 to the Trancas Street/Redwood Road exit. At the top of the exit ramp, turn west (left) onto Trancas Street. After you cross over Highway 29, the name of the road changes to Redwood. Follow Redwood Road west, bearing left at the fork that appears when the road narrows from four lanes to two. After this point, two signs on Redwood Road will direct you to the **Hess Collection.** Allow an hour or so to browse the excellent modern art collection before or after tasting the wines.

After your visit, backtrack on Redwood Road about 1¼ miles to Mt. Veeder Road and turn left. After a little more than 8 miles, turn right (east) onto Dry Creek Road. After ½ mile the road becomes signed as the Oakville Grade. From here, twist your way

back downhill to Highway 29 and turn north. (If you're prone to car sickness, take Redwood Road all the way back to Highway 29 and turn north.) On Highway 29 a bit north of the Oakville Grade you'll see the driveway to **Robert Mondavi** on your left. The introductory tour here is good for wine newbies. After visiting Mondavi, repair to the **Oakville Grocery** and put together a picnic you can enjoy right out back. For a serious wine-tasting experience, head east on Oakville Cross Road to **Silver Oak Cellars** for a library tasting of this winery's distinguished Cabernet Sauvignons.

Your trip down memory lane complete, backtrack west on Oakville Cross and south on Highway 29 to **Yountville,** where bakeries and boutiques tempt body and bank account. Stroll Washington Street and enjoy the scenery and the parade of well-heeled visitors. If you find yourself yearning for more tasting, slip into the **Ma(i)sonry Napa Valley, Hill,** or **Hestan** tasting rooms to sample wines from small-lot producers. As evening approaches, remain in Yountville for dinner or return to Napa.

wines—Cabernet Sauvignon, Chardonnay, Pinot Meunier, and Pinot Noir—are also worth a try. You can sip by the flight or the glass at the bar or begin there and sit at tables in the lounge and return to the bar as needed; in good weather, tables are set up outside. Tours, which cover Chandon's French and California histories and the basics of making sparkling wines, end with a seated tasting. For the complete experience, order a cheese board or other hors d'oeuvres on the lounge menu. ⊠ *1 California Dr., off Hwy. 29* ☎ *707/204–7530, 888/242–6366* ⊕ *www.chandon.com* 🍷 *Tastings $10–$22, tours $40* ⊙ *Daily 10–5; tour times vary.*

Hestan Vineyards. A contemporary structure of concrete, glass, hand-forged copper, and other materials, Hestan's downtown tasting room makes the most of its oddly shaped lot and inside further impresses with its use of travertine and Venetian plaster. Unlike at other tasting rooms, gleaming cookware—the owner manufactures upscale pots and pans for Williams-Sonoma and other stores—catches the eye before wine bottles do. Sit down for a tasting, though, and attention instantly focuses on the polished, almost voluptuous wines a team of acclaimed winemakers crafts from grapes grown amid the southern Vaca range. The Hestan and Stephanie Cabernet Sauvignons are particularly successful, and the Petit Verdot, a newer offering, proves exemplary. ⊠ *6548 Washington St., at Humboldt St.* ☎ *707/945–1002* ⊕ *www.hestan.com* ✉ *Tastings $20–$35* ⊙ *June–Oct., Sun.–Wed. 11–6, Thurs.–Sat. 11–7; Nov.–Mar., Sun.–Thurs. 11–5, Fri. and Sat. 11–6; Apr.–May, Sun.–Wed. 11–5, Thurs.–Sat. 11–6.*

Hill Family Estate. For years Doug Hill produced grapes for esteemed Napa Valley wineries, but at the urging of his son, Ryan, the family established its own line of Merlot, Cabernet Sauvignon, and other wines. Crafted by Alison Doran, a protégé of the late Napa winemaker André Tchelistcheff, these are subtle, refined wines you can sample in the family's downtown tasting salon, a cheery mélange of antiques alongside baseball, surfing, and other memorabilia—even a classic Fender guitar—ingeniously stained in Hill red wine. Seated tastings ($35), which include a cheese and charcuterie plate, require reservations, but you can also just taste at the bar. In summer and early fall, entertaining "secret garden" tours are conducted of **Jacobsen Orchards,** a small nearby farm that grows produce for The French Laundry and other top restaurants. ⊠ *6512 Washington St., at Mulberry St.* ☎ *707/944–9580* ⊕ *www.hillfamilyestate.com* ✉ *Tastings $20–$35; garden tour $65 (includes tasting)* ⊙ *Tasting room daily 10–6; garden tour by appointment, weather permitting.*

Fodor's Choice
★
Ma(i)sonry Napa Valley. An art-and-design gallery that also pours the wines of two dozen limited-production wineries, Ma(i)sonry occupies an atmospheric stone manor house constructed in 1904. Tasting flights can be sampled in fair weather in the beautiful garden, in a private nook, or at the communal redwood table, and in any weather indoors among the contemporary artworks and well-chosen *objets*—which might include 17th-century furnishings, industrial lamps, or slabs of petrified wood. ∎TIP➡ **Walk-ins are welcome space permitting, but during summer, at harvesttime, and on weekends and holidays it's best to book in advance.** ⊠ *6711 Washington St., at Pedroni St.* ☎ *707/944–0889* ⊕ *www.maisonry.com* ✉ *Tasting $15–$35* ⊙ *Sun.–Thurs. daily 10–6, Fri. and Sat. daily 10–7; check for later hrs in summer and early fall.*

Fodor's Choice
★
Robert Sinskey Vineyards. Although the winery produces a well-regarded Stags Leap Cabernet Sauvignon, two supple red blends called Marcien and POV, and white wines, Sinskey is best known for its intense, brambly Carneros District Pinot Noirs. All the grapes are grown in organic, certified biodynamic vineyards. The influence of Robert's wife, Maria Helm Sinskey—a chef and cookbook author and the winery's culinary director—is evident during the tastings, which are accompanied by a few bites of food with each wine. ∎TIP➡ **The Perfect Circle Tour ($75) takes in the winery's gardens and ends with a seated pairing of**

CLOSE UP

The Paris Wine Tasting of 1976

The event that changed the California wine industry forever took place half a world away, in Paris. To celebrate the American Bicentennial, Steven Spurrier, a British wine merchant, sponsored a comparative blind tasting of California Cabernet Sauvignon and Chardonnay wines against Bordeaux Cabernet blends and French Chardonnays. The tasters were French and included journalists and producers. The 1973 Stag's Leap Wine Cellars Cabernet Sauvignon came in first among the reds, and the 1973 Chateau Montelena Chardonnay edged out the French whites. The so-called Judgment of Paris stunned the wine establishment, as it was the first serious challenge to the supremacy of French wines. When the shouting died down, the rush was on. Tourists and winemakers streamed into the Napa Valley and wine prices rose so much that they even helped revitalize the Sonoma County wine industry.

3

POSTSCRIPT
In 2006, a re-creation of the earth-shaking 1976 tasting took place in Napa Valley and London. A panel of American, English, and French experts unanimously voted a 1971 Ridge California Cabernet Sauvignon the best of all. In fact, Californian Cabernet Sauvignons from the early 1970s swept the top five places—happy proof that California's wines can age as well as French vintages.

food and wine. ✉ *6320 Silverado Trail, at Yountville Cross Rd., Napa* ☎ *707/944–9090* ⊕ *www.robertsinskey.com* 🍷 *Tasting $25, tour $75* ☉ *Daily 10–4:30; tours by appointment weekdays at 11, weekends at 1.*

Stag's Leap Wine Cellars. A 1973 Stag's Leap Cabernet Sauvignon put this winery and the Napa Valley on the enological map by placing first in the famous Paris tasting of 1976. The grapes for that wine came from a vineyard visible from the new stone-and-glass Fay Outlook & Visitor Center, which opened in 2014. The tasting room has broad views of a second fabled Cabernet vineyard (Fay) and the promontory that gives both the winery and the Stags Leap District AVA their names. ■TIP➜ A $40 tasting includes the top-of-the-line estate-grown Cabernets, which sell for more than $100; a $25 tasting of more modestly priced wines is also available. ✉ *5766 Silverado Trail, at Wappo Hill Rd., Napa* ☎ *707/944–2020, 866/422–7523* ⊕ *www.cask23.com* 🍷 *Tastings $25–$40, tour with food and wine pairing $95* ☉ *Daily 10–4:30; tours by appointment.*

QUICK BITES

Bouchon Bakery. To satisfy that craving you didn't know you had—but soon will—for macarons (meringue cookies), stock up on hazelnut, pistachio, chocolate-dipped raspberry, and several other flavors at this bakery associated with the Thomas Keller restaurant of the same name. The brownies, pastries, and other baked goods are equally alluring. ✉ *6528 Washington St., at Yount St.* ☎ *707/944–2253* ⊕ *www.bouchonbakery.com.*

WORTH NOTING

Chimney Rock Winery. With its singularly ornate Cape (as in Cape of Good Hope) Dutch style of the 17th century, this winery owned by the Terlato family strikes an unconventional pose amid the austere Stags Leap landscape. The iconoclastic approach also plays out in the flagship Cabernet Sauvignon Stags Leap District wine, which is softer and suppler than most of its local counterparts. Chimney Rock is also known for its Bordeaux-style blend and several single-vineyard, estate-grown Cabernets. Whites include Sauvignon Gris—the grape is a clone of Sauvignon Blanc. The tasting room's decor complements the exterior, with high, wood-beamed ceilings and a fireplace that warms things up in winter. Tours are by appointment, but walk-ins are welcome as space permits. ⊠ *5350 Silverado Trail, at Capps Dr., Napa* ☎ *707/257– 2641* ⊕ *www.chimneyrock.com* ⊠ *Tastings $35–$65, tours $55–$130* ⊗ *Daily 10–5, tours by appointment.*

Clos du Val. A Napa Valley mainstay since the early 1970s, Clos du Val built its reputation on its intense reserve Cabernet Sauvignon, made with fruit from the Stags Leap District. Though known for this and other Cabernets, the winery also produces Merlot, Petit Verdot, Pinot Noir, and Primitivo reds, along with whites that include Chardonnay and a pleasing blend of Semillon and Sauvignon Blanc. On a sunny day, this last wine is perfect for enjoying in the shady olive grove beside the tasting room or at cabanas out front (reservations required for both). ■**TIP**➜ **The small-production Winemaker's Signature wines, worth investigating, are made from lots or varietals from a given vintage that capture winemaker Kristy Melton's fancy.** ⊠ *5330 Silverado Trail, just south of Capps Dr., Napa* ☎ *707/261–5251, 800/993–9463* ⊕ *www. closduval.com* ⊠ *Tasting $15–$35, tour $30* ⊗ *Daily 10–5; tour 10:30 and 2:30 by appointment.*

Jessup Cellars. Outgoing staffers and hip events entice younger than average patrons to this downtown Yountville tasting room and attached art gallery. Typical of the events is an evening series of short films screened in the gallery and "paired" with Jessup wines and flavor-infused popcorns. The house wine-making philosophy favors the maritime influences of the Carneros District for Chardonnay, Merlot, and Pinot Noir, and hotter, northern Napa Valley locales for Zinfandel, Petite Sirah, and Bordeaux varietals other than Merlot. The concept generally succeeds: the Pinot has the classic Carneros rich-berry earthiness, for instance, and you can tell the Zinfandel and Petite Sirah get the heat and hang time they require. ⊠ *6740 Washington St., at Pedroni St.* ☎ *707/944–8523, 888/537–7879* ⊕ *jessupcellars.com* ⊠ *Tastings $20* ⊗ *Daily 10–6, sometimes later for events; appointments recommended for gallery and private-room tastings.*

WHERE TO EAT

$$$$
MODERN
AMERICAN
Fodor's Choice
★

✕**Ad Hoc.** At this casual spot, superstar chef Thomas Keller offers a single, fixed-price menu ($52) nightly, with a small lineup of decadent brunch items served on Sunday. The dinner selection might include braised beef short ribs and creamy polenta, or a delicate *panna cotta* with a citrus glaze. The dining room is warmly low-key, with zinc-top tables, wine served in tumblers, and rock and jazz on the stereo. Call a day ahead to find out the next day's menu. ■TIP➔ **From Thursday through Saturday, except in winter, you can pick up a boxed lunch to go—the buttermilk fried chicken one is delicious—at the on-site and aptly named Addendum.** $ *Average main: $52* ⊠ *6476 Washington St., at Oak Circle* ☎ *707/944–2487* ⊕ *www.adhocrestaurant.com* ⌂ *Reservations essential* ☾ *No lunch Mon.–Sat. No dinner Tues. and Wed.*

$$$
FRENCH
Fodor's Choice
★

✕ **Bistro Jeanty.** French classics and obscure delicacies tickle patrons' palates at chef Philippe Jeanty's genteel country bistro. Jeanty prepares the greatest hits—escargots, cassoulet, *daube de boeuf* (beef stewed in red wine)—with the utmost precision and turns out pike dumplings and lamb tongue with equal élan. Regulars often start with the extraordinary, rich tomato soup in a flaky puff pastry before proceeding to sole meunière, slow-roasted pork shoulder, or coq au vin (always choosing the simple, suggested side: thin egg noodles cooked with just the right amount of butter and salt). Chocolate pot de crème, warm apple tart tartin, and other authentic desserts complete the French sojourn. $ *Average main: $27* ⊠ *6510 Washington St., at Mulberry St.* ☎ *707/944– 0103* ⊕ *www.bistrojeanty.com.*

$$$
ITALIAN

✕ **Bottega.** The food at chef Michael Chiarello's trattoria is simultaneously soulful and inventive, transforming local ingredients into regional Italian dishes with a twist. The antipasti shine: you can order grilled short-rib meatballs, house-made charcuterie, or incredibly fresh fish. Potato gnocchi might be served with pumpkin *fonduta* (Italian-style fondue) and roasted root vegetables, and hearty main courses such as a grilled acorn-fed pork shoulder loin with a honey-mustard glaze might be accompanied by cinnamon stewed plums and crispy black kale. The vibe is festive, with exposed-brick walls and an open kitchen, but service is spot-on, and the wine list includes interesting choices from Italy and California. $ *Average main: $26* ⊠ *V Marketplace, 6525 Washington St., near Mulberry St.* ☎ *707/945–1050* ⊕ *www.botteganapavalley.com* ☾ *No lunch Mon.*

$$$
FRENCH
Fodor's Choice
★

✕ **Bouchon.** The team that created The French Laundry is also behind this place, where everything—the lively and crowded zinc-topped bar, the elbow-to-elbow seating, the traditional French onion soup— could have come straight from a Parisian bistro. Roast chicken with sautéed chicken livers and button mushrooms, and steamed mussels served with crispy, addictive *frites* (french fries) are among the dishes served. ■TIP➔ **The adjacent Bouchon Bakery sells marvelous macarons (meringue cookies) in many flavors, along with brownies, pastries, and other baked goods.** $ *Average main: $27* ⊠ *6534 Washington St., near Humboldt St.* ☎ *707/944–8037* ⊕ *www.bouchonbistro.com* ⌂ *Reservations essential.*

$$
MODERN ITALIAN

✕ **Ciccio.** High-profile French and modern-American establishments may dominate the Yountville landscape, but recent arrival Ciccio instantly endeared itself with locals and visitors seeking inventive, reasonably priced—in this case, modern Italian—cuisine. Inside a remodeled former grocery store that retains a down-home feel, executive chef Polly Lappetito, formerly of the Culinary Institute of America, turns out pizzas and entrées, some of whose vegetables and herbs come from

DID YOU KNOW?

These tomatoes are headed for the kitchen of The French Laundry, one of the Napa Valley's most famous restaurants, where dinner will set you back $295—if you can get a reservation.

the garden of the owners, Frank and Karen Altamura. Seasonal grow-ing cycles dictate the ever-changing menu; Tuscan kale and white-bean soup, wood-fired sardines with salsa verde, and a mushroom, Taleg-gio, and crispy-sage pizza are among the recent offerings. Frank and Karen own Altamura Vineyards, whose wines are featured here, but their Napa Valley neighbors are also represented, and there's a Negroni cocktail bar. ⑤ *Average main: $19* ✉ *6770 Washington St., at Madison St.* ☎ *707/945–1000* ⊕ *www.ciccionapavalley.com* ⌕ *Reservations not accepted* ⊗ *Closed Mon. and Tues. No lunch.*

$$$$
AMERICAN
Fodor's Choice
★

✕ **The French Laundry.** An old stone building laced with ivy houses the most acclaimed restaurant in the Napa Valley—and, indeed, one of the most highly regarded in the country. The two nine-course prix-fixe menus (both $295), one of which highlights vegetables, vary, but "oysters and pearls," a silky dish of pearl tapioca with oysters and white sturgeon caviar, is a signature starter. Some courses rely on luxe ingredients like *calotte* (cap of the rib eye), while others take hum-ble foods such as fava beans and elevate them to art. Many courses also offer the option of "supplements"—sea urchin, for instance, or black truffles. ■ TIP➜ Reservations are hard-won here; to get one call two months ahead to the day at 10 am, on the dot. ⑤ *Average main: $295* ✉ *6640 Washington St., at Creek St.* ☎ *707/944–2380* ⊕ *www. frenchlaundry.com* ⌕ *Reservations essential* ⌂ *Jacket required* ⊗ *No lunch Mon.–Thurs.*

$$$$
MODERN
AMERICAN

✕ **Lucy Restaurant & Bar.** In a sleek modern space radiating offhand ele-gance, Lucy seduces with sophisticated flavors and suave service. Chef Victor Scargle builds his menu around produce from an on-site gar-den. As one of its farmers, he's intimately acquainted with its bounty, which includes the components of the (truly) freshly dug carrot salad. Sunchoke soup and ahi tuna ceviche also make excellent starters, and you can stay small even with the entrées, which come in full and half portions. A modern take on duck à l'orange is a consistent pleaser, but game diners can opt for a chop—in this case antelope—served with wild rice and tangy huckleberry jus. The sommelier, formerly of The French Laundry and New York City's Per Se, graciously guides diners through the well-conceived wine list. ⑤ *Average main: $33* ✉ *Bardessono, 6526 Yount St., at Finnell St.* ☎ *707/204–6030* ⊕ *www.bardessono.com/ restaurant_bar.*

$$$
AMERICAN

✕ **Mustards Grill.** Cindy Pawlcyn's Mustards fills day and night with fans of her hearty cuisine. The menu mixes updated renditions of traditional American dishes (what Pawlcyn dubs "deluxe truck stop classics")—among them barbecued baby back pork ribs and a lemon-lime tart piled high with browned meringue—with more fanciful choices such as sweet corn tamales with tomatillo-avocado salsa and wild mushrooms. A black-and-white marble tile floor and upbeat artworks keep the mood jolly. ⑤ *Average main: $27* ✉ *7399 St. Helena Hwy./Hwy. 29, 1 mile north of Yountville, Napa* ☎ *707/944–2424* ⊕ *www.mustardsgrill.com.*

$$
AMERICAN

✕ **Pacific Blues Cafe.** Because one can't take every meal at Bouchon or The French Laundry (or can one?), owner Jeff Steen graciously pro-vides Yountvillians and visitors with this comfort-food haven inside the town's restored 19th-century train depot. On sunny afternoons, nearly everyone's on the outdoor patio enjoying barbecue-salmon club sandwiches, pulled-pork sliders, turkey or beef burgers laid between Model Bakery buns, or generously portioned salads, perhaps accompanied by a well-made margarita. Some of these items also show up on the dinner menu, along with flat-iron steak, Niman Ranch pork chops, and mahimahi tacos. Lunch may be unnecessary if at breakfast you order the flat-iron with two eggs and hash browns or the huevos rancheros. Service can be uneven. ⑤ *Average main: $18* ✉ *6525 Washington St., at Yount St.* ☎ *707/944–4455* ⊕ *www.pacificbluescafe.com* ⌦ *Reservations not accepted.*

$$ ✗ **R+D Kitchen.** High-end eateries abound in Yountville, but the stone-
ECLECTIC   and-glass R+D satisfies without punching a huge hole in your wallet. As the name suggests, the chefs here are willing to experiment, starting with sushi plates that include hiramasa rolls topped with rainbow-trout caviar. The similar lunch and dinner menus both include a super-crispy chicken sandwich topped with Swiss cheese and a slow-roasted pork sandwich that pays homage to its Mexican roots. The Greek-style rotisserie chicken, one of several entrées popular with locals, swims in a frisky egg-lemon sauce. ■**TIP**➔ With Adirondack chairs, umbrellas, and a fountain, the outdoor patio attracts a crowd on sunny days to sip wine or fancy cocktails and munch on the Dip Duo (guacamole and pimento cheese) appetizer. ⑤ *Average main: $20* ✉ *6795 Washington St., at Madison St.* ☎ *707/945–0920* ⊕ *www.hillstone.com/#/restaurants/caferandd.*

$$$ ✗ **Redd.** The minimalist dining room here seems a fitting setting for chef
MODERN   Richard Reddington's up-to-date menu. The culinary influences include
AMERICAN   California, Mexico, Europe, and Asia, but the food always feels modern
Fodor's Choice   and never fussy. The glazed pork belly with apple puree, set amid a pool
★   of soy caramel, is a prime example of the East-meets-West style. The seafood preparations—among them petrale sole, clams, and chorizo poached in a saffron-curry broth—are deft variations on the original dishes. For the full experience, consider the five-course tasting menu ($80 per person, $125 with wine pairing). ■**TIP**➔ For a quick bite, order small plates and a cocktail and sit at the bar. ⑤ *Average main: $30* ✉ *6480 Washington St., at Oak Circle* ☎ *707/944–2222* ⊕ *www.reddnapavalley.com* ⌦ *Reservations essential.*

$$ ✗ **Redd Wood.** Chef Richard Reddington's casual restaurant specializes
ITALIAN   in thin-crust wood-fired pizzas and contemporary variations on rustic Italian classics. The nonchalance of the industrial decor mirrors the service, which is less officious than elsewhere in town, and the cuisine itself. A dish such as glazed beef short ribs, for instance, might seem like yet another fancy take on a down-home favorite until you realize how cleverly the sweetness of the glaze plays off the creamy polenta and the piquant splash of salsa verde. Redd Wood does for Italian comfort food what nearby Mustards Grill does for the American version: it spruces it up but retains its innate pleasures. ⑤ *Average main: $22* ✉ *North Block Hotel, 6755 Washington St., at Madison St.* ☎ *707/299–5030* ⊕ *www.redd-wood.com.*

WHERE TO STAY

$$$$ | 🏨 **Bardessono.** Although Bardessono bills itself as the "greenest luxury
RESORT | hotel in America," there's nothing spartan about its accommodations;
Fodor's Choice | arranged around four landscaped courtyards, the rooms have luxuri-
★ | ous organic bedding, gas fireplaces, and huge bathrooms with walnut
floors. **Pros:** large rooftop lap pool; exciting restaurant; excellent spa,
with in-room treatments available; polished service. **Cons:** expensive;
limited view from some rooms. $ *Rooms from: $650* ⊠ *6526 Yount
St.* ☎ *707/204–6000* ⊕ *www.bardessono.com* ↩ *56 rooms, 6 suites*
⊙ *No meals.*

$$$$ | 🏨 **Hotel Yountville.** The landscaped woodsy setting, resortlike pool area,
HOTEL | glorious spa, and exclusive yet casual ambience of the Hotel Yountville
attract travelers wanting to get away from it all yet still be close—but
not too close—to fine dining and tasting rooms. **Pros:** chic rooms; exclusive yet casual ambience; close, but not too close, to Yountville fine dining; glorious spa. **Cons:** occasional service lapses unusual at this price
point. $ *Rooms from: $625* ⊠ *6462 Washington St.* ☎ *707/967–7900,
888/944–2885 reservations* ⊕ *www.hotelyountville.com* ↩ *70 rooms,
10 suites* ⊙ *No meals.*

$$ | 🏨 **Lavender Inn.** On a quiet side street around the corner from The French
B&B/INN | Laundry restaurant, the Lavender Inn feels at once secluded and cen-
trally located. **Pros:** reasonable rates for Yountville; in residential area
but close to restaurants and shops; friendly staff. **Cons:** hard to book
in high season; lacks amenities of larger properties. $ *Rooms from:
$275* ⊠ *2020 Webber St.* ☎ *707/944–1388, 800/533–4140* ⊕ *www.
lavendernapa.com* ↩ *9 rooms* ⊙ *Breakfast.*

$ | 🏨 **Maison Fleurie.** A stay at this comfortable inn places you within easy
B&B/INN | walking distance of Yountville's fine restaurants. **Pros:** smallest rooms
a bargain; outdoor hot tub; pool (open in season); free bike rental.
Cons: breakfast room can be crowded at peak times. $ *Rooms from:
$160* ⊠ *6529 Yount St.* ☎ *707/944–2056, 800/788–0369* ⊕ *www.
maisonfleurienapa.com* ↩ *13 rooms* ⊙ *Breakfast.*

$$$ | 🏨 **Napa Valley Lodge.** Clean rooms in a convenient setting draw travelers
HOTEL | willing to pay more than at comparable lodgings in the city of Napa
to be within walking distance of Yountville's tasting rooms, restaurants, and shops. **Pros:** clean rooms; helpful staff; filling continental
breakfast; large pool area; cookies, tea, and coffee in lobby. **Cons:** no
elevator; lacks amenities of other Yountville properties. $ *Rooms from:
$340* ⊠ *2230 Madison St.* ☎ *707/944–2468, 888/944–3545* ⊕ *www.
napavalleylodge.com* ↩ *54 rooms, 1 suite* ⊙ *Breakfast.*

$ | 🏨 **Napa Valley Railway Inn.** Budget-minded travelers and those with kids
HOTEL | appreciate these very basic accommodations—inside actual railcars—
just steps away from most of Yountville's best restaurants. **Pros:** central
location; access to nearby gym. **Cons:** minimal service, because the
office is often unstaffed; rooms on the parking-lot side get some noise.
$ *Rooms from: $125* ⊠ *6523 Washington St.* ☎ *707/944–2000* ⊕ *www.
napavalleyrailwayinn.com* ↩ *9 rooms* ⊙ *No meals.*

$$$$ | 🏨 **North Block Hotel.** With a chic Tuscan style, this 20-room hotel has
HOTEL | dark-wood furniture and soothing decor in brown and sage. **Pros:**
extremely comfortable beds; attentive service; room service by Redd

3

Wood restaurant. **Cons:** outdoor areas get some traffic noise. $ *Rooms from: $420* ✉ *6757 Washington St.* ☎ *707/944–8080* ⊕ *northblockhotel.com* ↘ *20 rooms* ⦿ *No meals.*

$$$$
B&B/INN
Fodor's Choice
★
🍴 **Poetry Inn.** All the rooms at this splurgeworthy hillside retreat have full vistas of the lower Napa Valley from their westward-facing balconies; indoors, the polished service, comfortably chic decor, and amenities that include a private spa and a fully stocked wine cellar only add to the exquisite pleasure of a stay here. **Pros:** perfect for special occasions; valley views; discreet, polished service; gourmet breakfasts. **Cons:** pricey; party types might find the atmosphere too low-key. $ *Rooms from: $1030* ✉ *6380 Silverado Trail* ☎ *707/944–0646* ⊕ *poetryinn.com* ↘ *3 rooms, 2 suites* ⦿ *Breakfast.*

$$$$
RESORT
🍴 **Villagio Inn & Spa.** With a layout that resembles a Tuscan-inspired village, this relaxing haven has streamlined furnishings, subdued color schemes, and high ceilings that create a sense of spaciousness in the guest rooms, each of which has a wood-burning fireplace and, beyond louvered doors, a balcony or a patio. **Pros:** lavish buffet breakfast; no extra charge for the spa facilities; steps from many dining options. **Cons:** can be bustling with large groups; highway noise audible from many balconies or patios. $ *Rooms from: $595* ✉ *6481 Washington St.* ☎ *707/944–8877, 800/351–1133* ⊕ *www.villagio.com* ↘ *86 rooms, 26 suites* ⦿ *Breakfast.*

$$$$
RESORT
🍴 **Vintage Inn.** Amid downtown Yountville's 23-acre Vintage Estate complex, this inn consists of two-story villas with a French-inspired aesthetic. **Pros:** spacious bathrooms; generous buffet breakfast. **Cons:** highway noise is audible in some exterior rooms. $ *Rooms from: $595* ✉ *6541 Washington St.* ☎ *707/944–1112* ⊕ *www.vintageinn.com* ↘ *68 rooms, 12 suites* ⦿ *Breakfast.*

SPAS

North Block Spa. "Relax. Just Do It," reads a sign one passes down the staircase to the North Block Hotel's softly lit basement spa, and the well-trained massage and other therapists ensure this transpires. The signature treatments are a foot and back exfoliation followed by a massage; a full-body scrub with a blend of walnut shell powder, sweet almond, and blood orange prior to a massage involving pink grapefruit; and a "Playful Passion" session (for hotel guests only) that includes couples exfoliating each other, receiving dual massages, and playing a sensual game after relaxation sets in. Facials, acupuncture, skin regimens, and "Stiletto Blues" therapy for ladies betrayed by tall pointy heels are among the other treatments. ✉ *North Block Hotel, 6757 Washington St., near Madison St.* ☎ *707/944–8080* ⊕ *northblockhotel.com/spa* 🖼 *Treatments $120–$410* ☉ *Daily 8–8.*

Fodor's Choice
★
The Spa at Bardessono. Many of this spa's patrons are hotel guests who take their treatments in their rooms' large, customized bathrooms—all of them equipped with concealed massage tables—but the main facility is open to guests and nonguests alike. An in-room treatment popular with couples starts with massages in front of the fireplace and ends with a whirlpool bath and a split of sparkling wine. For the two-hour

Yountville Signature treatment, which can be enjoyed in-room or at the spa, a shea butter–enriched sugar scrub is applied, followed by a massage with antioxidant Chardonnay grape seed oil and a hydrating hair and scalp treatment. The spa engages massage therapists skilled in Swedish, Thai, and several other techniques. In addition to massages, the services include facials, waxing, and other skin-care treatments as well as manicures and pedicures. ⊠ *Bardessono Hotel, 6526 Yount St., at Mulberry St.* ☎ *707/204–6050* ⊕ *www.bardessono.com/spa* ⊡ *Treatments $65–$600* ⊗ *Spa 9–6, in-room service 8–8.*

Spa Villagio. The perks abound at this 13,000-square-foot Mediterranean-style spa facility equipped with 16 state-of-the-art treatment rooms and five private spa suites (complete with flat-screen TVs and wet bars) that are perfect for couples and groups. Noteworthy among the treatments are the four Signature Experiences, which draw on Arabian, Asian, Indian, and Mediterranean traditions. Each includes a matching wine-and-food pairing. Body treatments, facials, manicures, and massages are among the à la carte services. ⊠ *6481 Washington St., at Oak Circle* ☎ *707/948–5050, 800/351–1133* ⊕ *www.villagio.com/spavillagio* ⊡ *Treatments $75–$575.*

SPORTS AND THE OUTDOORS

BALLOONING

Napa Valley Aloft. Between 8 and 12 passengers soar over the Napa Valley in balloons that launch from downtown Yountville. The rates include preflight refreshments and a huge breakfast. ⊠ *V Marketplace, 6525 Washington St., near Mulberry St.* ☎ *707/944–4400, 855/944–4408* ⊕ *www.nvaloft.com* ⊡ *From $220.*

Napa Valley Balloons. The valley's oldest balloon company offers trips that are elegant from start to finish. Satisfied customers include Chelsea Clinton and *Today* show host Matt Lauer. ⊠ *Domaine Chandon, 1 California Dr., at Solano Ave., west of Hwy. 29* ☎ *707/944–0228, 800/253–2224* ⊕ *www.napavalleyballoons.com* ⊡ *$215 per person.*

BICYCLING

Fodor's Choice **Napa Valley Bike Tours.** With dozens of wineries within 5 miles, this shop
★ makes a fine starting point for vineyard and wine-tasting excursions. The outfit also rents bikes. ⊠ *6500 Washington St., at Mulberry St.* ☎ *707/944–2953* ⊕ *www.napavalleybiketours.com* ⊡ *From $99.*

SHOPPING

Finesse, the Store. This small store sells Thomas Keller gift sets of knives, olive oils, and other items, along with his culinary kits (costing several hundred dollars) for making caviar and blinis, black-truffle risotto, and the like. ⊠ *6540 Washington St., near Humboldt St.* ☎ *707/944–2380* ⊕ *store.tkrg.com* ⊗ *Closed Tues. and Wed.*

Kelly's Filling Station and Wine Shop. The fuel is more than petrol at this gas station/convenience store whose design recalls the heyday of Route 66 travel. The shop inside sells top-rated wines, designer sandwiches, gourmet chocolates and ice cream, and small gift items. Gas up, order coffee, espresso, or a cool drink to go, and be ever so merrily on your way. ⊠ *6795 Washington St., at Madison St.* ☎ *707/944–8165.*

V Marketplace. The clothing boutiques, art galleries, and gift stores amid this vine-covered market include celebrity chef Michael Chiarello's **NapaStyle,** which sells cookbooks, kitchenware, and prepared foods that are perfect for picnics. The aromas alone will lure you into **Kollar Chocolates,** whose not-too-sweet, European-style chocolates are made on-site with imaginative ingredients. ⊠ *6525 Washington St., near Mulberry St.* ☎ *707/944–2451* ⊕ *www.vmarketplace.com.*

OAKVILLE

2 miles northwest of Yountville.

Barely a blip on the landscape as you drive north on Highway 29, Oakville is marked only by its grocery store. Oakville's small size belies the big mark it makes in the wine-making world. Slightly warmer than Yountville and Carneros to the south, but a few degrees cooler than Rutherford and St. Helena to the north, the Oakville area benefits from gravelly, well-drained soil. This allows roots to go deep—sometimes more than 100 feet deep—so that the vines produce intensely flavored grapes. Cabernet Sauvignon from the most famous vineyard here, To Kalon, at the base of the Mayacamas range, goes into many top-rated wines from winemakers throughout the valley. Big-name wineries within this appellation include Silver Oak, Far Niente, and Robert Mondavi.

GETTING HERE AND AROUND

If you're driving along Highway 29, you'll know you've reached Oakville when you see the Oakville Grocery on the east side of the road. Here the Oakville Cross Road provides access to the Silverado Trail (head east). Oakville wineries are scattered along Highway 29, Oakville Cross Road, and the Silverado Trail in roughly equal measure.

You can reach Oakville from the town of Glen Ellen in Sonoma County by heading east on Trinity Road from Highway 12. The twisting route, along the mountain range that divides Napa and Sonoma counties, eventually becomes the Oakville Grade. The views of both valleys on this drive are breathtaking, though the continual curves make it unsuitable for those who suffer from motion sickness. VINE Bus 10 serves Oakville.

B Cellars chefs prepare gourmet bites for wine pairings right in the tasting room.

EXPLORING

TOP ATTRACTIONS

B Cellars. The chefs hold center stage in this tasting room's large open kitchen, and with good reason: creating food-friendly wines is B Cellars's raison d'être. Founded in 2003, the winery moved from Calistoga to its new Oakville facility, all steel beams, corrugated metal, and plate glass, in 2014. The flagship wines are a Chardonnay, Sauvignon Blanc, and Viognier blend and three red blends. One of the latter is a robust "super Tuscan" made with Cabernet Sauvignon, Sangiovese, Petite Sirah, and Syrah. You can taste the blends and other wines—among them single-vineyard Cabernets whose grapes come from top Napa Valley vineyards—at appointment-only seated tastings involving good-size bites from the kitchen that prove just how admirably winemaker Kirk Venge fulfills the B Cellars mission. ⊠ *703 Oakville Cross Rd., west of Silverado Trail* ☎ *707/709–8787* ⊕ *www.bcellars.com* ✉ *Tastings $45–$125* ⊘ *Daily 10–5 by appointment.*

Fodor's Choice ★ **Far Niente.** Though the fee for the combined tour and tasting is high, guests at Far Niente are welcomed by name and treated to a glimpse of one of the Napa Valley's most beautiful properties. Small groups are escorted through the historic 1885 stone winery, including some of the 40,000 square feet of aging caves, for a lesson on the labor-intensive method of making Far Niente's flagship wines: a Cabernet Sauvignon blend and a Chardonnay. The next stop is the Carriage House, which holds a gleaming collection of classic cars. The seated tasting of wines and cheeses that follows concludes on a sweet note with Dolce, a late-harvest wine made from Semillon and Sauvignon Blanc grapes. ⊠ *1350*

Acacia Dr., off Oakville Grade Rd. ☎ *707/944–2861* ⊕ *www.farniente. com* ✉ *Tasting and tour $65* ⊙ *Daily 10–3 by appointment.*

Fodor'sChoice **Nickel & Nickel.** A corral out front and a farm-style windmill add horse-
★ country flair to this winery that makes smooth, almost sensual, single-
vineyard Cabernet Sauvignons. Some of Nickel & Nickel's best ones
derive from the home-base Oakville AVA, with Cabernets from other
Napa Valley appellations—impressive wines themselves—supplying
the contrast. Tastings begin with Chardonnay in the immaculate 1884
Sullenger House, followed by a tour of historic vineyards, a rebuilt
18th-century barn, and underground aging caves. Tasting of more
wines resumes back at the house. ■TIP→ Cabernet lovers won't want
to miss this sister winery to elegant Far Niente. ✉ *8164 St. Helena
Hwy./Hwy. 129, north of Oakville Cross Rd.* ☎ *707/967–9600* ⊕ *www.
nickelandnickel.com* ✉ *Tasting and tour $65* ⊙ *Weekdays 10–3, week-
ends 10–2, by appointment.*

Fodor'sChoice **Silver Oak Cellars.** In what may been its decade's most addlepated prog-
★ nostication, the first review of Silver Oak's Napa Valley Cabernet Sauvignon declared the debut 1972 vintage not all that good—and overpriced
at $6 a bottle. Oops. The celebrated Bordeaux-style Cabernet blend, still
the only Napa Valley wine bearing its winery's label each year, evolved
into a cult favorite, and its only two creators, the late Justin Meyer
and current winemaker Daniel Baron, received worldwide recognition
for their artistry. At the august Oakville tasting room, constructed out
of reclaimed stone and other materials from a 19th-century Kansas
flour mill, you can sip the current Napa Valley vintage, the current
100% Cabernet from Silver Oak's Alexander Valley operation, and
some library wines ($20). Tours, private tastings, and food-wine pair-
ings elevate the experience. ✉ *915 Oakville Cross Rd., off Hwy. 29*
☎ *707/942–7022* ⊕ *www.silveroak.com* ✉ *Tastings $20–$60, tour $30*
⊙ *Tasting Mon.–Sat.–5, Sun. 11–5; tour Mon.–Thurs. 10 and 1, Fri. and
Sat. 10, 1, and 3, Sun. 11 and 1; no appointment required for current-
release ($20) tasting; all other tastings and the tour by appointment.*

WORTH NOTING

■ QUICK
BITES

Oakville Grocery. Built in 1881 as a general store, Oakville Grocery carries
high-end groceries and prepared foods. On busy summer weekends the
place is often packed with customers stocking up on picnic provisions: meats,
cheeses, breads, and gourmet sandwiches. During the week this is a mellow
pit stop where you can sit on a bench out front and sip an espresso or head
out back and have a picnic. ■TIP→ Patrons dropping by for savory breakfast burritos, scones and muffins, and high-test coffee drinks keep Oakville
bustling until right before lunchtime. ✉ *7856 St. Helena Hwy./Hwy. 29, at
Oakville Cross Rd.* ☎ *707/944–8802* ⊕ *www.oakvillegrocery.com.*

Opus One. In 1979 the Napa Valley's Robert Mondavi and France's
Baron Philippe de Rothschild joined forces to produce a single wine:
Opus One, a Bordeaux blend that was the first of Napa's ultrapremium
wines. From Highway 29 Opus One's futuristic limestone-clad structure, completed in 1991, seems to be pushing itself out of the earth,

Far Niente ages its Cabernets and Chardonnays in 40,000 square feet of caves.

though on satellite maps it's clear it was situated to look like a wine glass, with the tree-lined driveway as the stem and the barrels in the semicircular underground cellar the wine the glass holds. Tours focus on the combination of agriculture, science, and technology required to create Opus One and conclude with a tasting of the current vintage. ■TIP➔ **With a reservation, you can taste the wine without touring.** ✉ *7900 St. Helena Hwy./Hwy. 29* ☎ *707/944–9442, 800/292–6787* ⊕ *www.opusonewinery.com* 🍷 *Tasting $45, tours $75–$125* ☉ *Daily 10–4; tasting and tours by appointment.*

PlumpJack Winery. With its metal chandelier and wall hangings, the tasting room at this casual winery looks like a stage set for a modern Shakespearean production. (The name "PlumpJack" is a nod to Shakespeare's Falstaff.) A youngish crowd assembles here to sample vintages that include the citrusy reserve Chardonnay and a Merlot that's blended like a Cab, providing the wine sufficient tannins to ensure it can age at least another five years. The Syrah, from Atlas Peak and Carneros grapes, is available only through the winery. ■TIP➔ **The Hilltop Tasting takes in the cellar and grounds and ends with a seated tasting overlooking the vineyards. Limited to six guests, it books up quickly in summer.** ✉ *620 Oakville Cross Rd., off Silverado Trail* ☎ *707/945–1220* ⊕ *www.plumpjackwinery.com* 🍷 *Tastings $25–$50* ☉ *Daily 10–4; hilltop tasting in spring and summer by appointment.*

Robert Mondavi Winery. The arch at the center of the sprawling Mission-style building frames the lawn and the vineyard behind, inviting a stroll under the arcades. You can head for one of the two tasting rooms, but if you've not toured a winery before, the 90-minute Signature Tour and

The design of the Opus One winery combines space-age and Mayan elements.

Tasting ($30) is a good way to learn about enology, as well as the late Robert Mondavi's role in California wine making. Those new to tasting and mystified by all that swirling and sniffing should consider the 45-minute Wine Tasting Basics experience ($20). Serious wine lovers can opt for the one-hour $55 Exclusive Cellar tasting, during which a server pours and explains limited-production, reserve, and older-vintage wines. ■TIP→ Concerts, mostly jazz and R&B, take place in summer on the lawn; call ahead for tickets. ⊠ 7801 St. Helena Hwy./Hwy. 29 ☎ 888/766–6328 ⊕ www.robertmondaviwinery.com ⊠ Tastings $20–$55, tours $20–$50 ☉ Daily 10–5; tour times vary.

RUTHERFORD

2 miles northwest of Oakville.

The spot where Highway 29 meets Rutherford Road in the tiny community of Rutherford may well be the most significant wine-related intersection in the United States. With its singular microclimate and soil, Rutherford is an important viticultural center, with more big-name wineries than you can shake a corkscrew at, including Beaulieu, Inglenook, Mumm Napa, and St. Supéry.

Cabernet Sauvignon is king here. The soil is ideal for those vines, and since this part of the valley gets plenty of sun, the grapes develop exceptionally intense flavors. Legendary winemaker André Tchelistcheff's famous claim that "it takes Rutherford dust to grow great Cabernet" is quoted by just about every winery in the area that produces the stuff. That "Rutherford dust" varies from one part of the region to another, but the soils here are primarily gravel, sand, and loam, a well-drained home for Cabernet Sauvignon grapes that don't like to get their feet wet.

GETTING HERE AND AROUND

Wineries around Rutherford are dotted along Highway 29 and the parallel Silverado Trail just north and south of Rutherford Road/Conn Creek Road, which connect these two major thoroughfares. VINE Bus 10 serves Rutherford.

ESSENTIALS

Contact **Rutherford Dust Society** ☎ 707/255–7667 ⊕ www.rutherforddust.org.

3

EXPLORING

TOP ATTRACTIONS

Fodor's Choice ★ **Caymus Vineyards.** For a winery whose claims to fame include producing Special Selection Cabernet Sauvignon, the only two-time *Wine Spectator* Wine of the Year honoree, Caymus remains a remarkably accessible spot to taste current and past vintages of the celebrated wine. Chuck Wagner started making wine on this property in 1972 and still oversees Caymus production. His children craft most of the other wines in the Wagner Family of Wines portfolio, including the oaked and unoaked Mer Soleil Chardonnays and the Belle Glos Pinot Noirs. ■**TIP**→ **You can sample Caymus and other wines at the often crowded tasting bar for $25—in good weather, wines are also poured outside—but to taste library wines and learn more about the winery's history, consider booking a private tasting.** ⊠ *8700 Conn Creek Rd., off Rutherford Rd.* ☎ *707/967–3010* ⊕ *www.caymus.com* ⊡ *Tastings $25–$40* ☉ *Daily 9:30–4:30, last tasting at 4; private tasting by appointment.*

FAMILY
Fodor's Choice ★ **Frog's Leap.** John Williams, owner of Frog's Leap, maintains a sense of humor about wine that translates into an entertaining yet informative experience—if you're a novice, the tour here is a fun way to begin your education. You'll taste wines that might include Zinfandel, Merlot, Chardonnay, Sauvignon Blanc, and an estate-grown Cabernet Sauvignon. The winery includes a barn built in 1884, 5 acres of organic gardens, an eco-friendly visitor center, and a frog pond topped with lily pads. ■**TIP**→ **The tour is highly recommended, but you can also just sample wines either inside or on a porch overlooking the garden.** ⊠ *8815 Conn Creek Rd.* ☎ *707/963–4704, 800/959–4704* ⊕ *www. frogsleap.com* ⊡ *Tastings $15–$20, tour $20* ☉ *Tastings daily 10–4 by appointment only; tours weekdays at 10:30 and 2:30 by appointment.*

FAMILY **Honig Vineyard & Winery.** Sustainable farming is the big story at this family-run winery. Michael Honig, the grandson of founder Louis Honig, helped write the code of sustainable practices for the California Wine Institute and was a key player in developing the first certification programs for state wineries. The tour here, offered seasonally, focuses on the Honig family's environmentally friendly farming and production methods, which include the use of solar panels to generate a majority of the winery's power. The family produces only Cabernet Sauvignon and Sauvignon Blanc. You can taste whites and reds at a standard tasting for $20; the reserve tasting ($50) pairs single-vineyard Cabernets with small bites. ⊠ *850 Rutherford Rd., near Conn Creek Rd.* ☏ *800/929–2217* ⊕ *www.honigwine.com* 🖾 *Tastings $20–$50; tour $30* ☉ *Daily 10:30–4:30 (reserve tasting daily Mon.–Sat.), tour spring–fall Mon.–Thurs. at 10; tastings and tour by appointment.*

Inglenook. Filmmaker Francis Ford Coppola began his wine-making career in 1975, when he bought part of the historic Inglenook estate. Over the next few decades he reunited the original property acquired by Inglenook founder Gustave Niebaum, remodeled Niebaum's ivy-covered 1880s château, and purchased the rights to the Inglenook name. Various tours cover the estate's history, the local climate and geology, the sensory evaluation of wine, and the evolution of Coppola's signature wine, Rubicon, a Cabernet Sauvignon–based blend. Some tastings are held in an opulent, high-ceilinged room, others in a wine-aging cave. ■ TIP→ You can taste wines by the glass (or the bottle) at the Bistro, an on-site wine bar with a picturesque courtyard. ⊠ *1991 St. Helena Hwy./Hwy. 29* ☏ *707/968–1100, 800/782–4266* ⊕ *www.inglenook. com* 🖾 *Tastings $45–$60, tours $50–$85* ☉ *Daily 10–5; call for tour times.*

Mumm Napa. In well-known Mumm's light-filled tasting room or adjacent outdoor patio you can enjoy bubbly by the flute or the flight, but the sophisticated sparkling wines, elegant setting, and vineyard views aren't the only reasons to visit. An excellent gallery displays 27 original Ansel Adams prints and presents temporary exhibitions by acclaimed photographers. Winery tours cover the major steps making sparklers entails. For a leisurely tasting of several vintages of the top-of-the-line DVX wines, served with cheeses, nuts, and fresh and dried fruit, book an Oak Terrace tasting ($40; reservations recommended on Friday and weekends). ■ TIP→ Carlos Santana fans may want to taste the sparklers the musician makes in collaboration with Mumm's winemaker, Ludovic Dervin. ⊠ *8445 Silverado Trail, 1 mile south of Rutherford Cross Rd.* ☏ *707/967–7700, 800/686–6272* ⊕ *www.mummnapa.com* 🖾 *Tastings $8–$40, tour $25 (includes tasting)* ☉ *Daily 10–4:45; tour daily at 10, 11, 1, and 3.*

Fodor'sChoice ★ **Piña Napa Valley.** The Piña family, whose Napa Valley heritage dates to the 1850s, is known locally as much for its first-rate vineyard-management company as its modest winery that specializes in single-vineyard, 100% Cabernet Sauvignon wines. Winemaker Anna Monticelli crafts robust yet subtle Cabs from mostly hillside fruit, some estate grown. Though she doesn't blend in other varietals, commonly done to smooth out Cabernet, Piña doesn't release its wines until age has mellowed them. If he's not busy elsewhere, Larry Piña, the winery's genial managing partner and among his family's seventh generation involved in the wine business, often drops by the no-frills barrel-room tasting space. ■ TIP→ A short hillside path behind the barrel room leads to a picnic platform with views west to Rutherford. ⊠ *8060 Silverado Trail, 0.2 miles north of Skellenger La.* ☏ *707/738–9328* ⊕ *pinanapavalley.com* 🖾 *Tasting $20* ☉ *Daily 10–4 (appointment not necessary, but call 30 mins ahead to see if there's space).*

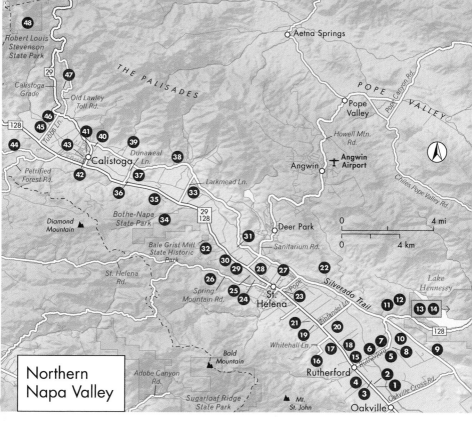

Northern Napa Valley

Round Pond Estate makes sophisticated wines and extra-virgin olive oils.

Round Pond Estate. Sophisticated wines come from Round Pond, but the estate also produces premium olive oils, most from olives grown and crushed on the property. Informative olive-related seminars pass through the high-tech mill, followed by tastings of the aromatic oils, both alone and with house-made red-wine vinegars. For a full wine tasting, head across the street to the winery. The basic tasting includes a Sauvignon Blanc and Round Pond's well-rounded reds. The flagship Estate Cabernet Sauvignon has the structure and heft of the classic 1970s Rutherford Cabs, but acknowledges 21st-century palates with smoother, if still sturdy, tannins. The estate tasting pairs small morsels with the wines. ■TIP→ The full Il Pranzo lunch incorporates products made and produce grown on-site, and there's a deservedly popular Sunday brunch. ✉ *875 Rutherford Rd., near Conn Creek Rd.* ☎ *707/302–2575, 888/302–2575* ⊕ *www.roundpond.com* ✉ *Wine tastings $25–$45, tour and tasting $55; olive mill tour and tasting $45* ⊙ *Daily 10–5, all tastings and tours by appointment 24–48 hrs in advance.*

Sequoia Grove. A stand of sequoias shades the outdoor areas and woodsy tasting room of this Cabernet Sauvignon producer. A standard tasting ($20) includes the Napa Valley Cabernet—a blend from several vineyards—along with wines that might include Sauvignon Blanc, Chardonnay, Merlot, or Syrah. For $40 you can taste several single-vineyard reserve Cabernets. A Taste for Cabernet ($50), a thoughtful seminar focused on the output of five vineyards, provides surprising insights into which tastes—sweet, sour, bitter, salty, and umami—best complement Cabernet Sauvignon. ✉ *8338 St. Helena Hwy./Hwy. 29, near Bella*

The National Prohibition Act, which passed in 1919 under the popular name of the Volstead Act, had far-reaching effects on California wineries. Prohibition forced many wineries to shut down altogether, but some, particularly Napa operations such as Beaulieu Vineyards, Beringer, and (on the site now occupied by the Culinary Institute of America) the Christian Brothers, stayed in business by making sacramental wines. Others took advantage of the exception permitting home wine making and sold grapes and in some cases do-it-yourself kits with "warnings" about the steps that would result in grape juice turning into wine. A few wineries kept their inventories in bond, storing their wine in warehouses certified by the Department of Internal Revenue and guaranteed secure by bonding agencies. Magically, wine flowed out the back doors of the bonded warehouses into barrels and jugs brought by customers, and just as magically it seemed to replenish itself. Now and then a revenuer would crack down, but enforcement seems to have been lax at best.

AFTER REPEAL
After the repeal of Prohibition in 1933, rebooting legitimate winemaking in California proved difficult. Wineries had lost many of their customers to bathtub gin and cheap cocktails, and those still drinking wine preferred sweet wines to dry ones. With the price of grapes and wine at a Depression-era low, it did not pay to replant grape acreage taken out of commission during Prohibition. In regions where vineyards had switched over to other crops or low-quality grapes, it made more financial sense to stick with the new regime than to go back to the old one.

STRUGGLE AND SURVIVAL
Prohibition did less damage in the Napa Valley, where grapes thrive but fruit trees grow poorly on the rocky and gravelly slopes, bench lands, and alluvial fans. Fewer Napa growers had been able to convert to other crops, and more had been able to survive with sacramental wine, so more vineyards could be brought back to fine-wine production after repeal. Several major wineries survived Prohibition, including Inglenook and Charles Krug (acquired in the 1940s by the Cesare Mondavi family). Considering the all-time low demand for their product—and the state of the American palate—these wineries made some amazingly good wines during this period. Nevertheless, the wine industry would struggle to regain its customer base well into the 1960s.

Oaks La. ☎ *707/944–2945, 800/851–7841* ⊕ *www.sequoiagrove.com* 🍷 *Tastings $20–$50* ☺ *Daily 10:30–5.*

WORTH NOTING
Beaulieu Vineyard. The influential André Tchelistcheff (1901–94), who helped define the California style of wine making, worked his magic here for many years. BV, founded in 1900 by Georges de Latour and his wife, Fernande, is known for its widely distributed Chardonnay, Pinot Noir, and Cabernet Sauvignon wines, but many others are produced in small lots and are available only at the winery. The most famous of

the small-lot wines is the flagship Georges De Latour Cabernet Sauvignon, first crafted by Tchelistcheff himself in the late 1930s. ■TIP➔ The engaging historic tour ($35) includes a peek at Prohibition-era artifacts and tastes of finished wines and ones still aging in their barrels. ⊠ *1960 St. Helena Hwy./Hwy. 29* ☎ *707/967–5233, 800/264–6918 Ext. 5233* ⊕ *www.bvwines.com* ✆ *Tastings $20–$75, tour $35* ☉ *Daily 10–5.*

Cakebread Cellars. The Cakebread family, at first Jack and Dolores and these days also their children, have been making complex Chardonnays, Cabernet Sauvignons, and Sauvignon Blancs since the 1970s. With a portfolio that now includes Merlot, Pinot Noir, Syrah, and other varietals, Cakebread has built its reputation on crafting food-friendly wines. Case in point: winemaker Julianne Laks's Sauvignon Blanc. Blended with Sèmillon and Sauvignon Musqué grapes and aged lightly in neutral French oak, it's both accessible and sophisticated and the ideal accompaniment to seafood and pasta dishes. A basic tasting includes six current releases; the all-reds option is popular with Cabernet and Merlot fans. ⊠ *8300 St. Helena Hwy./Hwy. 29* ☎ *707/963–5222 info, 800/588–0298 reservations* ⊕ *www.cakebread.com* ✆ *Tastings $15– $45, tour $25* ☉ *Daily 10–4; tour and all tastings by appointment.*

Hall Rutherford. The appointment-only sister winery to Hall St. Helena provides an exclusive, elegant wine and food pairing atop a Rutherford hillside. The visit includes a peek at the production facility's dazzlingly ornate stainless-steel aging tanks and the 14,000 square feet of caves under the Sacrashe vineyard, from whose steep slopes and rocky soils come grapes for some of Hall's best Cabernet Sauvignons. A tunnel lined with hand-stamped bricks salvaged from Habsburg-era Austrian buildings leads to a regal tasting room lit by a chandelier by artist Donald Lipski. Designed to mimic the roots of the grapevines above, it's adorned with nearly 2,000 Swarovski crystals. Tastings focus on wines from a single appellation—Hall makes wine from grapes grown in 13 of the 16 Napa Valley AVAs. ⊠ *56 Auberge Rd., off Silverado Trail* ☎ *707/967–2626* ⊕ *www.hallwines.com/hall-rutherford* ✆ *Tasting, tour, and wine-food pairing $125* ☉ *By appointment only.*

Rutherford Hill Winery. This winery is a Merlot lover's paradise in a Cabernet Sauvignon world. When its founders were deciding what grapes to plant, they discovered that the climate and soil conditions resembled those of Pomerol, a region of Bordeaux where Merlot is king. Now owned by the Terlato family, Rutherford Hill has extensive wine caves—nearly a mile of tunnels and passageways. You can glimpse the caves and the barrels inside them on tours that include the Bordeaux meets Napa Tasting Experience ($75), an educational seated tasting of reserve and older wines. Entertaining make-your-own-Merlot blending sessions ($105) take place on Saturday. The winery's hillside picnic area, amid oak and olive trees, is a magical spot. ■TIP➔ Picnic packages ($100–$150) include wine, glasses, and a linen-covered table. ⊠ *200 Rutherford Hill Rd., east of Silverado Trail* ☎ *707/963–1871* ⊕ *www. rutherfordhill.com* ✆ *Tastings $20–$75; tour $35* ☉ *Daily 10–5; tours daily at 11:30, 1:30, and 3:30.*

St. Supéry Estate Vineyards & Winery. Stylish, family-owned St. Supéry offers several tastings and interactive wine classes showcasing estate-grown wines. The pours might include Sauvignon Blanc, Chardonnay, Cabernet Sauvignon, Merlot, and even winery-exclusive vintages such as Cabernet Franc or Petit Verdot; all the wines are from estate-grown grapes. The tour provides a behind-the-scenes perspective of the entire wine-making process, from the vineyard to the glass. Outside, a small demonstration vineyard allows you to try your hand at the science of ampelography—identifying grapevines by observing the shape and color of their leaves. ⊠ *8440 St. Helena Hwy./Hwy. 29, near Manley La.* ☎ *707/963—4507* ⊕ *www.stsupery.com* ✉ *Tastings $15–$50, tour $25* ⊙ *Daily 10–5; some tastings by appointment, tour daily by appointment.*

WHERE TO EAT

$$$$
ITALIAN

✕ **Alex Italian Restaurant.** Often serene and uncrowded when the neighboring Rutherford Grill is all abustle, Alex also provides a culinary counterpoint with well-plated Italian classics. A huge stone fireplace anchors the softly lit dining room, which owner Alessandro "Alex" Sbrendol tends with smooth charm. He and his wife, Alessia (the other "Alex" here), both hail from Northern Italy, whose cuisines inspire the dishes they serve. The pasta course might include veal polpettine with papparedelle, and fresh fish prepared ever so delicately might appear as an entrée, but you could well see braised wild boar on the menu, perhaps accompanied by St. Louis–style boar ribs and sunchoke polenta. Both husband and wife are accomplished sommeliers; their lengthy wine list reflects their years of experience. ⑤ *Average main: $34* ⊠ *1140 Rutherford Rd., east of Hwy. 29* ☎ *707/967–5500* ⊕ *www.alexitalianrestaurant.com* ⊙ *Closed Mon. year-round. Closed Tues. Nov.–early Mar. No lunch Sun. year-round. No lunch Wed. and Thurs. Nov.–early Mar.*

$$$$
MODERN
AMERICAN
Fodor's Choice
★

✕ **Restaurant at Auberge du Soleil.** Possibly the most romantic roost for a dinner in all the Wine Country is a terrace seat at the Auberge du Soleil's illustrious restaurant, and the Mediterranean-inflected cuisine more than matches the dramatic vineyard views. The prix-fixe dinner menu ($105 for three courses, $125 for four; $150 for the six-course tasting menu), which relies largely on local produce, might include veal sweetbreads with hearts of palm and chanterelles in an orange glaze or prime beef pavé with white corn, potato croquettes, and a caramelized shallot sauce. The service is polished, and the wine list is comprehensive. ■**TIP**➔ **With a menu that embraces everything from muffins and gnocchi to Cabernet-braised short rib and (in season) a Maine lobster omelet, the weekend brunch here is delightfully over-the-top.** ⑤ *Average main: $105* ⊠ *Auberge du Soleil, 180 Rutherford Hill Rd., off Silverado Trail* ☎ *707/963–1211, 800/348–5406* ⊕ *www.aubergedusoleil.com* ⚵ *Reservations essential.*

$$$
AMERICAN
Fodor's Choice
★

✕ **Rutherford Grill.** Dark-wood walls, subdued lighting, and red-leather banquettes make for a perpetually clubby mood at this trusty Rutherford hangout. Many entrées—steaks, burgers, fish, succulent rotisserie chicken, and barbecued pork ribs—emerge from an oak-fired grill operated by master technicians. So, too, do starters such as the grilled jumbo artichokes and the iron-skillet corn bread, a ton of butter being the secret of success with both. The French dip sandwich is a local legend, and the wine list includes rare selections from Caymus and other celebrated producers at (for Napa) reasonable prices. You can also opt for a well-crafted cocktail. ■**TIP**➜ **In good weather the patio, popular for its bar, fireplace, and rocking chairs, is open for full meal service or drinks and appetizers.** $⑤$ *Average main: $25* ✉ *1180 Rutherford Rd., at Hwy. 29* ☎ *707/963–1792* ⊕ *www.rutherfordgrill.com* ⌂ *Reservations essential.*

WHERE TO STAY

$$$$ ⊡ **Auberge du Soleil.** Taking a cue from the olive-tree-studded landscape,
RESORT   this hotel with a renowned restaurant and spa cultivates a luxurious
Fodor's Choice   look that blends French and California style. **Pros:** stunning views over
★   the valley; spectacular pool and spa areas; the most expensive suites are fit for a superstar. **Cons:** stratospheric prices; least expensive rooms get some noise from the bar and restaurant. $⑤$ *Rooms from: $850* ✉ *180 Rutherford Hill Rd.* ☎ *707/963–1211, 800/348–5406* ⊕ *www. aubergedusoleil.com* ⤳ *31 rooms, 21 suites* ⦿│ *Breakfast.*

ST. HELENA

4 miles northwest of Oakville.

Fodor's Choice   Downtown St. Helena is a symbol of how well life can be lived in the
★   Wine Country. Sycamore trees arch over Main Street (Highway 29), where chic-looking visitors flit between boutiques, cafés, and storefront tasting rooms housed in sun-faded redbrick buildings. Genteel St. Helena pulls in rafts of Wine Country tourists during the day, though like most Wine Country towns it more or less rolls up the sidewalks after dark.

Many visitors never get away from the Main Street magnets—dozens of great restaurants and boutiques selling women's clothing, food and wine, and housewares—but you should explore a bit farther and stroll through the quiet residential neighborhoods. A few blocks west of Main Street you'll be surrounded by vineyards, merging into the ragged wilderness edge of the Mayacamas Mountains. Several blocks east of Main Street, off Pope Street, is the Napa River, which separates St. Helena from the Silverado Trail and Howell Mountain.

Around St. Helena the valley floor narrows between the Mayacamas and Vaca mountains. These slopes reflect heat onto the 9,000 or so acres below, and since there's less fog and wind, things get pretty toasty. In fact, this is one of the hottest AVAs in Napa Valley, with midsummer temperatures often reaching the mid-90s. Bordeaux varietals are the most popular grapes grown here—especially Cabernet Sauvignon but also Merlot. You'll also find Chardonnay, Petite Sirah, and Pinot Noir in the vineyards.

ST. HELENA HISTORY

Unlike many other parts of the Napa Valley, where milling grain was the primary industry until the late 1800s, St. Helena took to vines almost instantly. The town got its start in 1854, when Henry Still built a store. Still wanted company, so he donated land lots on his town site to anyone who wanted to erect a business. Soon he was joined by a wagon shop, a shoe shop, hotels, and churches. Dr. George Crane planted a vineyard in 1858, and was the first to produce wine in commercially viable quantities. A German winemaker named Charles Krug followed suit a couple of years later, and other wineries soon followed.

In the late 1800s, phylloxera had begun to destroy France's vineyards, and Napa Valley wines caught the world's attention. The increased demand for Napa wines spawned a building frenzy in St. Helena. Many of the mansions still gracing the town's residential neighborhoods were built around this time. During the same period, some entrepreneurs attempted to turn St. Helena into an industrial center to supply specialized machinery to local viticulturists. Several stone warehouses were built near the railroad tracks downtown. Other weathered stone buildings on Main Street, mostly between Adams and Spring streets and along Railroad Avenue, date from the same era. Modern facades sometimes camouflage these old-timers, but you can study the old structures by strolling the back alleys.

GETTING HERE AND AROUND

The stretch of Highway 29 that passes through St. Helena is called Main Street, and many of the town's shops and restaurants are clustered on two pedestrian-friendly blocks between Pope and Adams streets. Wineries are found both north and south of downtown along Highway 29 and the Silverado Trail, but some of the less touristy and more scenic spots are southwest of town on the slopes of Spring Mountain (to access Spring Mountain Road from Main Street, take Madrona Avenue or Elmhurst Avenue southwest a few blocks and turn right) and far east of downtown past Lake Hennessey off Highway 128. VINE Bus 10 and Bus 29 stop along Main Street.

ESSENTIALS

Contact St. Helena Chamber of Commerce ✉ *657 Main St., at Vidovich La.* ☎ *707/963–4456* ⊕ *www.sthelena.com.*

EXPLORING

TOP ATTRACTIONS

Beringer Vineyards. Arguably the Napa Valley's most beautiful winery, the 1876 Beringer Vineyards is also the oldest continuously operating property. In 1884 Frederick and Jacob Beringer built the Rhine House Mansion as Frederick's family home. Today it serves as the reserve tasting room, where you can sample wines surrounded by Belgian art-nouveau hand-carved oak and walnut furniture and stained-glass windows. The assortment includes a limited-release Chardonnay, a few big

Cabernets, and a Sauterne-style dessert wine. A less expensive tasting takes place in the original stone winery. ■TIP➜ The one-hour Taste of Beringer tour ($40), which includes a tasting with small food bites, provides a good overview of the valley's wine-making history. ⊠ *2000 Main St./Hwy. 29, near Pratt Ave.* ☎ *707/963–8989, 866/708–9463* ⊕ *www.beringer.com* ⊠ *Tastings $20–$50, tours $25–$40* ⊙ *June–mid-Oct. daily 10–6; mid-Oct.–May daily 10–5; many tours daily, call or check website for times.*

Fodor's Choice **Charles Krug Winery.** A historically sensitive renovation of its 1874 Red-
★ wood Cellar Building transformed the former production facility of the Napa Valley's oldest operating winery into an epic hospitality center with a tasting room and a café. Charles Krug, a Prussian immigrant, established the winery in 1861 and ran it until his death in 1892. Ital-ian immigrants Cesare Mondavi and his wife, Rosa, purchased Krug in 1943, and operated it with their sons Peter and Robert (who later opened his own winery). Krug, still run by Peter's family, specializes in small-lot Yountville and Howell Mountain Cabernet Sauvignons and makes Chardonnay, Merlot, Pinot Noir, Sauvignon Blanc, Zinfandel, and a Zinfandel Port. ■TIP➜ The café sells food to eat inside or at oak-shaded picnic tables (reservations recommended). ⊠ *2800 Main St./ Hwy. 29, across from Culinary Institute of America* ☎ *707/967–2229* ⊕ *www.charleskrug.com* ⊠ *Tastings $20–$50, tours $60 (includes tast-ing)* ⊙ *Daily 10:30–5; tours by appointment Mon.–Thurs. 10:30 and 12:30, Fri.–Sun. 10:30.*

Fodor's Choice **Corison Winery.** Respected for two 100% Cabernet Sauvignons, Cori-
★ son Winery harks back to simpler days with tastings that occur amid oak aging barrels stored inside an unadorned, barnlike facility. The straightforward approach suits the style of Cathy Corison, one of the Napa Valley's first women owner-winemakers, who eschews blending because she believes her sunny St. Helena AVA vineyards and others she selects can ripen Cabernet better than anywhere else in the world. Critics tend to agree, often waxing ecstatic about these classic wines. One Cabernet is poured at current-release tastings ($35), along with Cabernet Franc, Gewürztraminer, Rosé of Cabernet, or other wines. Library tastings ($55) include recent and older Cabernet Sauvignon vin-tages that collectively illustrate both her consistency as a winemaker and how gracefully her wines mature. ⊠ *987 St. Helena Hwy., at Stice La.* ☎ *707/963–0826* ⊕ *www.corison.com* ⊠ *Tastings $35–$55* ⊙ *Daily 10–5, by appointment.*

Culinary Institute of America. The West Coast headquarters of the coun-try's leading school for chefs are in the 1889 Greystone Winery, an imposing building that once was the world's largest stone winery. On the ground floor you can check out the quirky Corkscrew Museum and browse a shop stocked with gleaming gadgets and many cookbooks. At the adjacent Flavor Bar you can sample various ingredients (for example, chocolate or olive oil). Plaques upstairs at the Vintners Hall of Fame commemorate winemakers past and present. Beguiling one-hour cooking demonstrations (reservations required) take place on weekends. The student-run Bakery Café by Illy serves soups, salads, sandwiches, and baked goods; the Institute also operates a full restaurant. ⊠ *2555*

The Culinary Institute's well-stocked Spice Islands store tempts aspiring chefs.

Main St./Hwy. 29 ☎ *707/967–1100* ⊕ *www.ciachef.edu* ✉ *Museum and store free, cooking demonstrations $20, tastings $10–$15, tour $10* ☉ *Museum and store daily 10:30–6 (Mon.–Thurs. 11–5 in winter); tour 11:45, 2:45, 5.*

Duckhorn Vineyards. Merlot's moment in the spotlight may have passed, but you wouldn't know it at Duckhorn, whose fans gladly pay from $50 to nearly $100 a bottle for some of the world's finest wines from this varietal. You can taste Merlot, Sauvignon Blanc, Cabernet Sauvignon, and other wines in the airy, high-ceilinged tasting room, which looks like a sleek restaurant; you'll be seated at a table and served by staffers who make the rounds to pour. In fair weather, you may do your sipping on a fetching wraparound porch overlooking a vineyard. ■TIP➔ You don't need a reservation on weekdays to taste the current releases ($30), but you do on weekends, and they're required all the time for private and semiprivate tastings. ✉ *1000 Lodi La., at Silverado Trail N* ☎ *707/963–7108* ⊕ *www.duckhorn.com* ✉ *Tastings $30–$75* ☉ *Daily 10–4.*

Fodor'sChoice ★ **Hall St. Helena.** The award-winning Cabernet Sauvignons, Merlots, and an impeccable Syrah produced here are works of art—and of up-to-the-minute organic-farming science and wine-making technology. A glass-walled tasting room allows you to see in action some of the high-tech equipment director of winemaking Steve Leveque employs to craft the wines, which also include Cabernet Franc and late-harvest Sauvignon Blanc. The main guided tour provides a closer-up look at the facility and covers the winery's history and architecture and the three-dozen works—inside and out—by Patrick Dougherty, John Baldessari, Jesús

Moroles, and other major contemporary artists. ■**TIP→ The well-conceived seminars here include ones about the artworks, demystifying food and wine, and collecting Cabernet Sauvignons.** ⊠ *401 St. Helena Hwy./Hwy. 29, near White La.* ☎ *707/967–2626* ⊕ *www.hallwines.com* ☜ *Tastings $30–$100; tours $40–$75* ⊙ *Daily 10–5:30.*

Fodor's Choice ★ **Joseph Phelps Vineyards.** An appointment is required for tastings at the winery started by the legendary Joseph Phelps—his son Bill now runs the operation—but it's well worth the effort. Phelps makes fine whites, but the blockbuster wines are reds, particularly the Cabernet Sauvignon and the flagship Bordeaux-style blend called Insignia. The luscious-yet-subtle Insignia sells for more than $200 a bottle. Luckily, all tastings include the current vintage. The 90-minute seminars include one on wine-and-cheese pairing and another focusing on blending. Participants in the latter mix the various varietals that go into the Insignia blend. A new tasting room debuts in 2015 following a major renovation project. ⊠ *200 Taplin Rd., off Silverado Trail* ☎ *707/963–2745, 800/707–5789* ⊕ *www.josephphelps.com* ☜ *Tastings and seminars $60–$150 by appointment* ⊙ *Weekdays 10–4, weekends 10–3; tastings by appointment.*

QUICK BITES

Napa Valley Olive Oil Manufacturing Company. "There's a crazy little shack beyond the tracks," the song goes, but in this case the barnlike building just east of the railroad tracks sells tickle-your-taste-buds olive oils and vinegars, along with cheeses, meats, breads, and other delectables you can take with you on the road or enjoy at picnic tables right outside. This is old Napa—no frills, cash only—with a shout-out to old Italy. It's a fun stop even if you're not buying, though something will likely tempt you. ⊠ *835 Charter Oak Ave., off Main St.* ☎ *707/963–4173* ⊕ *oliveoilsainthelena.com.*

Spring Mountain Vineyard. Hidden off a winding road behind a security gate, the family-owned Spring Mountain Vineyard has the feeling of a private country estate, even though it's only a few miles from downtown St. Helena. Sauvignon Blanc, Pinot Noir, and Syrah wines are produced in limited quantities, but the calling card here is Cabernet Sauvignon—big and chewy, reflecting its mountain origin. A tasting of current releases ($40) gives you a good sense of these wines' charms. The estate tasting ($75) includes a meander through the elegant property, from the 19th-century caves to the beautifully preserved 1885 mansion. Other tastings explore library vintages of Cabernet Sauvignon ($100) and a vertical selection of the signature Bordeaux blend, Elivette ($200). ⊠ *2805 Spring Mountain Rd., off Madrona Ave.* ☎ *707/967–4188, 877/769–4637* ⊕ *www.springmountainvineyard.com* ☜ *Tastings $40–$200* ⊙ *Daily 10–4, tastings by appointment only.*

Fodor's Choice ★ **Tres Sabores Winery.** A long narrow lane with two sharp bends leads to splendidly workaday Tres Sabores, where the sight of sheep, guinea hens, pomegranate and other trees and plants, a slew of birds and bees, and a heaping compost pile help reinforce a simple point: despite the Napa Valley's penchant for glamour this is, first and foremost, farm country. Owner-winemaker Julie Johnson specializes in single-vineyard

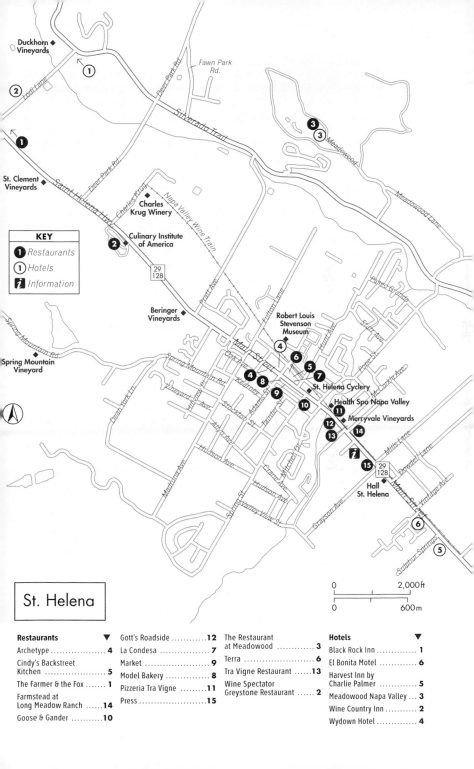

St. Helena

KEY

- **1** *Restaurants*
- **1** *Hotels*
- **i** *Information*

Duckhorn Vineyards

St. Clement Vineyards

Charles Krug Winery

Culinary Institute of America

Beringer Vineyards

Spring Mountain Vineyard

Robert Louis Stevenson Museum

St. Helena Cyclery

Health Spa Napa Valley

Merryvale Vineyards

Hall St. Helena

wines that include Cabernet Sauvignon, Sauvignon Blanc, and a quietly stunning Zinfandel made from Rutherford bench grapes. She also excels with Petite Sirah from dry-farmed Calistoga fruit and makes a zippy red blend called Por Qué No? (Why not?). *Tres sabores* is Spanish for "three flavors," which to Johnson represents the land, her vines, and her input as winemaker. Tastings here are informal, and often outside. ✉ *1620 S Whitehall La., off Hwy. 29* ☎ *707/967–8027* ⊕ *www.tressabores.com* 🍷 *Tasting and tour $30* ⊙ *Daily by appointment.*

WORTH NOTING

Bale Grist Mill State Historic Park. A short trail from the parking lot here leads to the water-powered Bale Grist Mill, erected in 1846 and partially restored in 1925. Exhibits explain the milling process and docents sometimes offer milling demonstrations. A trail leads from the park to **Bothe–Napa Valley State Park,** where you can pick up a number of hiking trails or linger for a picnic. ✉ *3369 St. Helena Hwy./Hwy. 29, 3 miles north of St. Helena* ☎ *707/942–4575* ⊕ *www.napavalleystateparks.org* 🍷 *Free, mill buildings $5* ⊙ *Park sunrise–sunset; mill June–Sept., Fri.– Mon. 10–5, Oct.–May, weekends 10–5 (last mill tour at 4 year-round).*

Cairdean Estate. A complex that includes a tasting room, a restaurant, a bakery, and shops, Cairdean Estate, which opened in 2014, has lawns and a hillside picnic area that invite lingering. The emphasis on hospitality begins with the complex's name—Scottish Gaelic for "friends." Co-owner Stacia Williams crafts the wines poured in the contemporary, vineyard-view **Cairdean Vineyards & Winery** tasting room. Williams uses oak in interesting ways, achieving a rounder feel, for instance, with Sangiovese than many winemakers do but without burying the flavor. Likewise, her polished Cabernet Franc blend illustrates what's special about that varietal. Cabernet Sauvignon, Pinot Noir, and Sauvignon Blanc are among the other noteworthy wines she makes. ✉ *3111 St. Helena Hwy. N/Hwy. 29, near Ehlers La.* ☎ *707/968–5434* ⊕ *www. cairdeanestate.com* 🍷 *Tastings $15–$50* ⊙ *Tasting room daily 11–8, bakery daily 7–5; shop hrs vary.*

Franciscan Estate. Cabernet Sauvignon and Merlot predominate at this bustling winery that in recent years has introduced two crowd-pleasing Sauvignon Blanc–based white blends. Winemaker Janet Myers's best reds—among them the Oakville Cabernet Sauvignon and the Cabernet-heavy Magnificat blend—are bold yet smooth, with just enough tannins to build character but not overwhelm. The Cuvée Sauvage Chardonnay, fermented using only natural yeasts, is another standout. Light streams through the full-length clerestory window of the main tasting space. You can also sip wines in small, private rooms and, on weekends in summer and fall, on an outdoor patio. ■**TIP→ Franciscan also pours the complex red wines—including the truly lofty Cabernet Sauvignon Elevation 1550—of its separate Mount Veeder Winery.** ✉ *1178 Galleron Rd., at Hwy. 29* ☎ *707/967–3830* ⊕ *www.franciscan.com* 🍷 *Tastings $15–$25; blending and sensory seminars $50.*

Merryvale Vineyards. Chardonnay and Cabernet Sauvignon are this ivy-covered winery's claims to fame, though you'll also find Pinot Noir and Merlot, along with small-lot estate Syrah, Zinfandel, and other wines.

Franciscan Estate's Cuvée Sauvage Chardonnay contributed to a revival in California of the practice of fermenting wines with natural instead of commercial yeasts.

The winery has been in existence as Merryvale for three decades, but the building it occupies, the former Sunny St. Helena Winery, is much older: this was the first winery completed after Prohibition. No reservations are needed for tastings of current releases of Chardonnay, Pinot Noir, Merlot, and Cabernet Sauvignon ($30), or of the top-of-the-line Silhouette Chardonnay and Profile red blend ($50). Profile, a Cabernet-Sauvignon–heavy Bordeaux-style blend of each vintage's best grapes, is also poured at private library tastings ($85) offered three times daily. ✉ *1000 Main St., at Charter Oak Ave.* ☎ *707/963–2225* ⊕ *www. merryvale.com* ✉ *Tastings $30–$85* ⊙ *Daily 10–5:30; reservations required for some tastings.*

Nichelini Family Winery. A scenic drive east of the Silverado Trail winds past Lake Hennessey to Nichelini, the Napa Valley's oldest continuously operated family-owned winery. Erected in the late 1800s by Anton Nichelini, an Italian-Swiss immigrant, the old winery buildings, still in use, cling to a steep embankment where the road skirts a cliff. The wines to taste—they're made by Anton's great-great-granddaughter Aimée Sunseri—are the Zinfandel, its Italian cousin the Primitivo, the Cabernet Sauvignon, the Petite Sirah, and the extra-crisp old-vine Muscadelle. The last grape often finds its way into white Bordeaux blends, but here it makes a single-varietal wine redolent of tropical fruit. ■ TIP→ The winery is open for drop-in tastings on Fridays and weekends, the rest of the week by easily made appointments. ✉ *2950 Sage Canyon Rd./ Hwy. 128, 8 miles east of Silverado Trail* ☎ *707/963–0717* ⊕ *www. nicheliniwinery.com* ✉ *Tastings $15–$20* ⊙ *Fri. and weekends 11–5, Mon.–Thurs. by appointment.*

Tastings in Raymond's atmospheric Barrel Cellar include wines that are still aging.

Raymond Vineyards. All the world's a stage to Jean-Charles Boisset, Raymond's charismatic owner—even his vineyards, where his five-act Theater of Nature includes a well-executed series of gardens and displays that explain biodynamic agriculture. The theatrics continue indoors in the disco-dazzling Crystal Cellar tasting room (chandelier and other accoutrements by Baccarat), along with several other spaces, some sedate and others equally expressive. Despite goosing up the glamour—gal pals out for a fun afternoon love this place—Boisset and winemaker Stephanie Putnam, formerly of Hess and Far Niente, have continued the winery's tradition of producing reasonably priced premium wines. The Cabernet Sauvignons and Merlots often surprise. ■**TIP**➔ **Concerned about dogs being left in hot cars during tasting, Boisset established the on-site Frenchie Winery, where canines lounge in comfort while their guardians sip wine.** ✉ *849 Zinfandel La., off Hwy. 29* ☎ *707/963–3141* ⊕ *www.raymondvineyards.com* ✉ *Tastings $25–$50; tour and tasting $45* ☉ *Daily 10–4.*

Robert Louis Stevenson Museum. If you have a soft spot for author Robert Louis Stevenson (*Treasure Island, Kidnapped*), drop by this small museum housing an impressive collection of memorabilia—rare manuscripts, first editions, photographs, childhood toys, and other artifacts—documenting Stevenson's life and literary career. One exhibit examines the months that Stevenson, at the time impoverished, spent in an abandoned mining town. The interlude later became the inspiration for the book *The Silverado Squatters.* ✉ *1490 Library La., at Adams St.* ☎ *707/963–3757* ⊕ *www.stevensonmuseum.org* ✉ *Free* ☉ *Tues.–Sat. noon–4.*

Rutherford Grove Winery. A 19th-century wine-bottling contraption, a Prohibition-era safe, and photos and documents spanning five generations enhance a visit to this winery run by the descendants of Albino Pestoni, its Swiss-Italian forebear. The pourers here, some of them family members, share the Pestoni story while dispensing wines made from grapes grown in choice vineyards acquired over the decades. The Merlots and Cabernet Sauvignons at reserve tastings ($25) nearly always impress, especially the Howell Mountain ones, and because the winery pours older vintages than most of its neighbors you can sense how well these wines will age. Estate tastings ($15) often include Sauvignon Blanc, Sangiovese, Petite Sirah, Zinfandel, and perhaps the field blend called "1892," named to commemorate the year Albino entered the wine business. ✉ *1673 St Helena Hwy./Hwy. 29, near Galleron Rd.* ☎ *707/963–0544* ⊕ *www.rutherfordgrove.com* ▱ *Tastings $15–$25* ☉ *Daily 10–5.*

St. Clement Vineyards. A winery steeped in history, St. Clement is blessed with such winning views of nearby vineyards and Howell Mountain beyond that you might drift into reverie even before tasting the signature Bordeaux-style blend, Oroppas. That's Sapporo spelled backward— the Japanese brewery once owned this property whose centerpiece, the 1878 Rosenbaum House, built in the Italianate style, looms over Highway 29. Fritz Rosenbaum, the wealthy merchant who commissioned it, purchased the surrounding land from his neighbor, the wine-maker Charles Krug. Seated tastings that include St. Clement's highly rated Oroppas and single-vineyard Cabernet Sauvignons unfold inside the 1970s stone winery behind the house. ✉ *2867 St. Helena Hwy. N/ Hwy. 29, near Deer Park Rd.* ☎ *707/967–3030* ⊕ *www.stclement.com* ▱ *Tasting $40* ☉ *Seated tastings at 11 and 3 by appointment* ☉ *Closed Tues. and Wed.*

Somerston Estate Vineyard & Winery. Sage Canyon Road (Highway 128) winds west for 9¼ miles past Lake Hennessey to remote, 1,628-acre Somerston Estate, which reserves some of the grapes it grows for major Wine Country players to make a few wines of its own. You can taste these wines—a Sauvignon Blanc, a Bordeaux-style red blend, a Cabernet Sauvignon, and sometimes a Port–like dessert wine—at seated tastings some guests precede with an exhilarating all-terrain-vehicle tour of portions of the hilly estate. Back at the high-tech winery, artisanal cheeses accompany the wines or, if you prefer, a prepared lunch. ∎**TIP➜** Somerston also has a tasting room in downtown Yountville. ✉ *3450 Sage Canyon Rd.* ☎ *707/967–8414* ⊕ *www.somerstonwineco.com* ▱ *Tasting only, $50; tour and tasting $75–$100* ☉ *Tasting and tour daily at 11, 1, and 3 by appointment.*

WHERE TO EAT

$$$
MODERN
AMERICAN
Fodor's Choice
★

✕ Archetype. Chef Ryder Zetts earned instant raves for his fancifully updated "Americana" cuisine at this establishment designed and owned by winery architect Howard Backen. The cream-color decor, twirling ceiling fans, and rattan settees and chairs set an upscale-homey tone in the main dining area and on the screened-in front porch. Seasonal appetizers might include textbook fried green tomatoes—but with burrata cheese—or peaches with Surryano ham served with creamily addictive mascarpone-pepper jelly. For lunch expect sandwiches such as smoked salmon pepped up by quick-pickled cucumbers. Dinner glides into a more serious realm with, perhaps, bacon-crusted Alaskan halibut or leg of lamb with lamb merguez sausage. ■TIP➔ **The $5 happy hour (daily from 5 to 7) and Monday burger night are popular with locals.** $ *Average main: $27* ⊠ *1429 Main St., near Adams St.* ☎ *707/968–9200* ⊕ *www.archetypenapa.com.*

$$
MODERN
AMERICAN
Fodor's Choice
★

✕ **Cindy's Backstreet Kitchen.** At her St. Helena outpost, Cindy Pawlcyn serves variations on the comfort food she made popular at Mustards Grill, but spices things up with dishes influenced by Mexican, Central American, and occasionally Asian cuisines. Along with mainstays such as meat loaf with garlic mashed potatoes and beef and duck burgers served with flawless fries, the menu might include a rabbit tostada or chicken served with avocado salsa and a two-cheese stuffed green chili. Two dessert favorites are the high-style yet homey warm pineapple upside-down cake and the nearly ethereal parfait. $ *Average main: $22* ⊠ *1327 Railroad Ave., at Hunt St., 1 block east of Main St.* ☎ *707/963–1200* ⊕ *www.cindysbackstreetkitchen.com.*

$$$
MODERN BRITISH

✕ **The Farmer & the Fox.** A Napa Valley reconception of a British gastro-pub and an instant hit since its 2014 debut, this pubby-clubby restaurant has already acquired an appealingly lived-in patina. Chef Joseph Humphrey, whose Wine Country resume includes Meadowood's restaurant and Auberge du Soleil, immediately wins over diners with clever appetizers such as smoked duck wings with blue cheese and lamb tartare on brioche chips. The entrées change seasonally but might include rabbit Wellington in "old school red wine sauce," a pub steak with whiskey-peppercorn sauce and fried onions, and grilled fish in béarnaise sauce. The lack of a corkage fee draws in the locals, who can be counted on for great Wine Country gossip—especially during crush (harvesttime)—if you dine at the brass-countered bar. $ *Average main: $23* ⊠ *Cairdean Estate, 3111 St. Helena Hwy. N/Hwy. 29, at Ehlers La.* ☎ *707/302–5101* ⊕ *www.cairdeanestate.com.*

$$
MODERN
AMERICAN

✕ **Farmstead at Long Meadow Ranch.** Housed in a former barn, Farmstead revolves around an open kitchen where chef Stephen Barber cooks with as many local and organic ingredients as possible. Many of them—including grass-fed beef and lamb, fruits and vegetables, eggs, extra-virgin olive oil, wine, and honey—come from the property of parent company Long Meadow Ranch. Entrées might include grilled rainbow trout with wild mushrooms, or potato gnocchi with beef ragout, herbs, and Parmesan. Tuesday is the popular pan-fried chicken night—$37 for a three-course meal. ■TIP➔ **The weekday happy hour, from 4 to 6 (good eats, too), is often hoppin'.** $ *Average main: $20* ⊠ *738 Main St., at Charter Oak Ave.* ☎ *707/963–4555* ⊕ *www.longmeadowranch.com/farmstead-restaurant.*

$$$
MODERN
AMERICAN
Fodor's Choice
★

✕ **Goose & Gander.** The pairing of food and drink at intimate Goose & Gander is as likely to involve cocktails as it is wine. Main courses such as wild king salmon with roasted delicata squash, lentils, applewood-smoked bacon, and celery root velouté work well with starters that in season might include cream of mushroom soup made from both wild and cultivated varieties. You can enjoy your meal with a top-notch Chardonnay or Pinot Noir—or a Manhattan made with three kinds of bitters and poured over a hand-carved block of ice. On cold days a fireplace warms the main dining room, and in good weather the outdoor patio is a fetching spot to dine alfresco. ■TIP→ Year-round the basement bar is a good stop for a drink. $ *Average main: $25* ⊠ *1245 Spring St., at Oak St.* ☎ *707/967–8779* ⊕ *www.gooseandgander.com.*

$ ✕ **Gott's Roadside.** A 1950s-style outdoor hamburger stand goes upscale
AMERICAN at this spot whose customers brave long lines to order breakfast sandwiches, juicy burgers, root-beer floats, and garlic fries. Choices not available a half century ago include the ahi tuna burger and the chili spice–marinated chicken breast served with Mexican slaw. ■TIP→ Arrive early or late for lunch, or all of the shaded picnic tables on the lawn might be filled. A second branch does business at Napa's Oxbow Public Market. $ *Average main: $12* ⊠ *933 Main St./Hwy. 29* ☎ *707/963–3486* ⊕ *www.gotts.com* ⚭ *Reservations not accepted* $ *Average main: $12* ⊠ *Oxbow Public Market, 644 1st St., at McKinstry St., Napa* ☎ *707/224–6900* ⚭ *Reservations not accepted.*

$$ ✕ **La Condesa.** The colors and cuisines of central Mexico, especially
MODERN Oaxaca, inspire the decor and menu at this blue-walled, high-ceilinged
MEXICAN contempo cantina. Starters include tortilla soup, pork belly with fig jam, and guacamole rendered spicy and smoky by chipotle puree. Among the entrées, the taco flight, for which you can choose three out of eight or so options, is a good way to experience the breadth of executive chef Chris Mortenson's offerings. The ones containing carnitas and chorizo lean more conventional; the duck breast and battered-shrimp ones play loose with tradition but still pass muster. ■TIP→ Taco Tuesday brings discounts and even more types of tacos. $ *Average main: $16* ⊠ *1320 Main St., near Hunt Ave.* ☎ *707/967–8111* ⊕ *lcnapa.com.*

$$ ✕ **Market.** Comfort reigns at this understated yet modern eatery whose
AMERICAN Mexico City–born chef, Ernesto Martinez, puts a clever Latin spin on American classics. Fried chicken comes with cheddar-jalapeño corn bread, for instance, and chipotle aioli accompanies the oyster po'boy. Martinez plays things straight with the Caesar salad, Dungeness crab Louis, and Zinfandel-braised lamb shank at dinner, but at his popular Sunday brunch offers fried-chicken-and-Belgian-waffle sliders and chilaquiles with eggs and Spanish sausage along with eggs Florentine and other standards. ■TIP→ For the most relaxed experience, stroll in at lunchtime midweek and linger over local wine from the extensive list. $ *Average main: $18* ⊠ *1347 Main St., near Hunt Ave.* ☎ *707/963–3799* ⊕ *marketsthelena.com.*

$ ✕ **Model Bakery.** Thanks in part to a Food Network plug by chef Michael
BAKERY Chiarello the English muffins here became so popular that takeout
Fodor's Choice customers are sometimes limited to purchases of six, but the scones,
★ croissants, breads, and other baked goods also dazzle. Breakfast brings pastries and English muffin sandwiches with scrambled eggs, bacon, and Canadian ham. The menu expands for lunch to include soups, salads, pizzas, and more sandwiches—turkey panini, Italian hoagies, muffalettas, and Cubans among them. After ordering at the counter you may have to wait for a table (inside or out), but you'll likely find

the results worth the effort. A second location is at the Oxbow Public Market in Napa. ⑤ *Average main: $10 ⊠ 1357 Main St., near Adams Ave.* ☎ *707/963–8192 ⊕ www.themodelbakery.com* ☺ *No dinner.*

$
PIZZA

✕ **Pizzeria Tra Vigne.** Early in the evening, families with kids flock to the outdoor tables at this casual pizzeria. Later on, young couples gather around the pool table or watch the game on the TV. At any time of day you'll find crisp, thin-crust pizzas, such as the unusual Positano, with sautéed shrimp, crescenza cheese, and fried lemons. Salads and pasta round out the menu. Service is friendly, if not particularly speedy, and the lack of a corkage fee makes it a good place to try out that bottle of Sangiovese you picked up at one of the wineries. ⑤ *Average main: $13 ⊠ 1016 Main St., at Charter Oak Ave.* ☎ *707/967–9999 ⊕ www. travignerestaurant.com* ⚋ *Reservations not accepted.*

$$$$
MODERN
AMERICAN
Fodor's Choice
★

✕ **Press.** Few taste sensations surpass the combination of a sizzling steak and a Napa Valley red, a union that the chef and sommeliers here celebrate with a reverence bordering on obsession. Beef from carefully selected local and international purveyors is the star—especially the rib eye for two—but chef Trevor Kunk also prepares pork chops and free-range chicken and veal on his cherry-and-almond-wood-fired grill and rotisserie. Kunk, hired in 2014, has added vegetarian offerings that include a roasted carrot "hot dog" and fried-green-tomato sandwiches. The cellar holds thousands of wines; if you recall having a great steak with a 1985 Mayacamas Mt. Veeder Cab, you'll be able to re-create, and perhaps exceed, the original event. Press's bartenders know their way around both rad and trad cocktails. ⑤ *Average main: $48 ⊠ 587 St. Helena Hwy./Hwy. 29, at White La.* ☎ *707/967–0550 ⊕ www. presssthelena.com* ⚋ *Reservations essential* ☺ *Closed Tues. No lunch.*

$$$$
MODERN
AMERICAN
Fodor's Choice
★

✕ **The Restaurant at Meadowood.** Chef Christopher Kostow has garnered rave reviews—and three Michelin stars for several years running—for creating a unique dining experience. After you reserve your table, you'll have a conversation with a reservationist about your party's desired culinary experience and dietary restrictions. Inspired by this conversation, chef Kostow will transform seasonal local ingredients, some grown on or near the property, into an elaborate, multicourse experience. If you choose the Tasting Menu option ($225 per person, $450 with wine pairings), you'll enjoy your meal in the romantic dining room, its beautiful finishes aglow with warm lighting. Choose the Counter Menu ($500, $850 with wine pairings), and you and up to three guests can sit inside the kitchen and watch Kostow's team prepare your meal. ∎ **TIP→** The restaurant also offers a limited, three-course menu ($90) at its bar. ⑤ *Average main: $225 ⊠ 900 Meadowood La., off Silverado Trail N* ☎ *707/967–1205, 800/458–8080 ⊕ www.therestaurantatmeadowood. com* ⚋ *Reservations essential* ☺ *Closed Sun. No lunch.*

$$$$
MEDITERRANEAN
Fodor's Choice
★

✕ **Terra.** For old-school romance and service, many diners return year after year to this quiet favorite in an 1884 fieldstone building. Chef Hiro Sone gives an unexpected twist to Italian and southern French cuisine, though for a few standouts, among them the signature sake-marinated black cod in a *shiso* broth, he draws on his Japanese background. Homey yet elegant desserts, courtesy of Sone's wife, Lissa Doumani, might include a chocolate mousseline with chocolate peanut butter crunch and toasted marshmallow. Meals here are prix-fixe—$78 for four courses diners choose from the menu, $93 for five, and $105 for six. ■**TIP→** Next door, Bar Terra serves cocktails, local wines, and a menu of lighter dishes—the succulent fried rock shrimp served with chive-mustard sauce is a local favorite. $ *Average main: $78* ⊠ *1345 Railroad Ave., off Hunt Ave.* ☎ *707/963–8931* ⊕ *www.terrarestaurant. com* ۞ *Closed Tues. No lunch.*

$$$ ✕**Tra Vigne Restaurant.** It's hard to say whether this restaurant is most
ITALIAN appealing in spring, when the wildflowers in the small vineyard out front are in full bloom, or on a rainy winter day, when the bright decor, hearty food, and friendly staff warm the chill in your bones. The menu by chef Nash Cognetti changes frequently, but smoked and braised beef short ribs and sage-infused pappardelle with rabbit ragout and wild mushrooms have been among recent offerings. The desserts include well-executed traditional favorites such as cannoli and the signature tiramisu. Sunday brunch is a colossal event throughout the year because of the dizzying array of options, from doughnuts to duck hash with a poached egg to kale-and-farro salad. $ *Average main: $25* ⊠ *1050 Charter Oak Ave., at Main St.* ☎ *707/963–4444* ⊕ *www. travignerestaurant.com.*

$$$ ✕**Wine Spectator Greystone Restaurant.** On busy nights at the Culinary
MEDITERRANEAN Institute's stone-walled restaurant you may find the student chefs toiling in their open stations more entertaining than your dining companions. The dishes prepared are Mediterranean in spirit and emphasize locally grown produce. Typical main courses include potato-crusted petrale sole and pan-seared duck breast with red flint polenta. For the Pop-Up Dinner Series, successful alumni chefs showcase new and signature dishes for a few evenings. ■**TIP→** On Sunday from spring into fall, small plates are served from 11 until sunset on the umbrella-shaded terrace, which has broad vineyard views. $ *Average main: $27* ⊠ *2555 Main St./Hwy. 29, near Deer Park Rd.* ☎ *707/967–1010* ⊕ *www.ciachef.edu* ۞ *No dinner Sun.; closed Sun. mid-Nov.–Apr.; closed Mon. year-round.*

WHERE TO STAY

$$$$ ⌂**Black Rock Inn.** Owner Jeff Orlik provides his guests such a gracious,
B&B/INN thoughtful experience that they tend to gush poetic about his suites, his gourmet breakfasts, but most of all his passion for ensuring a memorable time for everyone. **Pros:** winning host; gorgeous retreat; a gourmet breakfast to remember. **Cons:** rooms fill up quickly in season; somewhat pricey. $ *Rooms from: $425* ⊠ *3100 N. Silverado Trail* ☎ *707/968– 7893* ⊕ *www.blackrockinn.net* ⇲ *4 suites, 1 guesthouse* ❋❚ *Breakfast.*

$ ⌂**El Bonita Motel.** For budget-minded travelers the tidy rooms at this
HOTEL roadside motel are pleasant enough, and the landscaped grounds and picnic tables elevate this property over similar places. **Pros:** cheerful rooms; hot tub; microwaves and mini-refrigerators. **Cons:** road noise is a problem in some rooms. $ *Rooms from: $130* ⊠ *195 Main St./ Hwy. 29* ☎ *707/963–3216, 800/541–3284* ⊕ *www.elbonita.com* ⇲ *48 rooms, 4 suites* ❋❚ *Breakfast.*

CLOSE UP

A Great Northern Napa Drive

Dean & DeLuca in St. Helena opens early, making it a fine starting point for a day of exploring the northern Napa Valley. Purchase some food and drink, then drive north on Highway 29, turning east on Lincoln Avenue and driving through Calistoga to Tubbs Lane.

After turning left at Tubbs Lane, on your right you'll soon see the entrance to **Chateau Montelena** (which opens at 9:30). Enjoy the Beyond Paris & Hollywood wine tasting, then return to Highway 29 and turn left. The route winds steeply up the slopes of Mt. St. Helena until you reach the crest, where parking lots on either side of the road invite you to hike a bit in **Robert Louis Stevenson State Park,** named for the author who squatted here during a period of impoverishment.

Return to **Calistoga** on Highway 29 and enjoy lunch at **Solbar** or **Bosko's**

Trattoria. If you've made a reservation for one of the excellent tours at **Schramsberg** (the last one's at 2:30), head south on Highway 29 to Peterson Road, where you'll turn right and then quickly right again onto narrow Schramsberg Road. If sparkling wines aren't your thing or if you've a hankering for a medieval romp, opt for **Castello di Amorosa,** off Highway 29 a half-mile before Schramsberg. Either experience should leave you in a bubbly mood.

Return to Highway 29 and turn right to reach **St. Helena.** You'll have an hour or two to browse the shops along Main Street before they close for the evening. Numerous dining options await in St. Helena, but wherever you're going, stop beforehand at the handsome basement bar at **Goose & Gander** for a well-crafted cocktail.

$$$
HOTEL
Fodor's Choice
★

Harvest Inn by Charlie Palmer. Although this inn sits just off Highway 29, its patrons remain mostly above the fray, strolling 8 acres of landscaped gardens, enjoying views of the vineyards adjoining the property, partaking in spa services, and drifting to sleep in beds adorned with fancy linens and down pillows. **Pros:** garden setting; spacious rooms; well-trained staff. **Cons:** some lower-priced rooms lack elegance; high weekend rates. ⑤ *Rooms from: $359* ⊠ *1 Main St.* ☎ *707/963–9463, 800/950–8466* ⊕ *www.harvestinn.com* ⥀ *69 rooms, 5 suites* ⏏⃞ *Breakfast.*

$$$$
RESORT
Fodor's Choice
★

Meadowood Napa Valley. Founded in 1964 as a country club, Meadowood has evolved into a five-star resort, a gathering place for Napa's wine-making community, and a celebrated dining destination. **Pros:** superb restaurant; pleasant hiking trails; gracious service. **Cons:** very expensive; far from downtown St. Helena. ⑤ *Rooms from: $650* ⊠ *900 Meadowood La.* ☎ *707/963–3646, 800/458–8080* ⊕ *www.meadowood.com* ⥀ *85 rooms, suites, and cottages* ⏏⃞ *No meals.*

$$
B&B/INN

Wine Country Inn. A pastoral landscape of vine-covered hills surrounds this retreat, which was styled after the traditional New England inns its owners visited in the 1970s. **Pros:** free shuttle to some restaurants (reserve early); rates include hearty buffet breakfast and afternoon wine and appetizers; front desk operates 24/7; swimming pool is heated year-round. **Cons:** some rooms let in noise from neighbors; some areas could use updating. ⑤ *Rooms from: $267* ✉ *1152 Lodi La., east of Hwy. 29* ☎ *707/963–7077, 888/465–4608* ⊕ *www.winecountryinn.com* ⇨ *24 rooms, 5 cottages* ⦾ *Breakfast.*

$$$

HOTEL

Fodor'sChoice

★

🖰 **Wydown Hotel.** A smart boutique-hotel option near downtown shopping and dining, the Wydown delivers upscale comfort with a heavy dose of style. **Pros:** well run; eclectic decor; downtown location; quiet atrium rooms. **Cons:** lacks the amenities of larger properties. ⑤ *Rooms from: $329* ✉ *1424 Main St.* ☎ *707/963–5100* ⊕ *www.wydownhotel. com* ⇨ *12 rooms* ⦾ *No meals.*

NIGHTLIFE AND PERFORMING ARTS

Cameo Cinema. The art nouveau Cameo Cinema, built in 1913 and now beautifully restored, screens first-run and art-house movies and occasionally hosts live performances. ✉ *1340 Main St., near Hunt Ave.* ☎ *707/963–9779* ⊕ *www.cameocinema.com.*

SPAS

Health Spa Napa Valley. The focus at this local favorite is on health, wellness, and fitness, so there are personal trainers offering advice and an outdoor pool where you can swim laps in addition to the extensive regimen of massages and body treatments. The Harvest Mud Wrap, for which clients are slathered with grape-seed mud and French clay, is a more indulgent, less messy alternative to a traditional mud bath. Afterward you can take advantage of the sauna, hot tub, and eucalyptus steam rooms. ■**TIP→ Longtime patrons book treatments before noon to take advantage of the all-day access.** ✉ *1030 Main St., at Pope St.* ☎ *707/967–8800* ⊕ *www.napavalleyspa.com* 🖾 *Treatments $15–$235* ☉ *Weekdays 5:30 am–8:30 pm, weekends 6:45 am–8:30 pm.*

SPORTS AND THE OUTDOORS

BICYCLING

St. Helena Cyclery. Rent bikes by the hour ($15), as well as by the day (hybrids $40, road bikes from $70) at this shop that has a useful "Area Rides and Local Events" page on its website. ✉ *1156 Main St., at Spring St.* ☎ *707/963–7736* ⊕ *www.sthelenacyclery.com.*

SHOPPING

St. Helena's coolest stores are clustered around the 1200 and 1300 blocks of bucolic Main Street, where 19th-century redbrick buildings recall the town's past and make it a particularly pleasant place to while away an afternoon.

Caldwell Snyder. Inside the handsome Star Building (1900), this gallery exhibits contemporary American, European, and Latin American paintings and sculptures. ✉ *1328 Main St., near Hunt Ave.* ☎ *707/200–5050* ⊕ *www.caldwellsnyder.com.*

Dean & Deluca. The chain's Napa Valley branch sells a variety of kitchenware and has a large wine selection, but most visitors come for the terrific produce and deli items, all of which help you to picnic in style. ✉ *607 St. Helena Hwy./Hwy. 29, at White La.* ☎ *707/967–9980* ⊕ *www.deandeluca.com.*

Footcandy. Precariously steep stilettos and high-heeled boots are raised to an art form here. You'll also find ultracool handbags and other accessories. ✉ *1239 Main St., at Hunt Ave.* ☎ *707/963–2040* ⊕ *www. footcandyshoes.com.*

I. Wolk Gallery. This airy gallery exhibits abstract and contemporary realist paintings, works on paper, and sculpture. ✉ *1354 Main St., near Adams St.* ☎ *707/963–8800* ⊕ *www.iwolkgallery.com.*

Jan de Luz. Fine French table linens and high-quality items for home and garden fill this shop. ✉ *1219 Main St., at Spring St.* ☎ *707/963–1550* ⊕ *www.jandeluz.com.*

Fodor's Choice
★ **Pearl Wonderful Clothing.** Sweet Pearl carries the latest in women's fashions in a high-style space that makes dramatic use of the section of the historic stone building the shop occupies. Celebs find bags, shoes, jewelry, and outfits here, and you might, too. ✉ *1219C Main St.* ☎ *707/963–3236* ⊕ *pearlwonderfulclothing.com.*

St. Helena Olive Oil Company. Famous Napa chefs have been known to drop by this chic-looking store for its high-quality extra-virgin olive oil and vinegars. You'll also find artisanal honey, jams, herbs, mustards, and sauces, along with bath products made from all-natural ingredients. ✉ *1351 Main St., near Adams Ave.* ☎ *707/968–9260* ⊕ *www. sholiveoil.com.*

Woodhouse Chocolate. Elaborate confections made on the premises are displayed like miniature works of art at this shop that resembles an 18th-century Parisian salon. ✉ *1367 Main St., at Adams St.* ☎ *707/963– 8413, 800/966–3468* ⊕ *www.woodhousechocolate.com.*

CALISTOGA

3 miles northwest of St. Helena.

False-fronted shops, 19th-century hotels, and unpretentious cafés lining the main drag of Lincoln Avenue give Calistoga a slightly rough-and-tumble feel that's unique in the Napa Valley. With Mt. St. Helena rising to the north and visible from downtown, it looks a bit like a cattle town tucked into a remote mountain valley.

In 1859 Sam Brannan—Mormon missionary, entrepreneur, and vineyard developer—learned about a place in the upper Napa Valley, called Agua Caliente by settlers, that was peppered with hot springs and even had its own "old faithful" geyser. He snapped up 2,000 acres of prime property and laid out a resort. Planning a place that would rival New York's famous Saratoga Hot Springs, he built an elegant hotel, bathhouses, cottages, stables, observatory, and distillery (the last a questionable choice for a Mormon missionary). Brannan's gamble didn't pay off as he'd hoped, but Californians kept coming to "take the waters,"

The astounding Castello di Amorosa has 107 rooms.

supporting small hotels and bathhouses built wherever a hot spring bubbled to the surface. Many of them are still going, and you can come for an old-school experience of a mud bath or a dip in a warm spring-fed pool. In the 21st century, Calistoga began to get back to its roots, with new luxury properties springing up and old standbys getting a sprucing up. After the 2014 restoration of the Brannan Cottage Inn (⇨ see *Where to Stay, below*), you can even spend a night in part of the only Sam Brannan cottage still on its original site.

GETTING HERE AND AROUND

To get here from St. Helena or anywhere else farther south, take Highway 29 north and then turn right on Lincoln Avenue. Alternately, you can head north on Silverado Trail and turn left on Lincoln. VINE Bus 10 and Bus 29 serve Calistoga.

ESSENTIALS

Contact Calistoga Chamber of Commerce ✉ *1133 Washington St., near Lincoln Ave.* ☎ *707/942–6333* ⊕ *www.visitcalistoga.com.*

EXPLORING

TOP ATTRACTIONS

Ca' Toga Galleria d'Arte. The boundless wit, whimsy, and creativity of the Venetian-born Carlo Marchiori, this gallery's owner-artist, finds expression in paintings, watercolors, ceramics, sculptures, and other artworks. Marchiori often draws on mythology and folktales for his inspiration. A stop at this magical gallery may inspire you to tour **Villa Ca' Toga,** the artist's fanciful Palladian home, a tromp l'oeil tour de force that can be toured from May through October on Saturday only, at 11 am. ⊠ *1206 Cedar St., near Lincoln Ave.* ☎ *707/942–3900* ⊕ *www.catoga. com* ☽ *Closed Tues. and Wed.*

Castello di Amorosa. An astounding medieval structure complete with drawbridge and moat, chapel, stables, and secret passageways, the Castello commands Diamond Mountain's lower eastern slope. Some of the 107 rooms contain replicas of 13th-century frescoes (cheekily signed [the-artist's-name].com), and the dungeon has an actual iron maiden from Nuremberg, Germany. You must pay for a tour to see most of Dario Sattui's extensive eight-level property, though basic tastings include access to part of the complex. Wines of note include several Italian-style wines, including La Castellana, a robust "super Tuscan" blend of Cabernet Sauvignon, Sangiovese, and Merlot; and Il Barone, a praiseworthy cab made largely from Diamond Mountain grapes. ■**TIP→ The two-hour food- and-wine pairing ($75) by sommelier Mary Davidek is among the Wine Country's best.** ⊠ *4045 N. St. Helena Hwy./Hwy. 29, near Maple La.* ☎ *707/967–6272* ⊕ *www.castellodiamorosa.com* 🍷 *Tastings $20–$30, tours (with tastings) $35–$75* ☽ *Mar.–Oct., daily 9:30–6; Nov.–Feb., daily 9:30–5; tours and food-wine pairings by appointment.*

Chateau Montelena. Set amid a bucolic northern Calistoga landscape, this winery helped establish the Napa Valley's reputation for high-quality wine making. At the legendary Paris tasting of 1976, the Chateau Montelena 1973 Chardonnay took first place, beating out four white Burgundies from France and five other California Chardonnays. The 2008 movie *Bottle Shock* immortalized the event, and the winery honors its four decades of classic wine making with a special Beyond Paris & Hollywood tasting of the winery's Napa Valley Chardonnays ($40). You can also opt for a Current Release Tasting ($25) or a Limited Release Tasting ($50) that includes some stellar Cabernet Sauvignons. ⊠ *1429 Tubbs La., off Hwy. 29* ☎ *707/942–5105* ⊕ *www.montelena. com* 🍷 *Tastings $20–$50, tours $40; appointment required and restrictions apply for some tastings and tours* ☽ *Daily 9:30–4.*

Fodor'sChoice
★
Schramsberg. Founded in 1865, Schramsberg produces sparkling wines made using the *méthode traditionnelle*, also known as *méthode champenoise*. A fascinating tour precedes tastings. In addition to glimpsing the winery's historic architecture, you'll visit caves, some dug in late 19th century by Chinese laborers, where 2 million–plus bottles are stacked in gravity-defying configurations. Tastings include generous pours of very different bubblies. To learn more about them, consider the three-day **Camp Schramsberg,** held in fall and spring. Fall participants harvest grapes and learn about food and wine pairing, riddling (the process of turning the bottles every few days to nudge the sediment into the neck of the bottle), and other topics. In spring the focus is on blending. ⊠ *1400 Schramsberg Rd., off Hwy. 29* ☎ *707/942–4558, 800/877– 3623* ⊕ *www.schramsberg.com* 🍷 *Tasting and tour $60* ☽ *Tours at 10, 10:30, 11:30, 12:30, 1:30, and 2:30 by appointment.*

Storybook Mountain Vineyards. Tucked into a rock face in the Mayacamas range, Storybook occupies a picture-perfect site with rows of vines rising steeply in dramatic tiers. Zinfandel is king here, and there's even

CLOSE UP

Chinese in the Caves and Vineyards

In the late 19th century, many of the workers who dug the caves, constructed the stone wineries, and built the stone fences that still snake across Wine Country hillsides were Chinese. The Chinese had come to California to participate in the gold rush and later to help build the Transcontinental Railroad. After the railroad was built, they sought other work, sometimes in agriculture. Not only did the Chinese help build the wineries, they also cleared the land, tilled the soil, harvested the grapes, and in some cases, made the wine. However, many Chinese settlers were driven out of California agriculture in the 1880s because of anti-Asian sentiment. Immigrant workers from Italy and other regions of southern Europe took over their jobs.

3

a Zin Gris, an unusual dry Rosé of Zinfandel grapes. (In Burgundy, Vin Gris—a pale Rosé—is made from Pinot Noir grapes.) Tastings are preceded by a low-key tour that includes a short walk up the hillside and a visit to the atmospheric tunnels, parts of which have the same rough-hewn look as they did when Chinese laborers painstakingly dug them around 1888. ⊠ *3835 Hwy. 128, 4 miles northwest of town* ☎ *707/942–5310* ⊕ *www.storybookwines.com* 🖱 *Tasting and tour $25* ⊗ *Mon.–Sat. by appointment.*

Twomey Cellars. A fortuitous acquisition led to the creation of this winery and its flagship Merlot. Parent company Silver Oak Cellars, maker of a renowned Cabernet Sauvignon, purchased a Merlot vineyard intending to blend juice from its grapes into the Cabernet. Winemaker Daniel Baron realized early on that the vines' Merlot clones were among the world's finest and proposed making a stand-alone wine. Silver Oak only makes Cabernet, so the Twomey label was launched to sell the new wine. While sipping it, you can learn about the intricate *soutirage traditionnel* method Baron uses to age it. Tastings of Sauvignon Blanc and excellent Pinot Noirs precede the Merlot. ■TIP➔ The $10 fee here represents a true bargain for wines of this caliber. ⊠ *1183 Dunaweal La., off Hwy. 29* ☎ *707/942–7026* ⊕ *www.twomey.com* 🖱 *Tasting $10* ⊗ *Mon.–Sat. 10–5, Sun. 11–5.*

WORTH NOTING

Domaine Napa Valley. If you're looking to expand your wine knowledge or just want to discover wines you might not otherwise hear about, consider a visit to this bright-white, light-filled, high-ceilinged space inside downtown Calistoga's historic I.O.O.F building. The sophisticated yet affable sommeliers of Domaine Napa Valley conduct intimate tasting experiences, tailoring them to participants' interests and wine preferences. A typical tasting, by easily obtained appointment, might compare small-production Northern California wines with their counterparts around the world, or survey local and international sparkling wines. ■TIP➔ Even guidebook authors learn a thing or two from these well-informed somms. ⊠ *1345 Lincoln Ave., Suite B, near*

Washington St. ☎ *707/341–3038* ⊕ *www.domainenapavalley.com* 🍷 *Tastings $50–$75* ⊗ *Daily by appointment.*

Dutch Henry Winery. The casual style and lack of crowds at this pet-friendly winery make it a welcome change of pace from some of its overly serious neighbors. Towering

oak barrels hold excellent Cabernet Sauvignon, Pinot Noir, Zinfandel, Syrah, and other single-varietal wines, along with a well-regarded Bordeaux blend called Argos. Dutch Henry also sells a Sauvignon Blanc and a charming Rosé. A current-release tasting will introduce you to these wines; you can also visit the wine caves on one of two tours that include tastings. ✉ *4310 Silverado Trail, near Dutch Henry Canyon Rd.* ☎ *707/942–5771* ⊕ *www.dutchhenry.com* 🍷 *Tasting $25, tours $35–$50* ⊗ *Daily 10–4:30, tours by appointment.*

Frank Family Vineyards. As a former Disney film and television executive, Rich Frank knows a thing or two about entertainment, and it shows in the chipper atmosphere that prevails in the tasting room here. The site's wine-making history dates back to 1884, when it debuted as the Larkmead Winery—portions of the original structure, reclad in stone in 1906, remain standing today—and for decades this was the home of the Hanns Kornell sparkling-wine operation. Frank Family makes five sparklers itself, but the high-profile wines are the Cabernet Sauvignons, particularly the Rutherford Reserve and the Winston Hill red blend, which grace many Napa Valley restaurants' wine lists. ■TIP→ **With rows of tables shaded by elms, the lawn beside the tasting room is popular with picnickers.** ✉ *1091 Larkmead La., off Hwy. 29* ☎ *707/942–0859* ⊕ *www.frankfamilyvineyards.com.*

Jericho Canyon Vineyard. It takes a Polaris all-terrain vehicle to tour the vineyards at this family-owned winery whose grapes grow on hillsides that slope as much as 45 degrees. The rocky, volcanic soils of this former cattle ranch yield intensely flavored berries that winemaker Aaron Pott transforms into the flagship Jericho Canyon Cabernet Sauvignon and other wines. All tastings start with a Sauvignon Blanc and include the current flagship Cabernet and an older vintage. Winery tours pass through underground barrel caves redolent of French oak and red wine. Topics covered on the Polaris tour include the nuances of sustainable farming in this challenging environment. ✉ *3322 Old Lawley Toll Rd., off Hwy. 29* ☎ *707/331–9076* ⊕ *jerichocanyonvineyard.com* 🍷 *Winery tour and tasting $40, Polaris tour and tasting $80* ⊗ *Tastings and tours daily by appointment only.*

Kelly Fleming Wines. Given her previous career fashioning interiors for Ruth's Chris Steakhouse and other meat-centric eateries, it's perhaps fitting that upon opening her own winery Kelly Fleming gravitated toward steak-friendly Cabernet Sauvignon—and that her facility's design, by Taylor Lombardo Architects of San Francisco and Napa, was executed with the utmost precision. A similar attention to detail is in evidence in the vineyards, green and well pruned even during the dog days of summer, and in the wine made from those grapes, the elegant, aromatic estate Cabernet. Visits, by appointment only, begin with a glass of Sauvignon Blanc and a tour of the Tuscan-inspired winery and its caves, followed by Big Pour Napa Red (a Bordeaux-style blend), and the Cabernet. Small bites accompany the wines. ⊠ *2339 Pickett Rd., off Silverado Trail* ☎ *707/942–6849* ⊕ *www.kellyflemingwines.com* ✉ *Tasting and tour $60* ☉ *Daily 10–4, by appointment.*

Lava Vine Winery. The owners and staff of this jolly spot pride themselves on creating a family- and dog-friendly environment, and you're apt to hear rock, pop, and other tunes as you taste small-lot wines that include Cabernet Sauvignon, Chenin Blanc, Syrah, and Port. The wry Pete might even start playing the banjo. ■**TIP**➔ If they're available and you like mighty reds, be sure to taste the Suisun Valley Petite Sirah and the Knights Valley Reserve Cabernet. ⊠ *965 Silverado Trail N* ☎ *707/942–9500* ⊕ *www.lavavine.com* ✉ *Tasting $10* ☉ *Daily 10–5.*

Robert Louis Stevenson State Park. Encompassing the summit of Mt. St. Helena, this mostly undeveloped park is where Stevenson and his bride, Fanny Osbourne, spent their honeymoon in an abandoned bunkhouse of the Silverado Mine. This stay in 1880 inspired the writer's travel memoir *The Silverado Squatters,* and Spyglass Hill in *Treasure Island* is thought to be a portrait of Mt. St. Helena. A marble memorial marks the site of the bunkhouse. The 10-mile trail is steep and lacks shade in spots, but the summit is often cool and breezy. ■**TIP**➔ Bring plenty of water, and dress in layers. ⊠ *Hwy. 29, 7 miles north of Calistoga* ☎ *707/942–4575* ⊕ *www.parks.ca.gov/?page_id=472* ✉ *Free* ☉ *Daily sunrise–sunset.*

Sharpsteen Museum of Calistoga History. Walt Disney animator Ben Sharpsteen, who retired to Calistoga, founded this museum whose centerpiece is an intricate diorama depicting the Calistoga Hot Springs Resort during its 19th-century heyday. One exhibit examines the indigenous Wappo people who once lived here, and another focuses on Sharpsteen's career as an animator. ⊠ *1311 Washington St., at 1st St.* ☎ *707/942–5911* ⊕ *www.sharpsteen-museum.org* ✉ *$3* ☉ *Daily 11–4.*

FAMILY **Sterling Vineyards.** The approach to Sterling Vineyards, perched on a hilltop about a mile south of Calistoga, is the most spectacular in the valley. Instead of driving to the tasting room, you board an aerial tram to reach pristine white buildings that recall those in the Greek islands. (The founder often vacationed on Mykonos.) A tasting of current releases costs $29, which includes the tram ride and a self-guided tour, but consider ponying up the extra $10 for a Sterling Silver tasting, which includes reserve, single-vineyard, and limited-release wines. ■**TIP**➔ The short tram ride is one of the area's few kid-friendly attractions; the cost is $15 for guests under 21. ⊠ *1111 Dunaweal La., off Hwy. 29* ☎ *707/942–3300, 800/726–6136* ⊕ *www.sterlingvineyards.com* ✉ *Tastings $29–$39, includes tram ride, self-guided tour, and tasting* ☉ *Weekdays 10:30–5, weekends 10–5.*

Tamber Bey Vineyards. Endurance riders Barry and Jennifer Waitte share their passion for horses and wine at their glam-rustic winery north of Calistoga. Their 22-acre Sundance Ranch remains a working equestrian facility, but the site has been revamped to include a state-of-the-art winery with separate fermenting tanks for grapes from Tamber Bey's vineyards in Yountville, Oakville, and elsewhere. The winemakers produce two Chardonnays and a Sauvignon Blanc, but the winery's stars are several subtly powerful reds, including the flagship Cabernet Sauvignon, a Merlot, and blends dominated by Cabernet Franc, Cabernet Sauvignon, and Petit Verdot. ■TIP→ Appointments are required, but even on a few-minutes' notice they're generally easy to get. ✉ *1251 Tubbs La., at Myrtledale Rd.* ☎ *707/942–2100* ⊕ *www.tamberbey.com* 🍷 *Tastings $25–$55, tour and tasting $45* ⊙ *Daily 10–5, by appointment only.*

WHERE TO EAT

$$ ✕**All Seasons Bistro.** Flowers top the tables at this Calistoga mainstay,
AMERICAN   a delightful stop for lunch or dinner. The seasonal menu might include braised lamb shank with creamy polenta or seared salmon fillet with chive-scallion mashed potatoes, and year-round the grilled Angus-beef burger comes with super-crispy fries and a smoked-onion aioli. Among the homey desserts are a well-executed vanilla-bean crème brûlée and a warm dark-chocolate torte. ■TIP→ The extensive wine list includes some 1970s and 1980s gems, and there's full cocktail service. ⑤ *Average main: $21* ✉ *1400 Lincoln Ave., at Washington St.* ☎ *707/942–9111* ⊕ *www.allseasonsnapavalley.net* ⊙ *Closed Mon.*

$$ ✕**Barolo.** With red-leather seats, artsy lighting fixtures, and a marble
ITALIAN   bar indoors and café seating outside, this Italian-inflected wine bar is a fine spot for a glass of wine, including many from small producers you may not have heard of. Small plates that could have come straight from Italy—*polpettine* (braised pork-and-beef meatballs), risotto croquettes, a selection of *salumi* (dry-cured and other meats)—are great for sharing. Pastas, pizzas, and large plates such as chicken piccata and braised short ribs round out the menu. ⑤ *Average main: $19* ✉ *Mount View Hotel, 1457 Lincoln Ave., near Fair Way* ☎ *707/942–9900* ⊕ *www.barolocalistoga.com* ⊙ *No lunch.*

$$ ✕**Bosko's Trattoria.** Affable Bosko's provides tasty Italian cuisine at a fair
ITALIAN   price. The specialties include house-made pastas and thin-crust pizzas cooked in a wood-fired oven. Two of the hefty sandwiches worth trying are the free-range chicken breast sandwich on garlicky focaccia (also made in-house) and the Italian sausage on a sourdough roll. Both come with a salad or a bowl of minestrone or other soup. Nothing super-fancy here, just good value in a pleasant setting. ⑤ *Average main: $17* ✉ *1364 Lincoln Ave., at Washington St.* ☎ *707/942–9088* ⊕ *www.boskos.com* ⌕ *Reservations not accepted.*

$$$ ✕**Brannan's Grill.** Arts and Crafts–style lamps cast a warm glow over
AMERICAN   the tables and red leather booths at this casual hangout serving contemporary American cuisine. Rob Lam, the restaurant's original chef, returned in 2014 and restored longtime favorites, including hoisin-flavored barbecued baby back ribs, crispy whole fried fish, and grilled hanger steak. Lam also prepares lighter fare—an ahi tuna poke appetizer

set on crispy rice, for instance, and a pan-roasted salmon entrée. The antique mahogany bar is a congenial spot for cocktails, and live jazz on Friday and Saturday makes Brannan's a lively place for a weekend night out. ■TIP➔ **Look up at the vaulted ceiling, redwood beams, and hand-forged iron trestles; the building was constructed in 1903 as a garage.** ⑤ *Average main: $28* ✉ *1374 Lincoln Ave., at Washington St.* ☎ *707/942–2233* ⊕ *www.brannansgrill.com* ◷ *No lunch Mon.–Thurs.*

$$$
AMERICAN

✕ **Calistoga Inn Restaurant & Brewery.** Calistoga's comeback kid emerged from the ashes of a 2012 fire with a fresh look and a new menu, and the beers made on-site are better than ever. Starters might include clams and mussels steamed in wheat ale and fettuccine with avocado. Among the beer-friendly items, the garlic-crusted calamari appetizer and the country paella entrée stand out. Good with beer or wine are the vegetarian raviolis, the grilled rib-eye steak served with béarnaise butter, and the burger topped with Tillamook cheddar and applewood-smoked bacon. ■TIP➔ **When the weather's nice, the garden is a swell place to sip a brew.** ⑤ *Average main: $24* ✉ *1250 Lincoln Ave., at Cedar St.* ☎ *707/942–4101* ⊕ *www.calistogainn.com.*

$$
ITALIAN

✕ **Checkers.** A cheery spot filled with both locals and visitors, this Cal-Italian restaurant serves up a few surprises along with the standards. The entrées consist mostly of pasta (rigatoni with broccoli, linguini carbonara) and pizzas that include a tangy goat cheese pie with sundried tomatoes, mozzarella, and roasted garlic. An unusual but popular pick is the Thai pizza with chicken, cilantro, and peanuts. Among the best dishes are the hearty salads such as the sweet and tangy Napa Salad, served with apples, candied walnuts, Gorgonzola, and a poppy-seed dressing. The wine selection isn't nearly as imaginative, surprising for a sister property to nearby Brannan's Grill and Barolo, which have much better lists. ⑤ *Average main: $17* ✉ *1414 Lincoln Ave., at Washington St.* ☎ *707/942–9300* ⊕ *www.checkerscalistoga.com.*

$$
MODERN
AMERICAN

✕ **Evangeline.** The gaslamp-style lighting fixtures and charcoal-black hues of this 2015 newcomer evoke old New Orleans though, like the cuisine, with a California twist. Brandon Sharp, also the chef at nearby Solbar, puts a jaunty spin on classics such as oyster stew and po'boys, the latter with blackened petrale sole replacing the oysters. The lineup of daily specials includes duck cassoulet, fried buttermilk quail, and gumbo ya-ya. Open all day, Evangeline is a great late-afternoon spot to sip a palate-cleansing Sazerac or the signature old-fashioned while nibbling on shrimp cocktail with Cajon remoulade or Sharp's addictive fried pickles. The brick-lined courtyard outside is a sublime place to sit a spell. ⑤ *Average main: $19* ✉ *1226 Washington St., near Lincoln Ave.* ☎ *707/341–3131* ⊕ *www.evangelinenapa.com.*

$$$
ITALIAN
Fodor's Choice
★

✕ **Hotel D'Amici.** Italian and Italian-American influences abound at this restaurant operated by the Pestoni family, owners of Rutherford Grove Winery. A wall painted by San Francisco muralist Brian Barneclo riffs off Federico's Fellini's film *8½*; photos of Pestonis making Napa Valley wine (since 1892) are everywhere; and, perhaps most importantly, chef Joe Venezia is a protégé of the late cookbook author Marcella Hazan. Like Hazan, Venezia seeks out top-quality ingredients, strives for simplicity, and cooks sauces and his meals' other components long enough to permit the flavors to meld. He prepares all the classics, including gnocchi, spaghetti with seafood, and veal scaloppine, with finesse. Pestoni and other California vintages dominate the wine list, and there are Italian selections. ⓢ *Average main: $24* ⊠ *1440 Lincoln Ave., near Washington St.* ☎ *707/942–1400* ⊕ *www.hoteldamici.com.*

$$$
MODERN
AMERICAN

✕ **Jolē.** Local produce plays a starring role at this modern American restaurant, not surprising as chef Matt Spector is one of the area's biggest proponents of farm-to-table dining. Depending on when you visit, you might enjoy roasted cauliflower served with almonds, dates, capers, and balsamic; kale stew with Tasso ham, kabocha squash, and fingerling potatoes; and molasses-glazed quail with farro risotto, roasted pumpkin, and a maple-bourbon demi-glace. The menu is available à la carte, and there are four-, five-, and six-course prix-fixe options. With about four dozen wines by the glass, it's easy to find something to pair with each course. There's also a full bar, with a happy hour daily from 4 pm to 6 pm. ⓢ *Average main: $25* ⊠ *Mount View Hotel, 1457 Lincoln Ave., near Fair Way* ☎ *707/942–9538* ⊕ *jolerestaurant. com* ☉ *No lunch.*

$$$$
MODERN
AMERICAN
Fodor's Choice
★

✕ **Solbar.** Chef Brandon Sharp is known around the region for his subtle and sophisticated take on Wine Country cooking. As befits a restaurant at a spa resort, the menu here is divided into "healthy, lighter dishes" and "hearty cuisine." On the lighter side, the lemongrass-poached petrale sole comes with jasmine rice and hearts of palm. On the heartier side you might find a rib-eye steak served with Kennebec potatoes, creamed spinach, and sauce bordelaise. The service at Solbar is uniformly excellent, and in good weather the patio is a festive spot for breakfast, lunch, or dinner. ⓢ *Average main: $31* ⊠ *Solage Calistoga, 755 Silverado Trail, at Rosedale Rd.* ☎ *877/684–9146* ⊕ *www. solagecalistoga.com/solbar.*

WHERE TO STAY

$
HOTEL

🛏 **Best Western Plus Stevenson Manor.** Budget travelers get what they pay for—and a little bit more—at this motel a few blocks from Calistoga's downtown. **Pros:** great price for region; friendly staff; nice pool area; complimentary full breakfast. **Cons:** decidedly lacking in glamour. ⓢ *Rooms from: $165* ⊠ *1830 Lincoln Ave.* ☎ *707/942–1112, 800/780–7234* ⊕ *www.bestwestern.com* ⤳ *34 rooms* ⧉*Breakfast.*

$$
B&B/INN

🛏 **Brannan Cottage Inn.** A 2014 renovation injected glamour and vintage-yet-modern style into this small inn whose centerpiece is an 1860s cottage from Calistoga's original spa era. **Pros:** short walk from downtown; plush mattresses; helpful staff. **Cons:** noise from neighbors can be heard in some rooms; showers but no bathtubs in some rooms. ⓢ *Rooms from: $299* ⊠ *109 Wappo Ave., at Lincoln Ave.* ☎ *707/942–4200* ⊕ *www.brannancottageinn.com* ⤳ *6 rooms* ⧉*No meals.*

$$$$
RESORT
Fodor's Choice
★

🛏 **Calistoga Ranch.** Spacious cedar-shingle lodges throughout this posh, wooded property have outdoor living areas, and even the restaurant, spa, and reception space have outdoor seating and fireplaces. **Pros:** almost half the lodges have private hot tubs on the deck; lovely hiking trails on the property; guests have reciprocal privileges at Auberge du Soleil and Solage Calistoga. **Cons:** innovative indoor-outdoor organization works

Almost half the lodgings at the posh Calistoga Ranch have private hot tubs.

better in fair weather than in rain or cold. $ *Rooms from: $720* ✉ *580 Lommel Rd.* ☎ *707/254–2800, 800/942–4220* ⊕ *www.calistogaranch. com* ⌁ *50 guest lodges* ⦿ *No meals.*

$$$
B&B/INN

🖾 **Cottage Grove Inn.** A long driveway lined with freestanding cottages, each shaded by elm trees and with rocking chairs on the porch, looks a bit like Main Street, USA, but inside the skylighted buildings include all the perks necessary for a romantic weekend getaway. **Pros:** loaner bicycles available; plenty of privacy; huge bathtubs. **Cons:** no pool; some may find the decor too old school. $ *Rooms from: $395* ✉ *1711 Lincoln Ave.* ☎ *707/942–8400, 800/799–2284* ⊕ *www.cottagegrove. com* ⌁ *16 cottages* ⦿ *Breakfast.*

$$
RESORT

🖾 **Indian Springs Resort and Spa.** Stylish Indian Springs—operating as a spa since 1862—ably splits the difference between laid-back style and ultrachic touches. **Pros:** palm-studded grounds with outdoor seating areas; on-site restaurant; stylish for the price; enormous mineral pool; free touring bikes. **Cons:** lodge rooms are small; service could be more polished. $ *Rooms from: $259* ✉ *1712 Lincoln Ave.* ☎ *707/942–4913* ⊕ *www.indianspringscalistoga.com* ⌁ *77 rooms, 18 suites, 18 cottages, 3 houses* ⦿ *No meals.*

$$
B&B/INN
Fodor'sChoice
★

🖾 **Luxe Calistoga.** Extravagant hospitality defines the Napa Valley's luxury properties, but this inn takes the prize in the small-lodging category. **Pros:** attentive owners; marvelous breakfasts; good restaurants, tasting rooms, and shopping within walking distance. **Cons:** the hum (and sometimes scent) of street traffic is ever-present. $ *Rooms from: $269* ✉ *1139 Lincoln Ave.* ☎ *707/942–9797* ⊕ *luxecalistoga.com* ⌁ *5 rooms* ⦿ *Breakfast.*

$$
B&B/INN
Fodor's Choice
★

⊡ **Meadowlark Country House.** Two charming European gents run this laid-back but sophisticated inn on 20 wooded acres just north of downtown. **Pros:** charming innkeepers; tasty sit-down breakfasts; welcoming vibe that attracts diverse guests. **Cons:** clothing-optional pool policy isn't for everyone. ⑤ *Rooms from: $210* ⊠ *601 Petrified Forest Rd.* ☎ *707/942–5651, 800/942–5651* ⊕ *www.meadowlarkinn.com* ⇆ *5 rooms, 3 suites, 1 cottage, 1 guesthouse* ⑩ *Breakfast.*

$$
B&B/INN

⊡ **Mount View Hotel & Spa.** Although it's in a 1912 building that's been designated a National Historic Landmark, the Mount View feels completely modern, with freshly painted rooms, feather duvets, and iPod docking stations and other high-tech touches. **Pros:** convenient location; we-aim-to-please staff; good spa treatments; eco-friendly. **Cons:** outside noise can be heard in some rooms; ground-floor rooms are dark; some rooms feel cramped. ⑤ *Rooms from: $250* ⊠ *1457 Lincoln Ave.* ☎ *707/942–6877, 800/816–6877* ⊕ *www.mountviewhotel.com* ⇆ *18 rooms, 13 suites and cottages* ⑩ *Breakfast.*

$$$$
RESORT
Fodor's Choice
★

⊡ **Solage Calistoga.** The aesthetic at this 22-acre property is Napa Valley barn meets San Francisco loft, so the rooms have high ceilings, polished concrete floors, recycled walnut furniture, and all-natural fabrics in soothingly muted colors. **Pros:** great service; complimentary bikes; separate pools for kids and adults. **Cons:** the vibe may not suit everyone. ⑤ *Rooms from: $548* ⊠ *755 Silverado Trail* ☎ *855/942–7442, 707/226–0800* ⊕ *www.solagecalistoga.com* ⇆ *83 rooms, 6 suites* ⑩ *No meals.*

NIGHTLIFE AND PERFORMING ARTS

Calistoga is hardly a party town, but the bars at several restaurants, among them Solbar, the Calistoga Inn, Brannan's Grill (live jazz on Friday and Saturday), and JoLē are good stops for a nightcap. The Hydro Bar and Grill and Susie's have a more traditionally barlike feel.

Hydro Grill. Open until midnight on Friday and Saturday night with music and dancing, this may well be Calistoga's premiere all-purpose nightspot. That's not saying too much, but the atmosphere is festive. There's food, but dine elsewhere. ⊠ *1403 Lincoln Ave., at Washington St.* ☎ *707/942–9777.*

Susie's Bar. Calistoga's entrant in the dive-bar sweepstakes is on the demure side—but that's a good thing. Susie's is a cool place to toss back a top-shelf cocktail or a local brew after every place else in town has thrown in the bar towel. ⊠ *1365 Lincoln Ave., at Washington St.* ☎ *707/942–6710* ⊕ *susiescalistoga.com.*

SPAS

Baths at Roman Spa. Dispensing with high design and highfalutin treatments, this down-to-earth spa delivers the basics at reasonable prices. The decor, though utilitarian in spots, is generally soothing, and the staff members seem eager to provide an experience that transforms. The signature Deluxe Spa Combination consists of mud and mineral baths followed by a full-body massage of 85 or 110 minutes. You can have all these treatments à la carte, and aromatherapy and Reiki sessions are also an option. ■ TIP➔ **Not all Calistoga spas have rooms for couples, but this one does.** ⊠ *Roman Spa Hot Springs Resort, 1300 Washington St., at 1st St.* ☎ *707/942–2122, 800/404–4772* ⊕ *bathsromanspa.com* 🗔 *Treatments $70–$195* ☉ *Daily 9–5.*

Dr. Wilkinson's Hot Springs Resort. Newer, fancier establishments may have eclipsed Calistoga's oldest spa, but loyal fans appreciate its reasonable prices and unpretentious vibe. The mud baths here are a mix of volcanic ash and Canadian peat, warmed by the spa's own hot springs. Fun fact: back in 1952, "The Works"—a mud bath, steam room, blanket wrap, and a massage—cost $3.50. The charge now is $139. ⊠ *1507 Lincoln Ave., at Fair Way* ☎ *707/942–4102* ⊕ *www.drwilkinson.com* 🗔 *Treatments $69–$179* ☉ *Daily 8:30–5:30 (last spa treatment at 3:45).*

Indian Springs Spa. Even before Sam Brannan constructed a spa on this site in the 1860s, the Wappo Indians were building sweat lodges over its thermal geysers. Treatments include a Calistoga-classic pure volcanic-ash mud bath, followed by a mineral bath, after which clients are wrapped in a flannel blanket for a 15-minute cool-down session or until called for a massage if they've booked one. Facials using Intraceuticals and Pevonia products are another specialty. Spa clients have access to the Olympic-size mineral-water pool, kept at 92°F in summer and a toasty 102°F in winter. ⊠ *1712 Lincoln Ave., at Wappo Ave.* ☎ *707/942–4913* ⊕ *www.indianspringscalistoga.com* 🗔 *Treatments $70–$380* ☉ *Daily 9–9 (last treatment at 8).*

Fodor'sChoice
★ **Spa Solage.** This eco-conscious spa has reinvented the traditional Calistoga mud and mineral water therapies. Case in point: the hour-long "Mudslide," a three-part treatment that includes a mud body mask (in a heated lounge), a soak in a thermal bath, and a power nap in a sound/vibration chair. The mud here is a mix of clay, volcanic ash, and essential oils. Traditional spa services—combination Shiatsu-Swedish and other massages, full-body exfoliations, facials, and waxes—are available, as are fitness and yoga classes. ⊠ *755 Silverado Trail, at Rosedale Rd.* ☎ *707/226–0825, 855/790–6023* ⊕ *www.solagecalistoga.com/spa* 🗔 *Treatments $98–$470* ☉ *Daily 8–8.*

SPORTS AND THE OUTDOORS

BICYCLING

Calistoga Bikeshop. Options here include regular and fancy bikes that rent for $18 an hour and up, and there's a self-guided Cool Wine Tour ($90) that includes tastings at three or four small wineries. ⊠ *1318 Lincoln Ave., near Washington St.* ☎ *707/942–9687* ⊕ *www.calistoga bikeshop.net.*

SHOPPING

A stroll of the 1300 and 1400 blocks of Lincoln Avenue downtown will take you past most of Calistoga's best shops, with the remaining ones nearby. One outlier, Calistoga Pottery, is off Highway 29 just south of Lincoln.

A Man's Supply. An upscale store devoted to "class act" guys, this fun space stocks masculine outdoor clothing and gear and casual everyday wear. In addition to wallets and hats, the accessories here include cigars, knives, and manly-men gadgets. ⊠ *1343 Lincoln Ave., near Washington St.* ☎ *707/942–2280* ⊕ *amanssupply.com.*

Calistoga Pottery. You may recognize the dinnerware and other pottery sold by owners Jeff and Sally Manfredi—their biggest customers are the area's inns, restaurants, and wineries. Works by a few other potters are also sold here. ⊠ *1001 Foothill Blvd., at Pine St.* ☎ *707/942–0216* ⊕ *www.calistogapottery.com.*

Enoteca Wine Shop. The extensive tasting notes posted alongside nearly all of the wines sold here—among them some hard-to-find bottles from Napa, Sonoma, and around the world—help you make a wise choice. ⊠ *1348-B Lincoln Ave.* ☎ *707/942–1117* ⊕ *www.enotecawineshop.com.*

SONOMA
VALLEY

WELCOME TO SONOMA VALLEY

TOP REASONS TO GO

★ **California and wine history:** Sonoma's mission and nearby sites provide insights into California's history; at Bartholomew Park and Buena Vista you can explore the wine industry's roots.

★ **Literary and other trails:** Work off the wine and fine cuisine—and just enjoy the scenery—hiking the trails of Jack London and Sugar Loaf Ridge state parks; the former contains the ruins of London's Wolf House.

★ **Peaceful Glen Ellen:** As writers from London to M.F.K. Fisher discovered, peaceful Glen Ellen is a good place to decompress and tap into one's creativity. (Hunter S. Thompson found it too sedate.)

★ **Seated Pinot Noir tastings:** Patz & Hall, Sojourn, and other wineries host seated tastings focusing on high-quality Pinots from Los Carneros and beyond.

★ **Wineries with a view:** The views from the outdoor tasting spaces at Gundlach Bundschu, Ram's Gate, and Kunde encourage lingering over a glass of wine from your favorite varietal.

1 Sonoma. The Wine Country's oldest town has it all: fine dining, historical sites, and wineries from down-home to high style. Much of the activity takes place around Sonoma Plaza, where in 1846 some American settlers declared independence from Mexico and established the California Republic. The republic only lasted a month, but during the next decade, Count Agoston Haraszthy laid the foundation for modern California wine making. Much of the southern Sonoma Valley, including the western section of Los Carneros AVA, has a Sonoma address.

2 Glen Ellen. Sonoma Creek snakes through Glen Ellen's tiny "downtown," 8 miles northwest of Sonoma Plaza off Highway 12. The lodgings here are small, and the most high-profile winery, Benziger, is a family operation, two of the many reasons this town, which has several good restaurants, has retained its rural character.

Los Alamos Rd.
Sonoma Highway
Hood Mountain Regional Park
Bald Mountain
Adobe Canyon Rd.
12
Annadel State Park
Sugarloaf Ridge State Park
3 Kenwood
Warm Springs Rd.
S O N O M A
BENNETT VALLEY
Bennett Valley Rd.
Warm Springs Rd.
Jack London State Historic Park
2 Glen Ellen
Sonoma Mountain ▲
London Ranch Rd.
Eldridge
S O N O M A   M O U N T A I N S

3 Kenwood. St. Francis, Chateau St. Jean, and a few other name wineries straddle Highway 12 in Kenwood, whose vague center lies about 5 miles north of Glen Ellen. At Kunde Family Estate you can view the entire Kenwood scene during a Mountain Top Tasting; back down on the ground, most of the action takes place on or just off Highway 12.

GETTING ORIENTED

The Sonoma Valley lies just north of San Pablo Bay, itself an extension of the larger San Francisco Bay. The largest town, Sonoma, about 41 miles north of San Francisco's Golden Gate Bridge, is bisected by Highway 12, which continues north to Glen Ellen and Kenwood. About 11,000 people live in Sonoma proper, with another 22,000 within its orbit. Glen Ellen has about 800 residents, Kenwood a little more than 1,000.

4

The birthplace of modern California wine making, the Sonoma Valley seduces with its unpretentious attitude and pastoral landscape. Tasting rooms, restaurants, and historical sites abound near Sonoma Plaza, but beyond downtown Sonoma the wineries and attractions are spread out along gently winding roads. Sonoma County's half of the Carneros District lies within Sonoma Valley, whose other towns of note include Glen Ellen and Kenwood. Sonoma Valley tasting rooms are often less crowded than those in Napa or northern Sonoma County, especially midweek, and the vibe here, though sophisticated, is definitely less sceney.

That's not to suggest that the Sonoma Valley is undiscovered territory. On the contrary, along Highway 12, the main corridor through the Sonoma Valley, you'll spot classy inns, restaurants, and spas in addition to wineries. In high season Glen Ellen and Kenwood are filled with well-heeled wine buffs, and the best restaurants are packed. Still, the pace of life is generally slower here than elsewhere in the Wine Country—on some days you'll see as many bicyclists as limo drivers zipping from one winery to the next.

The historic Sonoma Valley towns offer glimpses of the past. Sonoma, with its tree-filled central plaza, is rich with 19th-century buildings. Two names pop up on many plaques affixed to them: General Mariano Guadalupe Vallejo, who in the 1830s and 1840s was Mexico's highest-ranking military officer in these parts, and Count Agoston Haraszthy, who opened Buena Vista Winery in 1857. Glen Ellen, meanwhile, has a special connection with the author Jack London. Kenwood claims a more recent distinction: in 1999 its Chateau St. Jean winery was the first one in Sonoma County to earn a "Wine of the Year" award from *Wine Spectator* magazine, one of several indications that Sonoma Valley wine making had come of age.

Bounded by the Mayacamas Mountains on the east and Sonoma Mountain on the west, this scenic valley extends north from San Pablo Bay nearly 20 miles to the eastern outskirts of Santa Rosa. The varied terrain, soils, and climate—cooler in the south because of the bay influence and hotter toward the north—allow grape growers to raise cool-weather varietals such as Chardonnay and Pinot Noir as well as Zinfandel, Merlot, Cabernet Sauvignon, and other heat-seeking grapes.

PLANNER

WHEN TO GO

As with the rest of Northern California's Wine Country, the best time to visit the Sonoma Valley is between late spring and early fall, when the weather is warm and wineries bustle with activity. September and October, when grape harvesting and crushing are in full swing, are the busiest months. Especially at this time—and on all summer weekends— lodging prices tend to be at their highest. Tasting rooms throughout the Sonoma Valley are generally not too crowded during the week even in high season except on holiday Mondays (and even then it's not bad).

PLANNING YOUR TIME

You can hit the Sonoma Valley's highlights in a day or two—a half or a full day exploring western Carneros District wineries and some in Sonoma proper, and the same amount of time to check out Glen Ellen and Kenwood. Most visitors stay in Sonoma. All the wineries covered in this chapter are within 15 miles of Sonoma Plaza, so traffic isn't an issue, except on Highway 12 north of Sonoma Plaza and the intersection of highways 116 and 121 during the morning and afternoon commutes.

Several of the star wineries—Patz & Hall, Scribe, and Sojourn among them—accept visitors by appointment only. On weekdays you may be able to reserve a space on short notice, but for weekend visits, especially during the summer and early fall, booking ahead is essential even when food pairings (which wineries need time to plan for) are not involved. A good strategy year-round is to book appointment-only wineries in the morning; this gives you more flexibility in the afternoon should lunch or other stops take longer than expected.

GETTING HERE AND AROUND

BUS TRAVEL

Vine Bus 25 travels between downtown Napa and Sonoma, where Sonoma Transit buses provide service within Sonoma and to Glen Ellen and Kenwood. ⇨ *For more information about arriving by bus, see Bus Travel in the Travel Smart chapter. For more information about local bus service, see the Bus Travel sections for the individual towns in this chapter.*

CAR TRAVEL

Traveling by car is the easiest way to tour the Sonoma Valley. Highway 12, also called the Sonoma Highway, is the main thoroughfare through the valley, running north–south through Sonoma, Glen Ellen, and Kenwood into Santa Rosa. To get to the Sonoma Valley from San Francisco, travel north on U.S. 101 to the city of Novato. Take the Highway 37

4

Tastings at Sojourn Cellars take place in a homey bungalow just off Sonoma Plaza.

turnoff (Exit 460A) to the east, continuing for about 7 miles to Highway 121, the main route through the Carneros District. Highway 12 leads north from Highway 121 into the town of Sonoma; the road is called Broadway in the blocks immediately south of Sonoma Plaza. From Napa, take Highway 29 south to Highway 121/12 and head west until Highway 12 splits off north from Highway 121.

From Oakville, head west over the Mayacamas range on the highly scenic—but slow and winding—Oakville Grade Road, which turns into Trinity Road before it reaches Highway 12. From Calistoga, travel north a few miles on Highway 29/128 and then west on Petrified Forest Road and later Calistoga Road to reach Highway 12 in Santa Rosa. From there, head south into the valley.

Most of the western Carneros wineries covered in this chapter are on or near Highway 121, often signed as the Carneros Highway, the Sonoma Highway, or Arnold Drive. The multiple names can lead to confusion. The Gloria Ferrer winery gives its address as 23555 Carneros Highway, for instance; the listed address of CornerStone, across the road, is 23570 Arnold Drive. Arnold Drive heads north from Highway 121 into Glen Ellen; on the north side of town it intersects with Highway 12. At this intersection, head north for Kenwood, south for Sonoma.

RESTAURANTS

With Sonoma's Friday farmers' market arguably the Wine Country's best, it's not surprising that farm-to-table influences can be felt not only at fancy establishments but also ethnic and comfort-food venues. Fine dining in the Sonoma Valley is generally low-key, with the major exception being Santé, the tony restaurant inside the Fairmont Sonoma

Mission Inn & Spa. Santé and Cafe La Haye, El Dorado Kitchen, and Harvest Moon Café, all in Sonoma, turn out thoughtful, complex cuisine that emphasizes locally produced meat, fish, cheese, vegetables, and fruit. La Salette, also in Sonoma, serves winning Portuguese-influenced dishes, and Aventine, inside a former sawmill and gristmill in Glen Ellen, is the best place for Italian; the town's Glen Ellen Star is the other must-do, but you can't go wrong at any of the fine-dining restaurants here. El Molino Central, modern in its use of organic ingredients but traditional in its preparations, is the top stop for Mexican, though Taqueria Los Primos takes the prize for downscale atmosphere. The Fremont Diner and Hot Box Grill both take comfort food to interesting places, with frying a major component in each case.

HOTELS

Sonoma has the valley's most varied accommodations, with motels and small inns, vacation condos, and boutique hotels all in the mix. Small inns are the norm in Glen Ellen and Kenwood. Spa lovers have two high-end choices at either end of the valley: the large and splashy Fairmont Sonoma Mission Inn & Spa in Sonoma and the Tuscan-style Kenwood Inn & Spa, in Kenwood.

For weekend stays in all towns it's wise to book a month or more ahead from late May through October. Most small lodgings require a two-night minimum stay on weekends at this time, three if Monday is a holiday. *Hotel reviews have been shortened. For full information, visit Fodors.com.*

WHAT IT COSTS				
	$	$$	$$$	$$$$
Restaurants	under $16	$16–$22	$23–$30	over $30
Hotels	under $201	$201–$300	$301–$400	over $400

Restaurant prices are the average cost of a main course at dinner, or if dinner isn't served, at lunch. Hotel prices are the lowest cost of a standard double room in high season.

VISITOR INFORMATION

Contacts Sonoma Valley Visitors Bureau ✉ *Sonoma Plaza, 453 1st St. E, Sonoma* ☎ *707/996–1090* ⊕ *www.sonomavalley.com* ✉ *23570 Arnold Dr., across from Gloria Ferrer, Sonoma.* **Wine Country Visitor Center at Corner-Stone** ✉ *23570 Arnold Dr., across from Gloria Ferrer, Sonoma.*

APPELLATIONS

Although Sonoma *County* is a large, diverse growing region encompassing several different appellations, the much smaller Sonoma *Valley*, at the southern end of Sonoma County, is comparatively compact and consists mostly of the **Sonoma Valley AVA**, which stretches northwest from San Pablo Bay toward Santa Rosa. The weather and soils here are unusually diverse. Pinot Noir and Chardonnay vineyards are most likely to be found in the AVA's southernmost parts, the sections cooled by fog from San Pablo Bay. (This part of the Sonoma Valley AVA overlaps with the Sonoma County portions of **Los Carneros AVA.**) Zinfandel, Cabernet Sauvignon, and Sauvignon Blanc grapes are more plentiful farther north, near Glen Ellen and Kenwood, both of which tend to be a few degrees warmer.

The **Sonoma Mountain AVA** rises to the west of Glen Ellen on the western border of the Sonoma Valley AVA. Benefiting from a sunny mountain location and rocky soil, the vineyards here produce deep-rooted vines and intensely flavored grapes that are made into unique, complex red wines, especially hearty Cabernet Sauvignons. Opposite Sonoma Mountain southeast across the Sonoma Valley sits its most recent subappellation, the **Moon Mountain District Sonoma County AVA.** This mountainside sliver, on the western slopes of the Mayacamas Mountains (just west of the Napa Valley's Mt. Veeder subappellation), contains some of California's oldest Zinfandel and Cabernet Sauvignon vines. The heavily sloped, rocky soils here produce smaller berries than vines on the valley floor, and the higher skin-to-juice ratio yields intense flavor.

Portions of the **Sonoma Coast AVA** overlap Los Carneros and Sonoma Valley. The tiny **Bennett Valley AVA**, also part of the Sonoma Valley AVA, falls within the city of Santa Rosa.

SONOMA

14 miles west of Napa; 45 miles northeast of San Francisco.

Fodor's Choice
★
One of the few towns in the valley with multiple attractions not related to food and wine, Sonoma has plenty to keep you busy for a couple of hours before you head out to tour the wineries. And you needn't leave town to taste wine. There are more than two dozen tasting rooms within steps of the plaza, some of which pour wines from more than one winery.

The valley's cultural center, Sonoma, founded in 1835 when California was still part of Mexico, is built around a large, tree-filled plaza. If you arrive from the south, on wide Broadway (Highway 12), you'll be retracing the last stretch of what long ago was California's most important road—El Camino Real, or "royal road," the only overland route through the state. During California's Spanish and Mexican periods, it ran past all of the state's 21 missions: beginning at San Diego de Alcala (1769) and ending at Mission San Francisco Solano (1823). This last mission still sits in the center of Sonoma.

GETTING HERE AND AROUND

To get to Sonoma from San Francisco by car, cross the Golden Gate Bridge, then head north on U.S. 101, east on Highway 37 toward Vallejo, and north on Highway 121, aka the Carneros Highway. At Highway 12, head north; several blocks before the highway dead-ends at Sonoma Plaza, the street's name changes to Broadway. There are three-hour unmetered parking spaces around the plaza. Free all-day parking can be found off 1st Street East a third of a block north of the plaza. Once you've parked, a pleasant stroll takes you past many of the town's restaurants, shops, and tasting rooms. High-profile and

CLOSE UP

Best Bets for Sonoma Valley Wineries

WINE TASTING

Deerfield Ranch Winery, Kenwood. You have to walk deep into the underground caves here to find the tasting room, where you'll sip "clean" red wines low in histamines and sulfites.

Sojourn Cellars, Sonoma. The tastings at Sojourn's bungalow focus on the variations among Chardonnays, Cabernet Sauvignons, and Pinot Noirs made from grapes grown in various climates and terrains.

Walt Wines, Sonoma. At this tasting room just north of Sonoma Plaza, it's all Pinot Noir all the time, with grapes sourced from Oregon's Willamette Valley to California's Central Coast.

WINERY TOURING

Benziger Family Winery, Glen Ellen. On this winery's tram tour, you'll learn about its unique microclimates and deep commitment to biodynamic farming principles.

Buena Vista Winery, Sonoma. Tours of the winery founded by wine pioneer Count Agoston Haraszthy pass through 19th-century caves dug by Chinese laborers.

Gloria Ferrer Caves and Vineyards, Sonoma. The sparkling-wine maker's tour takes in the aging caves and covers the winery's history and its contributions to wine science.

Kunde Estate Winery & Vineyards, Kenwood. The Mountain Top Tastings passenger-van tour winds 1,400 feet above the valley floor. On a shaded deck you'll enjoy memorable vistas while sipping reserve wines.

SETTING

Bartholomew Park Winery, Sonoma. Come for the wines and stay for the grounds, which include a woodsy picnic spot and miles of hiking trails.

Chateau St. Jean, Kenwood. Something's always in bloom in this winery's gardens, inspired by their rustic counterparts in Italy and France.

Ram's Gate Winery, Sonoma. Wherever you perch yourself—at the tasting bar, several lounging spaces, or strategically positioned outdoor areas—you'll take in sweeping (and often windswept) vistas.

Scribe, Sonoma. Most tastings at this winery opened by two sons of California walnut growers take place on an oak knoll overlooking vineyards holding Riesling, Sylvaner, and other grapes like those planted by German immigrants in this region more than a century ago.

FOOD-WINE PAIRING

Patz & Hall, Sonoma. The gourmet small bites at Salon Tastings at this respected winery show just how food-friendly its Chardonnays and Pinot Noirs are.

St. Francis Winery, Kenwood. The executive chef's small-dish pairings are among the Sonoma Valley's better deals. Local cheeses and meats are served by the fireplace in winter and on a patio in summer.

JUST PLAIN FUN

Gundlach Bundschu, Sonoma. The hills of "GunBun" are alive with the sounds of happy picnickers all summer; year-round the mood in the tasting room is festive and upbeat.

Loxton Cellars, Glen Ellen. Go retro at Loxton, where the personable owner-winemaker is often on the premises and the experience is down-home low-tech.

4

boutique wineries can be found a mile or so east; arrow-shape signs on East Spain Street and East Napa Street direct you.

Napa County VINE buses travel between Napa and Sonoma. Sonoma Transit buses connect Sonoma with other Sonoma County towns.

EXPLORING

TOP ATTRACTIONS

Gundlach Bundschu. Visitors may mispronounce this winery's name ("gun lock bun shoe" gets you close), but still they flock here to sample polished wines served by friendly pourers. Most of the winery's land has been in the Bundschu family since 1858. Cabernet Franc, Cabernet Sauvignon, Chardonnay, Merlot, and Tempranillo wines all are available in the standard $10 tasting. Add $10 to taste the signature Vintage Reserve red blend. For a more comprehensive experience, take the farm tour ($30), which ends with a cave tasting, or head into the vineyard ($50; available only between May and October). The Heritage Pairing ($75), involving gourmet bites and limited-release wines, takes place on weekends by appointment. ■**TIP**➔ On summer Fridays and weekends you can taste at vineyard-view tables outdoors. ⊠ *2000 Denmark St., at Bundschu Rd., off 8th St. E* ☎ *707/938–5277* ⊕ *www.gunbun.com* ⊠ *Tastings $10–$25, tours $30–$50; food-wine pairing $75* ⊗ *June– mid.-Oct., daily 11–5:30; mid.-Oct.–May, daily 11–4:30; food-wine pairing weekends by appointment.*

Fodor's Choice ★ **Patz & Hall.** Sophisticated single-vineyard Chardonnays and Pinot Noirs are the trademark of this respected winery that relocated from Napa to Sonoma in 2014. It's a Wine Country adage that great wines are made in the vineyard—the all-star fields represented here include Hyde, Durell, and Gap's Crown—but winemaker James Hall routinely surpasses peers with access to the same fruit, proof that discernment and expertise (Hall is a master at oak aging) play a role, too. Seated tastings hosted by knowledgeable pourers take place in a fashionable single-story residence 3 miles southeast of Sonoma Plaza. You can taste at the bar and on some days on the vineyard-view terrace beyond it, but to learn how food friendly these wines are, consider the Salon Tasting, at which they're paired with gourmet bites crafted with equal finesse. ⊠ *21200 8th St. E, near Peru Rd.* ☎ *707/265–7700* ⊕ *www.patzhall. com* ⊠ *Tastings $25–$75* ⊗ *Thurs.–Mon. 10–4, by appointment.*

Fodor's Choice ★ **Ram's Gate Winery.** Stunning views, ultrachic architecture, and wines made from grapes grown by acclaimed producers make a visit to Ram's Gate an event. The welcoming interior spaces—think Restoration Hardware with a dash of high-style whimsy—open up to the entire western Carneros. During fine weather you'll experience (in comfort) the cooling breezes that sweep through the area while sipping sophisticated wines, mostly Pinot Noirs and Chardonnays, but also Sauvignon Blanc, Cabernet Sauvignon, Syrah, late-harvest Zinfandel, and even a sparkler. With grapes sourced from the Sangiacomo, Hudson, and other illustrious vineyards, winemaker Jeff Gaffner focuses on creating balanced vintages that express what occurred in nature that year. One food-wine pairing ($60) includes tapas, wine tasting, and a winery

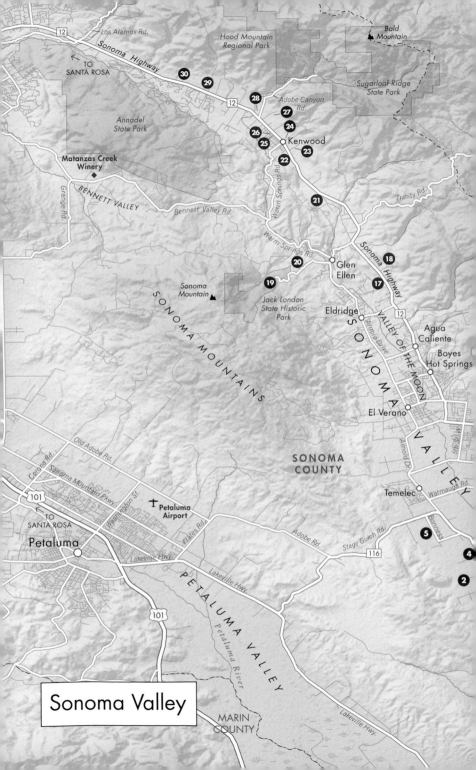

Sonoma Valley

tour; the other ($125; Thursday and Friday only) focuses on food and wine education. ✉ *28700 Arnold Dr./Hwy. 121* ☎ *707/721–8700* ⊕ *www.rams gatewinery.com* ✉ *Tasting $20–$125* ☉ *Thurs.–Mon. 10–6 by appointment.*

Fodor's Choice
★

WORD OF MOUTH

"Check out the accommodations around the very cute square in town in Sonoma. There are also a number of good wineries there. One of our favorites—with a great history—is Gundlach Bundschu."
—Tomsd

Scribe. Andrew and Adam Mariani, sons of California walnut growers, established Scribe in 2007 on land first planted to grapes in 1858 by Emil Dresel, a German immigrant. Dresel's claims to fame include cultivating Sonoma's first Riesling and Sylvaner, an achievement the brothers honor by growing both these varietals on land he once farmed. Using natural wine-making techniques they craft bright, terroir-driven wines from those grapes, along with Chardonnay, Pinot Noir, Syrah, and Cabernet Sauvignon. Tastings take place at weathered picnic tables on an oak-shaded knoll overlooking some of Scribe's vineyards. A 1915 Mission Revival–style hacienda nearby is being restored for use as a tasting space. During Prohibition it served as a hideout for bootleggers, and its basement harbored a speakeasy, two of many intriguing tales associated with this historic property. ✉ *2100 Denmark St., off Napa Rd.* ☎ *707/939–1858* ⊕ *scribewinery. com* ✉ *Tasting price varies; contact winery* ☉ *Daily by appointment.*

Fodor's Choice
★

Sojourn Cellars. Superior fruit sources and a winemaker with a wisely light touch have earned Sojourn Cellars high ratings from major wine critics for its Chardonnay, Pinot Noir, and Cabernet Sauvignon wines. The initial releases of this winery founded in 2001 were Cabernets, but it's best known these days for elegant, well-balanced single-vineyard Pinot Noirs from the Sonoma Coast and the Russian River Valley. A Sonoma Coast Chardonnay and a Pinot Noir, each with grapes from multiple vineyards, are also in the portfolio. In part because winemaker Erich Bradley uses oak in such a consistent way, the informative tastings at Sojourn's tasting room, in a homey bungalow just east of Sonoma Plaza, focus on the subtle variations caused by climate, terrain, and clone type depending on the vineyard. ✉ *141 E. Napa St., ½ block east of Sonoma Plaza* ☎ *707/938–7212* ⊕ *www.sojourncellars.com* ✉ *Tasting $25* ☉ *Daily 10–5 by appointment.*

Sonoma Mission. The northernmost of the 21 missions established by Franciscan friars in California, Sonoma Mission was founded in 1823 as Mission San Francisco Solano. It serves as the centerpiece of **Sonoma State Historic Park,** which includes several other sites in Sonoma and nearby Petaluma. Some early mission structures were destroyed, but all or part of several remaining buildings date to the days of Mexican rule over California. These include the **Sonoma Barracks,** a half block west of the mission at 20 East Spain Street, which housed troops under the command of General Mariano Guadalupe Vallejo, who controlled vast tracks of land in the region. The modest museum contains displays about the missions and information about the other historic sites. ✉ *114 E. Spain St., at 1st St. E* ☎ *707/938–9560* ⊕ *www.parks.*

Sonoma Mission was the last of California's 21 missions.

ca.gov/?page_id=479 ✉ *$3, includes same-day admission to other historic sites* ☙ *Daily 10–5.*

Sonoma Plaza. Dating from the Mission era, Sonoma Plaza is surrounded by 19th-century adobes, atmospheric hotels, and the swooping marquee of the Depression-era Sebastiani Theatre. A statue on the plaza's northeastern side marks the spot where California proclaimed its independence from Mexico on June 14, 1846. Despite its historical roots, the plaza is not a museum piece. On summer days it's a hive of activity, with children blowing off steam in the playground, couples enjoying picnics from gourmet shops, and groups listening to live music at the small amphitheater. The stone **City Hall** is also here. If you're wondering why the 1906 structure looks the same from all angles, here's why: its four sides were purposely made identical so that none of the plaza's merchants would feel that City Hall had turned its back to them. ✉ *North end of Broadway/Hwy. 12, bordered by E. Napa St., 1st St. E, E. Spain St., and 1st St. W.*

Fodor's Choice **Walt Wines.** You could spend a full day sampling wines in the tasting
★ rooms bordering Sonoma Plaza, but one not to miss is Walt, which specializes in Pinot Noir and makes two Chardonnays. Fruit-forward yet subtle, the Pinots win over even the purists who pine for the genre's days of lighter, more perfumey vintages. Some of the Pinots come from Sonoma County grapes but others are from ones grown in Mendocino County (just north of Sonoma County), California's Central Coast, and Oregon's Willamette Valley. Critics routinely bestow high ratings on all these wines. ✉ *380 1st St. W, at W. Spain St.* ☎ *707/933–4440* ⊕ *www. waltwines.com* ✉ *Tastings $20* ☙ *Daily 11–6.*

CLOSE UP

The Carneros District

The proximity of the compact Los Carneros AVA to San Francisco—it's less than an hour's drive away—makes it a favorite of in-the-know day-trippers and lovers of Pinot Noir and Chardonnay. This viticultural region, also known as the Carneros District or just the Carneros, stretches across the cool lower reaches of Sonoma and Napa counties. *Carneros* means "ram" in Spanish, and the slopes now covered with vines were once thought to be suitable only as sheep-grazing pasture.

To understand how different Los Carneros is from the other California wine-producing regions, notice how close it is to the northern reaches of San Francisco Bay, at this point called San Pablo Bay. On a gray day, the flat marshes and low hills near the water look moody, more like a Scottish moor than a typical California shore. During summer and autumn, strong west winds blow in from the ocean every afternoon, tempering the hot days.

The soil here is shallow and not particularly fertile, which means that the vines struggle to produce fruit. Though this would seem to be a drawback, it's in fact a plus. Vines that grow slowly and yield less fruit tend to produce concentrated, high-acid grapes that are ideal for wine making. Growers in the mid-19th century recognized this and planted vast tracts. Because of the low yields, some of the land was returned to sheep pasture after phylloxera destroyed the vines in the 1890s. But the reputation of the grapes survived, and shortly after the repeal of Prohibition, vines once again spread across the hills.

Pinot Noir and Chardonnay thrive on these exposed, windy slopes, but these days, winemakers are also trying out Merlot and Syrah, which are also well suited to the thin soil, moderate temperatures, and low rainfall. (Carneros generally gets less precipitation than elsewhere in Napa and Sonoma.) Even such warm-climate grapes as Cabernet Sauvignon can ripen well in favored Carneros locations.

WORTH NOTING

Anaba Wines. Reprising the greatest hits of Burgundy (Chardonnay, Pinot Noir) and the Rhône (Grenache, Mourvèdre, Syrah, Viognier), Anaba tries to be all things to most wine drinkers and generally succeeds. Pinot Noirs from Dutton Ranch and Soberanes Vineyard, the latter in Monterey County's Santa Lucia Highlands AVA, are the standouts, but all the wines are thoughtfully crafted. The winery's bungalow-like tasting room sits at the intersection of highways 121 and 116—turn west at the blinking red light. ■ TIP➔ A side patio faces the vineyards; if you don't mind a little highway noise, on a sunny day it's not a bad spot for a picnic put together at the deli across the street. ⊠ *60 Bonneau Rd., off Hwy. 116/121* ☏ *707/996–4188, 877/990–4188* ⊕ *www.anabawines.com* ▱ *Tasting $10* ⊗ *Daily 10:30–5:30.*

QUICK BITES

Angelo's Wine Country Deli. Many Bay Area locals stop here during Wine Country treks to get their jerky fix (10 types; generous free samples) or to pick up cheese, charcuterie, and sandwiches (huge and reasonably priced).

✉ *23400 Arnold Dr./Hwy. 121, near Wagner Rd.* ☎ *707/938–3688* ⊕ *ange-lossmokehouse.com/deli.htm* ⊙ *Daily 9–5.*

Bartholomew Park Winery. Although this winery was founded in 1994, grapes were grown in some of its vineyards as early as the 1830s. The emphasis here is on handcrafted, single-varietal wines—Cabernet Sauvignon, Chardonnay, Sauvignon Blanc, Syrah, and Zinfandel—made from organically farmed grapes. A small museum off the tasting room contains vivid exhibits about the history of the winery and the Sonoma region. Another plus is the beautiful, slightly off-the-beaten-path location amid a 375-acre private park about 2 miles from downtown Sonoma. Gather a lunch to enjoy on the woodsy grounds, one of Sonoma's prettier picnic spots, or hike 3 miles on the property's marked trails. ■TIP➜ To get here from Sonoma Plaza, head east on East Napa Street and follow the signs. ✉ *1000 Vineyard La., off Castle Rd.* ☎ *707/935–9511* ⊕ *www.bartpark.com* 🍷 *Tasting $10, tour $20* ⊙ *Daily 11–4:30; tours Fri. and Sat. at 11:30 and 2, Sun. at 2, by appointment.*

Buena Vista Winery. The site where modern California wine making got its start has been transformed into an entertaining homage to the accomplishments of the 19th-century wine pioneer Count Agoston Haraszthy. Tours pass through the original aging caves dug deep into the hillside by Chinese laborers, and banners, photos, and artifacts inside and out convey the history made on this site. Reserve tastings ($40) include library and current wines, plus ones still aging in barrels. The stylish former press house (used for pressing grapes into wine), which dates to 1862, hosts the standard tastings. ■TIP➜ Chardonnays and Pinot Noir, several inventive red blends, and a vibrant Petit Verdot are the strong suits here. ✉ *18000 Old Winery Rd., off E. Napa St.* ☎ *800/926–1266* ⊕ *www.buenavistawinery.com* 🍷 *Tastings $15–$40; tours $10–$35* ⊙ *Daily 10–5; tours by appointment.*

CornerStone Sonoma. A huge blue Adirondack chair on the east side of the road marks the way to this willful jumble of galleries, tasting rooms, and design and gift shops set amid 9 acres of landscape installations and outdoor sculptures. The sight of brides and bridesmaids scurrying along dirt-and-gravel paths to the weddings and receptions often held here adds to the visual mix. Sometimes closed a bit early on weekends when there are special events, the gardens are worth a 20-minute stroll. The Park 121 Café is a worthy stop for coffee or for lunch. ■TIP➜ The on-site Sonoma Valley Visitors Bureau office has coupons for free or discounted wine tastings in the western Carneros. ✉ *23570 Arnold Dr./ Hwy. 121, across from Gloria Ferrer winery* ☎ *707/933–3010* ⊕ *www.cornerstonesonoma.com* 🍷 *Free* ⊙ *Daily 10–5, gardens daily 10–4, sometimes later in summer.*

General Vallejo's Home (*Lachryma Montis*). General Mariano G. Vallejo commissioned this 1852 Victorian Gothic home that sits on several serene acres a few blocks west of Sonoma Plaza. It's a great place to picnic amid enormous cacti and learn about one of the region's early VIPs. The home blends Mexican and American styles and has opulent furnishings, including white-marble fireplaces and a French rosewood piano.

Wine-Making Pioneer

Count Agoston Haraszthy arrived in Sonoma in 1857 and set out to make fine wine commercially. He planted European vinifera varietals rather than mission grapes (the varietals Spanish missionaries brought to the Americas) and founded Buena Vista Winery the year he arrived.

Haraszthy deserves credit for two breakthroughs. At Buena Vista, he grew grapes on dry hillsides, instead of in the wetter lowlands, as had been customary in the Mission and Rancho periods. His success demonstrated that Sonoma's climate was moist enough to sustain grapes without irrigation. The innovative count was also the first to try aging his wine in redwood barrels, which were much less expensive than oak barrels. More affordable barrels made it feasible to ratchet up wine production. For almost 100 years, redwood barrels would be the California wine industry's most popular storage method (even though redwood can impart an odd flavor).

Despite producing inferior wines, the prolific mission grapes were preferred by California growers over better varieties of French, German, and Italian vinifera grapes through the 1860s and into the 1870s. But Haraszthy's success had begun to make an impression. A new red-wine grape, the Zinfandel, was becoming popular, both because it made excellent Claret (as good red wine was then called) and because it had adapted to the area's climate.

By this time, however, Haraszthy had disappeared, literally, from the scene. After a business setback during the 1860s, the count lost control of Buena Vista and ventured to Nicaragua to restore his fortune in the sugar and rum industries. While crossing a stream infested with alligators, the count lost his balance and plunged into water below. The body of modern California wine making's first promoter and pioneer was never recovered.

Buena Vista Winery and the nearby Bartholomew Park Winery now occupy Haraszthy's former land, and both have small museums with exhibits celebrating the count's legacy.

Another building holds a small museum. Occasional weekend tours are conducted by docents. ⊠ *W. Spain St., at 3rd St. W* ☎ *707/938–9559* 🖥 *$3, including same-day admission to Sonoma Mission* ⊙ *Fri.–Wed. 10–5.*

Gloria Ferrer Caves and Vineyards. A tasting at Gloria Ferrer is an exercise in elegance: at tables inside the Spanish hacienda–style winery or outside on the terrace (no standing at the bar at Gloria Ferrer), you can take in vistas of gently rolling hills while sipping sparkling and still wines. The Chardonnay and Pinot Noir grapes from the surrounding vineyards are the product of old-world wine-making knowledge—the same family started the sparkling-wine maker Freixenet in 16th-century Spain— and contemporary soil management techniques and clonal research. The tour covers the winery's history and its staff's contributions to advancing wine science. ⊠ *23555 Carneros Hwy./Hwy. 121, Sonoma*

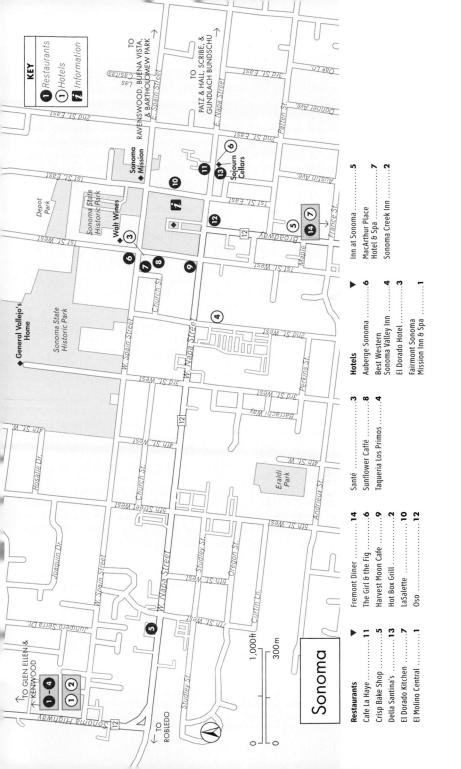

Sonoma

KEY
- ● Restaurants
- ① Hotels
- 🛈 Information

TO GLEN ELLEN & KENWOOD

TO ROBLEDO

RAVENSWOOD, BUENA VISTA, & BARTHOLOMEW PARK

TO PATZ & HALL, SCRIBE, & GUNDLACH BUNDSCHU

General Vallejo's Home

Sonoma State Historic Park

Depot Park

Sonoma State Historic Park

Walt Wines

Sonoma Mission

Sojourn Cellars

Eraldi Park

1,000 ft
300 m

Restaurants ▼
Cafe La Haye **11**
Crisp Bake Shop **5**
Della Santina's **13**
El Dorado Kitchen **7**
El Molino Central **1**

Fremont Diner **14**
The Girl & the Fig **6**
Harvest Moon Cafe **9**
Hot Box Grill **2**
LaSalette **10**
Oso **12**

Santé **3**
Sunflower Caffé **8**
Taqueria Los Primos **4**

Hotels ▼
Auberge Sonoma **6**
Best Western
Sonoma Valley Inn **4**
El Dorado Hotel **3**
Fairmont Sonoma
Mission Inn & Spa **1**

Inn at Sonoma **5**
MacArthur Place
Hotel & Spa **7**
Sonoma Creek Inn **2**

☎ *707/933–1917* ⊕ *www.gloriaferrer.com* ✉ *Tasting $6–$33, tour $20* ⊗ *Daily 10–5; tours at 11, 1, and 3.*

Ravenswood Winery. The punchy motto here is "no wimpy wines," and with its big, bold Zinfandels this winery nearly always succeeds. The Zins are sometimes blended with other varietals grown in the same field (this is called a "field blend"). Ravenswood also produces Bordeaux-style blends, early-harvest Gewürztraminer, and lightly sparkling Moscato. Tours, which focus on viticultural practices, include a barrel tasting of wines in the cellar. To learn even more about the wine-making process, make an appointment for one of the wine-blending sessions. ✉ *18701 Gehricke Rd., off E. Spain St., Sonoma* ☎ *707/933–2332, 888/669–4679* ⊕ *www.ravenswoodwinery.com* ✉ *Tastings $20, tour $20, blending session $50* ⊗ *Daily 10–4:30, tour daily at 10:30 by appointment; blending session by appointment.*

Robledo Family Winery. It's truly a family affair at this winery founded by Reynaldo Robledo Sr., a migrant worker from Michoacán, Mexico: all seven of his sons and two of his daughters—as well as matriarch Maria—are involved in its operations. You're likely to encounter a family member in the tasting room, where you'll learn the immigrant family's inspiring story while sipping Sauvignon Blanc, Pinot Noir, Merlot, Cabernet Sauvignon, and other wines, including a Chardonnay that comes from the vineyard right outside the door. ✉ *21901 Bonness Rd., off Hwy. 116* ☎ *707/939–6903, 888/939–6903* ⊕ *www. robledofamilywinery.com* ✉ *Tastings $10–$15, wine-and-cheese pairing $40* ⊗ *Mon.–Sat. 10–5, Sun. 11–4.*

WHERE TO EAT

$$$
AMERICAN
Fodor'sChoice
★

✕ **Cafe La Haye.** In a postage-stamp-size open kitchen, the skillful chef turns out main courses that star on a small but worthwhile seasonal menu emphasizing local ingredients. Chicken, beef, pasta, and fish get deluxe treatment without fuss or fanfare—the daily roasted chicken and the risotto specials are always good. Butterscotch pudding is a homey signature dessert. The dining room is compact, but the friendly owner, always there to greet diners, maintains a particularly welcoming vibe. ⑤ *Average main: $24* ✉ *140 E. Napa St., at 1st St. E* ☎ *707/935–5994* ⊕ *www.cafelahaye.com* ⊗ *Closed Sun. and Mon. No lunch.*

$
BAKERY

✕ **Crisp Bake Shop.** Only in the Wine Country would your local pastry chef, in this case Andrea Koweek, have honed her skills at The French Laundry. Much of what she bakes—croissants, cupcakes, mini-Bundt cakes, brioche sweet buns with ricotta and blueberries, chocolate sea-salt cookies—is so cute, it's difficult to take that first bite. Bacon, egg, and cheese pies for breakfast and sandwiches for lunch are among the more savory fare, which is overseen by executive chef Moaya Scheiman (also Andrea's husband). ■TIP➔ **Crisp is seven blocks west of Sonoma Plaza, but it's worth the walk or drive.** ⑤ *Average main: $8* ✉ *720 W. Napa St./Hwy. 12, at 7th St. W* ☎ *707/933–9999* ⊕ *www. crispbakeshop.com* ⚲ *Reservations not accepted* ⊗ *No dinner.*

$$
ITALIAN

✕ **Della Santina's.** Just east of the Plaza, Della Santina's serves cuisine influenced by its owners' Tuscan roots (they hail from Lucca). Daily

El Dorado Kitchen's chef Armando Navarro crafts flavorful dishes full of subtle surprises.

fish and veal specials join linguine with pesto, lasagna Bolognese, and other classic northern Italian dishes on the diverse menu. Of special note are the roasted meat dishes and, when available, petrale sole and fresh cracked Dungeness crab. The heated patio out back adds to the setting's down-to-earth charms. **Enoteca Della Santina,** the associated wine bar and retail shop next door, serves wines by the glass and the restaurant's full menu. ⑤ *Average main: $20* ⊠ *133 E. Napa St., near 1st St. E* ☎ *707/935–0576* ⊕ *www.dellasantinas.com.*

$$$

MODERN
AMERICAN

Fodor's Choice

★

✕ **El Dorado Kitchen.** The visual delights at this winning restaurant include its clean lines and handsome decor, but the eye inevitably drifts westward to the open kitchen, where chef Armando Navarro and his diligent crew craft flavorful dishes full of subtle surprises. Focusing on locally sourced ingredients, the menu might include bomba-rice paella awash with seafood and linguica sausage, or duck confit accompanied by farro salad, kale, mushrooms, and almonds. Even a simple dish like truffle-oil fries, liberally sprinkled with Parmesan, charms with its combination of tastes and textures. The noteworthy desserts include profiteroles with toasted marshmallow and chocolate ganache, and cornbread French toast with strawberries and buttermilk sherbet. ⑤ *Average main: $26* ⊠ *El Dorado Hotel, 405 1st St. W, at W. Spain St.* ☎ *707/996–3030* ⊕ *www.eldoradosonoma.com/restaurant.*

$

MEXICAN

✕ **El Molino Central.** Fans throughout the Bay Area purchase Karen Waikiki's tortillas and tamales—handmade from organic ingredients that include stone-ground heritage corn—at farmers' markets and other venues. At her El Molino restaurant she sells the full lineup, which includes tamales filled with Niman Ranch pork and guajillo chili, chicken and mole, black bean or roasted green chili and Monterey Jack, and barbecue chipotle bean with white cheddar. There are also nondairy editions. Tacos might be filled with beer-battered fish or crispy beef, and enchiladas and burritos are also on the menu. A breakfast favorite is chilaquiles Merida, with soft-scrambled eggs and tangy-smoky-spicy roasted tomato and chipotle salsa. ■TIP→ **Seating is sparse indoors (there are also tented and unprotected tables out back), so to-go is often the way to go; service can be erratic.** ⑤ *Average main: $11* ⊠ *11 Central Ave., at Hwy. 12, Boyes Hot Springs* ☎ *707/939–1010* 🍴 *Reservations not accepted.*

$$ ✕**Fremont Diner.** Locals mix with tourists at this retro-yet-au-courant
SOUTHERN diner whose menu favors rock-around-the-clock Southern favorites. With hefty breakfasts such as shrimp and grits with bacon, sausage, and poached eggs, no one leaves the Fremont hungry. Ditto for lunch, at which oyster po'boys, chili cheese dogs, and handmade hamburgers (no prefab patties here) fortify patrons for the next round of wine tasting. There's no let-up at dinner, where shrimp and grits reappear minus the eggs, and the Nashville Chicken puts a spicy spin on a down-home classic. The old-timey desserts include buttermilk cake with caramel, baked in a skillet, and butterscotch pudding. ⑤ *Average main: $18* ⊠ *2698 Fremont Dr., at Hwy. 121* ☎ *707/938–7370* ⊕ *www.thefremontdiner. com* 🍴 *Reservations not accepted* ☺ *No dinner Mon.–Wed.*

$$$ ✕**The Girl & the Fig.** Chef Sondra Bernstein transformed the historic bar
FRENCH   room of the Sonoma Hotel into a hot spot for inventive French cooking. You can always find a dish with the signature figs on the menu, whether it's a fig-and-arugula salad or an aperitif blending sparkling wine with fig liqueur. Also look for duck confit, a burger with matchstick fries, and wild flounder meunière. The wine list is notable for its emphasis on Rhône varietals, and a counter in the bar area sells artisanal cheese platters for eating here as well as cheese by the pound to go. The indulgent Sunday brunch lineup includes salmon eggs Benedict and croques monsieur with applewood-smoked ham. ⑤ *Average main: $24* ⊠ *Sonoma Hotel, 110 W. Spain St., at 1st St. W* ☎ *707/938–3634* ⊕ *www.thegirlandthefig.com.*

$$$ ✕**Harvest Moon Cafe.** It's easy to feel like one of the family at this little
AMERICAN restaurant with an odd, zigzagging layout. Diners seated at one of the
Fodor's Choice two tiny bars chat with the servers like old friends, but the husband-and-
★   wife team in the kitchen is serious about the food, much of which relies on local produce. The ever-changing menu might include homey dishes such as grilled pork loin with crispy polenta and artichokes, Niman Ranch rib-eye steak with a tomatillo salsa and Zinfandel reduction, or pan-seared Hawaiian Ono with jasmine rice, and eggplant. Everything is so perfectly executed and the vibe is so genuinely warm that a visit here is deeply satisfying. ■TIP→ **A spacious back patio with tables arranged around a fountain more than doubles the seating; a heated tent keeps this area warm in winter.** ⑤ *Average main: $25* ⊠ *487 1st St. W, at W. Napa St.* ☎ *707/933–8160* ⊕ *www.harvestmooncafesonoma. com* ☺ *Closed Tues. No lunch.*

$$$ ✕**Hot Box Grill.** Comfort foods aren't often described as *nuanced,* but
MODERN   the term aptly describes the locally sourced preparations at this modest
AMERICAN roadside restaurant. Take the fries (but not too many): they're cooked in

duck fat and served with malt-vinegar aioli, lending them a richness that lingers pleasingly in the memory. There's lots of frying going on—even Cornish game hen gets the treatment. Up against these dishes, the fish selections, wild-caught salmon, perhaps, or petrale sole or mahimahi—seem almost dainty. The appealing appetizers include spicy ahi tuna with a ponzu sauce, avocado mousse, and crispy wontons. The signature dessert, a creamy, high-test tiramisu, is amply dosed with mascarpone, rum, and espresso. ⑤ *Average main: $24* ✉ *18350 Sonoma Hwy./Hwy. 12, at Hawthorne St., Boyes Hot Springs* ☎ *707/939–8383* ⊕ *www.hotboxgrill.com* ☾ *Closed Mon. and Tues. No lunch.*

$$$
PORTUGUESE
✕ **LaSalette.** Born in the Azores and raised in Sonoma, chef-owner Manuel Azevedo serves dishes inspired by his native Portugal in this warmly decorated spot. The best seats are on a patio along an alleyway off Sonoma Plaza. Boldly flavored dishes such as pork tenderloin *recheado*, stuffed with olives and almonds and topped with a Port sauce, might be followed by a dish of rice pudding with Madeira-braised figs or a Port from the varied list. ■TIP➔ The daily seafood specials are well worth a try, especially the whole fish. ⑤ *Average main: $24* ✉ *452 1st St. E, near E. Spain St.* ☎ *707/938–1927* ⊕ *www.lasalette-restaurant.com.*

$$$$
MODERN
AMERICAN
✕ **Oso.** Owner-chef David Bush, who achieved national recognition for his food and wine pairings at St. Francis Winery, struck out on his own in late 2014, opening this restaurant whose name, Spanish for "bear," acknowledges the nearby spot where rebels raised a flag depicting a bear and declared California's independence from Mexico. Bush serves tapas-size dishes à la carte and prepares a five-course tasting menu with optional wine pairings. An early menu included pickled shrimp with a red cabbage, kale, and peanut slaw à la carte and Syrah-braised short ribs for the tasting. Oso's contemporary barlike space's design incorporates materials reclaimed from previous incarnations of its building, erected in the 1890s as a livery stable. ■TIP➔ Reservations are required for the tasting but aren't accepted otherwise. ⑤ *Average main: $32* ✉ *9 E. Napa St., at Broadway* ☎ *707/931–6926* ⊕ *ososonoma.com* ☾ *No lunch.*

$$$$
AMERICAN
Fodor'sChoice
★
✕ **Santé.** This elegant dining room has evolved into a destination restaurant through its focus on seasonal and locally sourced ingredients. The room is understated, with dark walls and soft lighting, but the food is anything but. Dishes such as the Sonoma Liberty duck breast and confit leg, served with pearl barley "risotto," sweet carrot puree, and maple duck jus, are sophisticated without being fussy. Others, like the sampler of Niman Ranch beef that includes a petite filet mignon, a skirt steak, and braised pavé beef à la bourguignonne, are pure decadence. The restaurant offers a seasonal tasting menu ($149). ⑤ *Average main: $43* ✉ *Fairmont Sonoma Mission Inn & Spa, 100 Boyes Blvd./Hwy. 12, 2½ miles north of Sonoma Plaza, Boyes Hot Springs* ☎ *707/938–9000* ⊕ *www.santediningroom.com* ☾ *No lunch.*

$
AMERICAN
✕ **Sunflower Caffé.** The food at this casual eatery, mostly salads and sandwiches, is simple but satisfying. Highlights include the smoked duck breast sandwich, served on a baguette and slathered with caramelized onions. A meal of soup and local cheeses is a good option if you just want to nibble. Both the pretty patio, which is in the back,

and the sidewalk seating area facing Sonoma Plaza are equipped with heating lamps and get plenty of shade, so they're comfortable in all but the most inclement weather. Cheerful artworks brighten up the interior, where locals hunker over their computers and take advantage of the free Wi-Fi. Omelets and waffles are the stars at breakfast. $ *Average main: $13* ⊠ *421 1st St. W, at W. Spain St.* ☎ *707/996–6645* ⊕ *www. sonomasunflower.com* ☾ *No dinner.*

$ ✕ **Taqueria Los Primos.** The ambience at this Mexican restaurant is decid-
MEXICAN edly downscale, but the food is tasty and there's plenty of it. Chefs from Sonoma's fancy restaurants have been known to slip over for carnitas, barbecue goat, and chicken, beef, and pulled-pork tacos. The breakfast burritos, egg plates, and other morning fare will fortify you for a day of wine tasting. ■ TIP➔ **The easiest place to park is south of the restaurant on Hawthorne Avenue.** $ *Average main: $10* ⊠ *18375 Hwy. 12, at Hawthorne Ave., Boyes Hot Springs* ☎ *707/935–3546* ⚊ *Reservations not accepted.*

WHERE TO STAY

$$$ ⊤ **Auberge Sonoma.** If you are traveling in a group of three or four, or
RENTAL just prefer lodgings that feel more like home, consider the two-bed-room suites at this charmer just off Sonoma Plaza. **Pros:** good value for couples traveling together; beautifully appointed; close to Sonoma Plaza shops, restaurants, and tasting rooms. **Cons:** two-night minimum (three on summer weekends). $ *Rooms from: $359* ⊠ *151 E. Napa St.* ☎ *707/939–5670 voice mail* ⊕ *www.aubergesonoma.com* ↴ *3 2-bed-room suites* ⦶ *No meals.*

$$ ⊤ **Best Western Sonoma Valley Inn.** This motel just off Sonoma Plaza has
HOTEL enthusiastic staffers who provide fine service, and public areas, includ-ing the lobby and a pool and spa, that are inviting, if not elegant. **Pros:** good value; complimentary continental breakfast; coupons for complimentary tastings at local wineries; within walking distance of Sonoma Plaza shops and restaurants. **Cons:** small fitness center; public areas nicer than the rooms; convention facilities and rooms in front can be noisy. $ *Rooms from: $269* ⊠ *550 2nd St. W* ☎ *800/334–5784, 707/938–9200* ⊕ *www.sonomavalleyinn.com* ↴ *73 rooms, 7 suites* ⦶ *Breakfast.*

$ ⊤ **El Dorado Hotel.** Rooms in this remodeled 1843 building strike a spare,
B&B/INN modern pose with their pristine white bedding, but the Mexican-tile floors hint at Sonoma's Mission-era past. **Pros:** stylish for the price; hip on-site restaurant; good café for breakfast; central location. **Cons:** rooms are small; lighting could be better; noisy. $ *Rooms from: $200* ⊠ *405 1st St. W* ☎ *707/996–3030* ⊕ *www.eldoradosonoma.com/hotel* ↴ *27 rooms* ⦶ *No meals.*

$$$$ ⊤ **Fairmont Sonoma Mission Inn & Spa.** The real draw at this Mission-style
RESORT resort is the extensive, swank spa with its array of massages and treat-ments, some designed for couples. **Pros:** enormous spa; excellent restaurant; free shuttle to downtown. **Cons:** standard rooms on the smaller side; lacks intimacy of similarly priced options. $ *Rooms from: $439* ⊠ *100 Boyes Blvd./Hwy. 12, 2½ miles north of Sonoma Plaza, Boyes*

Hot Springs ☎ *707/938–9000* ⊕ *www.fairmont.com/sonoma* ⤳ *166 rooms, 60 suites* ⊖| *No meals.*

$$
B&B/INN

🏨 **Inn at Sonoma.** They don't skimp on the little luxuries here: wine and cheese is served every evening in the lobby, and the cheerfully painted rooms are warmed by gas fireplaces. **Pros:** last-minute specials are a great deal; free soda available in the lobby; free Wi-Fi. **Cons:** on a busy street rather than right on the plaza. ⑤ *Rooms from: $220* ⊠ *630 Broadway* ☎ *707/939–1340, 888/568–9818* ⊕ *www.innatsonoma.com* ⤳ *27 rooms* ⊖| *Breakfast.*

$$$$
HOTEL
Fodor's Choice
★

🏨 **MacArthur Place Hotel & Spa.** Guests at this 7-acre boutique property five blocks south of Sonoma Plaza bask in ritzy seclusion in plush accommodations set amid landscaped gardens. **Pros:** secluded garden setting; high-style furnishings; on-site steak house. **Cons:** a bit of a walk from the plaza; some traffic noise audible in street-side rooms. ⑤ *Rooms from: $425* ⊠ *29 E. MacArthur St.* ☎ *707/938–2929, 800/722–1866* ⊕ *www.macarthurplace.com* ⤳ *62 rooms, 2 cottage suites* ⊖| *Breakfast.*

$
B&B/INN
FAMILY

🏨 **Sonoma Creek Inn.** The small but cheerful rooms at this motel-style inn are individually decorated with painted wooden armoires, cozy quilts, and brightly colored contemporary artwork. **Pros:** clean, well-lighted bathrooms; lots of charm for the price; popular with bicyclists. **Cons:** office not staffed 24 hours a day; a 10-minute drive from Sonoma Plaza. ⑤ *Rooms from: $145* ⊠ *239 Boyes Blvd., off Hwy. 12* ☎ *707/939–9463, 888/712–1289* ⊕ *www.sonomacreekinn.com* ⤳ *16 rooms* ⊖| *No meals.*

NIGHTLIFE AND PERFORMING ARTS

Aside from the hotel and restaurant bars, the nightlife scene in Sonoma is pretty subdued. The bar inside the El Dorado Kitchen is a good spot for a drink, as is the bar at the Ledson Hotel across Sonoma Plaza. The Epicurean Connection hosts live music from Wednesday through Saturday from about 7:30 to 10.

Sebastiani Theatre. This theater, built on Sonoma Plaza in 1934 by Italian immigrant and entrepreneur Samuele Sebastiani, schedules first-run films, as well as occasional musical and theatrical performances. ⊠ *476 1st St. E, near W. Spain St.* ☎ *707/996–2020* ⊕ *www.sebastianitheatre.com.*

Swiss Hotel. Old-timers head to the hotel's old-timey bar for a blast of Glariffee, a cold and potent cousin to Irish coffee that loosens the tongue. ⊠ *18 W. Spain St., at 1st St.* W ☎ *707/938–2884* ⊕ *www.swiss hotelsonoma.com.*

SHOPPING

Fodor's Choice
★

Chateau Sonoma. The fancy furniture, lighting fixtures, and objets d'art at this upscale shop make it a dangerous place to enter: after just a few minutes you may find yourself reconsidering your entire home's aesthetic. The owner's keen eye for style and sense of whimsy make a visit here a delight. ⊠ *153 W. Napa St., near 2nd St.* W ☎ *707/935–8553* ⊕ *www.chateausonoma.com.*

The Epicurean Connection. In addition to selling Délice de La Vallée, her award-winning cheese made from triple-cream cow and goat milk, Sheana Davis offers jams, sauces, tapenades, and other toppings from local producers. She also sells sandwiches and sweets, and stages good live music from Wednesday through Sunday evening and on Sunday afternoon. ⌧ *122 W. Napa St., at 1st St.* ☎ *707/935–7960* ⊕ *www. theepicureanconnection.com* ☉ *Closed Mon.*

Sign of the Bear. This locally owned shop sells the latest and greatest in kitchenware and cookware, as well as a few Wine Country–theme items, such as lazy Susans made from wine barrels. ⌧ *435 1st St. W, near W. Spain St.* ☎ *707/996–3722.*

Sonoma Cheese Factory. The town's touristy cheese shop offers samples of many local types. The store has everything you need for a picnic, from sandwiches to wine to homemade fudge. ⌧ *2 E. Spain St., near 1st St. E* ☎ *800/535–2855* ⊕ *www.sonomacheesefactory.com.*

Fodor's Choice ★ **Sonoma Valley Certified Farmers Market.** To discover just how bountiful the Sonoma landscape is—and how talented its farmers and food artisans are—head to Depot Park, just north of the Sonoma Plaza, on Friday morning. From April through October, the market gets extra play on Tuesday evening in Sonoma Plaza. ⌧ *Depot Park, 1st St. W, at Sonoma Bike Path* ☎ *707/538–7023* ⊕ *www.svcfm.org.*

Vella Cheese Company. A bit north and east of Sonoma Plaza, this old-world Italian cheese shop has been making superb cheeses, including raw-milk cheddars and several varieties of jack, since 1931. A bonus: plenty of free samples. ⌧ *315 2nd St. E, ½ block north of E. Spain St.* ☎ *707/938–3232, 800/848–0505* ⊕ *vellacheese.com* ☉ *Closed Sun.*

Williams-Sonoma. Yes, W-S is everywhere, but this location, opened in late 2014, occupies the original storefront where in 1956 Chuck Williams debuted the famous kitchenware brand. The orignal, unhyphenated, pineapple-logo sign hangs outside. ⌧ *605 Broadway, at Patten St.* ☎ *707/939–8974* ⊕ *www.williams-sonoma.com.*

SPAS

Willow Stream Spa at Fairmont Sonoma Mission Inn & Spa. With 40,000 square feet and 30 treatment rooms, the Wine Country's largest spa provides every amenity you could possibly want, including pools and hot tubs fed by local thermal springs. Although the place bustles with patrons in summer and on some weekends, the vibe is always soothing. The signature bathing ritual includes an exfoliating shower, dips in two mineral-water soaking pools, an herbal steam, a dry sauna, and cool-down showers. Other popular treatments include the warm ginger-oil float, which involves relaxation in a weightless environment, and the perennially popular caviar facial. The most requested room among couples is outfitted with a two-person copper bathtub. ⌧ *100 Boyes Blvd./Hwy. 12, 2½ miles north of Sonoma Plaza, Boyes Hot Springs* ☎ *707/938–9000* ⊕ *www.fairmont.com/sonoma/willow-stream* ⬚ *Treatments $65–$485.*

The Wine Country by Bicycle

Thanks to the scenic country roads winding through the region, bicycling is a nearly perfect way to get around the Wine Country (the lack of designated bike lanes in most places notwithstanding). Whether you're interested in an easy spin to a few wineries or a strenuous haul up a mountainside, there's a way to make it happen.

Cycle shops in most towns will rent you a bike and helmet for the day. In addition to providing maps and advice on the least-trafficked roads, staffers can typically recommend a route based on your interests and fitness level.

If you're concerned about the logistics of your trip, consider joining a one-day or multiday bike tour, which includes lunch, a guide, and a "sag wagon" in case you tire before you reach your destination.

SPORTS AND THE OUTDOORS

Sonoma Valley Bike Tours. This offshoot of Napa Valley Bike Tours a mile south of Sonoma Plaza rents bikes, conducts guided bicycle tours of wineries, and has a self-guided-tour option. ⌂ *1245 Broadway, at Woodworth La.* ☎ *707/996–2453* ⊕ *sonomavalleybiketours.com* ⊠ *From $25 for 2 hrs for bike rentals, $99 for self-guided tour from $109 for guided tours.*

Wine Country Cyclery. You can rent comfort/hybrid, tandem, and road bikes by the hour or the day at this mellow shop west of the plaza. ⌂ *262 W. Napa St., at 3rd St.* W ☎ *707/996–6800* ⊕ *winecountry cyclery.com* ⊠ *From $10 an hr, $30 a day.*

GLEN ELLEN

7 miles north of Sonoma.

Craggy Glen Ellen epitomizes the difference between the Napa and Sonoma valleys. Whereas small Napa towns like St. Helena get their charm from upscale boutiques and restaurants lined up along well-groomed sidewalks, in Glen Ellen the crooked streets are shaded with stands of old oak trees and occasionally bisected by the Sonoma and Calabasas creeks. Tucked among the trees of a narrow canyon, where Sonoma Mountain and the Mayacamas pinch in the valley floor, Glen Ellen looks more like a town of the Sierra foothills gold country than a Wine Country village.

Wine has been part of Glen Ellen since the 1840s, when a French immigrant, Joshua Chauvet, planted grapes and built a winery and the valley's first distillery. The winery machinery was powered by steam, and the boilers were fueled with wood from local oaks. In 1881 Chauvet built a stone winery to house his operations. Other valley farmers followed Chauvet's example, and grape growing took off. Wine was even made during Prohibition, when the locals took a liberal view of the 200 gallons each family was allowed to produce for personal consumption. There are still dozens of wineries in the area that beg to be visited, but sometimes it's hard not to succumb to Glen Ellen's slow pace and simply lounge poolside at your lodging or linger over a leisurely picnic. The renowned cook and food writer M. F. K. Fisher, who lived and worked in Glen Ellen for 22 years until her death in 1992, would surely have approved. (Hunter S. Thompson, who lived here for a spell before he became famous might not: he found the place too sedate.)

Glen Ellen's most famous resident, however, was Jack London, who epitomized the town's rugged spirit.

GETTING HERE AND AROUND

To get to Glen Ellen from Sonoma, drive west on Spain Street. After about a mile, take Highway 12 for 7 miles to Arnold Drive, which deposits you in the middle of town. Many of Glen Ellen's restaurants and inns are along a half-mile stretch of Arnold Drive. Sonoma Transit Bus 30 and Bus 38 serve Glen Ellen from Sonoma and Kenwood.

4

EXPLORING

TOP ATTRACTIONS

Fodor's Choice ★ **Benziger Family Winery.** One of the best-known Sonoma County wineries sits on a sprawling estate in a bowl with 360-degree sun exposure, the benefits of which are explored on popular tram tours that depart several times daily. Guides explain Benziger's biodynamic farming practices and give you a glimpse of the extensive cave system. The regular tram tour costs $25; another tour costing $50 concludes with a seated tasting. Noted for its Chardonnay, Cabernet Sauvignon, Merlot, Pinot Noir, and Sauvignon Blanc wines, the winery is a beautiful spot for a picnic. ■TIP→ Reserve a seat on the tram tour through the winery's website or arrive early in the day on summer weekends and during harvest season. ⊠ *1883 London Ranch Rd., off Arnold Dr.* ☎ *707/935–3000, 888/490–2739* ⊕ *www.benziger.com* ⊠ *Tastings $15–$40, tours $25–$50* ⊙ *Daily 10–5; tours daily 11–3:30 except noon on the ½ hr (reservation recommended).*

Fodor's Choice ★ **Jack London State Historic Park.** The pleasures are both pastoral and intellectual at the late writer Jack London's beloved Beauty Ranch. You could easily spend the afternoon hiking the 20-plus miles of trails that loop through meadows and stands of oaks, redwoods, and other trees. Manuscripts and personal artifacts depicting London's travels are on view at the House of Happy Walls Museum, which provides a tantalizing overview of the author's life and literary passions. A short hike away lie the ruins of Wolf House, which mysteriously burned down just before the writer was to move in. Also open to the public are a few farm outbuildings and the completely restored Cottage, a wood-framed building where London penned many of his later works. He's buried on the property. ⊠ *2400 London Ranch Rd., off Arnold Dr.* ☎ *707/938–5216* ⊕ *www.jacklondonpark.com* ⊠ *Parking $10 ($5 walk-in or bike), includes admission to museum; cottage $4* ⊙ *Mar.–Nov. park daily 9:30–5, museum 10–5, cottage noon–4; Dec.–Feb., Thurs.–Mon. park 9:30–5, museum 10–5, cottage noon–4.*

Benziger tram tours take to the fields to show biodynamic farming techniques in action.

Loxton Cellars. Back in the day, when tasting rooms were low-tech and the winemaker often poured the wines, the winery experience unfolded pretty much the way it does at Loxton Cellars today. The personable owner, Chris Loxton, who's on hand many days, crafts some stand-out Zinfandels, Syrahs, and a Cabernet Sauvignon, and some regulars swear by the delicate Pinot Noir from Russian River Valley grapes and the seductively smooth Syrah Port. To learn more about Loxton's wine-making philosophy and practices take the tour ($20), which is followed by a seated tasting. ■TIP➜ Walk-ins can sample a few current releases for free, with an appointment you can taste older and limited-release wines ($15). ✉ *11466 Dunbar Rd., at Hwy. 12* ☎ *707/935–7221* ⊕ *www.loxtonwines.com* ✉ *Tastings free–$15, tour $20* ☉ *Daily 11–5, tours on weekends by appointment.*

WORTH NOTING

Arrowood Vineyards & Winery. Its Sonoma Coast Chardonnay and Cabernet Sauvignon built a steady following for this winery between Glen Ellen and Kenwood. Winemaker Heidi von der Mehden also crafts single-vineyard wines from each of these varietals. The Monte Rosso Vineyard Cabernet, worth trying if it's being poured, comes from grapes grown in the recently minted Moon Mountain appellation. For $20 you can taste current releases; small-lot and older wines, some sold only in the tasting room, are served at reserve tastings ($25). ■TIP➜ In lieu of a tasting you can buy a glass of wine to enjoy on the wrap-around veranda outside the tasting room. ✉ *14347 Sonoma Hwy./ Hwy. 12* ☎ *707/935–2600, 800/938–5170* ⊕ *www.arrowoodwinery.*

com ✉ *Tastings $20–$35* ⊙ *Daily 10–4:30, reservation required for cheese-wine pairing only.*

B.R. Cohn. Classic-rock fans acknowledge this Glen Ellen winery's musical chops—Bruce Cohn, the longtime manager of the Doobie Brothers, founded it in 1984—but the oenological pedigree is equally noteworthy: the first winemaker was the now famous consultant Helen Turley, and Pinot Noir specialist Merry Edwards followed her. The wines, still crafted in Turley's fruit-forward style (by Tom Montgomery since 2004) include Sauvignon Blanc, Chardonnay, and Riesling whites, and Cabernet Sauvignon, Petite Sirah, Primitivo, and Zinfandel reds. A 1920s residence was expanded to create the tasting room, which bustles on most weekend afternoons. Between sips you can peruse Cohn's rock memorabilia. ■**TIP**➔ **A gourmet shop near the patio outside the tasting room sells olive oil from the property's 19th-century olive trees, along with vinegars and other food items.** ✉ *15000 Sonoma Hwy./Hwy. 12, ½ mile north of Madrone Rd.* ☎ *707/938–4064* ⊕ *brcohn.com* ✉ *Tastings $15–$50, tour and tasting $20* ⊙ *Daily 10–5; tour and some tastings by appointment only.*

WHERE TO EAT

$$
ITALIAN
Fodor'sChoice
★
Aventine Glen Ellen. A Wine Country cousin to chef Adolfo Veronese's same-named San Francisco and Hollywood establishments, this Italian restaurant occupies an 1839 sawmill from California's Mexican period. Evidence of the building's early lives—in 1856 it was converted into a gristmill—can be seen in the old-redwood walls and exposed ceiling beams. Veronese's varied menu includes a half dozen pizzas (the seasonal one with black truffle honey, béchamel, and wild arugula is a savory masterpiece), an equal number of pasta dishes, a risotto of the day, and several meat and fish entrées. All are deftly constructed, and the chicken parmigiana has aroused envy among local Sicilian grandmothers. ■**TIP**➔ **In good weather you can dine on a patio that overlooks Sonoma Creek, which powered the mill in days of yore.** Ⓢ *Average main: $19* ✉ *Jack London Village, 14301 Arnold Dr., ¾ mile south of downtown* ☎ *707/934–8911* ⊕ *www.aventineglenellen.com* ⊙ *Closed Mon. No lunch.*

$$
FRENCH
The Fig Cafe. The compact menu at this cheerful bistro, a Glen Ellen fixture, focuses on California and French comfort food—pot roast and duck confit, for instance, as well as thin-crust pizza. Steamed mussels are served with terrific crispy fries, which also accompany the sirloin burger. Weekend brunch brings out locals and tourists for French toast, pizza with applewood-smoked bacon and poached eggs, corned-beef hash, and other delights. ■**TIP**➔ **The unusual no-corkage-fee policy makes this a great place to drink the wine you discovered down the road.** Ⓢ *Average main: $18* ✉ *13690 Arnold Dr., at O'Donnell La.* ☎ *707/938–2130* ⊕ *www.thefigcafe.com* ✍ *Reservations not accepted* ⊙ *No lunch weekdays.*

$$
ECLECTIC
Glen Ellen Inn Oyster Grill & Martini Bar. Tucked inside a creekside 1940s cottage, this cozy restaurant exudes romance, especially if you sit in the shady garden or on the patio strung with tiny lights. After taking the

Jack London Country

The rugged, rakish author and adventurer Jack London is perhaps best known for his travels to Alaska and his exploits in the Pacific, which he immortalized in tales such as *Call of the Wild, White Fang,* and *South Sea Tales.* But he loved no place so well as the hills of eastern Sonoma County, where he spent most of his thirties and where he died in 1916 at the age of 40.

Between 1905 and 1916 London bought seven parcels of land totaling 1,400 acres, which he dubbed Beauty Ranch. When he wasn't off traveling, he dedicated most of his time to cultivating the land and raising livestock. He also maintained a few acres of wine grapes for his personal use.

DREAMS AND MYSTERIES

In 1913, London rhapsodized about his beloved ranch near Glen Ellen, writing, "The grapes on a score of rolling hills are red with autumn flame. Across Sonoma Mountain wisps of sea fog are stealing. The afternoon sun smolders in the drowsy sky. I have everything to make me glad I am alive. I am filled with dreams and mysteries."

Much of Beauty Ranch is now preserved as Jack London State Historic Park, worth visiting not only for its museum and other glimpses into London's life but also for the trails that skirt vineyards and meander through a forest of Douglas fir, coastal redwoods, oak, and madrones. London and his wife spent two years here constructing their dream house, Wolf House, before it burned down one hot August night in 1913, just days before they were scheduled to move in.

A look at the remaining stone walls and fireplaces gives you a sense of the building's grand scale. Within, a fireproof basement vault was to hold London's manuscripts. Elsewhere in the park stands the unusually posh pigsty that London's neighbors called the Pig Palace.

Outside the park, London-related attractions are relatively few. Downhill from the park entrance is the Jack London Saloon, which first opened in 1905 and has walls covered with photographs and other London memorabilia.

Parts of Beauty Ranch are still owned by London's descendants, who grow Cabernet Sauvignon, Zinfandel, and Merlot. For a taste of the wines made from these grapes, head a few miles north to Kenwood Vineyards, which uses them to produce Jack London Vineyard reserve wines.

edge off your hunger with some oysters on the half shell and an ice-cold martini, order from a menu that plucks elements from California, French, and other cuisines. You might find ginger tempura calamari with grilled pineapple salsa, or hanger steak with chimichurri sauce and a side of garlic fries. Desserts tend toward the indulgent; witness the signature sundae of French vanilla ice cream rolled in toasted coconut and served with a bittersweet caramel sauce. $ *Average main: $21* ⌧ *13670 Arnold Dr., at O'Donnell La.* ☎ *707/996–6409* ⊕ *www.glenelleninn. com* ☽ *No lunch Wed.*

$$ ✕**Glen Ellen Star.** Chef Ari Weiswasser honed his craft at The French
ECLECTIC Laundry, Daniel, and other bastions of culinary finesse, but the goal at
Fodor's Choice his Wine Country boîte is haute-rustic cuisine, much of which emerges
★ from a wood-fired oven that burns a steady 600°F. Pizzas such as the
crisp-crusted, richly sauced Margherita thrive in the torrid heat, as do
root and other vegetables roasted in small iron skillets. Ditto for entrées
that include juicy, tender roasted whole fish. Weiswasser signs each
dish with a sauce, emulsion, or sly blend of spices that jazzes things
up without upstaging the primary ingredient. The restaurant's decor
is equally restrained, with an open-beam ceiling, exposed hardwood
floors, and utilitarian seating. ■ **TIP→ Many regulars perch on a stool at
the kitchen-view counter to watch the chefs work.** ⓢ *Average main:
$22 ⊠ 13648 Arnold Dr., at Warm Springs Rd.* ☎ *707/343–1384* ⊕ *glen
ellenstar.com* ⌘ *Reservations essential* ⊗ *No lunch.*

$$$$ ✕**Olive & Vine.** With the cooks in the open kitchen backed by rows
MODERN of green-glazed tiles and lit like actors on a stage, there's a touch of
AMERICAN the theatrical to Olive & Vine, owner-chef Catherine Venturini's high-
ceilinged restaurant inside the former cask room of the historic Glen
Ellen Winery. The show these days revolves around what Venturini
calls "Sonoma style" cooking that emphasizes local ingredients. One
of the best examples of her approach initiates many a meal here: black
cod and bok choy dumplings in a broth of miso, lemongrass, and kaffir
lime that gracefully incorporates its pan-Asian influences. The entrées
change with the season, but Liberty duck served two ways—pan-seared
breast and confit leg—is frequently on the menu. The well-conceived
wine list favors California but heads farther afield. ⓢ *Average main:
$31 ⊠ 14301 Arnold Dr., ¾ miles south of downtown* ☎ *707/996–9152*
⊕ *oliveandvine.com.*

WHERE TO STAY

$ ⊡**Beltane Ranch.** On a slope of the Mayacamas range a few miles from
B&B/INN Glen Ellen, this 1892 ranch house, shaded by magnificent oak trees,
contains charmingly old-fashioned rooms, each individually deco-
rated with antiques and original artwork by noted artists. **Pros:** casual,
friendly atmosphere; reasonable prices; beautiful grounds with ancient
oak trees. **Cons:** downstairs rooms get some noise from upstairs rooms;
ceiling fans instead of air-conditioning. ⓢ *Rooms from: $195 ⊠ 11775
Sonoma Hwy./Hwy. 12* ☎ *707/996–6501* ⊕ *www.beltaneranch.com*
⌑ *3 rooms, 2 suites, 1 cottage* ⦿*Breakfast.*

$$ ⊡**Gaige House.** Asian objets d'art and leather club chairs cozied up to
B&B/INN the lobby fireplace are just a few of the graceful touches in this luxuri-
Fodor's Choice ous but understated bed-and-breakfast. **Pros:** beautiful lounge areas;
★ lots of privacy; excellent service; full breakfasts, afternoon wine and
appetizers. **Cons:** sound carries in the main house; the least expensive
rooms are on the small side. ⓢ *Rooms from: $275 ⊠ 13540 Arnold
Dr.* ☎ *707/935–0237, 800/935–0237* ⊕ *www.gaige.com* ⌑ *10 rooms,
13 suites* ⦿*Breakfast.*

4

$$
B&B/INN
Fodor's Choice
★

☷ **Olea Hotel.** The husband-and-wife team of Ashish and Sia Patel operate this boutique lodging that's at once sophisticated and down-home country casual. **Pros:** beautiful style; welcoming staff; chef-prepared breakfasts; complimentary wine throughout stay. **Cons:** fills up quickly on weekends; minor road noise in some rooms. ⑤ *Rooms from: $288* ⊠ *5131 Warm Springs Rd., west off Arnold Dr.* ☎ *707/996–5131* ⊕ *www.oleahotel.com* ➳ *10 rooms, 2 cottages* ◎ *Breakfast.*

KENWOOD

4 miles north of Glen Ellen.

Tiny Kenwood consists of little more than a few restaurants, shops, tasting rooms, and a historic train depot, now used for private events. But hidden in this pretty landscape of meadows and woods at the north end of Sonoma Valley are several good wineries, most just off the Sonoma Highway. Among the varietals grown here at the foot of the Sugarloaf Mountains are Sauvignon Blanc, Chardonnay, Zinfandel, and Cabernet Sauvignon.

GETTING HERE AND AROUND
To get to Kenwood from Glen Ellen, head northeast on Arnold Drive and north on Highway 12. Sonoma Transit Bus 30 and Bus 38 serve Kenwood from Glen Ellen and Sonoma.

EXPLORING

TOP ATTRACTIONS
B Wise Vineyards Cellar. Although the stylish roadside tasting room of this producer of small-lot red wines sits on the valley floor in Kenwood, B Wise's winery and vineyards, 8½ miles to the southeast, occupy a prime spot high in the new Moon Mountain appellation. Owner-winemaker Brion Wise made his name crafting big, bold Cabernets. One comes from Wise's mountain estate and another from the nearby Monte Rosso Vineyard, some of whose Cabernet vines are among California's oldest. These hearty mountain-fruit Cabs contrast pleasingly with a suppler one from the Napa Valley's Coombsville AVA. Wise also makes estate Syrah, Petite Sirah, Petit Verdot, and Zinfandel wines, along with Sonoma Coast and Willamette Valley (Oregon) Pinot Noirs and several red blends. ⊠ *9077 Sonoma Hwy., at Shaw Ave.* ☎ *707/282–9169* ⊕ *www.bwisevineyards.com* ▨ *Tastings $15–$25* ⊙ *Daily 10:30–5:30.*

Chateau St. Jean. At the foot of the Mayacamas Mountains stretch the impeccably groomed grounds of Chateau St. Jean, an old-country estate. Pick up a map in the tasting room: it will identify many of the flowers, trees, and hedges lining the neat pathways in the formal gardens. After a spin around the grounds, whose style harmonizes with the sprawling Mediterranean-style villa, step inside for a tasting of fine whites like Chardonnay and Fumé Blanc and reds that include Pinot Noir, Cabernet Sauvignon, Merlot, and Syrah. The unusually large gift shop sells clothing and housewares, including a fully equipped picnic backpack. Daily tours (weather permitting) focus on the garden. ⊠ *8555 Sonoma*

Hwy./Hwy. 12 ☏ *707/833–4134* ⊕ *www.chateaustjean.com* ✉ *Tastings $15–$45, tour $20* ⏱ *Daily 10–5, tour daily at 11 and 1; tour and some tastings by appointment.*

Deerfield Ranch Winery. The focus at Deerfield is on producing "clean wines"—ones low in histamines

WORD OF MOUTH

"In Kenwood, you must do the Mountain Top Tasting at Kunde—the view is spectacular." —juliecav

and sulfites—the better to eliminate the headaches and allergic reactions some red-wine drinkers experience. Winemaker Robert Rex accomplishes this goal with no loss of flavor or complexity. Deerfield wines are bold and fruit-forward, with a long finish. The lush DRX and Meritage Bordeaux-style red blends invite contemplation about the vineyards, weather, and wine-making skills involved in their creation. To sip these and other wines, including a finely tuned blend of four white grapes, you walk deep into a 23,000-square-foot cave for a seated tasting in a relaxed, loungelike space. ■TIP➔ Standard tastings ($15) include five wines; for an additional $5, you can sample more, including at least one older, library wine. ✉ *10200 Sonoma Hwy./Hwy. 12* ☏ *707/833–5215* ⊕ *www.deerfieldranch.com* ✉ *Tastings $15–$25* ⏱ *Daily 10:30–4:30.*

Kunde Estate Winery & Vineyards. On your way into Kunde you pass a terrace flanked by fountains, virtually coaxing you to stay for a picnic with views over the vineyard. Best known for its toasty Chardonnays, the winery also makes well-regarded Sauvignon Blanc, Cabernet Sauvignon, Merlot, and Zinfandel wines. Among the Destination wines available only through the winery, the Dunfillan Cuvée, a blend of Cabernet and Syrah grapes, is worth checking out. The free basic tour of the grounds includes the caves, some of which stretch 175 feet below a vineyard. ■TIP➔ Reserve ahead for the Mountain Top Tasting, a popular tour that ends with a sampling of reserve wines ($40). ✉ *9825 Sonoma Hwy./Hwy. 12* ☏ *707/833–5501* ⊕ *www.kunde.com* ✉ *Tastings $10–$40, tours free–$50* ⏱ *Daily 10:30–5, tours daily at various times.*

Landmark Vineyards. High-quality Chardonnays have always been Landmark's claim to fame, led by the flagship Overlook wine, with grapes from multiple vineyards going into each vintage. The winery also makes several single-vineyard Chardonnays, including ones from Rodgers Creek (Sonoma Coast) and Charles Heintz (Russian River Valley), and winemaker Greg Stach has earned high praise for his Sonoma Coast Grand Detour Pinot Noir. Following the Overlook Chardonnay approach, Stach also makes an Overlook Pinot Noir using grapes from multiple sources. Stop here to sample the wines, relax in the picnic area, and play a game of boccie ball. ■TIP➔ If you want to extend the pleasure of your visit, the winery has a cottage and guest suite available for overnight stays. ✉ *101 Adobe Canyon Rd., at Hwy. 12* ☏ *707/833–0053* ⊕ *www.landmarkwine.com* ✉ *Tastings $25–$35, tour and tasting $25* ⏱ *Daily 10–4:30, tour by appointment.*

Ledson Winery & Vineyards. The outrageously ornate French Normandy–style castle visible from the highway might persuade you to visit Ledson Winery even before you know it produces lovely wines, all of which are available only at the estate and at the wine bar at the Ledson Hotel & Centre Du Vin in downtown Sonoma. Although the winery's total production is only about 30,000 cases a year, Ledson offers several dozen largely single-varietal wines—everything from California stand-bys such as Zinfandel to Rhône varietals such as Syrah and Mourvèdre. The castle, intended as the Ledson family's home when its construction began in 1989, is now a warren of tasting rooms, special-event spaces, and a small market selling a good selection of cheeses and other pic-nic supplies. ⊠ *7335 Sonoma Hwy./Hwy. 12* ☎ *707/537–3810* ⊕ *www. ledson.com* ⊠ *Tastings $15–$25; $35 for private tasting* ☉ *Daily 10–5.*

St. Francis Winery. Nestled at the foot of Mt. Hood, St. Francis has earned national acclaim for its food-and-wine pairings. With its red-tile roof and dramatic bell tower, the winery's California Mission–style visitor center occupies one of Sonoma's most scenic locations. The charm of the surroundings is matched by the wines, most of them red, includ-ing rich, earthy Zinfandels from the Dry Creek, Russian River, and Sonoma valleys. Chef Bryan Jones's five-course small bites and wine pairings ($50)—Liberty duck breast cassoulet with one of the Zins, for example—are offered from Thursday through Monday; pairings with cheeses and charcuterie ($30) are available daily. ⊠ *100 Pythian Rd., off Hwy. 12* ☎ *888/675–9463, 707/833–6146* ⊕ *www.stfranciswinery. com* ⊠ *Tastings $10–$50* ☉ *Daily 10–5; tour Fri.–Sun at 11:30.*

WORTH NOTING

Kenwood Vineyards. The best of the Kenwood wines—Cabernet Sauvi-gnons, Zinfandels, Syrahs, and Merlots—come from Jack London's old vineyard, in the Sonoma Mountain AVA. Many of these, along with some value-priced reds and whites, are poured in a tasting room housed in one of the property's original barns. The crisp Sauvignon Blanc, though, is what wins the winery its highest accolades. Fine on its own, especially on a hot summer day, it pairs well with oysters, chicken, light fish, and vegetarian dishes. The premium spirits and wine distributor Pernod Ricard USA purchased Kenwood in 2014 and plans to expand its national reach. ⊠ *9592 Sonoma Hwy./Hwy. 12* ☎ *707/282–4228* ⊕ *www.kenwoodvineyards.com* ⊠ *Tastings $10–$15* ☉ *Daily 10–4:30.*

VJB Vineyards & Cellars. This Tuscan-inspired courtyard marketplace with tasting spaces and food shops is a fine spot to sip reasonably priced wines, enjoy a pizza or a deli sandwich, and just relax. The wines, most from Italian varietals (some rare in these parts), are like the complex, which is to say less rustic than in the old country and clearly adapted for contemporary American tastes. This isn't always a bad thing, and the best vintages—the Barbera, the Sangiovese, and the Primitivo—are lively and clean on the palate. ■TIP➔ **For gourmet dolci, check out Wine Truffle Boutique, which sells chocolates, Italian gelato, and wine-infused sorbets.** ⊠ *60 Shaw Ave., off Hwy. 12* ☎ *707/833–2300* ⊕ *www.vjbcellars.com* ⊠ *Tastings $10–$35* ☉ *Daily 10–5.*

WHERE TO EAT AND STAY

$ | ╳ **Café Citti.** Classical music in the background, a friendly staff, and a
ITALIAN | roaring fire when it's cold outside keep this roadside café from feeling too spartan. Order dishes such as roast chicken and slabs of tiramisu from the counter and they're delivered to your table, indoors or on an outdoor patio. The array of prepared salads and sandwiches means the café does a brisk business in takeout for picnic packers, but you can also choose pasta made to order. ⑤ *Average main: $13* ✉ *9049 Sonoma Hwy./Hwy. 12* ☎ *707/833–2690* ⊕ *www.cafecitti.com* ⌂ *Reservations not accepted.*

$$ | ╳ **The Kenwood Restaurant.** New owners took over the Kenwood and
MODERN | jettisoned much of the restaurant's French-inspired menu to promote
AMERICAN | "Sonoma Cuisine" paying tribute to the cultural and agricultural melting pot Sonoma County represents. Though the concept is still evolving, the early results show promise. Among dinner entrées you might see pan-seared, crispy-skin, wild California king salmon or organic beef and root vegetables over egg noodles with a sauce containing house-made sour cream. ■ **TIP →** This restaurant with a sloping wood-beamed ceiling is at its best on warm afternoons and evenings, when you can sit on the patio and bask in the views of the Kunde vineyards and the Sugarloaf Mountains. ⑤ *Average main: $21* ✉ *9900 Sonoma Hwy./Hwy. 12, at Kunde Winery Rd.* ☎ *707/833–6326* ⊕ *www.kenwoodrestaurant. com* ⊗ *Closed Mon. and Tues.*

$$$$ | 🏨 **Kenwood Inn and Spa.** Fluffy featherbeds, wood-burning fireplaces,
B&B/INN | and French doors opening onto terraces or balconies give the uncommonly spacious guest rooms at this inn a particularly romantic air. **Pros:**
Fodor'sChoice | large rooms; lavish furnishings; excellent restaurant; rich full breakfast; romantic. **Cons:** road or lobby noise in some rooms; expensive.
★ | ⑤ *Rooms from: $495* ✉ *10400 Sonoma Hwy./Hwy. 12* ☎ *707/833–1293, 800/353–6966* ⊕ *www.kenwoodinn.com* ↴ *25 rooms, 4 suites* 🍴 *Breakfast.*

SHOPPING

Figone's Olive Oil Co. At this family-owned roadside shop you can sample extra-virgin olive oils (the porcini-mushroom blend is outstanding), zest-infused olive oils, and balsamic vinegars. Figone's also carries cookbooks and tabletop accessories. From late spring to early fall, the outdoor Kenwood Farmers Market takes place here on Sunday morning. ✉ *9580 Sonoma Hwy./Hwy. 12, at Warm Springs Rd.* ☎ *707/282–9092* ⊕ *www.figoneoliveoil.com.*

SPAS

Fodor'sChoice | **Spa at Kenwood Inn.** A pretty setting, expert practitioners, and rejuve-
★ | nating therapies using products from iS Clinical, Intraceuticals, and the French line Caudalíe make a visit to this spa a marvelously ethereal experience. Caudalíe's wine-based Vinothérapie treatments and its beauty products come together admirably in the delicious-sounding Honey Wine Wrap, which involves a warming, full-body slathering of

4

A Great Drive in Sonoma Valley

It's easy to zip through the Sonoma Valley in a day—the drive from Sonoma at the south end to Kenwood to the north can be done in half an hour—but once you begin stopping at the historic sites and wineries, your visit could easily be spread over two days.

To hit the highlights, start in the town of Sonoma. Have breakfast at Sunflower Caffé or El Dorado Corner Cafe. After your coffee kicks in, take a quick spin around historic **Sonoma Plaza,** ending at either the Epicurean Connection or the Sonoma Cheese Factory, where you can pick up *picnic supplies.* Return to your car and drive east on East Napa Street. Turn south on East 8th Street and west onto Denmark Street to reach **Gundlach Bundschu Winery.** After a tasting, hike up the GunBun hill for your alfresco lunch.

Backtrack to East Napa Street, which becomes Highway 12 west of Broadway; head north on Highway 12 for about 20 minutes. At the northern end of Kenwood, the grand French Normandy–style castle of **Ledson Winery** gleams in the sun. Stop here or the nearby **St. Francis Winery,** an equally photogenic spot and a must for red-wine fans. Heading back south on Highway 12, look for **Kunde Estate** a few minutes down the road.

If you've managed to wrap up your wine tasting before 3 pm, continue south on Highway 12 and take Arnold Drive into the picturesque town of Glen Ellen. Turn right on London Ranch Road and wind your way uphill for a few minutes to reach **Jack London State Historic Park.** Take a short stroll through the grounds and a gander at some of the historic buildings near the parking area before the park closes at 5 pm. (Note: The park is closed on Tuesday and Wednesday from December through February.) Dine in Glen Ellen or return to Sonoma.

wine yeast and honey. The Crushed Cabernet Scrub, designed to stimulate and soften your skin, raises the sweetness ante by adding brown sugar to the honey, along with crushed grape seeds and grape-seed oil. The spa's other services include massages and facials. ✉ *10400 Sonoma Hwy./Hwy. 12* ☎ *707/833–1293, 800/353–6966* ⊕ *www.kenwoodinn. com/spa.php* ✆ *Treatments $125–$450.*

SPORTS AND THE OUTDOORS

Sugarloaf Ridge State Park. On a clear day you can see all the way to San Francisco and sometimes even east to the Sierra mountains at this hilltop park on the Napa–Sonoma border. With more than 25 miles of trails there's one to suit all hikers. The easiest trail follows Sonoma Creek for a mile from the visitor center; the hardest at 8.2 miles, heads over Bald Mountain for those superlative views. Wildflower viewing is a major pastime from spring to early summer. You can also mountain bike, and camping is permitted. ✉ *2605 Adobe Canyon Rd., off Hwy. 12* ☎ *707/833–5712* ⊕ *www.sugarloafpark.org* ✆ *$8* ☉ *Day use daily 6 am–8 pm.*

NORTHERN SONOMA, RUSSIAN RIVER, AND WEST COUNTY

WELCOME TO NORTHERN SONOMA, RUSSIAN RIVER, AND WEST COUNTY

TOP REASONS TO GO

★ **Back-roads biking:** The region's ultrascenic back roads include gentle hills and challenging terrain you can traverse with a guide or on your own.

★ **Diverse dining:** Area chefs tickle diners' palates with diverse offerings—everything from haute-French and Peruvian cuisine to playful variations on American standards.

★ **Hillside Cabs and old-vine Zins.** Alexander Valley hillside Cabernet Sauvignon and Dry Creek Valley old-vine Zinfandel grapes—as far as the eye can see in spots—thrive in the high heat here.

★ **Hip Healdsburg shopping:** Healdsburg wins the shopping wars fair and square with more captivating galleries, design-oriented shops, and clothing stores than anywhere in the Wine Country.

★ **Pinot aplenty and Chardonnay, too:** Russian River Valley and Sonoma Coast wineries large and small produce some of California's most celebrated Pinot Noirs and Chardonnays.

1 Healdsburg and Northern Sonoma. An hour's drive north of the Golden Gate Bridge on U.S. 101 (when there's no traffic), Healdsburg has a compact downtown surrounding a tree-filled central plaza. Though its population is small, Healdsburg sprawls in all directions from the plaza, lending its address to many acclaimed wineries. North of the plaza 8 miles, more sedate Geyserville straddles U.S. 101.

2 West County. The Russian River Valley's hotter eastern portions lie within Healdsburg proper, but the bulk of the AVA stretches southwest into Forestville, Guerneville, Freestone, Occidental, Sebastopol, Graton, and other small towns collectively known as West County. Its main roads include River Road, Highway 12, and Highway 116.

3 Santa Rosa. Sonoma County's largest city lies south of Healdsburg on U.S. 101 and north of the Sonoma Valley on Highway 12, which winds west from Santa Rosa into West County.

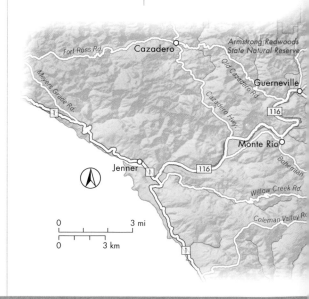

GETTING ORIENTED

Northern Sonoma County and Santa Rosa lie due north of San Francisco on U.S. 101. Highway 116 and Highway 12 lead west from U.S. 101 into Sebastopol, where 116 continues to north Forestville and 12 heads west to Freestone. From Freestone the Bohemian Highway leads north into Occidental and the Russian River town of Guerneville. River Road snakes west from U.S. 101 through Forestville and on to Guerneville, eventually dead-ending at the Pacific Ocean.

5

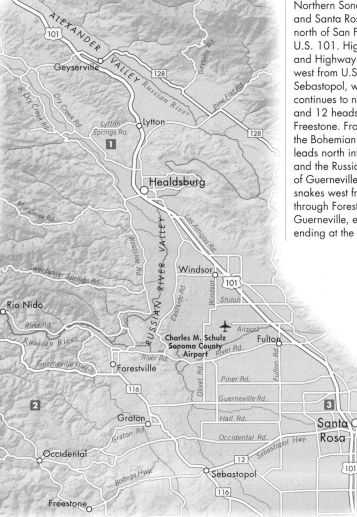

Sonoma County's northern and western reaches are a study in contrasts. Trendy hotels, restaurants, shops, and tasting rooms have transformed Healdsburg into a hot spot. Within a few miles, though, chic yields to bucolic, with only the occasional horse ranch, apple or peach orchard, or stand of oaks interrupting the rolling vineyard hills. The Russian River Valley is the grape-growing star, but Dry Creek and Alexander valleys and the Sonoma Coast also merit investigation. Office parks and tract housing diminish Santa Rosa's appeal, but wineries and cultural attractions, along with solid budget lodgings, can be found within its borders.

Healdsburg is the most convenient base for exploring northern Sonoma County. Not only does it have an easily walkable town center, swanky hotels, and a remarkable restaurant scene, but it's also at the confluence of the Russian River, Dry Creek, and Alexander valleys, three of northern Sonoma's blockbuster appellations. The wineries here produce some of the country's best Pinot Noirs, Cabernet Sauvignons, Zinfandels, and Chardonnays.

In the smaller West County towns of Forestville, Guerneville, and Sebastopol, high-style lodgings and fine dining are in shorter supply. Each town has a few charmers, however, along with dozens of wineries worth seeking out. The western reaches of Sonoma County, extending all the way to the Pacific Ocean, are more sparsely populated, although more and more vineyards are popping up where once stood orchards or ranches.

As the county's—and Wine Country's—largest city, workaday Santa Rosa may lack sex appeal, but it does contain the Charles M. Schulz Museum, Safari West, and other nonwine attractions, and the dining and lodging options here tend to be more reasonably priced than in the smaller towns.

Each of northern and western Sonoma County's regions claims its own microclimates, soil types, and most-favored varietals, but except for urban Santa Rosa all have something in common: peace and quiet. This area is less crowded than the Napa Valley and southern Sonoma. Healdsburg, in particular, is hardly a stranger to overnight visitors, but you'll find less company in most of the region's tasting rooms.

PLANNER

WHEN TO GO

High season runs from early June through October, but even then weekday mornings find many wineries blissfully uncrowded. Summers are warm and nearly always pleasant on the coast, and though inland the temperatures often reach 90°F, this is nothing a local Rosé of Pinot Noir can't cure. Fall brings harvest fairs and other local celebrations. Things slow down during winter, but with smaller crowds come more intimate winery visits. Two big events that break up the winter are Winter Wineland, in January, and Barrel Tasting, on two weekends in early March (⇨ *see Festivals and Seasonal Events in the Experience Napa and Sonoma for more information*). Roads along the Russian River are prone to flooding during heavy rains, as are a few in the Alexander Valley. Spring, when the grapevines are budding but the crowds are still thin, is a good time to visit.

PLANNING YOUR TIME

With hundreds of wineries separated by miles of highway—Sonoma County is as big as Rhode Island—you could spend weeks here and not cover everything, but to get a taste for what makes this region special, plan on a minimum of two or three days to hit the highlights. Healdsburg and the Russian River Valley are the must-sees, but it's worth venturing beyond them to the Alexander and Dry Creek valleys. If you still have time, head west toward the coast. Healdsburg makes a good base for Northern Sonoma and Russian River Valley touring, and Sebastopol, Forestville, and Guerneville are prime West County perches. Santa Rosa is convenient to both Northern Sonoma and the Russian River Valley, and it often has the best lodging rates.

GETTING HERE AND AROUND
BUS TRAVEL

Sonoma County Transit provides transportation to all the main towns in this region, though except for the routes from Santa Rosa to Healdsburg and to Sebastopol service isn't always frequent. Bus 60 travels from Santa Rosa to Healdsburg, where Bus 67, aka the Healdsburg Shuttle, loops through downtown. Buses 20, 22, 24, 26, and 28 serve Sebastopol and other West County towns. ⇨ *For more information about arriving by bus, see Bus Travel in the Travel Smart chapter. For more information about local bus service, see the Bus Travel sections for the individual towns in this chapter.*

5

CAR TRAVEL

Driving a car is by far the easiest way to get to and experience this region. From San Francisco, the quickest route to Northern Sonoma is north on U.S. 101 to Santa Rosa and Healdsburg. Highway 116 (also called the Gravenstein Highway), heads west from U.S. 101, taking you through Sebastopol and the hamlets of Graton and Forestville before depositing you along the Russian River near Guerneville. Traffic can be slow on U.S. 101, especially around Petaluma and Santa Rosa during rush hour and on summer weekends. Parking is easy nearly everywhere; even in downtown Healdsburg, Sebastopol, and Santa Rosa you'll rarely have to park more than a block or two from your destination, though in these towns you may have to park in a lot or feed a parking meter.

RESTAURANTS

Each year at the Sonoma County Harvest Festival and seasonally at local farmers' markets, the remarkable output of Northern Sonoma's farms and ranches is on display. Local chefs often scour the markets for seafood, meats, cheeses, and produce. With all these fresh ingredients readily at hand, it shouldn't surprise that farm-to-table cuisine predominates here, especially among the high-profile restaurants. Wood-fired pizzas are another local passion, as is modern Italian. Good delis and groceries abound, several of them located conveniently near wineries that allow picnics. Except in the region's most expensive restaurants, it's fine to dress casually.

HOTELS

Healdsburg's hotels and inns set this region's standard for bedding down in style, with plush rooms that top $1,000 a night in a few cases. In the more affordable category are traditional bed-and-breakfast inns and small hotels, and there are even some motel-style inns with down-to-earth prices. These last lodgings book up well in advance for high season, which is why Santa Rosa, just 15 miles away and home to decent chain and independent inns and hotels, is worth checking out year-round. Several secluded West County inns provide an elegant escape. Smaller properties throughout the region have two-night minimums on weekends (three nights on holiday weekends), though especially in winter this is negotiable. *Hotel reviews have been shortened. For full information, visit Fodors.com.*

WHAT IT COSTS				
	$	**$$**	**$$$**	**$$$$**
Restaurants	under $16	$16–$22	$23–$30	over $30
Hotels	under $201	$201–$300	$301–$400	over $400

Restaurant prices are the average cost of a main course at dinner, or if dinner isn't served, at lunch. Hotel prices are the lowest cost of a standard double room in high season.

APPELLATIONS

Covering about 329,000 acres, the **Northern Sonoma AVA,** itself within the larger Sonoma County "appellation of origin," a geopolitical designation, and the even larger multicounty **North Coast AVA,** is divided into nine smaller subappellations. Three of the most important subappellations meet at Healdsburg: the Russian River Valley AVA, which runs southwest along the river; the Dry Creek Valley AVA, which runs northwest of town; and the Alexander Valley AVA, which extends to the east and north. Also in this far northern area are four smaller AVAs whose names you're more likely to see on wine labels throughout the county than at the few visitable wineries within the appellations themselves: Knights Valley and Chalk Hill, east and south of Alexander Valley; Rockpile, which slices northwest from the Dry Creek AVA to the Mendocino County line; and Pine Mountain–Cloverdale Peak, which extends from the Alexander Valley's northeastern tip into Mendocino County.

The cool climate of the low-lying **Russian River Valley AVA** is perfect for fog-loving Pinot Noir grapes as well as Chardonnay. Although 25 years ago this was a little-known appellation, with as many farms, orchards, and redwood stands as vineyards, in recent years vines have sprouted up all over, and this is now one of Sonoma's most-recognized growing regions—with a significant subappellation of its own, the **Green Valley of the Russian River Valley AVA,** in the Forestville-Sebastopol area.

Although it's a small region—only about 16 miles long and 2 miles wide—**Dry Creek Valley AVA** is well known by Zin lovers. The coastal hills temper the cooling influence of the Pacific Ocean, making it ideal for such warm-climate grapes as Zinfandel. Even more acres are planted with Cabernet Sauvignon, and you'll find a smattering of Merlot, Chardonnay, Sauvignon Blanc, Syrah, and several other varietals growing in the diverse soils and climates (it's warmer in the north and cooler in the south).

Winemakers continue to experiment to determine which varietals grow best in the diverse soils and generally warm **Alexander Valley AVA,** but so far Chardonnay, Sauvignon Blanc, Zinfandel, and Cabernet Sauvignon seem to do well, and Petite Sirah and Italian varietals such as Sangiovese thrive here, too.

Much of the **Sonoma Coast AVA,** which stretches the length of Sonoma County's coastline, lies within the Northern Sonoma AVA. The classic combination of hot summer days and cooling evening fog and breezes (in some spots even cooler than the Russian River Valley) inspired major wine-making operations, including the Napa Valley's Joseph Phelps Vineyards, to invest in acreage here. The hunch paid off for Phelps and other area winemakers, whose Pinots and Chardonnays have been the darlings of national wine critics for nearly a decade. Because the Sonoma Coast AVA encompasses such varied terrain—its southeastern portion edges into the comparatively warmer Sonoma Valley, for instance—some West County growers and vintners have proposed subappellations that express what they promote as the "true" Sonoma Coast geology and microclimates. One subappellation granted approval was **Fort Ross–Seaview AVA,** whose hillside vineyards, mostly of Chardonnay and Pinot Noir, occupy hilly patches once thought too close to the Pacific Ocean to support grape growing.

With only 650 acres planted with vines, the idyllic **Bennett Valley AVA**—part of the Sonoma Valley AVA, but within the city of Santa Rosa—is one of California's smallest appellations. Surrounded by the mountains on three sides but cooled by coastal breezes that sneak through the wind gap at Crane Canyon, it's ideal for such cooler-weather grapes as Pinot Noir and Chardonnay, but also does well with Syrah, Cabernet Sauvignon, and Sauvignon Blanc.

HEALDSBURG AND NORTHERN SONOMA

Most of California's major grape varietals thrive in the disparate terrains and microclimates of Sonoma County's northern section, among them Zinfandel, which Italian immigrants such as Edoardo Seghesio planted in the Alexander Valley in the 1890s. Some of these vines survive to this day, but they were not the first grapes planted up this way. Five decades earlier, Cyrus Alexander, from whom the valley takes its name, planted grapevines on land now part of Alexander Valley Vineyards.

For years, most Alexander Valley grapes grown in the neighboring Dry Creek Valley found their way into bulk wines, and prune and other stone-fruit trees were far more common than grapevines. By the 1950s and 1960s, though, pioneers such as Evelyn and Leo Trentadue had begun planting the first vines in the Geyserville area since the Prohibition era. In the 1970s, Tom and Sally Jordan upped the ante when they set about producing French-style Chardonnays and Cabernet Sauvignons to rival those in the Napa Valley and France itself. More wineries followed, and by the early 2000s it was clear that Healdsburg, the area's winery hub, at the eastern edge of the Russian River Valley, was destined for stardom.

These days downtown Healdsburg contains so many tasting rooms that it's possible to sip fine wine at different places for days without venturing into the countryside to visit an actual winery. That would be a mistake, of course, because the scenery delights and surprises at nearly every curve in this area's many winding roads. The pace slows north of Healdsburg in less-splashy Geyserville, but wine connoisseurs, some in search of the Alexander Valley's distinctive Cabernet Sauvignons, devotedly make the rounds.

HEALDSBURG

17 miles north of Santa Rosa.

Fodor's Choice
★ Just when it seems that the buzz about Healdsburg couldn't get any bigger, there's another article published in a glossy food or wine magazine about properties such as the swingin' Spoonbar or the posh Hotel Les Mars. But you don't have to be a tycoon to enjoy Healdsburg. For every ritzy restaurant there's a great bakery serving reasonably priced sandwiches, and luxe lodgings are matched by modest bed-and-breakfasts.

Best Bets for Northern Sonoma County Wineries

WINE TASTING

Joseph Phelps Freestone Vineyards Guest Center, Freestone. A tasting here provides a splendid introduction to cool-climate Sonoma Coast Chardonnays and Pinot Noirs.

Locals Tasting Room, Geyserville. The flights are all of your own fancy at this room that pours the wines of small-lot producers. Sample Zins or Cabs, then decide which ones best suit your palate.

Merry Edwards Winery, Sebastopol. You can't amble up to the tasting bar—there isn't one—but you can book an informative sit-down session and sample acclaimed Pinot Noirs.

WINERY TOURING

Ferrari-Carano Winery, Healdsburg. Tours of the winery's over-the-top Italian villa take in the wine-making facilities, underground cellar, and manicured gardens.

Jordan Vineyard and Winery, Healdsburg. The pièce de résistance of the estate tour here is a Cabernet tasting at a 360-degree vista point overlooking acres of countryside.

Korbel Champagne Cellars, Guerneville. The pioneering efforts of the brothers Korbel and the making of sparkling wines using the French *méthode champenoise* are the topics of their winery's tour.

SETTING

Hartford Family Winery, Forestville. The opulent main winery and patio with views of vineyards and towering trees provide a gorgeous backdrop on a sunny summer day and even in the dead of winter.

Iron Horse Vineyards, Sebastopol. The vine-covered hills and valleys surrounding Iron Horse provide such compelling views the winery hosts its tastings outside.

Ridge Vineyards, Healdsburg. Outdoors in good weather and indoors year-round you can enjoy views of rolling vineyards while tasting intense Zinfandels and other well-rounded wines.

Rochioli Vineyards and Winery, Healdsburg. Stop at Healdsburg's Oakville Grocery to pick up food for a picnic, then drive to Rochioli to enjoy the views and serenity.

FOOD-WINE PAIRING

J Vineyards and Winery, Healdsburg. At these food-wine pairing sessions, J's best sparkling and still wines are paired with marvelous morsels in the plush Bubble Room.

Michel-Schlumberger. A gourmet chef prepares five substantial bites that demonstrate the versatility of this Dry Creek Valley AVA producer's French-style wines.

Paul Hobbs Winery, Sebastopol. The in-house chef at Paul Hobbs fashions three generous courses paired with Chardonnays, Pinot Noirs, and Cabernet Sauvignons.

JUST PLAIN FUN

Truett Hurst Winery, Healdsburg. A cool place to kick back, especially on weekends, when bands play, T-H has a creekside tasting area that's a treat all its own.

Unti Vineyards, Healdsburg. A favorite among Bay Area locals for its convivial vibe, Unti specializes in Rhône and Italian varietals.

5

Healdsburg is ideally located at the confluence of the Dry Creek Valley, Russian River Valley, and Alexander Valley AVAs, but you could easily spend a day or more exploring downtown. Around its old-fashioned plaza you'll find fashionable boutiques, art galleries, spas, hip tasting rooms, and some of the Wine Country's best restaurants.

Walking downtown, you realize that locals haven't been pushed aside to make way for tourists. This isn't by accident. For example, free summer concerts used to be held in Healdsburg Plaza on Sunday, but when they became so popular that locals stopped coming, the city moved the performances to Tuesday. The concerts are quite fine, by the way—you might hear anything from bluegrass to military marches. Set amid the plaza's fragrant trees and flowers, the scene is as pretty as a Norman Rockwell painting.

The countryside around Healdsburg is the sort you dream about when you're planning a Wine Country vacation, with orderly rows of vines alternating with beautifully overgrown hills. Set alongside relatively untrafficked roads, country stores and roadside farm stands offer just-plucked fruits and vine-ripened tomatoes. The wineries here are barely visible, often tucked behind groves of eucalyptus or hidden high on fog-shrouded hills.

GETTING HERE AND AROUND

To get to Healdsburg from San Francisco, cross the Golden Gate Bridge and continue north on U.S. 101. About 65 miles from San Francisco, take the Central Healdsburg exit and follow Healdsburg Avenue a few blocks north to Healdsburg Plaza. Many hotels and restaurants are on or around the scenic town square. From Santa Rosa, the drive along U.S. 101 takes about 15 minutes in light traffic. Wineries bearing Healdsburg addresses can be as far apart as 20 miles, so unless you plan to sample wines only at the many in-town tasting rooms, you'll need a car. Both Dry Creek Valley AVA and Russian River Valley AVA are west of U.S. 101; most of the Alexander Valley AVA is east of the freeway. Sonoma County Transit Bus 60 serves Healdsburg from Santa Rosa; Bus 67, a shuttle, serves portions of downtown and vicinity but isn't convenient for winery touring.

Getting to the Wineries: For wineries along Westside Road, head south on Center Street, then turn right at Mill Street. After Mill Street crosses under U.S. 101, the road's name changes to Westside Road. After about ½ mile, veer south to continue on Westside Road to reach the Russian River Valley wineries. Roughly following the curves of the Russian River, Westside Road passes vineyards, woods, and meadows along the way.

The route to wineries on Old Redwood Highway and Eastside Road is less scenic. Follow Healdsburg Avenue south to U.S. 101. Hop on the freeway, exiting after a mile at Old Redwood Highway. Veer right as you exit, and continue south. Just past the driveway that serves both Rodney Strong and J Vineyards, turn southwest to merge onto Eastside Road.

To reach the wineries along Dry Creek Road and West Dry Creek Road, head north on Healdsburg Avenue. After about a mile, turn west on

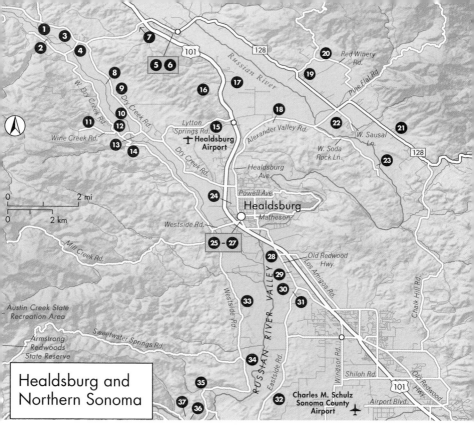

Healdsburg and Northern Sonoma

Dry Creek Road. West Dry Creek Road, which runs roughly parallel to Dry Creek Road, is accessible by the cross streets Lambert Bridge Road and Yoakim Bridge Road.

For Alexander Valley wineries, head north on Healdsburg Avenue. Reach Alexander Valley Vineyards by heading east on Alexander Valley Road. For Seghesio Family Vineyard, head west and then north onto Grove Street.

VISITOR INFORMATION

Healdsburg Chamber of Commerce & Visitors Bureau ⊠ *217 Healdsburg Ave., at Matheson St.* ☎ *707/433–6935* ⊕ *www.healdsburg.com.*

EXPLORING

TOP ATTRACTIONS

Fodor's Choice ★ **Acorn Winery.** For a throwback to the era when a hardworking couple forsook sensible careers and went all-in to become grape growers and vintners, visit this low-tech yet classy operation that's earned high praise for wines that include Cabernet Franc, Sangiovese, Zinfandel, and the rare-in-America Italian varietal Dolcetto. The gracious Betsy and Bill Nachbaur share their output in a garage-style, appointment-only tasting room amid their Alegría Vineyard. Each Acorn wine is a field blend of multiple grape varietals grown side by side and then crushed and co-fermented together. In the wrong hands, this old-world approach produces muddled, negligible wines, but these ones, made by Bill in consultation with local winemaker Clay Mauritson, soar. ⊠ *12040 Old Redwood Hwy., south of Limerick La.* ☎ *707/433–6440* ⊕ *acornwinery.com* ⊠ *Tasting $10* ⊗ *Daily 10:30–5:30 by appointment.*

Fodor's Choice ★ **Copain Wines.** Wells Guthrie, Copain's winemaker, is the kind of guy who spends his vacation working in a French vineyard, the better to understand how sun, soil, climate, and time-honored agricultural techniques combine to create great wines. This single-mindedness serves him well: his restrained yet accessible Chardonnays, Pinot Noirs, and Syrahs are marvelous examples of intuitive craftsmanship supported by deep knowledge. The Copain wines are among the most "European" ones produced in Sonoma County. The majority of the grapes come from elsewhere, mostly Mendocino and Monterey counties, and the wines' understated flavors reflect the cool climates and rocky coastal terrains of those areas. ■ TIP→ This winery occupies a hillside perch that begs you to sit, sip, and bask in the view. ⊠ *7800 Eastside Rd., near Ballard Rd.* ☎ *707/836–8822* ⊕ *www.copainwines.com* ⊠ *Tastings $20–$40* ⊗ *Daily 10–4 (last tasting 3 pm) by appointment.*

Fodor's Choice ★ **Dry Creek Peach & Produce.** If you happen by this farm stand in the summer, don't pass up the chance to sample the tree-ripened white and yellow peaches, some of which may have been harvested moments before you arrived. You can buy peaches in small quantities, as well as organic peach jam. How good are these peaches? The customers include the famed Chez Panisse Restaurant in Berkeley. ⊠ *2179 Yoakim Bridge Rd., near Dry Creek Rd.* ☎ *707/433–8121* ⊕ *www.drycreekpeach.com* ⊗ *July–mid-Sept., Wed. and Fri.–Sun. noon–5.*

Gary Farrell Winery. Pass through an impressive metal gate and wind your way up a steep hill to reach Gary Farrell, a spot with knockout

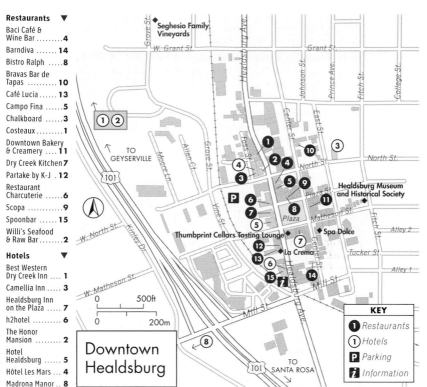

Downtown
Healdsburg

KEY

- ● Restaurants
- ① Hotels
- P Parking
- 𝒊 Information

views over the rolling hills and vineyards below. Though its Zinfandels and Chardonnays often excel, the winery is best known for its Russian River Valley Pinot Noirs, crafted these days by Theresa Heredia. At the tasting bar ($15) you can sample Sauvignon Blanc and other winery-only wines; depending on the weather, seated tastings ($25) focusing on single-vineyard Chardonnays and Pinot Noirs take place on an outdoor terrace or indoors near a fireplace. ■TIP→ The Pinots from the Hallberg and Rochioli vineyards are worth checking out. ✉ *10701 Westside Rd.* ☎ *707/473–2909* ⊕ *www.garyfarrellwinery.com* 🍷 *Tastings $15–$25, tours $35–$75* ☉ *Daily 10:30–4:30, tours by appointment.*

QUICK BITES

Flying Goat Coffee. Healdsburg locals are as obsessive about coffee as they are about wine. One hot stop for a cup of joe is FGC, whose earthy and potent Espresso No. 9 blend, redolent of molasses and milk chocolate, makes for a exceptionally satisfying cappuccino or latte. The lighter Optimist Blend, a town favorite, is made from all-organic beans. ■TIP→ A to-go-only satellite location is a block away at 419 Center Street. ✉ *324 Center St., near Plaza St.* ☎ *707/433–3599* ⊕ *www.flyinggoatcoffee.com* ☉ *Daily 7–7.*

J Vineyards and Winery. The dry sparkling wines made here, all from Pinot Noir and Chardonnay grapes planted in Russian River vineyards, have wonderfully complex fruit and floral aromas and good acidity. Best known for its sparklers, J also makes fine still wines, often from Pinot and Chardonnay grapes, as well as a brandy-fortified dessert wine and a pear eau-de-vie. You

can sample just the wines at the tasting bar, enjoy a private reserve tasting in the Legacy Lounge, or indulge yourself in the Bubble Room (reservations recommended), where top-end still and sparkling wines are paired with excellent morsels. Tours, a little more than an hour long, take place twice daily. ■TIP➜ From May through October, tastings also take place on a creekside terrace. ✉ *11447 Old Redwood Hwy., at Eastside Rd.* ☎ *707/431–3646* ⊕ *www.jwine.com* ✉ *Tastings $20–$75, tour free* ☉ *Daily 11–5, tours 11:30 and 2.*

Fodor's Choice
★

Jordan Vineyard and Winery. A visit to this sprawling property north of Healdsburg revolves around an impressive estate built in the early 1970s to replicate a French château. A seated one-hour Library Tasting of the current Cabernet Sauvignon and Chardonnay releases takes place in the château itself, accompanied by small bites prepared by executive chef Todd Knoll. The tasting concludes with an older vintage Cabernet Sauvignon paired with cheese. The 90-minute Winery Tour & Tasting includes the above, plus a walk through part of the château. ■TIP➜ For a truly memorable experience, splurge on the three-hour Estate Tour & Tasting, whose pièce de résistance is a Cabernet tasting at a 360-degree vista point overlooking 1,200 acres of vines, olive trees, and countryside. ✉ *1474 Alexander Valley Rd., on Greco Rd.* ☎ *800/654–1213, 707/431–5250* ⊕ *www.jordanwinery.com* ✉ *Library tasting $30, winery tour and tasting $40, estate tour and tasting $120* ☉ *Library tasting mid-Nov.–mid-Apr., Mon.–Sat. 10 and 2; mid-Apr.–mid.-Nov., Mon.–Sat. 10 and 2, Sun. 11, 1, and 3; winery tour mid-Nov.–mid-Apr.; Mon.–Sat. at 11; mid-Apr.–mid-Nov., Mon.–Sat. at 11, Sun. at 11; estate tour mid-Apr.–mid-Nov. at 9:45 Thurs.–Mon.*

Lambert Bridge Winery. Especially in spring and early summer when its front-porch wisteria arbor blooms a nostalgia-inducing light purple, the twin-dormered Lambert Bridge winery building looks far older than its four decades—the weathered structure has matured early and well, not unlike the powerful yet polished artisanal wines produced inside. The flagship offering, the silky and supple Limited Selection Cabernet Sauvignon, is blended from winery's best lots of Dry Creek and Alexander Valley grapes. Lambert Bridge has won praise for this and other reds—among them Cabernet Franc, Petit Verdot, Petite Sirah, and Zinfandel—but also makes fine whites. All can be sampled at the main tasting bar, fashioned from a single, intricately patterned old-growth curly redwood, and in the adjacent, candlelit barrel room. ✉ *4085 West Dry Creek Rd., ½ mile south of Lambert Bridge Rd.*

The ivy-covered château at Jordan Vineyard looks older than its four-plus decades.

☎ 800/975–0555, 707/431–4661 ⊕ www.lambertbridge.com ☞ Tastings $15–$50; harvest tour (Sept. and Oct.) $30 ☉ Daily 10:30–4:30; appointment required for some tastings.

Porter Creek Vineyards. About as down-home as you can get—there's just a small redwood-beam tasting room amid a modest family farm—Porter Creek makes notably good wines, some from estate-grown Chardonnay and Pinot Noir grapes. Its vineyards climb up steep hillsides of volcanic soil that imparts a slight mineral note to the Chardonnay; the cover crops planted between the vines provide erosion control in addition to nutrients. Winemaker Alex Davis, the son of George Davis, who founded the winery, also makes two distinctive wines from old-vine grapes, Carignane from Mendocino County and Zinfandel from Sonoma County, and his lineup includes Viognier and Syrah. The pourers here are uniformly gracious. ■ TIP→ Look closely for the winery's sign; the driveway is at a sharp bend in Westside Road. ⊠ 8735 Westside Rd. ☎ 707/433–6321 ⊕ www.portercreekvineyards.com ☞ Tasting $10 ☉ Daily 10:30–4:30.

Fodor's Choice ★ **Ridge Vineyards.** Ridge stands tall among California wineries, and not merely because one of its 1971 Cabernet Sauvignons placed first in a 2006 re-creation of the 1976 Judgment of Paris tasting. The winery built its reputation on Cabernet Sauvignons, Zinfandels, and Chardonnays of unusual depth and complexity, but you'll also find blends of Rhône varietals. Ridge makes wines using grapes from several California locales—including the Dry Creek Valley, Sonoma Valley, Napa Valley, and Paso Robles—but the focus is on single-vineyard estate wines such as the exquisitely textured Lytton Springs Zinfandel blend from grapes

The focus at Ridge Vineyards is on single-vineyard estate wines.

grown near the tasting room. In good weather you can taste outside, taking in views of rolling vineyard hills while you sip. ■TIP→ The $20 tasting option includes a pour of the top-of-the-line Monte Bello Cabernet Sauvignon blend from grapes grown in the Santa Cruz Mountains. ✉ 650 Lytton Springs Rd., off U.S. 101 ☎ 707/433–7721 ⊕ www. ridgewine.com ✉ Tastings $5–$20, tours $30–$40 ☉ June–Oct., Mon.–Thurs. 11–4, Fri. and weekends 11–5; Nov.–May, daily 11–4.

Fodor's Choice ★ **Rochioli Vineyards and Winery.** Claiming one of the prettiest picnic sites in the area, with tables overlooking the vineyards, this winery has an airy little tasting room with an equally romantic view. Production is small and fans on the winery's mailing list snap up most of the bottles, but the winery is still worth a stop. Because of the cool growing conditions in the Russian River Valley, the flavors of the Chardonnay and Sauvignon Blanc are intense and complex, and the Pinot Noir, which helped cement the Russian River's status as a Pinot powerhouse, is consistently excellent. ✉ 6192 Westside Rd. ☎ 707/433–2305 ⊕ www.rochioliwinery. com ✉ Tasting $10 ☉ Early Jan.–mid-Dec., Thurs.–Mon. 11–4, Tues. and Wed. by appointment.

Stuhlmuller Vineyards. Zinfandels and Cabernet Sauvignons from estate-grown grapes are the specialty of this off-the-beaten-path winery inside a distinctive redwood-stained building. Standout wines include the Rogers Schoolhouse Estate Zinfandel, crafted from small lots of old-vine grapes, and two estate Cabernets from specific grape blocks that grow side by side. Two Chardonnays and a Russian River Valley Pinot Noir from the noteworthy Starr Ridge Vineyard are also made here, and there's a rich dessert wine made from estate Cabernet fortified with brandy. Tastings take place in a room adjoining the aging cellar, and in good weather you can sip outdoors on a graveled patio near the vineyards. ■TIP➜ Picnickers are welcome here. ⌂ *4951 W. Soda Rock La., off Alexander Valley Rd.* ☎ *707/431–7745* ⊕ *www. stuhlmullervineyards.com* ⌕ *Tastings $10–$20, estate tour and tasting $25* ⊙ *Fri.–Mon. 11–4:30, Tues.–Thurs. by appointment only; tour Fri.–Mon. 11:30.*

Truett Hurst Winery. When the weather's fine, few experiences rate more sublime("pure magic," enthused one recent guest) than sitting on Truett Hurst's sandy, tree-shaded Dry Creek shoreline, sipping a Green Valley Pinot Noir or a Zinfandel Rosé, chatting with friends, and watching the water flow by. In addition to the Rosé, Truett Hurst makes six Zinfandels, a few of which are always poured in the contemporary, high-ceilinged tasting room or on the outdoor patio. The winemaker blends Petite Sirah into some of the Zins and makes a standalone Petite Sirah as well. Picnickers are welcome creekside or on the patio; meats, smoked fish, cheeses, and spreads are available for sale on-site. ■TIP➜ Bands, sometimes local, sometimes from beyond, liven things up in the tasting room on weekend afternoons. ⌂ *5610 Dry Creek Rd., 2 miles south of Canyon Rd.* ☎ *707/433–9545* ⊕ *www.truetthurst.com.*

Twomey Cellars. The draws at the Sonoma outpost of Twomey, founded by the owners of Silver Oak Cellars, include four Pinot Noirs, a Merlot crafted using a centuries-old French technique, and views of vineyards and the Mayacamas Mountains from a graceful, contemporary glass-walled tasting room. The Pinot Noirs, from grapes grown in prime California locales, are overseen by Daniel Baron, Silver Oak's Bordeaux-trained winemaker. For the Merlot, whose grapes come from a single Napa Valley vineyard, Baron employs the *soutirage traditionnel* method of transferring the wine from oak barrel to oak barrel multiple times during aging to soften the tannins and intensify the aromas. (It works.) ■TIP➜ If the weather's nice, you can enjoy your tasting on the patio facing the vineyards; picnickers are welcome here also. ⌂ *3000 Westside Rd., ¼ mile south of Felta Rd.* ☎ *707/942–7026* ⊕ *www. twomey.com* ⌕ *Tasting $10, tour free* ⊙ *Mon.–Sat. 10–5, Sun. 11–5; tours by appointment.*

WORTH NOTING

Alexander Valley Vineyards. The 1840s homestead of Cyrus Alexander, for whom the valley is named, is now the site of this winery known for Chardonnay, Cabernet Sauvignon, and a trio of Zinfandel wines, including the widely distributed Sin Zin. The standard tasting is free, but consider opting for the reserve tasting ($10) to sample the single-vineyard Cabernet Sauvignon, the Bordeaux blend called Cyrus, and other wines. A $25 wine-and-cheese pairing is also offered. A tour takes in the winery and wine caves dug deep into a nearby hillside. ■TIP➜ The winery welcomes picnickers, and there's a printable coupon on its website good for free reserve tastings. ⌂ *8644 Hwy. 128, at Sonnikson Rd.* ☎ *707/433–7209* ⊕ *www.avvwine.com* ⌕ *Tastings free–$25, tour free* ⊙ *Daily 10–5, tour at 11 and 2.*

Dry Creek Vineyard. Fumé Blanc is king at Dry Creek, where the refreshing white wine is made in the style of those in Sancerre, France. The winery also makes well-regarded Zinfandels, a zesty dry Chenin Blanc, a Pinot Noir, and a handful of Cabernet Sauvignon blends. Many wines sell for less than $30 a bottle (and some even $20), making this a popular stop for wine lovers looking to stock their cellars for a reasonable price. You can picnic on the lawn next to a flowering magnolia tree. Conveniently, a general store and deli is close by. ⊠ *3770 Lambert Bridge Rd., off Dry Creek Rd.* ☎ *707/433–1000, 800/864–9463* ⊕ *www.drycreekvineyard.com* ▧ *Tastings $5–$50, tour $20* ☉ *Daily 10:30–5, tour 11 and 1 by appointment.*

Ferrari-Carano Winery. Known for its over-the-top Italian villa and manicured gardens—not a stray blade of grass anywhere here—this winery produces mostly Chardonnays, Fumé Blancs, Zinfandels, and Cabernet Sauvignons. Though whites have traditionally been the specialty here, the reds garner attention, too, especially in recent years the Bordeaux-style blend called Trésor, and some guests come just for the dessert wines. Tours cover the wine-making facilities, underground cellar, and the gardens, where you can see a cork oak tree and learn about how cork is harvested. ■ TIP→ For a more relaxed experience than the main tasting room, head downstairs to the reserve tasting room. ⊠ *8761 Dry Creek Rd., at Yoakim Bridge Rd.* ☎ *707/433–6700, 800/831–0381* ⊕ *www.ferrari-carano.com* ▧ *Tastings $5–$35, tour free* ☉ *Daily 10–5, tour Mon.–Sat. 10 am by appointment.*

Foppiano Vineyards. Here's the rare Russian River Valley winery where Chardonnay and Pinot Noir, though on the tasting list, don't reign supreme: the flagship wine at family-owned Foppiano is a flavorful Petite Sirah from grapes grown in a nearby, warmer-than-average sliver of the AVA. The winery has operated continuously since 1896—the Foppiano clan weathered Prohibition in part by selling home wine-making kits to do-it-yourself vintners. The current winemaker, Natalie West, the daughter of longtime Dry Creek Valley grape growers, has revived the Chardonnay line, and the citrusy initial vintages have shown promise. ■ TIP→ If you like Petite Sirah, ask if the Gianna's Block, not made every year, is available for tasting. ⊠ *12707 Old Redwood Hwy., off U.S. 101* ☎ *707/433–7272* ⊕ *www.foppiano.com* ▧ *Tasting $5* ☉ *Daily 11–5.*

Healdsburg Museum and Historical Society. To take a short break from wine tasting, visit the Healdsburg Museum and its collection of local historical objects, including baskets and artifacts from native tribes. Other exhibits cover the Mexican Rancho period, the founding and growth of Healdsburg in the 1850s, and the history of local agriculture. ⊠ *221 Matheson St., at Fitch St.* ☎ *707/431–3325* ⊕ *www.healdsburgmuseum. org* ▧ *Free* ☉ *Wed.–Sun. 11–4.*

La Crema. The tasteful decor of La Crema's tasting room perfectly suits the high-profile brand's well-composed Chardonnays and Pinot Noirs. A basic tasting provides an overview of the offerings, but consider requesting a Pinot Noir appellation tasting, which allows you to sample wines whose grapes derive from several coastal AVAs. The extra heat that grapes from the Russian River Valley receive makes that area's

The Russian River Valley AVA extends from Healdsburg west to Guerneville.

wine the perkiest of the bunch, but each wine has its virtues. You can almost taste the sand and seashells in the more ascetic Sonoma Coast Shell Ridge Pinot Noir, and the Anderson Valley wine is soft, sweet, and mildly flowery. ■ TIP→ For a slightly higher fee you can taste the more exclusive 9 Barrels vintages. ⊠ *235 Healdsburg Ave., near Matheson St.* ☎ *800/314–1762, 707/431–9400* ⊕ *www.lacrema.com* ✉ *Sun.–Thurs. 10:30–5:30, Fri. and Sat. 10:30–7* ⊗ *Tastings $10–$30.*

Michel-Schlumberger. Down a narrow road at the westernmost edge of the Dry Creek Valley, Michel-Schlumberger specializes in Bordeaux varietals but also makes Burgundian- and Rhône-style wines. Seated tastings—there's no tasting bar—take place in an elegant white-stucco California Mission–style building, on its side terrace, or near the reflecting pool of the large rectangular courtyard. The winery's initial reputation rested on Cabernet Sauvignons, but the Chardonnays, Rosé of Merlot, Malbec, and Syrah also impress, as do Faux Pas, a suavely potent 50–50 blend of Cabernet Sauvignon and Syrah, and the classic Port. ■ TIP→ A splendid way to experience the versatility of the M-S lineup is to sign up for chef Michael Pryor's leisurely, generously portioned five-course wine and food pairing. ⊠ *4155 Wine Creek Rd., off W. Dry Creek Rd.* ☎ *707/433–7427, 800/447–3060* ⊕ *michelschlumberger.com* ✉ *Tastings $10–$20, tour $30, wine and food pairing $59* ⊗ *Daily 11–5; tour at 11 and 2, by appointment; wine and food pairing Wed. 1 and 3, Thurs.–Sun. 11, 1, and 3.*

Moshin Vineyards. If you've ever wondered how your college math professor might fare as a winemaker, slip over to this friendly place acclaimed for its small-lot, single-vineyard Pinot Noirs. Rick Moshin, formerly of

CLOSE UP

Dry Creek Valley AVA

If you drive north along Healdsburg Avenue and turn left onto Dry Creek Road, you'll soon feel like you've slipped back in time. Healdsburg looks totally urban in comparison with the pure, unspoiled countryside of Dry Creek Valley. Although the region has become renowned for its wines, it preserves a rural simplicity rarely found in California's Wine Country today. The valley's well-drained, gravelly floor is planted with Chardonnay grapes to the south, where an occasional sea fog creeping in from the Russian River cools the vineyards. Sauvignon Blanc is planted in the north, where the vineyards are warmer. The red decomposed soils of the benchlands bring out the best in Zinfandel—the grape for which Dry Creek has become famous—but they also produce great Cabernet Sauvignon. And these soils seem well suited to such Rhône varieties as Cinsault, Mourvèdre, and Marsanne, which need heat to ripen properly. Wineries within this AVA include Dry Creek, Ferrari-Carano, Preston, Quivira, and Ridge.

San Jose State University's math department, started out small in 1989, but by the mid-2000s demand for his meticulously crafted Pinots was sufficiently strong to support construction of a four-tier, gravity-flow winery on his hillside property. Brief but interesting tours cover the winery's layout and Moshin's penchant for picking grapes earlier than most of his neighbors (to preserve the acidity that helps his wines pair well with food). In the tasting room, which always has a curated art exhibit, guests sip Pinot Noirs along with Chardonnay, Merlot, Sauvignon Blanc, Zinfandel, and other wines. ⊠ *10295 Westside Rd., off Wohler Rd.* ☎ *707/433–5499, 888/466–7446* ⊕ *moshinvineyards.com* 🍷 *Tasting $10, tour $20* ☯ *Daily 11–4:30.*

QUICK BITES

Moustache Baked Goods. This shop specializes in sweets incorporating local, organic ingredients: cupcakes (try the one with maple-spice frosting and local bacon), snickerdoodles, whoopie pies, and macarons, to name a few. ⊠ *381 Healdsburg Ave., at North St.* ☎ *707/395–4111* ⊕ *moustache-bakedgoods.com* ☯ *Daily 10–6.*

Papapietro Perry. Pinot Noir and Zinfandel are the mainstays of this small operation in the heart of the Dry Creek Valley, but the winery also produces small lots of Chardonnay. Most of the grapes come from the Russian River Valley, though there's a Pinot from Sonoma Coast grapes and another from fruit grown in neighboring Mendocino County; one Zin is made from Dry Creek fruit. Standard tastings ($10) at the copper-topped bar include five pours, and it always pays to ask what else is open in the back—the 777 Clones Pinot is particularly delicious. Pinot on the Patio wine and cheese tastings ($45) are by appointment only. ⊠ *4791 Dry Creek Rd., at Timber Crest Farms* ☎ *707/433–0422, 877/467–4668* ⊕ *www.papapietro-perry.com* 🍷 *Tastings $10–$45* ☯ *Daily 11–4:30; 24-hr notice required for wine-cheese tasting.*

FAMILY **Preston of Dry Creek.** The long driveway at convivial Preston, flanked by vineyards and punctuated by the occasional olive tree, winds down to farmhouses encircling a shady yard with picnic tables. Year-round a selection of organic produce grown in the winery's gardens is sold at a small shop near the tasting room; house-made bread and olive oil are also available. Owners Lou and Susan Preston are committed to organic growing techniques and use only estate-grown grapes in their wines, which include a perky Sauvignon Blanc (the best option for a picnic here), Barbera, Petite Sirah, Syrah, Viognier, and Zinfandel. ✉ *9282 W. Dry Creek Rd., at Hartsock Rd. No. 1* ☎ *707/433–3372* ⊕ *www. prestonvineyards.com* 🍷 *Tasting $10* ☉ *Daily 11–4:30.*

Quivira Vineyards and Winery. An unassuming winery in a modern wooden barn topped by solar panels, Quivira produces some of Dry Creek's most interesting wines. Hugh Chappelle, the winemaker since 2010, crafts well-balanced reds, among them a lush Syrah, several hearty Zinfandels, and a Petite Sirah that showcases this unheralded varietal's noblest attributes. He also makes a zesty yet refined Sauvignon Blanc. The excellent tour provides information about the winery's bio-dynamic and organic farming practices and offers a glimpse of the beautiful garden and the property's pigs, chickens, and beehives. ■ TIP➜ You can take a free self-guided tour through the garden, some of whose bounty—including estate-grown olive oil—is available for sale. ✉ *4900 W. Dry Creek Rd., near Wine Creek Rd.* ☎ *707/431–8333, 800/292–8339* ⊕ *www.quivirawine.com* 🍷 *Tasting $10, tour $20* ☉ *Daily 11–5; tours daily at 10 by appointment.*

Rodney Strong Vineyards. The late Rodney Strong was among the first winemakers to plant Pinot Noir grapes in the Russian River Valley; his namesake winery still makes Pinot Noirs, but it's known more for Cabernet Sauvignon–based wines. The headliners include the Bordeaux-style blend Symmetry and three single-vineyard Alexander Valley Cabernets: Alexander's Crown, Rockaway, and Brothers Ridge. You can sample Cabs and Pinots—along with Sauvignon Blanc, Chardonnay, Malbec, Zinfandel, and other wines—in the octagonal tasting room and, in good weather, on an umbrella-shaded terrace. A self-guided tour provides a good view of the fermentation tanks and machinery, and guided tours also take place. ■ TIP➜ The winery hosts popular outdoor jazz and rock concerts during summer. ✉ *11455 Old Redwood Hwy., north of Eastside Rd.* ☎ *707/431–1533, 800/678–4763* ⊕ *www. rodneystrong.com* 🍷 *Tastings $10–$30, tour free* ☉ *Daily 10–5, tour at 11 and 3.*

Seghesio Family Vineyards. The ancestors of the current winemaker, Ted Seghesio, planted some of the Alexander Valley's earliest Zinfandel vines. The grapes harvested here produce sophisticated wines, among them the Home Ranch Zinfandel. Seghesio crafts most of his wines—including old-vine Zinfandel, Sangiovese, and Omaggio, a super-Tuscan blend of Cabernet Sauvignon and Sangiovese—using estate-grown fruit from the Alexander, Dry Creek, and Russian River valleys. ■ TIP➜ The $75 Family Tables Tasting pairs food prepared by chef Peter Janiak with limited-release wines. ✉ *700 Grove St., off W. Grant St.*

☎ 707/433–3579 ⊕ *www.seghesio.com* ▣ *Tastings $15–$75* ⊙ *Daily 10–5; Family Tables Tasting Fri.–Sun. by appointment.*

Stonestreet. From the broad patio that fronts Stonestreet Alexander Mountain Estate's stablelike building you can see some of the steep, rugged terrain where grapes for the winery's full-bodied Chardonnays and wild-as-a-stallion Cabernet Sauvignons are grown. At 5,100 acres (900 planted), this is among the world's largest mountain vineyards. Farming these steep hills is difficult and labor intensive, but the hard-won output finds its way into top boutique wines in addition to Stonestreet's. You can taste a flight of whites, reds, or a combination; for stunning views and to experience the vineyards close up, take the mountain tour, which includes lunch. ■TIP➔ Stonestreet also has an in-town tasting room, near Healdsburg Plaza at 337 Healdsburg Avenue. ⊠ *7111 Hwy. 128, off W. Sausal La.* ☎ *800/355–8008 estate winery, 707/473–3377 Healdsburg Ave. tasting room* ⊕ *www.stonestreetwines.com* ▣ *Estate winery tastings, some with food $12–$50, mountain tour $75; Healdsburg Ave. tasting room $12–$15* ⊙ *Estate winery daily 11–4:30, mountain tour by appointment; Healdsburg Ave. tasting room Sun.–Thurs. 10:30–5:30, Fri. and Sat. 10:30–7.*

Thumbprint Cellars Tasting Lounge. With its exposed-brick walls, sleek leather chairs, silk curtains, and artwork on the walls, this stylish tasting room has the feel of a very hip friend's San Francisco loft. The alluringly named wines—among them Arousal, Four Play, and Three Some—come primarily from Russian River, Dry Creek, and Alexander valley grapes. ⊠ *102 Matheson St., at Healdsburg Ave.* ☎ *707/433–2393* ⊕ *www. thumbprintcellars.com* ▣ *Tasting $5 and up* ⊙ *Daily 11–6.*

Unti Vineyards. There's a reason why Unti, known for Zinfandel and wines made from sometimes obscure Rhône and Italian varietals, often bustles even when business is slow elsewhere in Dry Creek—this is a fun, casual place. You'll often find the convivial co-founder, Mick Unti, who manages the winery, chatting up guests and pouring wine in the rustic-not-trying-to-be-chic tasting room. Tastings often begin with Cuvée Blanc, a blend of Vermentino, Grenache Blanc, and Picpoul grapes, followed by a white or two more and then Barbera, Sangiovese, and Syrah. The Segromigno blend showcases the estate-grown Sangiovese and Montepulciano grapes. ■TIP➔ Visits here require appointments, but it's usually possible to get one on short notice. ⊠ *4202 Dry Creek Rd., ¾ north of Lambert Bridge Rd.* ☎ *707/433–5590* ⊕ *www. untivineyards.com* ▣ *Tasting $5* ⊙ *Daily 10–4.*

WHERE TO EAT

$$$

ITALIAN

✕ **Baci Café & Wine Bar.** Tourists keep this neighborhood trattoria bustling during high season, but after things die down locals continue dropping by for pizza, a long list of pasta plates, and osso buco, saltimbocca, and other stick-to-your ribs Italian standards. The Iranian-born chef, Shari Sarabi, applies a pan-Mediterranean sensibility to locally sourced, mostly organic ingredients, and his dishes satisfy without being overly showy. His wife, Lisbeth Holmefjord, of Norway, runs the dining room with infectious enthusiasm and is a sage sommelier. A feed store in the 19th century, the contemporary space has cream-yellow walls, zinc-top tables, and colorful artwork and banners. ■**TIP→ Many menu items, including pasta dishes, can be made gluten-free.** $\boxed{\$}$ *Average main: $24* ✉ *336 Healdsburg Ave., at North St.* ☎ *707/433–8111* ⊕ *www. bacicafeandwinebar.com* ⊗ *Closed Tues. No lunch.*

$$$$
AMERICAN

✕**Barndiva.** This hip joint abandons the homey vibe of many Wine Country spots for a more urban feel. Electronic music plays quietly in the background while servers ferry inventive seasonal cocktails. The food is as stylish as the couples cozying up next to each other on the banquette seats. Make a light meal out of yellowfin sashimi or a kale Caesar with pickled pearl onions, or settle in for the evening with wild king salmon served with gnocchi and avocado or roasted chicken with chanterelles and ricotta and egg yolk ravioli. ■**TIP→ During warm weather the open-air patio is the place to be.** $\boxed{\$}$ *Average main: $31* ✉ *231 Center St., at Matheson St.* ☎ *707/431–0100* ⊕ *www.barndiva. com* ⊗ *Closed Mon. and Tues.*

$$$
FRENCH

✕**Bistro Ralph.** There was a time when Bistro Ralph was *the* good restaurant in downtown Healdsburg, and long before the concept of "fresh, simple, local" became culinary gospel, that hallowed refrain coursed through the kitchen of this northern Sonoma County pioneer. The menu shifts seasonally. In spring, for example, you might find extraordinary grilled marinated asparagus; at other times look for grilled Columbia River sturgeon or Dungeness crab ravioli. Standbys include fried Szechuan-pepper calamari, chicken livers (locals love 'em), lamb burgers, and cassoulet. ■**TIP→ The wines are all from Healdsburg, but with dozens of wineries within city limits, the selection is more than sufficiently varied.** $\boxed{\$}$ *Average main: $27* ✉ *109 Plaza St., near Healdsburg Ave.* ☎ *707/433–1380* ⊕ *www.bistroralph.com* ⊗ *No dinner Sun.*

$$$
SPANISH
Fodor'sChoice
★

✕**Bravas Bar de Tapas.** Spanish-style tapas and an outdoor patio in perpetual party mode make this restaurant headquartered in a restored 1920s bungalow a popular downtown perch. Contemporary Spanish mosaics set a perky tone inside, but unless something's amiss with the weather nearly everyone heads out back for cocktails, sangrias, beers, or flights of sherry (a tapas-bar staple in Spain) to prep the palate for the onslaught of flavors. Reliable items include the paella, Spanish cured ham, *pan tomate* (tomato toast), farm-fried duck eggs, pork-cheek sliders, croquettes, skirt steak, and crispy fried chicken with pickled peppers. ■**TIP→ On a hot Healdsburg day, the watermelon salad or gazpacho will instantly reset your internal thermostat.** $\boxed{\$}$ *Average main: $26* ✉ *420 Center St., near North St.* ☎ *707/433–7700* ⊕ *www. starkrestaurants.com/bravas.html.*

$$$
PORTUGUESE

✕**Café Lucia.** The flavors of Portugal dazzle diners at this restaurant run by Healdsburg native Lucia Azevedo Fincher. You can go the tapas-only route—the fried Sonoma goat cheese and the crispy pig's ear are two standouts—or order a few small plates before moving on to a full entrée. A fine accompaniment either way is *caldo verde,* a potato-thickened beef consommé with thinly sliced collard greens and linguiça sausage. Among the noteworthy mains is *feijoada completa,* the Brazilian national dish, a thick mass of stewed beef, pork, smoked sausage, and black beans. The Portuguese variation on paella is also a

The Russian River Valley's hot summer days and cool nights create ideal conditions for growing Chardonnay and Pinot Noir.

winner. $ *Average main: $24* ✉ *235 Healdsburg Ave., near Matheson St.* ☎ *707/431–1113* ⊕ *www.cafelucia.net.*

$$
ITALIAN
Fodor's Choice
★

✕**Campo Fina.** Ari Rosen, the owner of popular Scopa (⇨ *see below*), converted a storefront that once housed a bar notorious for boozin' and brawlin' into a second showcase for his contemporary-rustic Italian cuisine. Sandblasted red brick, satin-smooth walnut tables, and old-school lighting fixtures strike an appropriately retro note for a dinner menu built around pizzas and a few other Scopa gems such as Rosen's variation on his grandmother's tomato-braised chicken with creamy-soft polenta. Locals love Campo Fina for lunch, especially on the outdoor patio, beyond which lies a boccie court that looks out of a movie set. The Sally Peppers sandwich—house-made sausage, provolone, sweet and spicy peppers, and caramelized onions on a ciabatta roll—is a memorable medley. $ *Average main: $18* ✉ *330 Healdsburg Ave., near North St.* ☎ *707/395–4640* ⊕ *www.campofina.com* ✍ *Reservations essential.*

$$
MODERN
AMERICAN
Fodor's Choice
★

✕**Chalkboard.** Unvarnished oak flooring, wrought-iron accents, and a vaulted white ceiling create a polished yet rustic ambience for the playfully ambitious cuisine of chef Shane McAnelly. Starters such as pork-belly biscuits might at first glance seem frivolous, but the silky flavor blend—maple glaze, pickled onions, and chipotle mayo playing off feathery biscuit halves—signals a supremely capable tactician at work. Likewise with vegetable sides such as fried brussels sprouts perched upon a perky kimchi puree, or moist and crispy buttermilk fried quail. House-made pasta dishes favor rich country flavors—the robust Sonoma lamb *sugo* (sauce) with Pecorino-Romano tickles the entire palate—while desserts named the Candy Bar and Donuts O' the Day aim to please (and do). The canny wine selections ably support McAnelly's cuisine. ⑤ *Average main: $19* ✉ *Hotel Les Mars, 29 North St., west of Healdsburg Ave.* ☎ *707/473–8030* ⊕ *chalkboardhealdsburg.com.*

$ | ✕**Costeaux.** This French-style bakery and café has won numerous
FRENCH | awards for its bread, and the croissants are among Sonoma County's best. Breakfast, served all day, includes homemade quiche, the signature omelet (sun-dried tomatoes, applewood-smoked bacon, and Brie), and French toast made from thick slabs of cinnamon-walnut bread. Among the lunch items are two au courant variations on classic sandwiches: a French dip made from house-roasted rib eye and a Monte Cristo (turkey, ham, and Jarlsberg cheese) on that addictive cinnamon-walnut bread. ■**TIP**➜ **Arrive early on weekends to grab a seat on the open-air patio.** ⑤ *Average main: $13* ✉ *417 Healdsburg Ave., at North St.* ☎ *707/433–1913* ⊕ *www.costeaux.com* ⚑ *Reservations not accepted* ⊙ *No dinner.*

$ | ✕**Downtown Bakery & Creamery.** To catch the Healdsburg spirit, hit the
BAKERY | plaza in the early morning to down a cup of coffee and a fragrant
Fodor's Choice | sticky bun or a too-darlin' *canelé*, a French-style pastry with a soft
★ | custard center surrounded by a dense caramel crust. Until 2 pm you can also go the full breakfast route: pancakes, granola, poached farm eggs on polenta, or perhaps the dandy bacon-and-egg pizza. For lunch there are sandwiches, pizzas, and calzones. ⑤ *Average main: $8* ✉ *308A Center St., at North St.* ☎ *707/431–2719* ⊕ *www.downtownbakery.net* ⚑ *Reservations not accepted* ⊙ *No dinner.*

$$$$ | ✕**Dry Creek Kitchen.** Chef Charlie Palmer's ultramodern destination res-
MODERN | taurant enchants diners with clever combinations of flavors and textures
AMERICAN | in dishes based on seasonal, often local ingredients. A perennial favorite among the starters is the diver scallops with fennel in a thin and flaky pastry shell, with a caviar-Pernod beurre blanc sauce. Expect a similar level of complexity with main courses that might include crispy-skin Petaluma chicken and smoked duck breast with Pinot Noir–braised cabbage. ■**TIP**➜ **The restaurant waives the corkage fee on wines from Sonoma County, which can take the edge off your final tab.** ⑤ *Average main: $33* ✉ *Hotel Healdsburg, 317 Healdsburg Ave., near Matheson St.* ☎ *707/431–0330* ⊕ *www.drycreekkitchen.com* ⊙ *No lunch Mon.–Thurs.*

$$$ | ✕**Partake by K-J.** Kendall-Jackson's downtown restaurant opened with a
MODERN | novel wine-oriented tasting menu that has evolved into a more straight-
AMERICAN | forward appetizers-salads-entrées format, but the emphasis on pairing
Fodor's Choice | top-tier Jackson-label wines and food remains. Much of chef Justin
★ | Wangler's produce finds its way from K-J's 3-acre Santa Rosa organic farm to diners' tables in a mere few hours. With ingredients this fresh, Wangler wisely displays a light touch: summertime heirloom-tomato dishes, for instance, might have no dressing at all, the same for salads of tender mixed baby greens. Popular appetizers include lamb sliders; duck breast and local salmon are consistent main-course favorites. ■**TIP**➜ Tempura maitake mushrooms, the tour de force side, are served with a sweet Korean soy sauce that plays well off the wafflelike notes in the tempura batter. ⑤ *Average main: $23* ✉ *241 Healdsburg Ave., near*

5

Matheson St. ☎ 707/433–6000 ⊕ www.partakebykj.com ⊘ Restaurant closed Mon. and Tues. No lunch.

$$$ ✕ **Restaurant Charcuterie.** French-born chef Patrick Martin's bistro just
ECLECTIC north of Healdsburg Plaza tilts Provençal, but traditional and contemporary American and Italian culinary influences broaden its appeal. You might find anything from an all-American chicken-salad sandwich and an excellent house-cured pork tenderloin sandwich on the lunch menu to Italian favorites such as fusilli and smoked chicken in a basil cream sauce for dinner. Several of the most accomplished dishes are French through and through, among them baked Brie, escargots in a garlicky herb butter, and a charcuterie plate that includes pork-pepper pâté, duck rillette, and garlic salami. $ *Average main: $23* ⊠ *335 Healdsburg Ave., at North St.* ☎ *707/431–7213* ⊕ *www.charcuteriehealdsburg.com.*

$$ ✕ **Scopa.** At his tiny, deservedly popular eatery, chef Ari Rosen pre-
ITALIAN pares rustic Italian specialties such as *sugo Calabrese* (tomato-braised
Fodor's Choice beef and pork rib) and house-made ravioli stuffed with ricotta. Simple
★ thin-crust pizzas, including one with mozzarella, figs, prosciutto, and arugula, make fine meals, too. Locals love the restaurant for its lack of pretension: wine is served in juice glasses, and the friendly hostess makes the rounds to ensure everyone is satisfied. You'll be packed in elbow-to-elbow with your fellow diners, but for a convivial evening over a bottle of Nebbiolo, there's no better choice. $ *Average main: $20* ⊠ *109A Plaza St., near Healdsburg Ave.* ☎ *707/433–5282* ⊕ *www. scopahealdsburg.com* ⊘ *No lunch.*

$$$ ✕ **Spoonbar.** Cantina doors that open onto Healdsburg Avenue make
MODERN this trendy eatery especially appealing in summer, when a warm breeze
AMERICAN wafts into the stylish space. Midcentury modern furnishings, concrete walls, and a long communal table fashioned from rough-hewn acacia wood create an urbane setting for contemporary American fare. Chef Louis Maldonado, a 2014 finalist on Bravo TV's *Top Chef* and a champion on the network's *Last Chance Kitchen,* divides his menu into five sections, from which diners mix and match to create a meal. The mains might include lamb rib-eye stuffed with merguez sausage and escargots or barbecue-glazed flounder served with rock shrimp and corn and scallion ragout. ■TIP➔ The bar, known for inventive seasonal and historical cocktails, is the real draw for many locals. $ *Average main: $25* ⊠ *h2hotel, 219 Healdsburg Ave., at Vine St.* ☎ *707/433–7222* ⊕ *www. h2hotel.com/spoonbar* ⊘ *No lunch.*

$$$ ✕ **Willi's Seafood & Raw Bar.** The festive crowd at Willi's likes to enjoy
SEAFOOD specialty cocktails at the full bar before sitting down to a dinner of
Fodor's Choice small, mostly seafood-oriented plates. The warm Maine lobster roll
★ with garlic butter and fennel conjures up a New England fish shack, while the ceviches and the scallops served with a ginger-lime aioli suggest Latin America. Gluten-, dairy-, nut-, and seed-free options are available for diners with dietary restrictions. Desserts are a big deal here, with the key lime cheesecake and caramelized banana split among the most popular. The wine list favors Sonoma County but also includes entries from Australia, France, Greece, Portugal, and other locales. $ *Average main: $25* ⊠ *403 Healdsburg Ave., at North St.* ☎ *707/433– 9191* ⊕ *www.willisseafood.net* ⊂ *Reservations not accepted Fri.–Sun.*

An 1883 Italianate Victorian is the centerpiece of the photogenic Honor Mansion.

WHERE TO STAY

$
HOTEL
Best Western Dry Creek Inn. Easy access to downtown restaurants, tasting rooms, and shopping as well as outlying wineries and bicycle trails makes this Spanish Mission–style motel near U.S. 101 a good budget option. **Pros:** laundry facilities; some pet-friendly rooms; frequent Internet discounts. **Cons:** thin walls; highway noise audible in many rooms. $ *Rooms from: $172* ⊠ *198 Dry Creek Rd.* ☎ *707/433–0300, 800/222–5784* ⊕ *www.drycreekinn.com* ⤳ *163 rooms* ⦿*Breakfast.*

$$
B&B/INN
Camellia Inn. In a well-preserved Italianate Victorian completed in 1871, this colorful B&B sits on a quiet residential street a block from the main square. **Pros:** reasonable rates; family-friendly atmosphere; within easy walking distance of restaurants. **Cons:** a few rooms have a shower but no bath; all rooms lack TVs. $ *Rooms from: $215* ⊠ *211 North St.* ☎ *707/433–8182, 800/727–8182* ⊕ *www.camelliainn.com* ⤳ *8 rooms, 1 suite* ⦿*Breakfast.*

$$$
B&B/INN
Fodor's Choice
★
h2hotel. Eco-friendly touches abound at this hotel, from the plant-covered "green roof" to wooden decks made from salvaged lumber. **Pros:** stylish modern design; popular bar; complimentary bikes. **Cons:** least expensive rooms lack bathtubs; no fitness facilities. $ *Rooms from: $313* ⊠ *219 Healdsburg Ave.* ☎ *707/922–5251* ⊕ *www.h2hotel. com* ⤳ *28 rooms, 8 suites* ⦿*Breakfast.*

$$
B&B/INN
Healdsburg Inn on the Plaza. A genteel antidote to Healdsburg's mania for tech-chic accommodations, this inn occupies a 19th-century office building whose former tenants include a Wells, Fargo & Co. **Pros:** central location; competent service. **Cons:** garish room lighting; so-so beds; slightly impersonal feel for a B&B; street noise audible in plaza-facing

The spa at the Hotel Healdsburg sources many of its treatments' ingredients from area farms.

rooms. 💲 *Rooms from: $295* ✉ *112 Matheson St.* ☎ *800/431–8663* ⊕ *www.healdsburginn.com* ⤴ *12 rooms* ¶○¶ *Breakfast.*

$$$ 📺 **The Honor Mansion.** An 1883 Italianate Victorian houses this pho-
B&B/INN togenic hotel; rooms in the main home preserve a sense of the build-
Fodor'sChoice ing's heritage, whereas the larger suites are comparatively understated.
★ **Pros:** homemade sweets available at all hours; spa pavilions by pool available for massages in fair weather. **Cons:** almost a mile from Healdsburg Plaza; walls can seem thin. 💲 *Rooms from: $325* ✉ *891 Grove St.* ☎ *707/433–4277, 800/554–4667* ⊕ *www.honormansion. com* ⤴ *5 rooms, 7 suites, 1 cottage* ⊗ *Closed 2 wks around Christmas* ¶○¶ *Breakfast.*

$$$$ 📺 **Hotel Healdsburg.** Across the street from the tidy town plaza, this
RESORT spare, sophisticated hotel caters to travelers with an urban sensibility.
Pros: several rooms overlook the town plaza; comfortable lobby with a small attached bar; extremely comfortable beds. **Cons:** exterior rooms get some street noise; rooms could use better lighting. 💲 *Rooms from: $449* ✉ *25 Matheson St.* ☎ *707/431–2800, 800/889–7188* ⊕ *www. hotelhealdsburg.com* ⤴ *49 rooms, 6 suites* ¶○¶ *Breakfast.*

$$$$ 📺 **Hôtel Les Mars.** This Relais & Châteaux property takes the prize for
HOTEL opulence with guest rooms spacious and elegant enough for French
Fodor'sChoice nobility, 18th- and 19th-century antiques and reproductions, canopy
★ beds dressed in luxe linens, and gas-burning fireplaces. **Pros:** large rooms; just off Healdsburg's plaza; fancy bath products; room service by Chalkboard restaurant. **Cons:** very expensive. 💲 *Rooms from: $675* ✉ *27 North St.* ☎ *707/433–4211* ⊕ *www.hotellesmars.com* ⤴ *16 rooms* ¶○¶ *Breakfast.*

$$
B&B/INN
Fodor's Choice
★

▦ **Madrona Manor.** This Victorian mansion dating from 1881 is surrounded by 8 acres of wooded and landscaped grounds; rooms in the three-story mansion, the carriage house, and the three separate cottages are gloriously ornate, with mirrors in gilt frames and paintings covering every wall. **Pros:** old-fashioned and romantic (especially rooms 203 and 204); pretty veranda perfect for a cocktail. **Cons:** pool heated from May through October only. ⑤ *Rooms from: $260* ⊠ *1001 Westside Rd.* ☎ *707/433–4231, 800/258–4003* ⊕ *www.madronamanor.com* ⤶ *18 rooms, 5 suites* ⊺◎⊺ *Breakfast.*

NIGHTLIFE AND PERFORMING ARTS

In addition to the dependable Bear Republic brewpub and retro-hip Bergamot Alley wine-and-beer bar, a few Healdsburg's restaurants, most notably Spoonbar, Chalkboard, and Campo Fina *(⇨ see above),* have bars helmed by talented mixologists equally comfortable fashioning the latest potions or time-honored libations. The Raven arts center presents mostly classical, jazz, and theater performances.

Bear Republic Brewing Company. Lovers of the brew make pilgrimages to Bear Republic to sample the flagship Racer 5 IPA, the Hop Rod Rye, the mighty Big Bear Black Stout, and many other offerings at this craft-brew pioneer. The brewery's spacious pub is a good stop for a casual lunch or dinner—all kinds of burgers (beef, salmon, veggie, and more), chili, pastas, and artisanal-cheese and charcuterie plates. ∎**TIP→** In warm weather there's often a wait for the seats outdoors, but there's usually room inside. ⊠ *345 Healdsburg Ave., at North St.* ☎ *707/433–2337* ⊕ *www.bearrepublic.com.*

Fodor's Choice
★

Bergamot Alley. The welcoming vibe of the largely under-30 crowd at this retro-hip but chill wine-and-beer bar is exceeded only by that of the charming hosts. Congeniality aside, the other draws here include the craft brews on tap, the change-of-pace selection of international wines (nothing from California), and the live-music, movie, and other event nights. ⊠ *328 Healdsburg Ave., at North St.* ☎ *707/433–8720* ⊕ *bergamotalley.com.*

Raven Performing Arts Theater. The Philharmonia Healdsburg orchestra and the Raven Players theater group are this venue's resident companies. Healdsburg Jazz Festival events take place here every year. ⊠ *115 North St., at Center St.* ☎ *707/433–6335* ⊕ *www.raventheater.org.*

SHOPPING

Healdsburg is the Wine Country's most pleasant spot for an afternoon of window-shopping, with dozens of art galleries, boutiques, and high-end design shops clustered on or around Healdsburg Plaza. The town's food fetish extends to the specialty grocers and markets, but there are plenty of stores selling nonedibles, too. Should you weary of shopping, there are countless cafés and tasting rooms where you can revive yourself.

ART GALLERIES

Christopher Hill Gallery. In a town with many worthy galleries, Christopher Hill's brick-walled space stands out for both the quality of the art and his willingness to exhibit edgier styles and subject matter

5

than most of his counterparts. ✉ *326 Healdsburg Ave., at Plaza St.* ☏ *707/395–4646* ⊕ *www.chgallery.com* ⊙ *Wed.–Mon. 10–5:30, Tues. by appointment.*

Gallery Lulo. A collaboration between a local artist and jewelry maker and a Danish-born curator, this museumlike gallery presents changing exhibits of exquisite jewelry, sculpture, and objets d'art. ✉ *303 Center St., at Plaza St.* ☏ *707/433–7533* ⊕ *www.gallerylulo.com.*

Healdsburg Center for the Arts. A block off the plaza, this center displays work by local artists. In addition to larger-scale paintings and photography, look for suitcase-friendly jewelry and fine crafts. ✉ *130 Plaza St., at Center St.* ☏ *707/431–1970* ⊕ *www.healdsburgcenterforthearts. com* ⊙ *Closed Tues.*

BOOKSTORE

Copperfield's Books. In addition to magazines and best-selling books, this store, part of a local indie chain, stocks a wide selection of discounted and remaindered titles, including many cookbooks. ✉ *106 Matheson St., at Healdsburg Ave.* ☏ *707/433–9270* ⊕ *copperfieldsbooks.com/ stores/healdsburg.*

CRAFTS

Fodor's Choice
★

One World Fair Trade. Independent artisans in developing countries create the clothing, household items, jewelry, gifts, and toys sold in this bright, well-designed shop whose owner has a shrewd eye for fine craftsmanship. ✉ *104 Matheson St., at Healdsburg Ave.* ☏ *707/473–0880* ⊕ *www.oneworldfairtrade.net.*

FOOD AND WINE

Big John's Market. If the sandwich line is too long at Healdsburg's fancier markets, head north of the plaza 11 blocks and save time and money at Big John's, a full-service grocery that sells excellent gourmet sandwiches, sushi made on the spot, artisanal cheeses, and bread from Costeaux and other local bakers. ✉ *1345 Healdsburg Ave., at Dry Creek Rd.* ☏ *707/433–7151* ⊕ *www.bigjohnsmarket.com.*

Dry Creek General Store. The Dry Creek Valley is so picture-perfect, it would be a shame to pass up the opportunity to picnic at one of the wineries. For breakfasts, sandwiches, bread, cheeses, and picnic supplies, stop by the general store, established in 1881 and still a popular spot for locals to hang out on the porch or in the bar. ✉ *3495 Dry Creek Rd., at Lambert Bridge Rd.* ☏ *707/433–4171* ⊕ *www.drycreek generalstore1881.com.*

Fodor's Choice
★

Healdsburg Farmers' Market. The long-running market, held from late spring into the fall, showcases locally produced cheeses, breads, herbs, meats, and oils, in addition to the usual (ultratasty) fruits and vegetables. The flavors and smells arouse the senses, and the passion of the participating artisans warms the heart. ✉ *North and Vine Sts., 1 block west of Healdsburg Plaza* ☏ *707/431–1956* ⊕ *www.healdsburgfarmersmarket. org* ⊙ *May–Nov., Sat. 9–noon; June–Oct., Wed. 3:30–6.*

Jimtown Store. The Alexander Valley's best picnic-packing stop has great espresso and a good selection of deli items, including the signature Brie-and-chopped-olive sandwich. While you're here, take a few minutes to browse through the gifts, which include housewares and old-fashioned toys like sock monkeys. ■TIP→ Chef Peter Brown's Sunday brunch, from 9 to 2, is right fine. ✉ *6706 Hwy. 128, near W. Sausal La.* ☎ *707/433–1212* ⊕ *www.jimtown.com* ☙ *Mon., Wed., and Thurs. 7:30–4; Fri.–Sun. 7:30–5.*

Oakville Grocery. The Healdsburg branch of this Napa-based store is filled with wine, condiments, and deli items, and sells sandwiches and other picnic fixings. A terrace with ample seating makes a good place for an impromptu meal, but you might want to lunch early or late to avoid the crowds. ✉ *124 Matheson St., at Center St.* ☎ *707/433–3200* ⊕ *www.oakvillegrocery.com.*

Fodor'sChoice ★ **The Shed.** Inside a glass-front, steel-clad variation on a traditional grange hall, this shop-cum-eatery celebrates local agriculture with specialty foods. It also stocks seeds and plants, gardening and farming implements, cookware, and everything a smart pantry should hold. ✉ *25 North St., west of Healdsburg Ave.* ☎ *707/431–7433* ⊕ *healdsburg-shed.com.*

Tip Top Liquor Warehouse. Shopping for wine at this nondescript liquor barn 11 blocks north of the plaza is a bit like poking around a thrift shop, but you might find some Napa and Sonoma rarities, often priced well below what you'd pay at their wineries. ✉ *90 Dry Creek Rd., at Healdsburg Ave.* ☎ *707/431–0841.*

HOUSEHOLD ITEMS AND FURNITURE

Lime Stone. Owned by Dry Creek Kitchen chef Charlie Palmer and his wife, Lisa, this shop carries wine-related items, kitchen accoutrements, and household accessories. The hip and tasteful Lisa does all the buying. ✉ *Hotel Healdsburg, 318 Healdsburg Ave., near Matheson St.* ☎ *707/433–3080* ⊕ *www.limestonehealdsburg.com.*

Plaza Gourmet. You'll find not only wine-related gadgets but also a wide selection of kitchenware and serving pieces at this appealing shop. ✉ *108 Matheson St., at Healdsburg Ave.* ☎ *707/433–7116.*

Saint Dizier Home. With its selection of furniture and contemporary items for the home, this shop reminds mere mortals why the universe provides us with decorators and designers—they really do know best. ✉ *259 Center St., at Matheson St.* ☎ *707/473–0980* ⊕ *www.saintdhome.com.*

Fodor'sChoice ★ **Urban Lumber Company.** Master woodworker Seth San Filippo creates contemporary, designer-quality furniture out of reclaimed, salvaged, and sustainably harvested hardwoods. The one-of-a-kind pieces include tables, cabinets, chairs, counters, and bar tops. ✉ *328 Healdsburg Ave., at Plaza St.* ☎ *707/756–5044* ⊕ *www.urbanlumber.co.*

SPAS

Spa Dolce. Owner Ines von Majthenyi Scherrer has a good local rep, having run a popular nearby spa before opening this stylish facility just off Healdsburg Plaza. Spa Dolce specializes in skin and body care for men and women, and waxing and facials for women. Curved white walls and fresh-cut floral arrangements set a subdued tone for such treatments as the exfoliating Hauschka body scrub, which combines organic brown sugar with scented oil. There's a romantic room for couples to enjoy massages for two. ■ TIP➔ Many guests come just for the facials, which range from a straightforward cleansing to an anti-aging peel. ⊠ *250 Center St., at Matheson St.* ☎ *707/433–0177* ⊕ *www.spadolce. com* ⊠ *Treatments $55–$240* ⊙ *Tues.–Sun. 10–7.*

The Spa Hotel Healdsburg. Taking a page from its restaurant's farm-to-table approach, the Hotel Healdsburg's spa also sources many of its treatments' ingredients from area farms. The plush robes for patrons, an outdoor Jacuzzi, and soothing minimalist decor make this a tranquil choice for massages, body wraps, facials, and hand and foot treatments. The most popular ones include the Meyer lemon body polishes, herbal wraps, and massages and the lavender-and-peppermint restorative massage, all of which leave the skin tingling and rejuvenated. The hotel's signature Swedish-style massage involves aromatic oils, hot stones, and, as necessary, acupressure. ⊠ *327 Healdsburg Ave., at Matheson St.* ☎ *707/433–4747* ⊕ *www.hotelhealdsburg.com/spa* ⊠ *Treatments $45–$240* ⊙ *Daily 9–8.*

SPORTS AND THE OUTDOORS
BICYCLING

A mostly gentle 20-mile loop starting and ending in Healdsburg Plaza will take you past several good wineries—and infinitely beautiful scenery that includes vineyard-covered hills, the rolling Russian River, and a gently rusting trestle bridge. Start by heading south from the plaza on Healdsburg Avenue. Turn west onto Mill Street, whose name changes to Westside Road after you cross under U.S. 101. Follow Westside for almost 10 miles, stopping at wineries (among them Rochioli) as time permits. Unless you're heading to Gary Farrell Winery or Moshin Vineyards, which are a little farther south, turn east on Wohler Road and then north on Eastside Road. Copain is among the wineries along this view-filled portion of the ride. Head north again at Old Redwood Highway—J Vineyards and Rodney Strong are at this intersection. The name of the road changes to Healdsburg Avenue after you cross under U.S. 101; the avenue leads back to the plaza.

Wine Country Bikes. This shop in downtown Healdsburg is perfectly located for single or multi-day treks into the Dry Creek and Russian River valleys. Bikes, including tandems, rent for $39 to $145 a day. One-day tours start at $149. ⊠ *61 Front St., at Hudson St.* ☎ *707/473–0610, 866/922–4537* ⊕ *www.winecountrybikes.com.*

BOATING
Russian River Adventures. This outfit rents inflatable canoes for self-guided, full- and half-day trips down the Russian River. Pack a swimsuit and a picnic lunch and shove off. You'll likely see wildlife on the shore

and can stop at fun swimming holes and even swing on a rope above the water. The fee includes a shuttle ride back to your car. The full-day trip is dog-friendly. ⊠ *20 Healdsburg Ave., at S. University St.* ☎ *707/433–5599, 800/280–7627* ⊕ *www.russianriveradventures.com* ⌸ *$47.50 per person ½ day, $60 full day, $10 dogs* ⊙ *Mid-Apr.–mid-Oct.*

GEYSERVILLE

8 miles north of Healdsburg.

Several of the Alexander Valley AVA's high-profile wineries, including Silver Oak Cellars and the splashiest of them all, the Francis Ford Coppola Winery, can be found in the town of Geyserville. Not long ago Geyserville was a dusty farm town with little to offer travelers besides a grocery store. Downtown retains its dusty character, but the restaurants, shops, and tasting rooms along the short main drag make it worth a stroll.

GETTING HERE AND AROUND

From Healdsburg, the quickest route to downtown Geyserville is north on U.S. 101 to the Highway 128/Geyserville exit. Turn right at the stop sign onto Geyserville Avenue and follow the road north to the small downtown. For a more scenic drive, head north from Healdsburg Plaza along Healdsburg Avenue. About 3 miles north, jog west (left) for a few hundred feet onto Lytton Springs Road, then turn north (right) onto Geyserville Avenue. In town, the avenue merges with Highway 128. Sonoma County Transit Bus 60 serves Geyserville from downtown Healdsburg.

VISITOR INFORMATION

Geyserville Chamber of Commerce ☎ 707/857–3745 ⊕ www.geyservillecc.com.

EXPLORING
TOP ATTRACTIONS

David Coffaro Estate Vineyard. David Coffaro himself tends to every aspect of the wine-making process at his namesake winery, where memorabilia of his beloved Oakland Raiders lines the wall behind the bar. (On game days, you might find staffers watching the action on a large screen tucked between the barrels.) Despite the relaxed attitude, Coffaro is serious about wines. He specializes in reasonably priced single-varietal wines—Zinfandel and Petite Sirah are strong suits. He also makes wines using Lagrein, Aglianico, and other less familiar grapes, which also find their way into his unique blends. ⊠ *7485 Dry Creek Rd., near Yoakim Bridge Rd.* ☎ *707/433–9715* ⊕ *www.coffaro.com* ⌸ *Tasting $5, tour free* ⊙ *Daily 11–4, tour Fri. at 11 and 1.*

Fodor's Choice
★

Locals Tasting Room. Though trending upscale, downtown Geyserville remains little more than a crossroads with a few shops and restaurants. But if you're serious about wine, Carolyn Lewis's tasting room is alone worth a trek. Connoisseurs come to sample the output of a dozen or so small wineries, most without tasting rooms of their own. There's no fee for tasting—a bargain for wines of this quality—and the extremely knowledgeable staff is happy to pour you a flight of several wines so

A Great Drive in Northern Sonoma County

Dabble in three AVAs in one day on a scenic loop drive that begins in downtown Healdsburg. Before departing, break your fast at **Flying Goat Coffee** or **Downtown Bakery & Creamery,** then pick up everything you need for a picnic at nearby **Oakville Grocery.** Thus prepared, hop in the car and head south on Healdsburg Avenue.

RUSSIAN RIVER VALLEY AVA

A few blocks south of Healdsburg Plaza, stay left to avoid accessing U.S. 101. About ½ mile past the bridge over the Russian River, Healdsburg Avenue becomes Old Redwood Highway. Just past the driveway for the J and Rodney Strong wineries (and by all means stop at one of them if you're eager to start tasting), make a right onto Eastside Road and continue past Copain Wines to Wohler Road and turn right. Before long you'll cross the rusting, highly photogenic Wohler Bridge. At Westside Road, turn north to reach **Rochioli Vineyards and Winery**—if it's Tuesday or Wednesday, when the winery is open by appointment only, turn south and drive a few miles to **Gary Farrell Winery.** In either case, after your tasting head north on Westside Road about 5 miles past Rochioli.

DRY CREEK VALLEY AVA

Turn northwest at the intersection of Westside and West Dry Creek roads— **Madrona Manor,** worth a peek for its well-tended estate garden, borders them both—and continue on West Dry Creek for about 9 miles to **Preston of Dry Creek.** Sample some wines and perhaps purchase one—the peppy Sauvignon Blanc is a natural on a hot summer day—to enjoy while picnicking on the property.

From Preston, head southeast on West Dry Creek Road and east on Yoakim Bridge Road. If it's summer and the Dry Creek Peach Produce stand is open, stop to sample the fruit; otherwise continue directly to Dry Creek Road and turn south, heading east after about ¼ mile onto Canyon Road. After 2 miles, just after you pass under U.S. 101, turn south onto Highway 128 east, also signed as Geyserville Avenue.

ALEXANDER VALLEY AVA

Let your mood determine your stop in the Alexander Valley. Taste flights of wines from small producers at the **Locals Tasting Room,** or for breathtakingly balanced Chardonnays and Bordeaux reds, continue east on Highway 128, turning left on Geysers Road and right on Red Winery Road to **Robert Young Estate Winery.** If Hollywood glitz is more your speed, head south on Geyserville Avenue to U.S. 101, hop on the freeway for 1 mile, and take the Independence Lane exit. Follow signs west from the exit to **Francis Ford Coppola Winery.**

After your Alexander Valley stop, either enjoy dinner at **Diavola Pizzeria & Salumeria** or **Catelli's** in Geyserville, or head back to Healdsburg, south on Geyserville Avenue, briefly east (left) onto Lytton Springs Road, and south on Healdsburg Avenue.

you can compare, say, different Cabernet Sauvignons. ✉ *21023A Geyserville Ave., at Hwy. 128* ☎ *707/857–4900* ⊕ *www.tastelocalwines. com* 🍷 *Tasting free* ⊗ *Daily 11–6.*

Fodor's Choice
★ **Robert Young Estate Winery.** The whitewashed colonial-style residence and barnlike winery building at Robert Young lend an appropriate air of permanence to this longtime grower whose Chardonnays and Cabernet Sauvignons wine critics routinely applaud. The first Youngs began farming this land in the mid-1800s, but it was the late Robert Young, of the third generation, who planted two Chardonnay clones now named for him. Grapes from them go into the Area 27 Chardonnay, noteworthy for the quality of its fruit and craftsmanship. Winemaker Kevin Warren also shines with the reds—not to be missed if being poured are the Petit Verdot, Cabernet Franc, and the Cabernet Sauvignons. ▪**TIP**➜ Tables for picnickers are set up outside the two entrances to the winery's caves. ✉ *4960 Red Winery Rd., off Hwy. 128* ☎ *707/431–4811* ⊕ *www.ryew.com* 🍷 *Tasting $10, wine-and-cheese pairing $25* ⊗ *Daily 10–4:30, wine-and-cheese pairing Fri. only, by appointment.*

Fodor's Choice
★ **Silver Oak Cellars.** The placid, well-appointed, Tudor-modern Geyserville facility of the same-named Napa Valley winery produces just one wine each year: a taut, robust, well-balanced Alexander Valley Cabernet Sauvignon. Unlike many Wine Country Cabernets, this one is aged in American rather than French oak barrels (half new, half once-used) for 24 months. You can taste the current Alexander Valley Cabernet and the Cabernet-heavy Napa Valley Bordeaux blend for $10; these two wines plus two older vintages ($20); or Silver Oak wines and ones of sister property Twomey ($30). ▪**TIP**➜ GPS navigation doesn't always locate the winery precisely; Chianti Road is parallel to and just west of U.S. 101/Highway 128. ✉ *24625 Chianti Rd., off Canyon Rd.* ☎ *707/942–7082* ⊕ *www.silveroak.com/visit-us/alexander* 🍷 *Tastings $10–$30, tour and tasting $10* ⊗ *Mon.–Sat. 10–5, Sun. 11–5.*

WORTH NOTING

FAMILY **Francis Ford Coppola Winery.** The film director's over-the-top fantasyland is the sort of place the mid-level Mafiosi in his *The Godfather* saga might declare had real class—the "everyday wines" poured here are pretty much beside the point. The fun here is all in the excess, and you may find it hard to resist having your photo snapped standing next to Don Corleone's desk from *The Godfather* or beside memorabilia from other Coppola films, including some directed by his daughter, Sofia. A bandstand reminiscent of one in *The Godfather Part II* is the centerpiece of a large pool area where you can rent a changing room, complete with shower, and spend the afternoon lounging poolside, perhaps ordering food from the adjacent café. A more elaborate restaurant, Rustic, overlooks the vineyards. ✉ *300 Via Archimedes, off U.S. 101* ☎ *707/857–1400* ⊕ *www.franciscoppolawinery.com* 🍷 *Tastings free–$20, tours $20–$75, pool pass $30* ⊗ *Tasting room daily 11–6, restaurant daily 11–9; pool hrs vary seasonally.*

The Meeker Vineyard. Old teller windows, a heavy steel vault, and a bowing tile floor supply atmosphere aplenty at this tasting room inside the circa-1900s former Bank of Geyserville building. Winemaker Charles

Alexander Valley AVA

The Alexander Valley, one of Sonoma's least-visited regions, extends northeast of Healdsburg through Geyserville all the way to Mendocino County. Driving through the rolling hills along Highway 128, you're more likely to have to slow down for tandem bicyclists than for other drivers. And you might find you're the only visitor in the tasting room at some of the small, family-owned wineries.

The Alexander Valley AVA got a boost in 2006, when director and winemaker Francis Ford Coppola bought the old Chateau Souverain winery and opened a tasting room, but some combination of distance from San Francisco (a drive here takes a little under 2 hours on a day with light traffic) and

hairpin switchback roads seems to have preserved the unpretentious, rustic nature of this region. Restaurants and inns are relatively few and far between, and this remains a spot to enjoy life in the slow lane.

As recently as the 1980s the Alexander Valley was mostly planted in walnuts, pears, prunes, and bulk grapes, so one might argue that experimentation here has hardly begun. So far, Chardonnay, Sauvignon Blanc, Zinfandel, and Cabernet Sauvignon seem to do well in places. Italian grapes such as Sangiovese or the Rhône varieties, which do so well in the Dry Creek Valley, are also beginning to make great wines in the valley's warmer sections.

Meeker, whose resume also includes a spell as the president of MGM, specializes in high-powered reds, most with good stories behind them. A harvest intern's mistake, for instance, led to the first vintage of Barberian, a robust (and then some) blend of Barbera and Zinfandel, and each bottle of Winemaker's Handprint Merlot receives individual handprints from winery workers and volunteers. Meeker also makes Chardonnays and dessert wines; his son and assistant winemaker, Lucas, expresses his individuality with lighter Lucas J Cellars Pinot Noirs and a Syrah. ✉ *21035 Geyserville Ave., at Hwy. 128* ☎ *707/431–2148* ⊕ *meekerwine.com* 🍷 *Tasting $10* ☼ *Daily 10:30–6.*

Stryker Sonoma. A wisteria-draped pergola fronts the main building of Stryker Sonoma, worth a visit for its estate-grown wines, glass-walled tasting room, and fine vineyard views. Cabernet Sauvignon is a specialty here, and Chardonnay and Zinfandel figure prominently in tastings, but if Petit Verdot and Tannat are on the menu, consider trying these rarer reds as well. For $10 you can sample several popular wines; small-production and club-only wines are poured at seated tastings ($25). The tour ($40) takes in the vineyards and concludes on the observation deck overlooking them. ■TIP→ **The picnic area is a marvelous place to bask in the quiet of the Alexander Valley countryside.** ✉ *5110 Hwy. 128, at Beleson Cemetery Rd.* ☎ *707/433–1944, 800/433–1944* ⊕ *www.strykersonoma.com* 🍷 *Tastings $10–$25, tour and tasting $40* ☼ *Daily 10:30–5.*

Trentadue Winery. Sangiovese, Zinfandel, and La Storia Cuvée 32—a blend of Sangiovese, Cabernet Sauvignon, Merlot, and sometimes other grapes—are among the strong suits of this Alexander Valley stalwart established in 1959 by the late Leo Trentadue and his wife, Evelyn. Tastings, $5 for the Trentadue Family wines and a worthwhile $10 for La Storia reserve selections, take place inside an ivy-covered villa. The diverse lineup includes a sparkler made from Chardonnay grapes, along with Sauvignon Blanc, Zinfandel Rosé, Merlot, Cabernet Sauvignon, Petite Sirah, Zinfandel, and dessert wines, all reasonably priced. ✉ *19170 Geyserville Ave., off U.S. 101* ☎ *707/433–3104* ⊕ *www.trentadue.com* 🍷 *Tastings $5–$25, tour and tasting $25* ☉ *Daily 10–5, tours by appointment.*

WHERE TO EAT AND STAY

$$
ITALIAN
Fodor's Choice
★

✕ **Catelli's.** Cookbook author and *Iron Chef* judge Domenica Catelli teamed up with her brother Nicholas to revive their family's American-Italian restaurant, a longtime Geyserville fixture. Contemporary abstracts, reclaimed-wood furnishings, and a color palette that favors muted grays and chocolatey browns signal the changing times, but you'll find good-lovin' echoes of traditional cuisine in the sturdy meat sauce that accompanies Catelli's signature lasagna dish. Also available vegetarian style, it's made with 10 layers of paper-thin pasta that merge seamlessly with the ricotta and herb-cheese filling. Another star is the three-meat (beef, pork, and chicken) ravioli made with similarly thin pasta. ■TIP➜ **In good weather, the large, marble-floor back patio, flanked by gardens with organic plants Domenica uses in her cooking, is a glamorously festive oasis.** ⑤ *Average main: $20* ✉ *21047 Geyserville Ave., at Hwy. 128* ☎ *707/857–3471* ⊕ *www.mycatellis.com* ☉ *Closed Mon.*

$$
ITALIAN
Fodor's Choice
★

✕ **Diavola Pizzeria & Salumeria.** A dining area with hardwood floors, a pressed-tin ceiling, and exposed-brick walls provides a fitting setting for the rustic cuisine at this Geyserville charmer. Chef Dino Bugica studied with several artisans in Italy before opening this restaurant that specializes in pizzas pulled from a wood-burning oven and several types of house-cured meats. A few salads and meaty main courses round out the menu. ■TIP➜ **If you're impressed by the antipasto plate, you can pick up some smoked pork belly, pancetta, or spicy Calabrese sausage to take home.** ⑤ *Average main: $19* ✉ *21021 Geyserville Ave., at Hwy. 128* ☎ *707/814–0111* ⊕ *www.diavolapizzeria.com* ⚐ *Reservations not accepted.*

$
HOTEL

🛏 **Geyserville Inn.** Clever travelers give the Healdsburg hubbub and prices the heave-ho but still have easy access to outstanding Dry Creek and Alexander Valley wineries from this modest, well-run inn. **Pros:** pool; second-floor rooms in back have vineyard views; picnic area. **Cons:** occasional noise bleed-through from corporate and other events. ⑤ *Rooms from: $155* ✉ *21714 Geyserville Ave.* ☎ *707/857–4343, 877/857–4343* ⊕ *www.geyservilleinn.com* ⚐ *41 rooms* ⦿*No meals.*

WEST COUNTY

The portion of Sonoma County west of Healdsburg and Santa Rosa goes by the name West County. The towns in this area, many of them along or near the Russian River, include Forestville, Guerneville, Occidental, Freestone, Sebastopol, and Graton. Redwoods tower over much of the region, which since the 1980s has increasingly seen grapes supplant apples and other crops on its many farms. Long before that, West County was a getaway for city and suburban dwellers, but despite the increased awareness wine making has brought, West County remains generally unfussy and resolutely rural, especially the farther west you head.

FORESTVILLE

13 miles southwest of Healdsburg.

To experience the Russian River AVA's climate and rusticity, follow the river's westward course to the town of Forestville, home to a highly regarded restaurant and inn and a secluded winery that looms large in the hearts of Pinot Noir aficionados.

GETTING HERE AND AROUND

To reach Forestville from U.S. 101, drive west from the River Road exit north of Santa Rosa. From Healdsburg, follow Westside Road west to River Road and then continue west. Sonoma County Transit Bus 20 serves Forestville.

EXPLORING

Fodor's Choice **Hartford Family Winery.** Pinot Noir lovers appreciate the subtle differ-
★ ences in the wines Hartford's Jeff Stewart crafts from grapes grown in Sonoma County's three top AVAs for the varietal—Los Carneros, Russian River Valley, and the Sonoma Coast—along with one from the Anderson Valley, just north in Mendocino County. The Pinot Noirs win praise from major wine critics, and Stewart also makes highly rated Chardonnays and old-vine Zinfandels. A reserve tasting ($15) includes a flight of six wines; a tour of the winery is part of the seated private library tasting ($40). ■ TIP→ If the weather's good and you've made a reservation, your reserve tasting can take place on the patio outside the opulent main winery building. ✉ *8075 Martinelli Rd., off Hwy. 116 or River Rd.* ☎ *707/887–8030, 800/588–0234* ⊕ *www.hartfordwines.com* 🍷 *Tastings $15–$40* ☉ *Daily 10–4:30, tours by appointment.*

Kozlowski Farms. Three generations of Kozlowskis produce the pies and jams, jellies, chutneys, and other specialty foods at one of Sonoma County's first farms to embrace organic agriculture. There are plenty of items to sample, and you can pick up pie tarts, apple strudel, and cookies to go. ✉ *5566 Gravenstein Hwy. N/Hwy. 116, near Ross Station Rd.* ☎ *707/887–1587* ⊕ *www.kozlowskifarms.com* 🍷 *Free* ☉ *Daily 9–5.*

WHERE TO EAT AND STAY

$$$ ✕ **The Backyard.** The folks behind this casually rustic modern Ameri-
MODERN can restaurant regard Sonoma County's farms and gardens as their
AMERICAN "backyard" and proudly list their purveyors on the menu. Dinner entrées, which change seasonally, might include roast chicken on a bed of creamy kale, wild line-caught salmon with a smoked-tomato vinaigrette, and tagliatelle with ricotta (both housemade) and lamb bacon. A yellow-walled alcove and a sliver of counter seating with a view of the kitchen provide cozy seating indoors, but in fine weather the front patio, shaded in its entirety by a gigantic poplar, sees all the action.

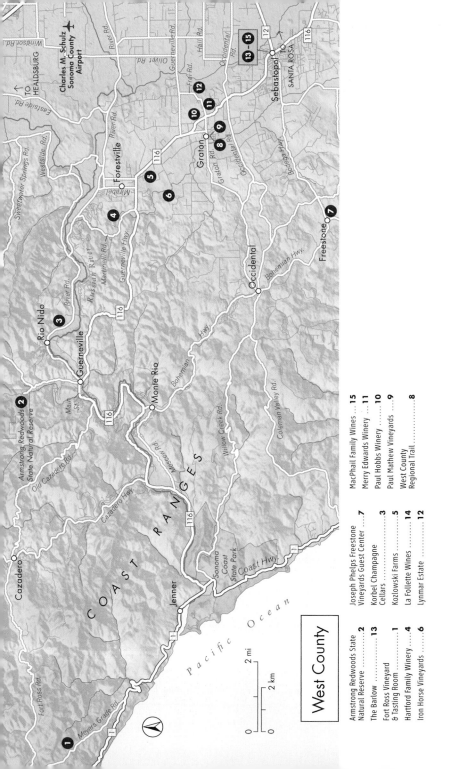

West County

Russian River Valley AVA

As the Russian River winds its way from Mendocino to the Pacific Ocean, it carves out a valley that's a near-perfect environment for growing certain grape varietals. Because of its low elevation, sea fog pushes far inland to cool the soil, yet in summer it burns off, giving the grapes enough sun to ripen properly. Fog-loving Pinot Noir and Chardonnay grapes are king and queen in the Russian River Valley AVA, which extends from Healdsburg west to the town Guerneville. The namesake river does its part by slowly carving its way downward through many layers of rock, depositing a deep layer of gravel that in parts of the valley measures 60 or 70 feet. This gravel forces the roots of grape-vines to go deep in search of water and nutrients. In the process, the plants absorb trace minerals that add complexity to the flavor of the grapes.

■TIP➔ **The three-course Wednesday-night special—a deal at $32—centers on buttermilk fried chicken served with mashed potatoes, lamb-sausage gravy, and buttermilk biscuits.** ⑤ *Average main: $24* ⊠ *6566 Front St./Hwy. 116, at 1st St.* ☎ *707/820–8445* ⊕ *backyardforestville. com* ☽ *Closed Tues.*

$$$$
FRENCH
Fodor'sChoice
★

✕ **The Farmhouse Inn.** From the sommelier who assists you with wine choices to the servers who describe the provenance of the black truf-fles shaved over the intricate pasta dishes, the staff matches the qual-ity of this restaurant's French-inspired cuisine. The signature dish, "Rabbit Rabbit Rabbit," a trio of confit of leg, rabbit loin wrapped in applewood-smoked bacon, and roasted rack of rabbit with a whole-grain mustard sauce, is typical of preparations that are both rustic and refined. The menu is prix-fixe (three courses $79, four $94). ■TIP➔ **The inn is a favorite of wine-industry foodies, so reserve well in advance; if it's full, you might be able to dine in the small lounge.** ⑤ *Average main: $79* ⊠ *7871 River Rd., at Wohler Rd.* ☎ *707/887–3300, 800/464–6642* ⊕ *www.farmhouseinn.com* ⌂ *Reservations essential* ☽ *Closed Tues. and Wed. No lunch.*

$$$$
B&B/INN
Fodor'sChoice
★

⌂ **The Farmhouse Inn.** With a rustic-farmhouse-meets-modern-loft aes-thetic, this low-key but upscale getaway with a pale-yellow exterior con-tains spacious rooms filled with king-size four-poster beds, whirlpool tubs, and hillside-view terraces. **Pros:** fantastic restaurant; luxury bath products; full-service spa. **Cons:** mild road noise audible in rooms clos-est to the street. ⑤ *Rooms from: $495* ⊠ *7871 River Rd.* ☎ *707/887–3300, 800/464–6642* ⊕ *www.farmhouseinn.com* ⇱ *19 rooms, 6 suites* ⑩ *Breakfast.*

SPORTS AND THE OUTDOORS

Burke's Canoe Trips. You'll get a real feel for the Russian River's flora and fauna on a leisurely 10-mile paddle downstream from Burke's to Guerneville. A shuttle bus returns you to your car at the end of the journey, which is best taken from late May through mid-October and, in summer, on a weekday. Summer weekends can be crowded and

On a hot summer day the shady paths of Armstrong Redwoods State Natural Reserve provide cool comfort.

raucous. ✉ *8600 River Rd., at Mirabel Rd.* ☎ *707/887–1222* ⊕ *www.burkescanoetrips.com* ✉ *$65 per canoe.*

GUERNEVILLE

7 miles northwest of Forestville; 15 miles southwest of Healdsburg.

Although most visitors to the Russian River Valley stay in Healdsburg, there's a lot to be said for peaceful Guerneville, a popular destination for gay and lesbian travelers who stay in the rustic resorts and sunbathe on the bank of the river. The town's most famous winery is Korbel Champagne Cellars, established here nearly a century and a half ago. Even older are the stands of redwoods that except on the coldest of winter days make Armstrong Redwoods State Natural Reserve such a perfect respite from wine tasting.

GETTING HERE AND AROUND

To get to Guerneville from Healdsburg, follow Westside Road south to River Road and turn west. From Forestville, head west on Highway 116; alternatively, you can head north on Mirabel Road to River Road and then head west. Sonoma County Transit Bus 20 serves Guerneville.

VISITOR INFORMATION

Guerneville Visitor Center ✉ 16209 1st St, at Armstrong Woods Rd. ☎ 707/869–9000, 877/644–9001 ⊕ www.russianriver.com.

EXPLORING

FAMILY
Fodor'sChoice
★

Armstrong Redwoods State Natural Reserve. Here's your best opportunity in the western Wine Country to wander amid *sequoia sempervirens,* also known as coast redwood trees. The oldest example in this 805-acre state park, the Colonel Armstrong Tree, is thought to be more than 1,400 years old. A half-mile from the parking lot, the tree is easily accessible, and you can hike a long way into the forest before things get too hilly. ■ TIP→ During hot summer days, Armstrong Redwoods's tall trees help the park keep its cool. ⊠ *17000 Armstrong Woods Rd., off River Rd.* ☎ *707/869–2958 visitor center, 707/869–2015 park headquarters* ⊕ *www.parks.ca.gov* ⊜ *$8 per vehicle, free to pedestrians and bicyclists* ☉ *Park daily 8 am–1 hr after sunset; visitor center daily 11–3.*

OFF THE BEATEN PATH

Fort Ross Vineyard & Tasting Room. The Russian River and Highway 116 snake west from Guerneville through redwood groves to the coast, where Highway 1 twists north past rocky cliffs to this windswept ridgetop winery. Until recently many experts deemed the weather here too chilly even for cool-climate varietals, but Fort Ross Vineyard and other Fort Ross–Seaview AVA wineries are proving that Chardonnay and Pinot Noir can thrive above the fogline. The sea air and rocky soils here produce wines generally less fruit-forward than their Russian River Valley counterparts but equally sophisticated and no less vibrant. Many coastal wineries are appointment-only or closed to the public; with its rustic-chic, barnlike tasting room and wide outdoor patio, Fort Ross provides an appealing introduction to this up-and-coming region's wines. ⊠ *15725 Meyers Grade Rd., off Hwy. 1, Jenner* ✛ *From Guerneville take Hwy. 116 west 12 miles, then Hwy. 1 north 6 miles to Meyers Grade Rd.* ☎ *707/847–3460* ⊕ *www.fortrossvineyard.com* ⊜ *Tasting $15* ☉ *Apr.–Nov., daily 10–6, Dec.–Mar., daily 10–5.*

Korbel Champagne Cellars. The three brothers Korbel (Joseph, Francis, and Anton) planted Pinot Noir grapes in the Russian River Valley in the 1870s, pioneering efforts that are duly noted on 50-minute tours of the well-known brand's Guerneville facility. Tours include a clear explanation of the *méthode champenoise* used to make the company's sparkling wines, a walk through ivy-covered 19th-century buildings, and tastings of Korbel's reasonably priced bubblies and still wines. You can also taste without touring. ■ TIP→ If you have the time, stroll through the rose garden, home to more than 250 varieties. ⊠ *13250 River Rd., west of Rio Nido* ☎ *707/824–7000* ⊕ *www.korbel.com* ⊜ *Tasting and tour free* ☉ *Winery daily 10–4:30, tours daily 11–3:45; garden tour mid-Apr.–mid-Oct., Tues.–Sun. 1 and 3.*

WHERE TO EAT

$$$$
MODERN AMERICAN
Fodor'sChoice
★

✕**Applewood Inn Restaurant.** Fruit orchards and redwoods surround this California-Mediterranean restaurant built in the style of a French country barn. The agrarian sensibility runs deeper than mere design, however: much of the produce in the stylishly presented dishes comes from 6 acres of on-site organic gardens. The menu changes seasonally, but beef tenderloin, king salmon, and rack of California lamb rubbed with cocoa are among the signature offerings. Summer might bring a cooling gazpacho of Galia melon, winter a bone-warming crispy pork belly topped with a quail egg and served with turnips. ■ TIP→ The five-course tasting menu, $75 per person for the whole table only, is an excellent option; on Sunday the chefs prepare a three-course prix-fixe dinner for $35 ($60 with wine pairing). ⑤ *Average main: $34* ⊠ *13555*

Hwy. 116, near Mays Canyon Rd. ☎ *707/869–9093, 800/555–8509* 🌐 *www.applewoodinn.com.*

$ MODERN AMERICAN ✕ **Big Bottom Market.** Foodies love this culinary pit stop and grocery for its breakfast biscuits, inventive sandwiches, and savory salads to go or eat here. The house-special biscuit, made with cheddar and thyme, comes with honey butter and a rich jam of your choice, and heartier breakfast fare is prepared as well. Popular sandwiches include the Vietnamese Veggie (lentil-walnut pâté, sliced marinated portobello, and spicy Asian carrots) and Colonel Armstrong (curried chicken salad with currants and cashews on a brioche). 💲 *Average main: $11* ✉ *16228 Main St., near Church St.* ☎ *707/604–7295* 🌐 *www.bigbottommarket.com* ✍ *Reservations not accepted* ⏲ *Closed Tues. No dinner.*

$$ MODERN AMERICAN Fodor's Choice ★ ✕ **boon eat+drink.** A casual storefront restaurant on Guerneville's main drag, boon eat+drink has a menu built around small, "green" (salads and cooked vegetables), and main plates assembled for the most part from locally produced organic ingredients. Polenta lasagna, a beguilingly creamy mix of ricotta salata cheese and polenta served on greens sautéed in garlic, all of it floating upon a spicy marinara sauce, is among the signature dishes. Typical of chef-owner Crista Luedtke's adventurous sensibility, it deviates significantly from the lasagna norm but succeeds on its own merits. **■ TIP→ All the wines served here come from the Russian River Valley, making this a good place to sample what area wineries, many of them close by, have to offer.** 💲 *Average main: $19* ✉ *16248 Main St., at Church St.* ☎ *707/869–0780* 🌐 *eatatboon.com* ✍ *Reservations not accepted* ⏲ *No lunch Wed. late-May–Oct. Closed Wed. Nov.–late-May.*

$ CAFÉ ✕ **Coffee Bazaar.** A fine spot for a pastry and a well-crafted coffee—and for three-plus decades *the* place to gossip and gab—the Coffee Bazaar has free Wi-Fi and serves light meals and snacks. The locally baked banana nut and zucchini bread pair well with a double espresso. 💲 *Average main: $8* ✉ *14045 Armstrong Woods Rd.* ☎ *707/869–9706* ✍ *Reservations not accepted* ⏲ *No dinner.*

WHERE TO STAY

$$ B&B/INN 🏨 **Applewood Inn, Restaurant and Spa.** On a knoll sheltered by towering redwoods, this romantic three-building inn is a short drive from downtown Guerneville. **Pros:** secluded location; excellent restaurant; great breakfasts; outdoor pool and large whirlpool. **Cons:** may feel too remote to some; sounds can carry in Villa Casa Grande. 💲 *Rooms from: $225* ✉ *13555 Hwy. 116* ☎ *707/869–9093, 800/555–8509* 🌐 *www.applewoodinn.com* 🛏 *19 rooms* 🍴 *Breakfast.*

$ HOTEL Fodor's Choice ★ 🏨 **boon hotel+spa.** Redwoods, Douglas firs, and palms supply shade and seclusion at this lushly landscaped resort ¾ mile north of downtown Guerneville. **Pros:** congenial staff; lush landscaping; on-site spa; memorable breakfasts; complimentary bikes; Coyuchi organic cotton linens, tent rooms in summer. **Cons:** lacks amenities larger properties can offer. 💲 *Rooms from: $155* ✉ *14711 Armstrong Woods Rd.* ☎ *707/869–2721* 🌐 *boonhotels.com* 🛏 *14 rooms, 3 tent rooms (summer only)* 🍴 *Breakfast.*

5

SPORTS AND THE OUTDOORS

River Riders. The gung-ho River Riders crew delivers and picks up high-quality mountain, hybrid, or other rental bikes within 15 miles of Guerneville. Nearby places to ride include the town, many wineries, and Armstrong Redwoods State Natural Reserve. ☎ *707/483–2897* ⊕ *www.riverridersrentals.com* ⌨ *From $25 for 4 hrs.*

OCCIDENTAL

11 miles south of Guerneville.

A village surrounded by redwood forests, orchards, and vineyards, Occidental is a former logging hub with a bohemian vibe. The small downtown, which contains several handsome Victorian-era structures, has a whimsically decorated bed-and-breakfast inn, two good restaurants, and a handful of art galleries and shops worth poking around.

GETTING HERE AND AROUND

From Guerneville, head west on Highway 116 for 4 miles to the town of Monte Rio, then turn south on Church Street and travel past the old Rio Theater and over the bridge spanning the Russian River. At this point the road is signed as the Bohemian Highway, which takes you into town, where the road's name changes to Main Street. Taking public transit isn't a convenient way to travel here.

WHERE TO EAT AND STAY

$$$
FRENCH
Fodor's Choice
★

✕ **Bistro des Copains.** A green structure scarcely bigger than a shack holds this Provençal-inflected restaurant popular with winery staffers and food fans. Appetizers and small plates include escargots in a puff pastry and a mushroom crème brûlée that's a clever, savory play on the French dessert. The menu and preparations change with the seasons, but rabbit is generally included in some form—perhaps braised in mustard cream and served with fettuccine. Another favorite is the Liberty Farms duck breast, its flavors enhanced perchance by a touch of fried sage. The wines are well selected and reasonably priced; there's no corkage fee on Thursday night for Sonoma County wines. ■TIP→ **The three-course chef's tasting menu (price varies) is a often a very good deal.** $ *Average main: $23* ✉ *3782 Bohemian Hwy., at Occidental Rd.* ☎ *707/874–2436* ⊕ *www.bistrodescopains.com* ⌲ *Reservations essential* ⊙ *No lunch.*

$
AMERICAN

✕ **Howard Station Cafe.** The mile-long list of morning fare at Occidental's go-to spot for breakfast and weekend brunch includes vegetarian and gluten-free items. Biscuits and gravy, huevos rancheros, omelets, and eggs Benedict with ham, salmon, veggie, or crab are among the specialties, but the menu also includes waffles, pancakes, French toast, and "healthy alternatives" such as tofu rancheros, oatmeal, and house-made granola. Soups, salads, burgers, and monstrous sandwiches are served for lunch. Organic ingredients go into many of the dishes at this café and juice bar whose neo-hippie aura only adds to its charm. ■TIP→ **Arrive early for weekend brunch.** $ *Average main: $11* ✉ *3611 Main St./Bohemian Hwy., at 2nd St.* ☎ *707/874–2838* ⊕ *www.howardstationcafe.com* ⌲ *Reservations not accepted* ⊟ *No credit cards* ⊙ *No dinner.*

$$
B&B/INN

⌕ **The Inn at Occidental.** Quilts, folk art, and original paintings and photographs fill this colorful and friendly inn. **Pros:** whimsical decor;

most rooms have private decks and jetted tubs; friendly. **Cons:** not for those with minimalist tastes; not for kids. $ *Rooms from: $249* ✉ *3657 Church St.* ☎ *707/874–1047, 800/522–6324* ⊕ *www.innatoccidental. com* ⤴ *13 rooms, 3 suites, 1 cottage* ⦿ *Breakfast.*

SPORTS AND THE OUTDOORS

Sonoma Canopy Tours. Zip through the trees with the greatest of ease—at speeds up to 25 mph—at this zip-lining center 2½ miles north of Occidental. The friendly guides prepare guests well for their 2½-hour natural high. ■ **TIP→ Participants must be at least 10 years old and weigh between 70 and 250 pounds.** ✉ *6250 Bohemian Hwy.* ☎ *888/494–7868* ⊕ *www.sonomacanopytours.com* ⧢ *From $99.*

SHOPPING

Laurence Glass Works. A true find, this glass-arts gallery displays the works of its Parisian-born namesake owner, who creates bowls, plates, and other items from recycled, recast glass. Laurence achieves her imaginative colors and shapes in part by etching the glass while it's in the kiln. Works by other glass artists are also sold here. ✉ *74 Main St./Bohemian Hwy., at 1st. St.* ☎ *707/874–3465.*

Verdigris. Designer Howard Dernberger makes stylish lamps out of everything from old samovars and fire extinguishers to antique movie projectors. They're quite original, and the small shop they're sold in is a minor delight. ✉ *72 Main St./Bohemian Hwy., at 1st St.* ☎ *707/874–9018* ⊕ *www.1lightartlamps.com* ⊗ *Closed Tues. and Wed.*

FREESTONE

4 miles south of Occidental; 6 miles west of Sebastopol.

A few decades ago, calling tiny Freestone (population 92) a sleepy village was overstating the case. Not so anymore, and the rebranding of the local tasting room as the Joseph Phelps Freestone Vineyards Guest Center a few years back conferred all-star status on a wine-making operation that was already attracting a steady stream of Pinot-loving pilgrims. Oh yes, and bread lovers. The marvelous Wild Flour Bread has adherents nearly as fervent as the wine lovers. The guest center is open daily, but in keeping with Freestone's laid-back traditions, the bakery is open only four days a week.

GETTING HERE AND AROUND

To get to Freestone from Occidental, drive south on the Bohemian Highway. From central Sebastopol, drive west on Highway 12, following signs toward Bodega Bay. Turn north at the Bohemian Highway, and you've arrived. Taking public transit isn't a convenient way to travel here.

EXPLORING

Fodor's Choice **Joseph Phelps Freestone Vineyards Guest Center.** The renowned Napa Valley
★ winery's West County outpost is a serene spot to learn about the cool-weather Sonoma Coast AVA and the Chardonnays and Pinot Noirs it produces. Phelps wines have always garnered praise for their expression of *terroir* (the land and microclimate), and the ascetic quality of the ones made here mirrors the rugged terrain. Tastings take place in an

CLOSE UP

Crush Camp in Sonoma County

The harvest in late summer and early fall is a prime time to connect with the beauty of sprawling Sonoma County, the rhythms of agricultural life, and the passionate professionalism of its grape farmers and winemakers. To go behind the scenes and meet the people who make the wine, consider attending a "crush camp" like the **Sonoma County Grape Camp**, 2½ days of immersion in grape harvesting, wine blending, and food-and-wine pairing. You'll see the inner workings of the wineries and even blend your own bottle. And yes, you'll taste wine: dozens of Pinot Noirs, Chardonnays, Zinfandels, Cabernets, Sauvignon Blancs, and other vintages.

A friendly blending competition was a highlight of a recent crush camp, as teams of four crafted a wine by blending a French Burgundy and two California Pinot Noirs. In a nod to marketing—wine making is about farming, science, and the subtleties of taste, but it's also a business—the teams named their blends and created labels. The winners won a bottle of Pinot Noir from a top winery.

THE BOTTOM LINE

There's a premium fee for this curated access to wine professionals and outstanding food: $2,000 per person, which includes accommodations, food and wine, and transportation during the trip. As for your fellow attendees, expect wine lovers enthusiastic about learning, not wine snobs.

After this unique communal experience—celebrated on the final day at a lavish dinner—you'll never drink a glass of wine the same way. For information contact the Sonoma County Winegrape Commission (☎ *707/522–5864* ⊕ *www.sonomagrapecamp.com*).

upscale-rural space or at picnic tables out front. A $20 tasting includes the current Sonoma Coast wines—the estate-grown Pinot Noir is always worth trying—and for $35 you can sample them and Insignia, Phelps Napa Valley's flagship Bordeaux-style red blend. ■TIP➔ Each month on the second Sunday the guest center hosts fun and reasonably priced food events; Pinot Noir and Hawaiian barbecue and Chardonnay and crab cakes are two perennial favorites. ✉ *12747 El Camino Bodega, at Bohemian Hwy.* ☎ *707/874–1010* ⊕ *www.josephphelps.com* ✍ *Tastings $20–$50* ⊗ *May–Oct., daily 11–5; Nov.–Apr., Thurs.–Mon. 11–5.*

WHERE TO EAT

$

BAKERY

✕ **Wild Flour Bread.** The sticky buns at Wild Flour are legendary in western Sonoma, as are the rye breads and sock-it-to-me scones in such flavors as double chocolate, espresso, and hazelnut. There's a long table inside, but most patrons enjoy their baked goods on the benches outside. ■TIP➔ Get here early: on weekend afternoons the most popular items sell out quickly. ⓢ *Average main: $5* ✉ *140 Bohemian Hwy., at El Camino Bodega* ☎ *707/874–2938* ⊕ *www.wildflourbread.com* ✍ *Reservations not accepted* ⊟ *No credit cards* ⊗ *Closed Tues.–Thurs. No dinner.*

SHOPPING

Fodor'sChoice
★ **Enduring Comforts.** This shop showcases what it calls "antiques and other delights," and owner Thea Doty has an eye for the unusual. Among the antiques are small items—lamps, vintage jewelry, stained glass—that might fit in your luggage. You might also consider scented candles, fragrant French soaps, and contemporary handbags, jewelry, and men's and women's hats. ✉ *142 Bohemian Hwy., off El Camino Bodega* ☎ *707/874–1111* ⊙ *Closed Tues.–Thurs.*

Fodor'sChoice
★ **Freestone Artisan Cheese.** "Try this one!" are the three favorite words of Omar Mueller, this shop's sociable monger of quality cheeses from Sonoma, nearby counties, and a few places beyond. Omar also sells gourmet food and kitchen items and makes crepes. The one with Nutella is a hit with kids and adults. ✉ *380 Bohemian Hwy., near Freestone St.* ☎ *707/874–1030* ⊕ *www.freestoneartisan.com* ⊙ *Closed Tues. and Wed.*

SPAS

Osmosis Day Spa Sanctuary. The signature treatment at this locally popular spa is a traditional Japanese detoxifying bath. You'll slip into a deep redwood tub filled with damp cedar shavings and rice bran that are naturally heated to 140°F by the action of enzymes. Attendants bury you up to the neck and throughout the 20-minute bath session bring sips of water and place cool cloths on your forehead. After a shower, you can lie down and listen to brain-balancing music through headphones or have a massage, perhaps in one of the creek-side pagodas. Aromatherapy, body wraps, facials, and other treatments are also available. Reservations are recommended. ✉ *209 Bohemian Hwy.* ☎ *707/823–8231* ⊕ *www.osmosis.com* ✉ *Treatments $99–$299* ⊙ *Daily 9–9.*

SEBASTOPOL

6 miles east of Freestone; 7 miles southwest of Santa Rosa.

A stroll through downtown Sebastopol, a town formerly known more for Gravenstein apples than for grapes, but these days a burgeoning wine hub, reveals glimpses of the distant and recent past and perhaps the future, too. Before entering the district of browsable, if mostly modest, shops, you may notice a sign declaring Sebastopol a "Nuclear Free Zone." Many hippies settled here in the 1960s and 1970s and, as the old Crosby, Stills, Nash & Young song goes, they taught their children well—the town remains steadfastly, if not entirely, countercultural.

Another strain of nostalgia runs even deeper, though, as evidenced by the popularity of the remarkably well-preserved Foster's Freeze stand (banana split, anyone?). Those hankering for a 1960s flashback can truck on over to the Grateful Bagel, complete with Grateful Dead logo.

Sebastopol has always had really good, if somewhat low-profile, wineries, among them Iron Horse, Lynmar Estate, and Merry Edwards. With the opening of a cluster of artisanal food and wine vendors at the Barlow, on the site of a former apple-processing plant, the town may be poised for a Healdsburg-style transformation. Then again, maybe not. Stay tuned.

Iron Horse produces sparklers that make history.

GETTING HERE AND AROUND
Sebastopol can be reached by driving east on El Camino Bodega from Freestone or west on Highway 12 from Santa Rosa. From Forestville, head south for 7 miles on Highway 116. Sonoma County Transit buses 20, 22, 24, and 26 serve Sebastopol.

VISITOR INFORMATION
Sebastopol Visitor Center ⊠ 265 S. Main St., at Willow St. ☎ 707/823–3032 ⊕ www.sebastopol.org.

EXPLORING
TOP ATTRACTIONS
The Barlow. On the site of a former apple cannery, this cluster of buildings celebrates Sonoma County's "maker" culture with an inspired combination production space and marketplace. The complex contains microbreweries and wine-making facilities, along with areas where people create or sell crafts, large-scale artworks, and artisanal food, herbs, and beverages. There's even a studio where artists using traditional methods are creating the world's largest *thangka* (Tibetan painting). Only club members can visit the anchor wine tenant, Kosta Browne, but La Follette, MacPhail, and other small producers have tasting rooms open to the public. Warped Brewing Company and Woodfour Brewing Company make and sell ales on-site, and you can have a nip of gin or bourbon at Spirit Works Distillery. ■**TIP→ From July through October the complex hosts a Thursday-night street fair, with live music and even more vendors.** ⊠ 6770 McKinley St., at Morris St., off Hwy. 12 ☎ 707/824–5600 ⊕ www.thebarlow.net ✉ Free to complex; tasting fees at wineries, breweries, distillery ☺ Daily, hrs vary.

Fodor'sChoice **Iron Horse Vineyards.** A meandering one-lane road leads to this win-
★ ery known for its sparkling wines and estate Chardonnays and Pinot
Noirs. The sparklers have made history: Ronald Reagan served them at
his summit meetings with Mikhail Gorbachev; George Herbert Walker
Bush took some along to Moscow for treaty talks; and Barack Obama
has included them at official state dinners. Despite Iron Horse's brushes
with fame, a casual rusticity prevails at its outdoor tasting area (large
heaters keep things comfortable on chilly days), which gazes out on
acres of rolling, vine-covered hills. Regular tours ($25) take place on
weekdays at 10 am. ■TIP➜ When his schedule permits, winemaker
David Munksgard leads a private tour by truck ($50) at 10 am on Mon-
day. ⊠ *9786 Ross Station Rd., off Hwy. 116* ☎ *707/887–1507* ⊕ *www.
ironhorsevineyards.com* ☕ *Tasting $20, tours $25–$50 (includes tast-
ing)* ⊗ *Daily 10–4:30, tour (by appointment) weekdays at 10.*

Fodor'sChoice **La Follette Wines.** Greg La Follette made his early reputation researching
★ vine physiology and how different yeasts affect a wine's "mouthfeel," but
for all his technical expertise, the sheer fruity joy of his namesake winery's
single-vineyard, cool-climate Chardonnays and Pinot Noirs is the impression that lingers. A sought-after consultant, La Follette is respected for his
ability to match varietals and clone types to the right microclimates and
soils, and these wines reflect the disparate Sonoma and Mendocino locales
they derive from. He describes Pinot Noir, notoriously finicky in both field
and aging barrel, as an "exacting mistress," but it's clear from the richly
layered Pinots the affair's a success. Tastings take place in a spare, light-
filled space in The Barlow artisan-producers' complex. ⊠ *The Barlow,
180 Morris St., at McKinley St.* ☎ *707/395–3902* ⊕ *www.lafollettewines.
com* ☕ *Tastings $10–$55* ⊗ *Daily 11–6, until 8 Thurs. night July–Oct.*

Fodor'sChoice **MacPhail Family Wines.** A two-story cascade of crumpled ruby-red Radio
★ Flyer wagons—meant to mimic wine pouring out of a bottle—grabs
immediate attention inside this swank industrial space, a showcase for
the distinguished Pinot Noirs of namesake winemaker James MacPhail.
The wagons represent family and continuity to MacPhail, who, peers
sometimes joke, "never met a vineyard he didn't like." Maybe so, but
he knows how to pick them. His bright, classy Pinots, none of which
taste alike, fully express their places of origin, which include Oregon's
Willamette Valley, Mendocino County's Anderson Valley, several prime
Sonoma County spots, and the Santa Rita Hills of California's Central
Coast. MacPhail also makes Chardonnay and Rosé (of Pinot Noir, of
course). ⊠ *The Barlow, 6761 McKinley St., off Morris St.* ☎ *707/824–
8400* ⊕ *macphailwine.com* ☕ *Tastings $20–$50* ⊗ *Daily 11–6, until 8
Thurs. night July–Oct.*

Fodor'sChoice **Merry Edwards Winery.** Winemaker Merry Edwards describes the Russian
★ River Valley as "the epicenter of great Pinot Noir," and she produces
wines that express the unique characteristics of the soils, climates, and
Pinot Noir clones from which they derive. (Edwards's research into
Pinot Noir clones is so extensive that there's even one named after
her.) The valley's advantages, says Edwards, are warmer-than-average
daytime temperatures that encourage more intense fruit, and evening
fogs that mitigate the extra heat's potential negative effects. Group
tastings of the well-composed single-vineyard and blended Pinots take

5

place throughout the day, and there are five sit-down appointment slots available except on Sunday. Edwards also makes a fine Sauvignon Blanc that's lightly aged in old oak. Tastings end, rather than begin, with this singular white wine so as not to distract guests' palates from the Pinot Noirs. ✉ *2959 Gravenstein Hwy. N/Hwy. 116, near Oak Grove Ave.* ☎ *707/823–7466, 888/388–9050* ⊕ *www.merryedwards.com* ✉ *Tasting free* ☉ *Daily 9:30–4:30; call for appointment or drop in and join next available tasting.*

Paul Hobbs Winery. Major wine critics routinely bestow high-90s scores on the Chardonnays, Pinot Noirs, Cabernet Sauvignons, and a Syrah produced at this appointment-only winery set amid gently rolling vineyards in northwestern Sebastopol. Owner-winemaker Paul Hobbs's university thesis investigated the flavors that result from various oak barrel toasting levels, and he continued his education—in both vineyard management and wine making—at the Robert Mondavi Winery, Opus One, and other storied establishments before striking out on his own in 1991. Tastings take place in a space designed by winery specialist Howard Backen's architectural firm. Guests on a Signature tour ($45) visit the vineyards and winery and taste several wines; the Small Bites experience ($100) includes the tour plus three marvelous courses, each paired with two wines. ✉ *3355 Gravenstein Hwy. N, near Holt Rd.* ☎ *707/824–9879* ⊕ *www.paulhobbswinery.com* ✉ *Signature tour $45, Small Bites $100* ☉ *Signature tour Mon., Tues., Thurs., and Fri. 10 and 1:30, Wed. 1:30 only; Small Bites tasting Tues. and Thurs. at 1.*

WORTH NOTING

Lynmar Estate. *Elegant* and *balanced* describe Lynmar's landscaping and contemporary architecture, but the terms also apply to the wine-making philosophy. Expect genteel, handcrafted Chardonnays and Pinot Noirs with long, luxurious finishes, especially on the Pinots. The attention to refinement and detail extends to the tasting room, where well-informed pourers serve patrons enjoying garden and vineyard views through two-story-tall windows. The consistent winner here is the Quail Hill Pinot Noir, a blend of some or all of the 14 Pinot Noir clones grown in the vineyard outside, but the Russian River Pinot Noir and the Summit Pinot Noir are also exceptional. Most of the wines can be bought only online or at the winery, which also offers food and wine pairings. ✉ *3909 Frei Rd., off Hwy. 116* ☎ *707/829–3374* ⊕ *www.lynmarestate. com* ✉ *Tastings $15–$50* ☉ *Daily 10–4:30.*

WHERE TO EAT

$ ✕ **Hole in the Wall.** In a region where bios usually tally up culinary degrees
AMERICAN and stints at famous restaurants, this strip-mall spot's description of its chef is refreshingly modest: "Starting at age 15, Adam Beers began his first culinary job stirring gumbo." Good for him, and good for you, because as with the gumbo he serves now, the food here is down-home tasty with unexpected delights. Locals love the breakfasts, especially the challah French toast and the short ribs, hash, and eggs. Burger options include the usual beef and turkey, but also portobello mushroom and black-bean editions for the crunchola crowd. The prize, though, goes to the duck burger for the accompanying cranberry-horseradish aioli. Other menu favorites include the savory and dessert crepes. ⑤ *Average*

The views, architecture, wines, and cuisine make a visit to Paul Hobbs Winery special.

main: $8 ✉ 972 Gravenstein Hwy. S, at Fellers La. ☎ 707/861–3777 ⊕ www.holeinthewallsebastopol.com ♨ Reservations not accepted ☾ No dinner Mon. and Tues.

$$ **✕ Vignette.** At the helm of what may well be the Wine Country's cut-
PIZZA est pizza oven—a cobalt-blue-tile, igloo-shape affair from Naples that burns almond wood at 850°F to 900°F—chef Mark Hopper turns out thin-crust pies in less than two minutes. Hopper, formerly of Thomas Keller's The French Laundry and Bouchon, assembled a straightforward menu of antipasti, salads, and pizzas for Vignette, which debuted in mid-2014. Among the early pizza faves were the mushroom Alfredo, with garlic cream, roasted mushrooms, stracciatella cheese, and toma-toes, and a pie topped with meatballs, tomatoes, Parmesan, and moz-zarella. ⑤ *Average main: $17* ✉ *The Barlow, 6750 McKinley St., off Morris St.* ☎ 707/861–3897 ⊕ *www.vignettepizzeria.com* ♨ *Reserva-tions not accepted.*

$$$ **✕ Zazu Kitchen + Farm.** "Know the face that feeds you" is the motto at
MODERN Zazu, and some of the local ingredients in dishes here come from the
AMERICAN owners themselves: executive chef Duskie Estes and her husband, John Stewart, the house salumist (specialist in all things pig). Small plates such as *chicharrones* (fried pork rinds), tamarind Petaluma chicken wings, and baby back ribs can add up to a meal, or you can sample a few appetizers before moving on to a bacon burger, porcini noodle and Sebastopol mushroom stroganoff, or a tomahawk steak for two and fries. In good weather the industrial-looking space's huge doors lift up to admit the breeze that often graces the open-air patio, which is surrounded by raised garden beds that supply produce and spices for diners' meals. ⑤ *Average main: $23* ✉ *The Barlow, 6770 McKinley*

St., No. 150, off Morris St. ☎ 707/523–4814 ⊕ *www.zazukitchen.com* ⊙ *Closed Tues. No lunch Mon.*

WHERE TO STAY

$$$ ⊞ **Avalon Bed & Breakfast.** Set amid redwoods and impeccably furnished, **B&B/INN** the Tudor-style Avalon provides romance, luxury, and seclusion in a **Fodor's Choice** creekside setting. **Pros:** lavish breakfasts; woodsy, romantic setting; private entrances; plush furnishings; fireplaces in all rooms. **Cons:** maximum occupancy of two for all rooms; two-night minimum for some stays; atmosphere may be too low-key for some. ⑤ *Rooms from: $299* ⊠ *11910 Graton Rd.* ☎ 877/328–2566, 707/824–0880 ⊕ *avalonluxuryinn.com* ⇆ *3 suites* ⑩ *Breakfast.*

$ ⊞ **Fairfield Inn & Suites Santa Rosa Sebastopol.** A safe West County bet **HOTEL** that often has rooms when other inns and hotels are full up, the three-story Fairfield, a fairly new property a bit south of Sebastopol's core, is a competently run chain hotel. **Pros:** clean rooms; good-size outdoor pool and spa; noon checkout; friendly staff; convenient to West County wineries and Santa Rosa; fitness center; frequent Internet specials. **Cons:** hardly a unique Wine Country experience; occasional service letdowns. ⑤ *Rooms from: $149* ⊠ *1101 Gravenstein Hwy. S* ☎ 707/829–6677 ⊕ *www.marriott.com* ⇆ *81 rooms, 1 suite* ⑩ *Breakfast.*

$ ⊞ **Sebastopol Inn.** The cheerful rooms clustered around this reasonably **HOTEL** priced inn's courtyard are steps from the Barlow, a hip collection of **FAMILY** restaurants, wine-tasting rooms, brewpubs, galleries, and other spaces. **Pros:** good rates; friendly staff; across from Barlow complex; near noteworthy wineries. **Cons:** no frills; bland decor. ⑤ *Rooms from: $129* ⊠ *6751 Sebastopol Ave.* ☎ 707/829–2500 ⊕ *www.sebastopolinn.com* ⇆ *29 rooms, 2 suites* ⑩ *No meals.*

GRATON

½ mile west of Sebastopol.

Mere steps from Sebastopol and not far from Occidental and Freestone, the tiny hamlet of Graton has a one-block main drag one can stroll in two minutes, though it's possible to while away a few hours at the block's artist-run gallery, nostalgia-inducing antiques shop, a small winery's tasting room (open from Thursday through Sunday), and one of two notably fine restaurants. For more strolling, you can hit the local hiking trail.

GETTING HERE AND AROUND

To reach Graton from Sebastopol, head west from Highway 116 a half-mile on Graton Road. Sonoma County Transit bus 20 passes through Graton.

EXPLORING

Paul Mathew Vineyards. With experience that includes stints as a winery tour guide, cellar rat, sales rep, vineyard developer, and finally winemaker, owner Mat Gustafson of Paul Mathew Vineyards knows how to make and market his Pinot Noirs and other wines. Gustafson specializes in spare, low-alcohol, food-friendly Russian River Valley Pinots and makes Chardonnay, a surprisingly light Cabernet Franc, and Valdiguie, also known as Napa Gamay. On a hot summer day his Rosé of Pinot Noir makes for delightful sipping in the picnic area behind the tasting room, which occupies a century-old Edwardian storefront along Graton's main drag. ⊠ *9060 Graton Rd., at Ross Rd.* ☎ *707/865–2505* ⊕ *www.paulmathewvineyards.com* ⊡ *Tasting $10* ☉ *Thurs.–Sun. 10:30–4:30, by appointment Mon.–Wed.*

West County Regional Trail. Oaks, poplars, and other trees shade this trail that winds north from Graton's main drag through land once used by the local railway line. In summer you'll see plenty of blackberries (and sometimes local pickers) along the 3-mile stretch between Graton and Forestville. The path is so quiet it's hard to believe that nearby in 1905 raged the Battle of Sebastopol Road between crews of two rival rail lines. ■ TIP→ **There's free trailhead parking behind the old Graton Fire Station.** ⊠ *Entrance off Graton just west of Ross Rd.* ☎ *707/565–2041* ⊕ *parks.sonomacounty.ca.gov* ⊡ *Free* ☉ *Sunrise–sunset.*

WHERE TO EAT

$$$

MODERN
AMERICAN

Fodor'sChoice
★

✕ **Underwood Bar & Bistro.** Run by the same people who operate the Willow Wood Market Cafe across the street, this restaurant with a sophisticated Continental ambience has a seasonally changing menu based on smaller and larger dishes. The tapas and other petite offerings might include anything from glazed ribs and tuna tartar to Chinese broccoli; depending on the season, osso bucco, mushroom-leek ravioli, or Catalan fish stew might be among the entrées. ■ TIP→ **The bar here emulates those of a bygone era with a full array of ports, cognacs, and sweet wines, good alone or with the desserts and well-chosen after-dinner cheeses.** ⑤ *Average main: $25* ⊠ *9113 Graton Rd., about ½ mile west of Hwy. 116* ☎ *707/823–7023* ⊕ *www.underwoodgraton. com* ☉ *Closed Mon. No lunch Sun.*

$$

MODERN
AMERICAN

✕ **Willow Wood Market Cafe.** This café across the street from the Underwood Bar & Bistro serves simple, tasty soups, salads, and sandwiches. The brunches are amazing, but even daily breakfast—the specialties include hot, creamy polenta and house-made granola—is modern-American down-home solid. Lunch and dinner bring equally hearty hot and cold sandwiches and ragouts on polenta. ■ TIP→ **Take a few minutes to poke around the quirky general store while you're waiting for your food.** ⑤ *Average main: $16* ⊠ *9020 Graton Rd., about ½ mile west of Hwy. 116* ☎ *707/823–0233* ⊕ *willowwoodgraton.com* ⌂ *Reservations not accepted* ☉ *No dinner Sun.*

SHOPPING

Graton Gallery. The West County hills are alive with talented fine-arts painters, sculptors, and photographers, and this artist-run gallery in downtown Graton displays their works and those of their counterparts nearby and beyond. ⊠ *9048 Graton Rd., at Ross Rd.* ☎ *707/829–8912* ⊕ *www.gratongallery.com* ☉ *Closed Mon.*

Fodor'sChoice
★

Mr. Ryder & Company. Named for its impresario's deceased pooch, this co-op of a baker's dozen antiques dealers distinguishes itself with its pleasing layout and tastefully offbeat selections of a century-plus of mostly Americana. Even *Martha Stewart Living* has taken note. ⊠ *9040 Graton Rd., near Ross Rd.* ☎ *707/824–8221* ⊕ *www.mrryderantiques.com.*

5

SANTA ROSA

6 miles east of Sebastopol; 52 miles north of San Francisco.

Urban Santa Rosa isn't as popular with tourists as many Wine Country destinations—not surprising, because there are more office parks than wineries within its limits. However, this hardworking town is home to a couple of interesting cultural offerings and a few noteworthy restaurants and vineyards. The city's chain motels and hotels can be handy if you're finding that everything else is booked up, especially since Santa Rosa is roughly equidistant from Sonoma, Healdsburg, and the western Russian River Valley, three of Sonoma County's most popular wine-tasting destinations.

GETTING HERE AND AROUND

To get to Santa Rosa from Sebastopol, drive east on Highway 12. From San Francisco, cross the Golden Gate Bridge and continue north on U.S. 101 to the downtown Santa Rosa exit. Santa Rosa's hotels, restaurants, and wineries are spread over a wide area; factor in extra time when driving around the city, especially during morning and evening rush hour. To get here from downtown San Francisco take Golden Gate Transit. Several Sonoma County Transit buses serve the city and surrounding area.

VISITOR INFORMATION

Visit Santa Rosa ⊠ *9 4th St., at Wilson St.* ☎ *800/404–7673* ⊕ *www.visitsanta rosa.com.*

EXPLORING

TOP ATTRACTIONS

Fodor's Choice ★ **Martinelli Winery.** In a century-old hop barn with the telltale triple towers, Martinelli has the feel of a traditional country store, but the sophisticated wines made here are anything but old-fashioned. The winery's reputation rests on its complex Pinot Noirs, Syrahs, and Zinfandels, including the $125-a-bottle Jackass Hill Vineyard Zin, made with grapes from 130-year-old vines. You can sip these acclaimed wines—going back a decade or more—during a private Library Tasting ($50). A standard tasting ($10) focuses on current releases, a Chardonnay, three reds, and a Muscat that tastes like honeysuckle. Winemaker Helen Turley set the Martinelli style—fruit forward, easy on the oak, reined-in tannins—in the 1990s. The current winemaker Bryan Kvamme, a Turley protégé, continues the tradition. ⊠ *3360 River Rd., east of Olivet Rd., Windsor* ☎ *707/525–0570, 800/346–1627* ⊕ *www.martinelliwinery. com* 🍷 *Tastings $10–$50* ☉ *Daily 10–5; library tasting and wine-cheese pairing by appointment only with 48-hr notice.*

Fodor's Choice ★ **Matanzas Creek Winery.** The visitor center at Matanzas Creek sets itself apart with an understated Japanese aesthetic, extending to a tranquil fountain, a koi pond, and a vast field of lavender. The winery makes Sauvignon Blanc, Chardonnay, Merlot, and Pinot Noir wines under the Matanzas Creek name and three equally well-regarded wines—a Bordeaux red blend, a Chardonnay, and a Sauvignon Blanc—with the Journey label. All tours take in the beautiful estate and include tastings.

Matanzas Creek Winery is a star of the tiny Bennett Valley AVA.

The Signature tour concludes with tastings of limited-production and library wines paired with artisanal cheeses. ■TIP➔ An ideal time to visit is in May and June, when lavender perfumes the air. ✉ *6097 Bennett Valley Rd.* ☎ *707/528–6464, 800/590–6464* ⊕ *www.matanzascreek. com* ✑ *Tastings $10–$25, tours $10–$35* ⊙ *Daily 10–4:30; estate tour ($10) daily at 10:30, others by appointment at least 48 hrs in advance.*

FAMILY **Safari West.** An unexpected bit of wilderness in the Wine Country, this African wildlife preserve covers 400 acres. A visit begins with a stroll around enclosures housing lemurs, cheetahs, giraffes, and rare birds such as the brightly colored scarlet ibis. Next, climb with your guide onto open-air vehicles that spend about two hours combing the expansive property, where more than 80 species—including gazelles, cape buffalo, antelope, wildebeests, and zebras—inhabit the hillsides. If you'd like to extend your stay, lodging in well-equipped tent cabins *(⇨ see Where to Stay, below)* is available. ✉ *3115 Porter Creek Rd., off Mark West Springs Rd.* ☎ *707/579–2551, 800/616–2695* ⊕ *www.safariwest. com* ✑ *$70–$95 ($32–$35 ages 3–12)* ⊙ *Safaris Mid-Mar.–early Sept. at 9, 10, 1, 2, and 4; hrs vary rest of year.*

WORTH NOTING

FAMILY **Charles M. Schulz Museum.** Fans of Snoopy and Charlie Brown will love this museum dedicated to the late Charles M. Schulz, who lived his last three decades in Santa Rosa. Permanent installations include a re-creation of the cartoonist's studio, and temporary exhibits often focus on a particular theme in his work. ■TIP➔ Children and adults can take a stab at creating cartoons in the Education Room. ✉ *2301 Hardies La., at W. Steele La.* ☎ *707/579–4452* ⊕ *www.schulzmuseum.org* ✑ *$10*

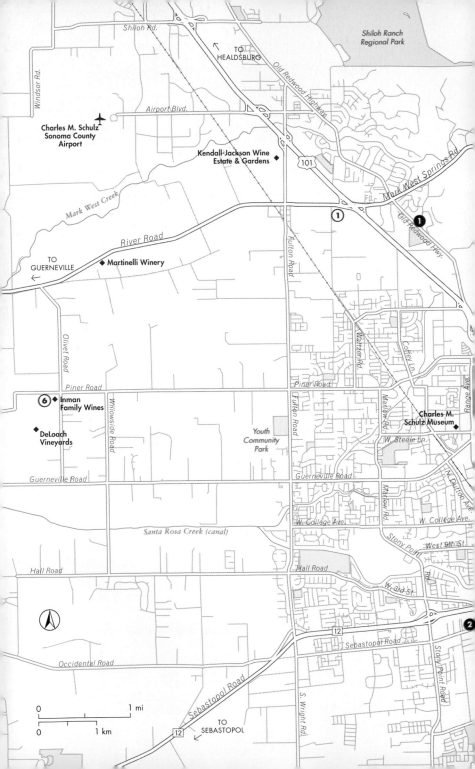

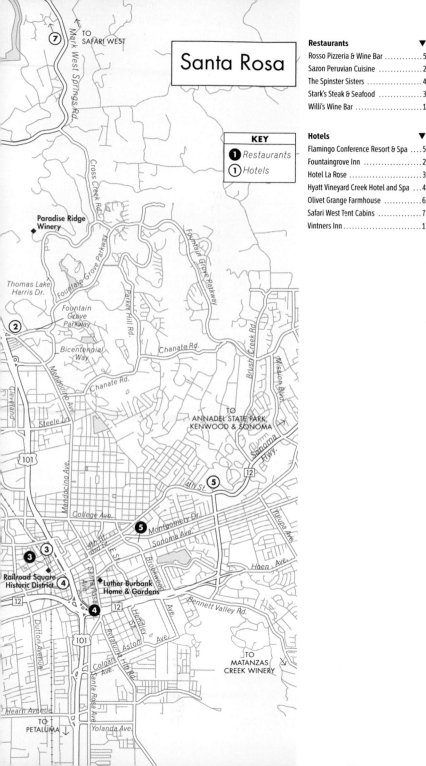

Santa Rosa

KEY

1 *Restaurants*
1 *Hotels*

A familiar-looking hat provides shade at the Charles M. Schulz Museum.

⊘ *Labor Day–Memorial Day, Mon. and Wed.–Fri. 11–5, weekends 10–5; Memorial Day–Labor Day, weekdays 11–5, weekends 10–5.*

DeLoach Vineyards. Best known for its Russian River Valley Pinot Noirs, DeLoach also produces Chardonnays, old-vine Zinfandels, and a few other wines. Some of the reds are made using open-top wood fermentation vats that have been used in France for centuries to intensify a wine's flavor. Tours focus on these and other wine-making techniques and include a stroll through organic gardens and vineyards. You can also take wine-blending a seminar, compare California and French Chardonnays and Pinot Noirs, or (on weekends only) relax with a wood-fired pizza and a glass of wine. ■TIP➔ The sparklers and still wines of the JCB label, whose letters match the initials of its dapper creator, DeLoach's Burgundy-born owner, Jean-Charles Boisset, are poured in a separate tasting room. ⊠ *1791 Olivet Rd., off Guerneville Rd.* ☎ *707/526–9111* ⊕ *www.deloachvineyards.com* ✉ *Tastings $15–$100, tour $20* ⊘ *Daily 10–5, tour daily at noon.*

Inman Family Wines. "The winemaker is in," reads a driveway sign when owner Kathleen Inman, who crafts her winery's delicate Chardonnay, Pinot Noir, and other western Russian River Valley wines, is present. She's often around, and it's an extra treat to learn directly from the source about her farming, fermenting, and aging methods. Her restrained, balanced wines complement sophisticated cuisine so well that San Francisco's The Slanted Door and other top-tier restaurants include them on their menus. Inman shows equal finesse with Rosé of Pinot Noir, two sparkling wines, and a Pinot Gris. Her zeal to recycle is in evidence everywhere, most conspicuously in the tasting room, where redwood reclaimed from an on-site barn was incorporated into the design, and crushed wine-bottle glass was fashioned into the bar. ✉ *3900 Piner Rd., at Olivet Rd.* ☎ *707/293–9576* ⊕ *www. inmanfamilywines.com* 🍷 *Tasting $15* ☉ *Thurs.–Mon. 11–4.*

Kendall-Jackson Wine Estate & Gardens. Seven gardens devoted to cuisine, flowers, and the understanding of wine descriptors such as "black cherry" and "green grass," make a visit to this colorful estate as much about food and wine education as about sipping the famous brand's limited-release whites and reds. It's possible, of course, merely to sample a few wines in the window-filled, high-ceilinged tasting room or on an umbrella-shaded vineyard-view terrace, but a guided or self-guided spin through the gardens enhances the experience. Back in the tasting areas, food and wine pairings involve fruits, vegetables, and flowers, some quite exotic, freshly plucked from the 3-acre organic garden. Many of the accompanying wines—Chardonnays, Pinot Noirs, Cabernet Sauvignons, and dessert wines among them—are from the well-regarded Jackson Estate and Highland Estates labels. ✉ *5007 Fulton Rd., off River Rd.* ☎ *707/571–7500* ⊕ *www.kj.com* 🍷 *Tastings $10–$50, garden tour $25, wine-food pairing $35* ☉ *Tasting room daily 10–5; garden tour at 11, 1, and 3; wine-food pairing by appointment.*

Luther Burbank Home & Gardens. Renowned horticulturist Luther Burbank lived and worked on these grounds and made great advances using the modern techniques of selection and hybridization. The 1.6-acre garden and greenhouse showcase the results of some of Burbank's experiments to develop spineless cactus and such flowers as the Shasta daisy. Instructions for the free self-guided garden tour, which uses your cell phone, are posted near the carriage house. In the music room of Burbank's home, a modified Greek Revival structure, a dictionary lies open to a page on which the verb *burbank* is defined as "to modify and improve plant life." Docent-led tours, required to see the house, take place from April through October. ✉ *204 Santa Rosa Ave., at Sonoma Ave.* ☎ *707/524–5445* ⊕ *www.lutherburbank.org* 🍷 *Gardens free, tour $7* ☉ *Gardens daily 8–dusk; home and gift shop Apr.–Oct., Tues.–Sun. 10–4, docent tours every ½ hr.*

Paradise Ridge Winery. Eastern Santa Rosa's suburbs may be encroaching on this hillside winery, but its 4-acre contemporary-sculpture garden and Russian River Valley views still inspire. Wines to seek out include the estate Zinfandel and Elevation Cabernet Sauvignon, the latter from Rockpile AVA grapes grown 2,000 feet up the mountain. Locals and tourists show up on Wednesday evenings from mid-May through mid-October to sip wine, catch the sunset, listen to local bands, and sample food from area vendors. ■**TIP→** The sunset event often sells out, so it's wise to purchase tickets through the winery's website, which also has two-for-one tasting coupons. ✉ *4545 Thomas Lake Harris Dr., off Fountaingrove Pkwy.* ☎ *707/528–9463* ⊕ *www.prwinery.com* 🍷 *Tasting $10; Wed. sunset event $8, wine available by glass or bottle* ☉ *Daily 11–5 for tasting; mid-May–mid-Oct., Wed. until sunset.*

5

Luther Burbank Home and Gardens showcases the results of its namesake's many botanical experiments.

Railroad Square Historic District. The location of Santa Rosa's former Northwestern Pacific Railroad depot—built in 1903 by Italian stonemasons and immortalized in Alfred Hitchcock's coolly sinister 1943 film *Shadow of a Doubt*—provides the name for this revitalized neighborhood west of U.S. 101. The depot is now a visitor center, and Fourth Street between Wilson and Davis streets contains restaurants, bar, and antiques and thrift shops worth checking out, as do nearby lanes. ⊠ *Depot visitor center, 9 4th St., at Wilson St.* ☎ *707/577–8674* ⊕ *railroadsquare.net.*

WHERE TO EAT

$$
PIZZA
Fodor's Choice
★

✕ **Rosso Pizzeria & Wine Bar.** Ask local wine pourers where to get the best pizza, and they'll often recommend lively Rosso, also acclaimed for its diverse wine selection. Neapolitan-style pizzas emerge from the brick-lined Tuscan oven with thin crusts and imaginative ingredients atop red and white bases. Two perennial favorites are the Moto Guzzi, with house-smoked mozzarella and spicy Caggiano sausage, and the Funghi di Limone, with oven-roasted mixed mushrooms and Taleggio and fontina cheese. Rosso's other crowd-pleaser, and perfect for the non-pizza crowd, is fried chicken. Made extra crispy by double frying, it's served with pancetta bits and seductive sweet-and-sour sauce. Salads and gluten-free dishes are also on the menu. ⑤ *Average main: $17* ⊠ *Creekside Center, 53 Montgomery Dr., at Brookwood Ave.* ☎ *707/544–3221* ⊕ *www.rossopizzeria.com.*

$$$
PERUVIAN
Fodor'sChoice
★

✕ **Sazon Peruvian Cuisine.** Take a break from the usual Cali cuisine at this strip-mall Peruvian restaurant run by a father-son team from Lima. You'll often see the son and lead chef, José Navarro, scurrying about the kitchen or out greeting guests, many of them Peruvian locals enjoying a taste of back home. *Sazon* means "flavor" or "seasoning," and Navarro's skillful spicing sets his restaurant apart. The half-dozen ceviches— ordered singly or in a trio at a discount—show the range of tastes he and his team conjure up. You can order small and large plates to share family-style; the latter include *arroz con mariscos,* a velvety, seafood-only paella whose allure derives from heavy cream and turmeric used in place of saffron. ⑤ *Average main: $24* ✉ *1129 Sebastopol Rd., at Roseland Ave.* ☎ *707/523–4346* ⊕ *sazonsr.com.*

$$$
MODERN
AMERICAN

✕ **The Spinster Sisters.** A rectangular, polished-redwood bar with two dozen stools anchors this concrete and glass hot spot for snappy cuisine and wine-world gossip. Modern, well-sourced variations on eggs Benedict and other standards are served at weekday breakfast and weekend brunch, both highly popular. The dinner menu consists of shareable bites and small and large plates—kimchi-and-bacon deviled eggs, sweet corn and coconut fritters, and crispy pork shoulder being three respective examples. The stellar lineup of local and international wines earned The Spinster Sisters a slot on *Wine Enthusiast* magazine's 2014 top-100 list of wine restaurants nationwide. ■ TIP→ **The bites are served daily between 3 and 5, making this a quality late-afternoon pit stop.** ⑤ *Average main: $26* ✉ *401 S. A St., at Sebastopol Ave.* ☎ *707/528–7100* ⊕ *thespinstersisters.com.*

$$$$
STEAKHOUSE

✕ **Stark's Steak & Seafood.** The low lighting, well-spaced tables, and gas fireplaces at this Railroad Square Historic District restaurant create a congenial setting for dining on generous slabs of steak, seafood from the raw bar, and sustainable fish. With entrées that include a 20-ounce, dry-aged rib eye and a 32-ounce porterhouse for two, there's not a chance that meat eaters will depart unsated, and nonsteak options such as tamarind barbecue prawns and halibut with roasted grapes, almonds, and capers are a cut above those at your average temple to beef. ■ TIP→ **The full menu is available in the adjoining, less formal lounge, which is renowned for its happy hour (from 3 to 6, except Sunday).** ⑤ *Average main: $36* ✉ *521 Adams St., at 7th St.* ☎ *707/546–5100* ⊕ *starkssteakhouse.com* ⊘ *No lunch weekends.*

$$$
ECLECTIC
Fodor'sChoice
★

✕ **Willi's Wine Bar.** Don't let the name fool you: instead of a sedate spot serving wine and delicate nibbles, you'll find a cozy warren of rooms where boisterous crowds snap up small plates from the globe-trotting menu. Dishes such as the pork-belly pot stickers represent Asia, and duck prosciutto and Moroccan-style lamb chops are two of the Mediterranean-inspired foods. Several cheese and charcuterie plates are among the many using California-sourced ingredients. Wines are available in 2-ounce pours, making it easier to pair each of your little plates with a different glass. ■ TIP→ **It can get noisy inside on busy nights, so consider a table on the covered patio.** ⑤ *Average main: $28* ✉ *4404 Old Redwood Hwy., at Ursuline Rd.* ☎ *707/526–3096* ⊕ *williswinebar.net* ⊘ *No lunch Sun. and Mon.*

5

WHERE TO STAY

$ ▦ **Flamingo Conference Resort & Spa.** If Don Draper from the TV show
RESORT *Mad Men* popped into Santa Rosa, he'd feel right at home in this
1950s-style resort just beyond downtown. **Pros:** cool pool; retro vibe;
good value, especially the gray-tone rooms renovated in 2014 (request
one of these). **Cons:** 30-minute walk to downtown; small bathrooms in
some rooms. ⑤ *Rooms from: $119* ✉ *2777 4th St.* ☏ *707/545–8530,
800/848–8300* ⊕ *www.flamingoresort.com* ⌦ *170 rooms* ⦿ *No meals.*

$ ▦ **Fountaingrove Inn.** Rooms at this hotel off U.S. 101 often cost half the
HOTEL price of their equivalents in Healdsburg, yet the town's plaza is only
a 15-minute drive away. **Pros:** frequent Internet specials; amenities for
business travelers; room service; attractive lobby. **Cons:** small pool;
some public areas look tattered; uneven housekeeping. ⑤ *Rooms from:
$199* ✉ *101 Fountaingrove Pkwy., at Mendocino Ave.* ☏ *800/222–6101*
⊕ *www.fountaingroveinn.com* ⌦ *124 rooms* ⦿ *No meals.*

$ ▦ **Hotel La Rose.** The obvious choice for travelers seeking historic atmo-
HOTEL sphere and proximity to Railroad Square restaurants, nightlife, and
shopping, Hotel La Rose delivers a comfortable stay, if one lacking the
boutique-hotel style and polished service the grand stone exterior might
imply. **Pros:** reasonable rates; convenient to Railroad Square; historic
atmosphere. **Cons:** inconsistent hospitality; some rooms feel cramped;
no pool or fitness center; street noise heard in some rooms; some travelers may find the surrounding neighborhood scruffy. ⑤ *Rooms from:
$130* ✉ *308 Wilson St.* ☏ *707/579–3200, 707/527–6738* ⊕ *hotellarose.
com* ⌦ *48 rooms* ⦿ *No meals.*

$$ ▦ **Hyatt Vineyard Creek Hotel and Spa.** Relentlessly corporate but easy
HOTEL on the eyes and well maintained, the Hyatt wins points for its con-
venient downtown location, decent-size pool, courteous staff, and
arbor-lined sculpture garden. **Pros:** well-maintained property; pool and
garden; convenient to Railroad Square dining and shopping; frequent
online specials. **Cons:** the many events booked here detract from the
leisure-traveler experience. ⑤ *Rooms from: $209* ✉ *170 Railroad St.*
☏ *707/284–1234* ⊕ *vineyardcreek.hyatt.com* ⌦ *139 rooms, 16 suites*
⦿ *No meals.*

$$$ ▦ **Olivet Grange Farmhouse.** A deal for large groups, especially those stay-
RENTAL ing for more than a few days, this farmhouse at a working winery has
modern conveniences but retains a nostalgic ambience. **Pros:** spacious;
nostalgic ambience; get-away-from-it-all feel; vineyard views; quality
linens; washer and dryer; full kitchen; garden; discounts for longer
stays. **Cons:** two-night minimum; may be too isolated for some guests;
lacks the usual hotel amenities. ⑤ *Rooms from: $350* ✉ *Inman Family
Wines, 3900 Piner Rd.* ☏ *707/293–9576* ⊕ *www.inmanfamilywines.
com/about-us/farmhouse-rental* ⌦ *1 house* ⦿ *No meals.*

$$ ▦ **Safari West Tent Cabins.** The swank Botswana-made tent cabins at
B&B/INN this African wildlife preserve overlook the living areas of giraffes, ante-
lopes, flamingos, and other animals. **Pros:** outdoorsy feel without all
the work; plush bedding; private bathrooms; get-away-from-it-all feel;
online package deals. **Cons:** the squawking of flamingos and cranes
can be heard in some cabins (for silence and solitude request one away

from them); summer evenings can be hot. $ *Rooms from: $260* ✉ *3115 Porter Creek Rd.* ☎ *707/579–2551* ⊕ *www.safariwest.com/visit/spend-the-night* ⤴ *30 tent cabins* ⊘ *Closed Jan. and Feb.* ⑩ *Breakfast.*

$$
HOTEL
Fodor's Choice
★

Vintners Inn. The owners of Ferrari-Carano Vineyards operate this oasis set amid 92 acres of vineyards that's known for its comfortable lodgings. **Pros:** spacious rooms with comfortable beds; jogging path through the vineyards; online deals pop up year-round. **Cons:** occasional noise from adjacent events center. $ *Rooms from: $265* ✉ *4350 Barnes Rd.* ☎ *707/575–7350, 800/421–2584* ⊕ *www.vintnersinn.com* ⤴ *38 rooms, 6 suites* ⑩ *No meals.*

NIGHTLIFE AND PERFORMING ARTS

NIGHTLIFE

BREWPUBS

Fodor's Choice
★

Russian River Brewing Company. It's all about Belgian-style ales, "aggressively hopped California ales," and barrel-aged beers at this popular brewery's large pub. The legendary lineup includes Pliny the Elder (and Younger, but only in February), Blind Pig I.P.A., Mortification (nuances of clove, toffee, and roasted malts), and so many more. ■ **TIP→ Happy hour (from 4 to 6:30 on weekdays and all day Sunday) is a jolly time to visit.** ✉ *725 4th St., near D St.* ☎ *707/545–2337* ⊕ *www. russianriverbrewing.com.*

CASINO

Graton Resort & Casino. Slots predominate at this spiffy casino that opened in late 2013. Blackjack, baccarat, and a few other table games are also available. The several mid- to upscale restaurants include a steak house and a Chinese restaurant by Martin Yan of *Yan Can Cook* fame, and there's a pricey food court. ✉ *288 Golf Course Dr. W, west off U.S. 101's Golf Course Dr. exit, Rohnert Park* ☎ *707/588–7100* ⊕ *www.gratonresortcasino.com.*

PERFORMING ARTS

ARTS CENTERS

Joan and Sanford I. Weill Hall. The acoustically sophisticated hall, which debuted in 2012, hosts classical (the San Francisco and Santa Rosa symphonies), jazz (Jazz at Lincoln Center with Wynton Marsalis), pop (Gispy Kings), and other ensembles, as well as solo performers such as Audra McDonald, Laurie Anderson, and Bill Maher. During summer, the hall's back wall opens out to include a terraced lawn. ■ **TIP→ If driving, park in lots L through O.** ✉ *Sonoma State University, Rohnert Park Expwy. and Petaluma Hill Blvd., east off U.S. 101, Rohnert Park* ☎ *866/955–6040* ⊕ *www.gmc.sonoma.edu/events.*

Spreckels Performing Arts Center. A short drive south of downtown Santa Rosa, the center presents the Broadway-style musicals of the resident Spreckels Theatre Company, along with dance and other performances. ✉ *5409 Snyder La., Rohnert Park Expwy., east off U.S. 101, Rohnert Park* ☎ *707/588–3400* ⊕ *www.spreckelsonline.com.*

Wells Fargo Center for the Arts. This cultural hub, configured theater-style or open-floor depending on the performance, books acts as varied as Steve Winwood, Colbie Caillat, the Peking Acrobats, Les Ballets Trockadero, and Cesar "The Dog Whisperer" Millan. ⊠ *50 Mark West Springs Rd., east off U.S. 101* ☏ *707/546–3600* ⊕ *wellsfargocenter arts.org.*

SPORTS AND THE OUTDOORS

Annadel State Park. More than 40 miles of hiking, mountain biking, and equestrian trails lace this day-use park that swarms with locals in April and May when the wildflowers bloom around Lake Ilsanjo. The rest of the year you can take to the trails or fish for black bass or bluegill (state fishing license required). ⊠ *6201 Channel Dr., off Montgomery Dr.* ☏ *707/539–3911* ⊕ *www.parks.ca.gov/?page_id=480* ⊠ *$8 per vehicle* ☉ *Park daily 8 am–sunset; Channel Dr. entrance 9–6.*

Getaway Adventures. Owner Randy Johnson and his energetic crew lead excursions down the Russian River and conduct biking and hiking tours to wineries, organic farms, and other locales. ☏ *707/568–3040, 800/499–2453* ⊕ *www.getawayadventures.com* ⊠ *From $99 (hiking), $149 (biking), and $155 (kayaking).*

Up & Away Ballooning. Being so close to the coast means that if the balloon you're in gets high enough, you'll have ocean views on a sunny day. You'll also take in plenty of vineyard vistas. Journeys conclude with a sparkling-wine brunch at Kendall-Jackson winery. ⊠ *Sonoma County Airport, 2200 Airport Blvd., off U.S.101* ☏ *707/836–0171, 800/711–2998* ⊕ *www.up-away.com* ⊠ *$235 per person.*

SHOPPING

Fodor'sChoice ★ **Hot Couture Vintage Fashion.** Locals love Hot Couture for its knowledgeable owner, Marta, and eclectic, well-curated, and reasonably priced vintage fashions and accessories from the 1900s into the 1980s. ⊠ *101 3rd St., at Wilson St.* ☏ *707/528–7247.*

Whistlestop Antiques. The granny's-attic ambience of this mélange of antiques, art, and bric-a-brac makes for an engaging, nostalgic shopping experience. The prices aren't bad, either. ⊠ *140 4th St., at Davis St.* ☏ *707/542–9474* ⊕ *whistlestop-antiques.com.*

TRAVEL SMART
NAPA AND SONOMA

Visit Fodors.com for advice, updates, and bookings

GETTING HERE AND AROUND

Most travelers to the Wine Country start their trip in San Francisco. Getting to southern Napa or Sonoma takes less than an hour in normal traffic. Using public transportation can be time-consuming. If you base yourself the Napa Valley towns of Napa, Yountville, or St. Helena, or in Sonoma or Healdsburg in Sonoma County, you'll be able to visit numerous tasting rooms and nearby wineries on foot.

The 511 SF Bay website (⊕ *www.511.org*) can help you plan trips to and within the Wine Country. *See the Planning sections at the front of each chapter for more public transit information.*

Contact 511 SF Bay ⊕ *511.org.*

▎ AIR TRAVEL

Nonstop flights from New York to San Francisco take about 5½ hours, and with the three-hour time change, it's possible to leave JFK by 8 am and be in San Francisco by 11 or 11:30 am. Some flights require changing planes midway, making the total excursion between 8 and 9½ hours.

More than three dozen airlines serve San Francisco's airport, and a few of the same airlines also serve the airports in Oakland and Sacramento. Fares to San Francisco are often the cheapest, but the two smaller airports can sometimes be more convenient, especially if your destination is southern Napa. Alaska, American, Delta, jetBlue, Southwest, and US Airways serve all three airports. United serves San Francisco and Sacramento. Frontier and Virgin America serve San Francisco. Alaska's subsidiary, Horizon Air, serves Sacramento and Santa Rosa's Charles M. Schulz Sonoma County Airport.

Airline Contacts Alaska Airlines ☎ *800/252–7522* ⊕ *www.alaskaair.com.* **American Airlines** ☎ *800/433–7300* ⊕ *www. aa.com.* **Delta Airlines** ☎ *800/221–1212* ⊕ *www.delta.com.* **Frontier Airlines**

☎ *800/432–1359* ⊕ *www.flyfrontier.com.* **jetBlue** ☎ *800/538–2583* ⊕ *www.jetblue. com.* **Southwest Airlines** ☎ *800/435–9792* ⊕ *www.southwest.com.* **United Airlines** ☎ *800/864–8331* ⊕ *www.united.com.* **US Airways** ☎ *800/428–4322* ⊕ *www.usairways. com.* **Virgin America** ☎ *877/359–8474* ⊕ *www.virginamerica.com.*

AIRPORTS

The major gateway to the Wine Country is San Francisco International Airport (SFO), 60 miles from the city of Napa. Oakland International Airport (OAK), almost directly across San Francisco Bay, is actually closer to Napa, which is 50 miles away. Most visitors choose SFO, though, because it has more daily flights. Yet another option is to fly into Sacramento International Airport (SMF), about 68 miles from Napa and 76 miles from Sonoma. Wine Country regulars often fly into Santa Rosa's Charles M. Schulz Sonoma County Airport (STS), which receives daily nonstop flights from San Diego, Los Angeles, Portland, and Seattle. The airport is only 15 miles from Healdsburg. Avis, Budget, Enterprise, Hertz, and National rent cars here. ▎TIP➔ **Alaska allows passengers flying out of STS to check up to one case of wine for free.**

Airport Information Charles M. Schulz Sonoma County Airport (STS). ☎ *707/565– 7243* ⊕ *www.sonomacountyairport.org.* **Oakland International Airport** (OAK). ✉ *1 Airport Dr., Oakland* ☎ *510/563–3300* ⊕ *www. flyoakland.com.* **Sacramento International Airport** (SMF). ☎ *916/929–5411* ⊕ *www. sacramento.aero/smf.* **San Francisco International Airport** (SFO). ✉ *McDonnell and Link Rds., San Francisco* ☎ *800/435–9736, 650/821–8211* ⊕ *www.flysfo.com.* **San Jose International Airport** (SJC). ✉ *1701 Airport Blvd., San Jose* ☎ *408/392–3600* ⊕ *www. flysanjose.com.*

GROUND TRANSPORTATION

To the Wine Country Two shuttle services serve Napa and Sonoma from both San Francisco International Airport and Oakland International Airport. Evans Airport Service, affiliated with California Wine Tours, is an option for travelers without cars staying in Napa or Yountville. The service, which costs $45 per person, drops you off at any hotel. If you're heading elsewhere, the company will arrange for taxi service from its drop-off point. The Sonoma County Airport Express shuttles passengers between the airports and the cities of Santa Rosa, Rohnert Park, and Petaluma for $34. Ask the driver to call ahead so that a taxi is waiting for you when you arrive.

If you'll be staying in the town of Napa, it's possible to take BART from SFO or OAK to the El Cerrito Del Norte station and then board VINE Bus 29. If you're headed to the town of Sonoma, transfer in Napa to Bus 25. Private limousine service costs up to $300, depending on your destination. SF Limo Express charges $149 to take up to four people to the town of Sonoma, $189 to Calistoga, and $270 to Healdsburg.

Charles M. Schulz Sonoma County Airport is just off U.S. 101 in Santa Rosa. Healdsburg is north of the airport via U.S. 101. For the town of Sonoma, drive south to Highway 12 and head east.

To San Francisco If you're headed to downtown San Francisco, a taxi ride from San Francisco International Airport costs from $50 to $55. More economical are GO Lorrie's Airport Shuttle and SuperShuttle, both of which take you anywhere within the city limits for $17 per person. Both can be found on the airport's lower level near baggage claim. SF Limo Express charges $49 for a town car ride. The rates of request-a-ride services such as Uber, Lyft, and Sidecar, whose drivers are summoned by downloadable smartphone apps, vary depending on the type of vehicle selected and the travel time. Taking the smallest-size Uber vehicle, for instance, costs between $95 and $123 to Sonoma, $99 and $128 to Napa, and $109 and $142 to Santa Rosa. The fare is comparable on Lyft and lower on Sidecar.

Bay Area Rapid Transit (BART) commuter trains take you directly to downtown San Francisco. The trip takes about 30 minutes and costs $8.65. BART trains depart from the international terminal every 15 minutes or 20 minutes, depending on the time of day. Two SamTrans buses provide another inexpensive option: the 292 (one hour, $2) and the KX (35 minutes, $5; only one small carry-on bag permitted). Board SamTrans buses on the lower level.

A taxi from Oakland International Airport to downtown San Francisco costs from $40 to $45. You must make reservations for shuttle service. BayPorter Express provides private service only ($70 for up to seven passengers). With SuperShuttle ($27 for the first passenger, $15 for each additional passenger), other travelers may join the ride.

The best public-transit option is BART. Follow signs in the terminal to the driverless BART shuttle train, which operates between the airport and the Coliseum station. After exiting the shuttle, you can purchase a ticket whose price covers the cost of shuttle and the train to your destination. The fare to San Francisco is $10.05.

Limos, Shuttles, and Ride Services BayPorter Express ☏ *415/467–1800, 510/864–4000* ⊕ *www.bayporter.com.* **Evans Airport Service** ✉ *Napa Office and Airporter Terminal, 4075 Solano Ave., Napa* ☏ *707/255–1559* ⊕ *www. evanstransportation.com.* **GO Lorrie's Airport Shuttle** ☏ *415/334–9000* ⊕ *www.gosfovan. com.* **Lyft** ⊕ *www.lyft.com.* **SF Limo Express** ☏ *415/990–6364* ⊕ *www.sflimoexpress. net.* **Sidecar** ⊕ *www.side.cr.* **Sonoma County Airport Express** ☏ *707/837–8700, 800/327–2024* ⊕ *www.airportexpressinc.com.* **SuperShuttle** ☏ *800/258–3826* ⊕ *www. supershuttle.com.* **Uber** ⊕ *www.uber.com.*

Public Transit Bay Area Rapid Transit
(*BART*). ☎ *415/989–2278* ⊕ *www.bart.gov.*
SamTrans ☎ *800/660–4287* ⊕ *www.samtrans.*
com.

▌BUS AND COMMUTER TRAIN TRAVEL

The knee-jerk local reaction to the notion of getting to tasting rooms—or the Wine Country—via public transit is that it's impossible or will take forever, but it's definitely possible. The two easiest towns to visit are Napa and Sonoma, and both have numerous tasting rooms, restaurants, and lodgings in their downtown areas.

To Napa: From San Francisco or Oakland, you can take a BART train to the El Cerrito Del Norte station and then pick up VINE Express Bus 29, which stops at the Soscol Gateway Transit Center in downtown Napa. Once in Napa you can connect with VINE buses that travel up the entire valley to Calistoga. VINE Bus 25 connects the towns of Napa and Sonoma.

To Sonoma and Santa Rosa: To get to the town of Sonoma from downtown San Francisco, you can take any of several Golden Gate Transit buses to San Rafael and transfer to Sonoma County Transit Bus 38, which stops near Sonoma Plaza. Golden Gate Transit also serves Santa Rosa, from whose Transit Mall you can transfer to buses serving Healdsburg, Sebastopol, and other Sonoma County destinations. From San Francisco, Greyhound serves Santa Rosa via Oakland and then San Rafael, in Marin County, a circuitous route. You're better off taking Golden Gate Transit from San Francisco, and Greyhound from Oakland.

Bus Lines Golden Gate Transit
☎ *415/455–2000* ⊕ *www.goldengatetransit.
org.* **Greyhound** ☎ *800/231–2222* ⊕ *www.
greyhound.com.* **Sonoma County Transit**
☎ *707/576–7433, 800/345–7433* ⊕ *www.
sctransit.com.* **VINE** ✉ *Soscol Gateway Transit
Center, 625 Burnell St., Napa* ☎ *707/251–2800,
800/696–6443* ⊕ *www.ridethevine.com.*

▌CAR TRAVEL

A car is the most logical and convenient way to navigate Napa and Sonoma. Although some thoroughfares can be congested, especially during rush hour and on summer weekends, there are plenty of less trafficked routes. Parking is generally not a problem.

To drive to the Wine Country from San Francisco International, follow signs north out of the airport to Interstate 380, which leads to Interstate 280. As you approach San Francisco, follow signs for the Golden Gate Bridge. By the time you begin crossing the bridge, you're on U.S. 101. Head north for northern Sonoma County. For southern Sonoma County and the Napa Valley, head east on Highway 37 at the town of Novato, then follow Highway 121 into southern Sonoma. At Highway 12, turn north to reach the town of Sonoma. For the Napa Valley, continue east on Highway 121 to Highway 29 and head north.

From Oakland International, the best way to get to Sonoma County is via Interstate 880 north. Follow signs for Interstate 80 East/Interstate 580 West, which takes you across the Richmond–San Rafael Bridge. After you cross the bridge, follow the signs to U.S. 101 North. From here, continue north for northern Sonoma County or head east of Highway 37 for southern Sonoma County and the Napa Valley. A quicker option if you're heading to the Napa Valley is to stay on Interstate 80 to Highway 37 in Vallejo. Head west on Highway 37 and north on Highway 29, following the signs for Napa.

If you fly into Sacramento International, take Interstate 5 South to Interstate 80 West. Exit onto Highway 12 and continue west to Highway 29 north for the city of Napa. For the town of Sonoma continue west on Highway 121 and north on Highway 12.

From Sonoma's airport, take U.S. 101 south to Santa Rosa and then east and south on Highway 12 to reach Kenwood,

Glen Ellen, and Sonoma; head north on U.S. 101 for Healdsburg; and head south on Laughlin Road and west on River Road for Guerneville, Forestville, Sebastopol, and other Russian River Valley towns. To reach the Napa Valley, take U.S. 101 south to the River Road exit and head east on Mark Springs West Road, Porter Creek Road, and Petrified Forest to Calistoga.

CAR RENTALS

If you're flying into the area, it's almost always easiest to pick up a car at the airport. You'll also find rental companies in the major towns around the Wine Country. The beautiful landscapes make it a popular place for renting specialty vehicles, especially convertibles. Exotic Car Collection by Enterprise or the locally based City Rent-a-Car rent such vehicles. ■TIP→ When renting a specialty car, ask about mileage limits. Some companies stick you with per-mile charges if you exceed 100 miles a day.

Most rental companies require you to be at least 20 years old to rent a car, but some agencies won't rent to those under 25; check when you book. Super Cheap Car Rentals, near San Francisco International, has competitive prices and, unlike many agencies, rents to drivers between 21 and 24 for no extra charge.

Car-rental costs in the area vary seasonally, but in San Francisco generally begin at $50 a day and $275 a week for an economy car with unlimited mileage. Rates can be slightly higher in Oakland and substantially higher in Sacramento, often offsetting any airfare savings. This doesn't include car-rental taxes and other surcharges and fees, which can add another 20% to the per-day rate.

Rental agencies in California aren't required to include liability insurance in the price of the rental. If you cause an accident, you may be liable. When in doubt about your own policy's coverage, take the liability coverage the agency offers.

Automobile Associations American Automobile Association (*AAA*). ☎ *415/565–2141* ⊕ *www.aaa.com.* **National Automobile Club** ☎ *800/622-2136* ⊕ *www.thenac.com.*

Local Agencies City Rent-a-Car ✉ *1433 Bush St., near Van Ness Ave., Van Ness/Polk, San Francisco* ☎ *415/359-1331, 866/359-1331* ⊕ *www.cityrentacar.com.* **Super Cheap Car Rental** ✉ *10 Rollins Rd., at Millbrae Ave., Millbrae* ☎ *650/777-9993* ⊕ *www. supercheapcar.com.*

Major Agencies Alamo ☎ *800/462-5266* ⊕ *www.alamo.com.* **Avis** ☎ *800/633-3469* ⊕ *www.avis.com.* **Budget** ☎ *800/218-7992* ⊕ *www.budget.com.* **Exotic Car Collection by Enterprise** ☎ *650/238-5338, 866/456-9227* ⊕ *exoticcars.enterprise.com/sanfrancisco.* **Hertz** ☎ *800/654-3131* ⊕ *www.hertz.com.* **National Car Rental** ☎ *877/222-9058* ⊕ *www.nationalcar.com.*

GASOLINE

Gas is readily available on all but the most remote back roads. Expect to pay from 10% to 20% more than you would back home.

PARKING

Parking is rarely a problem in the Wine Country, as wineries and hotels have ample free parking. In some communities, street parking is limited to two or three hours during the day. There are often reasonably priced municipal lots downtown; signs will generally point you in the right direction.

ROAD CONDITIONS

Whether they are four-lane highways or winding country lanes, the roads in the Wine Country are generally well maintained. Traffic jams do occur, though the biggest tie-ups you'll experience will likely be in and around San Francisco. Trying to negotiate morning and afternoon rush hours will add considerable time to your trip. On Sunday evenings you'll encounter lots of traffic as you head back to San Francisco, but it's nothing compared with the crush of cars trying to leave San Francisco on a Friday afternoon. Traffic can be equally bad heading north from Oakland to Napa along Interstate 80, especially during the afternoon rush hour. For up-to-the-minute traffic info, visit ⊕ *www.traffic.511.org* or tune your radio to 740 AM and 106.9 FM, which broadcast traffic news every 10 minutes.

Once you've reached the Wine Country, the roads become less crowded and more scenic. Expect heavier traffic during rush hours, generally between 7 and 9 am and 4 and 6 pm. Things can also get congested on Friday and Sunday afternoons, when weekenders add to the mix. Highway 29, which runs the length of Napa Valley, can be slow going in summer, especially on weekends, and it can slow to a crawl around the town of St. Helena.

ROADSIDE EMERGENCIES

Dial 911 to report accidents on the road and to reach police, the highway patrol, or the fire department. The American Automobile Association and the National Automobile Club provide roadside assistance to members.

RULES OF THE ROAD

To encourage carpooling during rush hour, some freeways have special lanes for so-called high-occupancy vehicles (HOVs)—cars carrying more than one or two passengers. Look for the white diamond in the middle of the lane. Signs next to or above the lane indicate the hours that carpooling is in effect. If you get stopped for not having enough passengers, expect a fine of nearly $500.

State law bans drivers from using handheld mobile telephones while operating a vehicle, and the use of seat belts in both front- and backseats is required. Children must ride in a properly secured child passenger safety restraint in the backseat until they are eight years old or 4 feet 9 inches tall. The speed limit on city streets is 25 mph unless otherwise posted. A right turn after stopping at a red light is legal unless posted otherwise.

■ **TIP→** If you're wine tasting, either select a designated driver or be careful of your wine intake—the police keep an eye out for tipsy drivers.

■ FERRY TRAVEL

From late April through October the San Francisco Bay Ferry sails from the Ferry Building and Pier 41 in San Francisco to Vallejo, where you can board VINE Bus 11 to the town of Napa. Buses sometimes fill in for the ferries.

Contact San Francisco Bay Ferry
☎ *510/522-3300* ⊕ *sanfranciscobayferry.com.*

■ TAXI TRAVEL

Taxis aren't a common sight in the Wine Country—most visitors are driving a rental car. Still, you might want to take a cab to and from dinner, especially if you want to indulge in a cocktail or a few glasses of wine. All cabs are metered: expect to pay $3 upon pickup and another $2.50 to $3 per mile thereafter, depending on the city you're in. Taxi drivers usually expect a 15%–20% tip for good service. Cabs must be called rather than hailed.

A to Z Cab serves the entire Napa Valley. Napa Valley Cab is another option. All City Taxi serves Santa Rosa, Healdsburg, Rohnert Park, and Sebastopolns. Vern's Taxi serves the Sonoma Valley (Sonoma, Glen Ellen, Kenwood, Santa Rosa). Yellow Cab serves Santa Rosa and Kenwood. A-C Taxi, which owns Healdsburg Taxi, serves the entire county.

Taxi Companies A-C Taxi of Santa Rosa
✉ *Santa Rosa* ☎ *707/777-7777.* **A to Z Cab** ✉ *St. Helena* ☎ *707/666-1555* ⊕ *www.atozcab.com.* **All City Taxi** ✉ *Santa Rosa* ☎ *707/333-3333* ⊕ *allcitytaxiservice.com.* **Healdsburg Taxi Cab Company** ✉ *Healdsburg* ☎ *707/433-7088.* **Napa Valley Cab** ✉ *Napa* ☎ *707/257-6444* ⊕ *www.napavalleycab.com.* **Vern's Taxi** ☎ *707/938-8885* ⊕ *www.vernstaxi.com.* **Yellow Cab** ☎ *707/544-4444* ⊕ *www.yellowtaxirides.com.*

ESSENTIALS

▌ ACCOMMODATIONS

Wine Country inns and hotels range from low-key to sumptuous, and generally maintain high standards. Many inns are in historic Victorian buildings, and when rates include breakfast the preparations often involve fresh local produce. The newer hotels tend to have a more modern, streamlined aesthetic and elaborate, spalike bathrooms, and many have excellent restaurants on-site.

Accommodations generally have lower rates on weeknights, and prices are about 20% lower in winter. The towns of Napa and Santa Rosa have the widest selection of moderately priced rooms. On weekends, two- or even three-night minimum stays are commonly required at smaller lodgings. Book well ahead for stays at such places during the busy summer or fall season. If your party will include travelers under age 16, inquire about policies regarding younger guests; some smaller lodgings discourage (or discreetly forbid) children.

INFORMATION AND RESERVATIONS

BedandBreakfast.com has details about member inns in the Napa and Sonoma County. The Napa Valley Hotels & Resorts page on the Visit Napa Valley website lists hotels, inns, and other accommodations throughout Napa County. The Sonoma Hotels & Lodging page on the Visit Sonoma site has similarly comprehensive listings for Sonoma County. The members of the Sonoma Valley Bed & Breakfast Association operate noteworthy small inns and vacation-rental properties throughout the valley; Wine Country Inns represents 20 small lodgings throughout Sonoma County. You can check availability at its members' inns on the website, which can save you time. The various innkeepers share phone duties, so the level of assistance offered varies depending on whose turn it is.

Reservations are a good idea, especially from late spring through the fall harvest season and on many weekends. Two- or even three-night minimum stays are commonly required, especially at smaller lodgings. If you'd prefer to stay a single night, innkeepers are more flexible in winter. Some lodgings aren't suitable for kids, so ask before you make a reservation.

Contacts BedandBreakfast.com ☎ *800/462–2632, 512/322–2710* ⊕ *www. bedandbreakfast.com.* **Napa Valley Hotels & Resorts** ☎ *707/251–9188, 855/333–6272* ⊕ *www.visitnapavalley.com/napa_valley_ hotels.htm.* **Sonoma Hotels & Lodging** ⊕ *www.sonomacounty.com/hotels-lodging.* **Wine Country Inns** ⊠ *Cloverdale* ☎ *800/946– 3268* ⊕ *www.winecountryinns.com.*

FACILITIES

When pricing accommodations, always ask what's included. Some small inns may not have air-conditioning, so be sure to ask if you're visiting in July or August, when temperatures can reach 90°F. Most hotels have Wi-Fi, although it's not always free. Most large properties have pools and fitness rooms; those without usually have arrangements at nearby gyms, sometimes for a fee.

PRICES

Wine Country lodging prices, which on average exceed those even in high-end San Francisco, may come as an unpleasant surprise. Even the humblest accommodations start at nearly $200 a night in high season. If you're having difficulty finding something in your price range, remember that Napa and Santa Rosa have the widest selection of moderately priced rooms. Rates vary widely; call the property directly, but also check its website and online booking agencies.

Our local writers vet every hotel to recommend the best overnights in each price category, from budget to expensive. Unless otherwise specified, you can expect private bath, phone, and TV in your room. *Prices in the reviews are the lowest cost of a standard double room in high season. For expanded reviews, visit Fodors.com.*

CATEGORY	COST
$	under $201
$$	$201–300
$$$	$301–$400
$$$$	over $400

▮ COMMUNICATIONS

INTERNET

Given the California Wine Country's proximity to Silicon Valley and San Francisco, it's no surprise that it's easy to get connected almost everywhere you go. Most cafés in the Wine Country also offer Wi-Fi service, often for free if you order something.

▮ EATING OUT

Excellent meals can be found in all the major Wine Country towns, and tiny Yountville has become a culinary crossroads under the influence of chef Thomas Keller. In St. Helena the elegant Restaurant at Meadowood has achieved almost as much critical acclaim as Keller's The French Laundry, yet is easier to get into. And the buzzed-about restaurants in Sonoma County, including Glen Ellen Star and the Farmhouse Inn, offer plenty of mouthwatering options.

The Wine Country's top restaurants tend to serve what is often called "California cuisine," which incorporates elements of French and Italian cooking and emphasizes the use of fresh, local products. If the restaurant scene here has a weakness, it's the absence of a greater variety of cuisines. However, the number of immigrants from Latin America ensures that in almost any town you'll find good, inexpensive spots selling tacos, fajitas, and similar fare.

Vegetarians shouldn't have any trouble finding excellent choices on Wine Country menus. The region's bounty of fresh produce and California's general friendliness toward vegetarians mean that restaurants are usually willing to go out of their way to accommodate you.

The Wine Country's restaurants, though excellent, can really dent your wallet. If you're on a budget, many high-end delis prepare superb picnic fare. Stopping for lunch or brunch can be a cost-effective strategy at pricey restaurants, as can sitting at the bar and ordering appetizers instead of having a full meal. It also doesn't hurt to ask about a restaurant's corkage policy: some restaurants eliminate their corkage fee one night a week, or even every night, hoping to attract locals in the wine industry who would rather drink bottles from their own cellar than the restaurant's.

The sheer number of restaurants means you can always find an empty table somewhere, but it pays to call ahead for a reservation, even if only a day or two before you visit. For the big-name restaurants such as Press, Terra, Goose & Gander, and Farmhouse Inn, calling a few weeks in advance is advised, though you can often get in on short notice if you're willing to eat early or late. (For The French Laundry, you must call two months ahead to the day.)

Except as noted in individual restaurant listings, dress is informal. Where reservations are indicated as essential, book a week or more ahead in summer and early fall. *Prices in the reviews are the average cost of a main course at dinner or, if dinner is not served, at lunch.*

CATEGORY	COST
$	under $16
$$	$16–$22
$$$	$23–$30
$$$$	over $30

MEALS AND MEALTIMES

Lunch is typically served from 11:30 to 2:30 or 3, and dinner service in most restaurants starts at 5 or 5:30 and ends around 9 or 10. The Wine Country is short on late-night dining, so don't put off eating until any later than 10. Most hotels and inns offer breakfast service—anything from a basic continental breakfast to a lavish buffet to an individually prepared feast—but if yours doesn't, you'll find a good bakery in just about every Wine Country town.

Some restaurants close for a day or two a week, most often on Tuesday or Wednesday, when the number of visitors is fewest, so be sure to check in advance if you're planning on dining midweek. Unless otherwise noted, the restaurants listed here are open daily for lunch and dinner.

PAYING

Almost all restaurants in the Wine Country accept credit cards. On occasion, you might find a bakery or a casual café that takes cash only. *For guidelines on tipping see ⇨ Tipping, below.*

RESERVATIONS AND DRESS

Restaurants throughout the Wine Country tend to be fairly casual, especially in Sonoma. This is less true in the Napa Valley, where you're unlikely to see jeans or shorts at dinner except at casual restaurants. Jackets, however, are very rarely required for men. At The French Laundry, though, they're necessary for both lunch and dinner. At top-tier restaurants like The Restaurant at Meadowood and the Farmhouse Inn, they would certainly be appropriate.

Regardless of where you are, it's a good idea to make reservations if you can.

We mention them specifically only when essential (there's no other way you'll ever get a table) or when they are not accepted. For popular restaurants, book as far ahead as you can (often 30 days), and reconfirm as soon as you arrive. (Large parties should always call ahead to check the reservations policy.) We mention dress only when men are required to wear a jacket or a jacket and tie.

Online reservation services make it easy to book a table before you even leave home. Tables at many Wine Country restaurants are available through the OpenTable and Urbanspoon sites.

Contacts Open Table ⊕ *www.opentable.com.* **Urbanspoon** ⊕ *www.urbanspoon.com.*

WINES, BEER, AND SPIRITS

Nowhere in the United States are you more likely to see someone enjoying a glass or two of wine not only with dinner, but with lunch as well. Only the smallest dives and most casual cafés lack a wine menu; lists here are usually strongest in local bottles, with other West Coast wines and perhaps some French and Italian wines as well. Upscale restaurants generally have full bars. Though it's legal to serve alcohol as late as 2 am in California, most restaurants close down by 10 pm or so.

▌ HOURS OF OPERATION

Winery tasting rooms are generally open from 10 or 11 am to 4:30 or 5 pm. Larger wineries are usually open every day, but some of the smaller ones may open only on weekends or for three or four days. Tuesday and Wednesday are the quietest days of the week for wine touring. If you have a particular winery in mind, check its hours before you visit, and keep in mind that many wineries are open by appointment only.

MONEY

The sweet life costs a pretty penny in most Wine Country areas, where even a basic hotel tends to cost around $200 a night. That said, it is possible to stick to a lower budget if you're willing to stay in a fairly basic motel, eat at some of the less expensive restaurants, and take advantage of the many picnicking opportunities.

ITEM	AVERAGE COST
Cup of Coffee (Not a Latte!)	$2.50
Glass of Wine	$11
Glass of Beer	$7
Sandwich	$9
One-Mile Taxi Ride	$6
Museum Admission	$5

Prices here are given for adults. Substantially reduced fees are almost always available for children, students, and senior citizens.

SAFETY

The Wine Country is generally a safe place for travelers who observe all normal precautions. Most visitors will feel safe walking at night in all the smaller towns and in the downtown area of towns like Sonoma. Still, the largest towns, such as Napa and Santa Rosa, have a few rougher areas (typically far from the tourist spots), so you should check with a local before you go wandering in unknown neighborhoods. Car break-ins are not particularly common here, although it's always best to remove valuables from your car, or at least keep them out of sight.

The main danger you face in the Wine Country is the threat of drunk drivers. Keep an eye out for drivers who may have had one too many glasses of wine, as well as for bikers who might be hidden around the next bend in the road.

SHIPPING

Because alcoholic beverages are regulated by individual states, shipping wine back home can be easy or complicated, depending on where you live. Some states, among them Alabama, Pennsylvania, and Utah, prohibit all direct shipments from wineries. Others allow the shipment of limited quantities—a certain number of gallons or cases per year—if a winery has purchased a permit to do so. The penalties for noncompliance can be steep—it's a felony, for instance, to ship wines to Kentucky or Utah (this includes shipping the wines yourself). Since selling wine is their business, wineries are well versed in the regulations.

If you decide to send wines back home, keep in mind that most states require that someone 21 or older sign for the delivery. The Wine Institute, which represents California wineries, has up-to-date information about shipping within the United States and abroad.

Information Wine Institute ⊕ *www. wineinstitute.org/initiatives/stateshippinglaws.*

SPECIAL-INTEREST TOURS AND EDUCATION

BICYCLING TOURS

Bicycling tours of the Wine Country range from one-day excursions to weeklong vacations with lavish picnic lunches, leisurely dinners, and stays at some of the region's fanciest inns. You might pay less than $100 for a half- or full-day trip; multiday excursions can cost from $250 to $500 per day, including accommodations.

Backroads. This Berkeley-based outfit conducts several premium multiday guided tours of various levels of difficulty. A typical Sonoma County tour might start in the Russian River Valley and take in Dry Creek Valley and Alexander Valley wineries as well. Some Napa Valley tours cover out-of-the-way wineries and the greatest hits. Overnight stays are at top hotels, luggage transfers and other logistics are taken care of, and support vans are stocked with all the comforts and necessities riders need. ☎ 800/462–2848 ⊕ www.backroads.com ✉ From $2,900.

Getaway Adventures. Randy Johnson's Santa Rosa–based outfit conducts guided short and multiday biking, hiking, and kayaking tours of the Napa Valley and Sonoma County. Excursions include a foodie biking tour of Healdsburg, a hike to the top of Mt. St. Helena, kayaking on the Napa River, and a combined biking and kayaking tour of the Russian River with winery stops. ☎ 707/568–3040 ⊕ getawayadventures.com ✉ From $69.

Napa & Sonoma Valley Bike Tours. Afternoon and all-day guided tours of wineries, vineyards, and other sights are this company's specialty. The pace is leisurely, and all-day tours include a picnic lunch at a winery. One combination tour starts with an early-morning balloon ride. ☎ 707/251–8687 for Napa trips, 707/996–2453 for Sonoma trips ⊕ www. napavalleybiketours.com ✉ From $99.

Wine Country Bikes. This family-owned Healdsburg outfitter rents bikes by the day and organizes one-day and multiday trips throughout Sonoma County. ☎ 707/473–0610, 800/922–4537 ⊕ www. winecountrybikes.com ✉ From $149 for all-day trips.

CULINARY TOURS AND CLASSES

Tours usually include one or more of the following: cooking classes, festive dinners at fine restaurants, excursions to local markets, and the opportunity to meet some of the area's top chefs. Tours can last from a few days to a week and start at around $500 per day, accommodations included. Epiculinary and Food and Wine Trails are two well-regarded tour companies. Staff and guest instructors at the Culinary Institute of America and Ramekins teach cooking classes and give demonstrations.

Culinary Institute of America. The chef-instructors at the institute's Greystone campus in St. Helena present live one-hour cooking demonstrations on most weekends. Attendees taste the dish made, accompanied by a glass of wine. Hands-on cooking classes cover topics such as baking, grilling, making sauces, and pairing food and wine. ✉ 2555 Main St., St. Helena ☎ 707/967–1100 ⊕ enthusiasts.ciachef.edu ✉ Demonstrations $20, classes from $95 ☾ Call or visit website for schedules.

Epiculinary. Hands-on cooking lessons and workshops are the centerpiece of this company's two- to five-night tours. Flavors of the Napa Valley includes trips to wineries or local farms or ranches; several restaurant stops are part of Bounty of Sonoma; and though two classes take up most of Wine Country Weekend there's still time for a massage. ☎ 520/488–2792 ⊕ www.epiculinary.com ✉ From $1,100.

Food and Wine Trails. Providing its clients with insights into more than just Napa and Sonoma's wines and wine making is the goal of this company that folds spa and restaurant trips and nonwine activities into its custom itineraries. ☎ 800/367–5348 ⊕ www.foodandwinetrails.com ✉ Price varies depending on itinerary and time of year; call for rates.

Ramekins Culinary School. Locals and visitors attend the wine-and-food events and hands-on and demonstration cooking classes at Ramekins. The topics range from the cuisine of Umbria to the flavors of fall and how to shop at a farmers' market; current and former Wine Country restaurant chefs teach some of the courses. Winemaker dinners often introduce up-and-coming talents. ✉ 450 W. Spain St., Sonoma ☎ 707/933–0450 ⊕ www.ramekins.com.

WINE EDUCATION

Many wineries hold seminars in blending, pairing wine and food pairing, and how to taste wine, and other topics; the San Francisco Wine School holds professional classes that visitors can attend.

San Francisco Wine School. David Glancy, a master sommelier, provides professional training at his well-respected school, but attendees of individual evening, day-long, and three-day-intensive classes also include wine lovers wishing to get up to speed on such topics as California appellations, detecting flaws in wine, and Rhône varietals. A few classes take place in Napa and Sonoma, but most are held in South San Francisco, near San Francisco's airport. ☎ 415/644–8461 ⊕ *sanfranciscowineschool.com* ✉ *From $125.*

WINERY TOURS

With several million visitors to the Wine Country every year, dozens of tour companies have sprung up to provide tours. Many of these are well organized and will chauffeur you to places you might not otherwise find on your own. Whether you're content to tour the Wine Country in a full-size bus with dozens of other passengers or you want to spring for your own private limo to take you to your favorite wineries, there are plenty of operators who can accommodate you. If you know the wineries, regions, or even the grape varietals that interest you, these operators can help you develop a satisfying itinerary. All visit both Napa and Sonoma wineries.

Most companies offer a range of tours, usually lasting five to seven hours and stopping at four or five wineries. Rates vary widely, from $80 per person for a day of touring to $250 or more, depending on the type of vehicle and whether the tour includes other guests. You can also book a car and driver by the hour for shorter trips. Rates for limo generally run from $50 to $85 per hour, and there's usually a two- or three-hour minimum.

★ **Fodor's Choice** | **Perata Luxury Tours & Car Services.** Perata's customized private tours, led by well-trained, knowledgeable drivers, are tailored to its patrons' interests—you can create your own itinerary or have your guide craft one for you. Tours, in luxury SUVs, cover Napa and Sonoma. The options include exclusive, appointment-only boutique wineries. ☎ 707/227–8271 ⊕ *www.perataluxurycarservices.com* ✉ *From $325 per day, plus fuel surcharge ($25–$35), tasting fees, and 18% gratuity charge.*

★ **Fodor's Choice** | **Platypus Wine Tours.** The emphasis at Platypus is on "fun" experiences at off-the-beaten-path wineries. Expect intimate winery experiences with jolly, well-informed guides. You can join an existing tour with other guests or book a private one. ☎ 707/253–2723 ⊕ *www.platypustours.com* ✉ *From $99, excluding tasting fees.*

Valley Wine Tours. Historic, family-owned wineries are the specialty of this Sonoma-based company that provides a gourmet picnic lunch—on china with cloth napkins, no less. The Valley Wine tour rate includes tasting fees. ☎ 707/975–6462 ⊕ *www.valleywinetours.com* ✉ *From $135.*

Woody's Wine Tours. The amiable, well-informed Woody Guderian favors small wineries but will customize a tour to suit your taste and budget. In addition to winery tours in both Napa and Sonoma, Woody also conducts tours of local craft breweries. ☎ 707/396–8235 ⊕ *www.woodyswinetours.com* ✉ *From $80 per hr, excluding tasting fees.*

▌ TAXES

Sales tax is 8% in Napa County and from 8¼% to 9¼% in Sonoma County. Non-prepared foods bought in grocery stores are exempt. The tax on hotel rooms adds from 9% to 14% to your bill in Sonoma County and 14% in Napa County.

▌ TIME

California is on Pacific Time. Chicago is two hours ahead of the West Coast, and New York is three hours ahead. Depending on whether daylight saving time is in effect, London is either 8 or 9 hours ahead and Sydney is 17 or 18 hours ahead.

■ TIPPING

TIPPING GUIDELINES FOR NAPA AND SONOMA	
Bartender	About 15%, starting at $1 a drink at casual places
Bellhop	$1 to $5 per bag, depending on the level of the hotel
Hotel concierge	$5 or more, if he or she performs a service for you
Hotel doorman, room service, or valet	$2–$3
Hotel maid	$3–$5 a day (either daily or at the end of your stay, in cash)
Taxi Driver	15%–20%, but round up the fare to the next dollar amount
Tour Guide	10% of the cost of the tour
Waiter	15%–20%, with 20% being the norm at high-end restaurants; nothing additional if a service charge is added to the bill

■ VISITOR INFORMATION

To begin your pretrip planning, visit the websites of the Wine Country's official tourism bureaus, Visit Napa Valley and Visit Sonoma. Three visitor centers are worth checking out while you're in the Wine Country: the California Welcome Center in Santa Rosa, the Napa Valley Welcome Center in downtown Napa, and the Sonoma Valley Visitors Center in Sonoma Plaza.

The Discover California Wines website has information about Napa and Sonoma wineries in its North Coast section. Other useful websites include those of local associations and wineries and grape growers. Many wineries require reservations for tours, seminars, and tastings. You can book winery experiences through the CellarPass and VinoVisit websites, as well as plan your itinerary. Wine Country and Winery Finder, two mobile apps, give you discounts on tasting fees and provide information about restaurants.

Visitor Centers California Welcome Center ⊠ *9 4th St., at Wilson St., Santa Rosa* ☎ *800/404-7673* ⊕ *www.visitcalifornia.com/california-welcome-centers/santa-rosa.* **Napa Valley Welcome Center** ⊠ *600 Main St., at 5th St., Napa* ☎ *707/251-5895* ⊕ *www.visitnapavalley.com/welcome_centers.htm.* **Sonoma Valley Visitors Center** ⊠ *453 1st St. E, east side of Sonoma Plaza, Sonoma* ☎ *707/996-1090, 866/996-1090* ⊕ *www.sonomavalley.com.*

Visitor Information Sonoma County Tourism Bureau ⊠ *3637 Westwind Blvd., Santa Rosa* ☎ *707/522-5800, 800/576-6662* ⊕ *www.sonomacounty.com.* **Sonoma Valley Visitors Bureau** ☎ *707/996-1090, 866/996-1090* ⊕ *www.sonomavalley.com.*

Visit Napa Valley ☎ *707/251-5895* ⊕ *www.visitnapavalley.com.* **Visit Sonoma** ☎ *707/522-5800, 800/576-6662* ⊕ *www.sonomacounty.com.*

Websites and Apps CellarPass ☎ *707/255-4390* ⊕ *www.cellarpass.com.* **VinoVisit** ☎ *888/252-8990* ⊕ *www.vinovisit.com.* **Wine Country** ⊕ *www.winecountry.com.* **Winery Finder** ⊕ *www.econcierges.com.*

Wines and Wineries Alexander Valley Winegrowers ☎ *888/289-4637* ⊕ *www.alexandervalley.org.* **Carneros Wine Alliance** ☎ *707/996-4140* ⊕ *www.carneros.com.* **Discover California Wines** ☎ *415/512-0151* ⊕ *www.discovercaliforniawines.com.* **Heart of Sonoma Valley Winery Association** ☎ *707/431-1137, 866/794-9463* ⊕ *www.heartofsonomavalley.com.* **Napa Valley Vintners Association** ☎ *707/963-3388* ⊕ *www.napavintners.com.* **Russian River Wine Road** ☎ *707/433-4335, 800/723-6336* ⊕ *www.wineroad.com.* **Sonoma County Vintners** ☎ *707/522-5840* ⊕ *www.sonomawine.com.* **Sonoma Valley Vintners & Growers Alliance** ☎ *707/935-0803* ⊕ *www.sonomavalleywine.com.* **West Sonoma Coast Vintners** ⊕ *www.westsonomacoast.com.* **Winegrowers of Dry Creek Valley** ☎ *707/433-3031* ⊕ *www.wdcv.com.*

INDEX

NOT[?]

2 WEEKS

PHOTO CREDITS

Front cover: Javarman / Shutterstock [Description: Vineyards of Napa Valley]. 1, Ljupco Smokovski/ Shutterstock. 2, Rebecca Gosselin Photography. 6, 8, and 9, Robert Holmes. Chapter 1: Experience Napa and Sonoma: 10, Tori Wilder. 11 (left), Robert Holmes. 11(right), sddbb, Fodors.com member. 14 (left), Terry Joanis/Frog's Leap. 14 (top right), Round Pond Estate. 14 (bottom right), French Laundry. 15 (top left), Vincent Thompson, Fodors.com member. 15 (left), Napa Valley Bike Tours. 15 (bottom left), The Culinary Institute of America. 16 (left), Far Niente+Dolce+Nickel & Nickel. 16 (top right), Artesa Vineyards and Winery. 16 (bottom right), Rocco Ceselin. 17 (top left), Eric Risberg/Schramsberg Vineyards. 17 (right), The Hess Collection. 17 (bottom left), M. J. Wickham. 18 (left). Merry Edwards Winery. 18 (top right), Laurence G. Sterling/Iron Horse Vineyards. 18 (bottom right), Copain Wines. 19 (top left), Robert Holmes. 19 (right), Matanzas Creek. 19 (bottom right), Rocco Ceselin/Ram's Gate Winery. 20, Fairmont Hotels & Resorts. 21, RENAULT Philippe / age fotostock. 22, Sonoma County Tourism. 23, ZUMA Wire Service / Alamy. 25 (left), Robert Holmes. 25 (right), Courtesy of Meadowood Napa Valley. 29, Mustards Grill. Chapter 2: Visiting Wineries and Tasting Rooms: 31-49, Robert Holmes. 52, Warren H. White. Chapter 3: Napa Valley: 65, Robert Holmes. 67 (top), Megan Reeves Photography. 67 (bottom), Courtesy of Napa Valley Balloons, Inc.. 68, Andy Dean Photography / Shutterstock. 71, Robert Holmes. 74, Napa Valley Wine Train. 78, Avis Mandel. 81 and 85, Robert Holmes. 88, di Rosa. 90, Teodora George | Dreamstime.com. 94, OPENKITCHENPhotography. 100, Robert Holmes. 107, Michael Venera. 109, Far Niente+Dolce+Nickel & Nickel. 110, Opus One. 114, Olaf Beckman. 121, The Culinary Institute of America. 125, Avis Mandel. 126, Scott Chebagia. 135, Smcfeeters | Dreamstime.com. 143, Calistoga Ranch. Chapter 4: Sonoma Valley: 147, ivanastar/iStockphoto. 148, James Fanucchi. 149 (top), James Fanucchi. 149 (bottom), Stevan Nordstrom. 150, Robert Holmes Photography. 152, Stevan Nordstrom. 157, Rocco Ceselin/Ram's Gate Winery. 161, Nigel Wilson/Flickr. 167, 2012 LeoGong. 171, Fairmont Hotels & Resorts. 176, Benziger Family Winery. Chapter 5: Northern Sonoma, Russian River and West Country: 185, M. J. Wickham. 186, Sonoma County Tourism. 187 (left), Martinelli Winery. 187 (right), Copain Wines. 188, Helio San Miguel. 199, Matt Armendariz. 200, Robert Holmes. 203 and 208, Warren H. White. 211, The Honor Mansion. 212, Cesar Rubio. 225, Sonoma County Tourism. 232, Laurence G. Sterling/Iron Horse Vineyards. 235, Mitch Tobias, courtesy of Paul Hobbs Winery. 239, Matanzas Creek. 242, Joe Shlabotnik/Flickr. 244, Jeffrey M. Frank/Shutterstock. Back cover: Lee Jorgensen; Glen Ellen Star; Napa Valley Wine Train. Spine: Sonoma County Tourism.

About Our Writer: Daniel Mangin, courtesy of J Rodby.

NOTES

ABOUT OUR WRITER

 Daniel Mangin returned to California, where he's maintained a home for three decades, after two stints at the Fodor's editorial offices in New York City, the second one as the Editorial Director of Fodors.com and the Compass American Guides. While at Compass he was the series editor for the *California Wine Country* guide and commissioned the *Oregon Wine Country* and *Washington Wine Country* guides. A wine lover whose earliest visits to Napa and Sonoma predate the Wine Country lifestyle, Daniel is delighted by the evolution in wines, wine making, and hospitality. With several dozen wineries less than a half-hour's drive from home, he often finds himself transported as if by magic to a tasting room bar, communing with a sophisticated Cabernet or savoring the finish of a smooth Pinot Noir.

← Barcode